English G 21

B5

für Realschulen

Vokabeltrainer-App

Verfügbar für: iOS, Android und Windows Phone

Cornelsen

English G 21 • Band B 5

Im Auftrag des Verlages herausgegeben von
Prof. Hellmut Schwarz, Mannheim
Wolfgang Biederstädt, Köln

Erarbeitet von
Barbara Derkow Disselbeck, Köln
Allen J. Woppert, Berlin
Susan Abbey, Nenagh, Irland
Laurence Harger, Wellington, Neuseeland
sowie Claire Lamsdale, Llangybi, Wales

unter Mitarbeit von
Wolfgang Biederstädt, Köln
Joachim Blombach, Herford
David Christie, Banbury, England
Helmut Dengler, Limbach
Jennifer Seidl, München
Andrea Ulrich, Berlin
sowie Uwe Chormann, Einselthum; Udo Wagner, Voerde

in Zusammenarbeit mit der Englischredaktion
Dr. Christiane Kallenbach (Projektleitung);
Klaus G. Unger (verantwortlicher Redakteur);
Susanne Bennetreu (Bildredaktion); Britta Bensmann;
Dr. Philip Devlin; Bonnie S. Glänzer; Uwe Tröger
sowie Ulrike Berendt

Beratende Mitwirkung
Anja Bersch, Waldstetten; Peer Brändel, Gütersloh;
Matthew George, Frankfurt (Main); Prof. Dr. Liesel Hermes, Karlsruhe; Bernhard Hunger, Dettingen;
Gabriele Künstler, Altlußheim; Ulrike Rath, Aachen;
Lutz Salvi, Braunschweig; Michael Semmler, Lünen;
Karl Starkebaum, Diekholzen; Elke Storz, Freiburg i. Br.

Illustrationen
Silke Bachmann, Hamburg; Roland Beier, Berlin;
Carlos Borrell, Berlin; Dylan Gibson, Pitlochry;
Christian Görke, Berlin; Alfred Schüssler, Frankfurt/Main

Layoutkonzept
Aksinia Raphael; Korinna Wilkes

Technische Umsetzung
Aksinia Raphael; Korinna Wilkes;
Stephan Hilleckenbach; Rainer Bachmaier

Umschlaggestaltung
Klein & Halm Grafikdesign, Berlin

Für die freundliche Unterstützung bei den Aufnahmen für *English connects* danken wir: GLS Sprachenzentrum Berlin; Yildiz Restaurant, Berlin; DressFaktor, Berlin

www.cornelsen.de
www.EnglishG.de

Druck und Bindung: Livonia Print, Riga

1. Auflage, 9. Druck 2020
ISBN 978-3-06-031314-3
broschiert

1. Auflage, 4. Druck 2016
ISBN 978-3-06-031364-8
gebunden

PEFC
PEFC/12-31-006

PEFC zertifiziert
Dieses Produkt stammt aus nachhaltig bewirtschafteten Wäldern und kontrollierten Quellen.
www.pefc.de

Dein Englischbuch enthält folgende Teile:

Units 1 2 3 4	die vier Kapitel des Buches
Getting ready for a test	Hier kannst du dich gezielt auf einen Test vorbereiten.
EXTRA: Text File	viele interessante Texte zum Lesen (passend zu den Units)
Skills File (SF)	Beschreibung wichtiger Lern- und Arbeitstechniken
Grammar File (GF)	Zusammenfassung der Grammatik der Units; Übersichten über die Zeitformen (*present, past, future*)
Vocabulary	Wörterverzeichnis zum Lernen der neuen Wörter jeder Unit
Dictionary	alphabetisches englisch-deutsches Wörterverzeichnis

Die Units bestehen aus diesen Teilen:

Lead-in	Einstieg in das neue Thema
Part A, B, C, D	neuer Lernstoff mit vielen Aktivitäten
Practice	Übungen
How am I doing?	Hier kannst du dein Wissen und Können überprüfen.

In den Units findest du diese Überschriften und Symbole:

Exploring language	Hier lernst du anhand von Beispielen, neue sprachliche Strukturen zu verstehen und richtig anzuwenden.
STUDY SKILLS	Einführung in Lern- und Arbeitstechniken
Dossier	Schöne und wichtige Arbeiten kannst du in einer Mappe sammeln.
SPEAKING COURSE	Sprechkurs in vier Kapiteln
EVERYDAY ENGLISH	Übungen zum Bewältigen wichtiger Alltagssituationen
ENGLISH FOR JOBS	Übungen zur Vorbereitung auf typische berufliche Situationen
MEDIATION	Hier vermittelst du zwischen zwei Sprachen.
VIEWING	Aufgaben zu Filmausschnitten
Now you	Hier sprichst und schreibst du über dich selbst.
REVISION	Übungen zur Wiederholung
WORDS	Übungen zu Wortfeldern und Wortverbindungen
Extra	zusätzliche Aktivitäten und Übungen
	Partnerarbeit / Gruppenarbeit
	nur auf CD / auf CD und im Schülerbuch
	Filmausschnitte auf DVD
	Textaufgaben

Inhalt

Australia

The world of work

Teen world

Big city life

Unit 1 Australia

Judith's blog

About me

Name Judith
Age 15
From born and grew up in Cologne (Germany); now in Melbourne, Victoria, Australia (my dad's had a job here since July)

- **Comments**
  Please write to me here.
- **Photo Gallery**
  I have posted some more photos of kangaroos, koalas, the outback etc.
- Click here for my sound file to go with the photos.

19th July
Just arrived – too excited to sleep! As we flew across Australia, south towards Melbourne, I looked out of the window and saw red earth – just red earth for miles. I suddenly understood why everyone talks about how huge Australia is: I felt very, very small and a bit scared. When I got off the plane in Melbourne I got a shock! I'd left Cologne on a hot July day, but here 'Down Under' things are different, of course: it was a cold winter day.

22nd July
Melbourne is very beautiful and very big: 3 million people live here. My first view of the city was awesome – the Yarra River, the skyscrapers, the sea – magical.

1

24th July
Life is less magical now – school has started! There are four terms a year in Australia and the third has just started. Here the school day begins at 8.30 – quite nice, but then you have to stay there until 3.15 pm! After 3.15 students also have lots of extracurricular school activities like sport, music or debates. And when that's all over, there's homework. I suppose school is going to fill my days now. :-(

30th September
It's spring holiday time and I've just come back from a really exciting trip – a 5-day hike in the bush. It was amazing, but a bit scary too. One evening I was about to go to bed when one of the girls shouted 'Stop!' There was a snake inside my sleeping bag! She saved my life!

14th October
I'm learning to surf – it's fantastic the way the waves carry you to the beach! Here, lots of kids my age know how to surf.

19th November
It's getting hot now! Just back from a 'barbie' (barbecue!). When you're under 18 here you aren't allowed to drink alcohol, smoke cigarettes or visit clubs, pubs or bars without an adult. So it's a common thing to have a party at someone's place. It's all very relaxed and I now have lots of Australian friends.

2

3

4

5

6

1 What's special about Australia?

a) *What does Judith tell us about Australia? Read her blog and take notes. Compare your notes with a partner.*

b) *What is different about your lives and Judith's life in Australia? Would you like to go to Australia? Why (not)?*

c) Extra *Write a comment for Judith's blog.*

2 Pictures of Australia

Listen to Judith's sound files and take notes on what you find most interesting about each photo. Then write a caption for each. Compare and discuss with a partner.

► *SF Describing pictures (p. 121)*

3 Extra About Australia – a project

Choose one of the topics from 'The Australia Project' in Text File 1. Then collect useful ideas, information, words and phrases as you go through the unit.

► Text File 1 *(pp. 98–99)* • Text File 2 *(pp. 100–101)* • *WB 1 (p. 2)*

AUSTRALIA – FACTS AND FIGURES

1 READING Group puzzle (part 1)
Divide the class into four groups (A, B, C, D). Group A studies A, Group B studies B, etc. Take notes so that you can pass on the information you've found. In your group agree on the most important information.

Quick facts ★ ★ ★

Area: 7,686,850 sq km
Population: 21.2 million
Capital: Canberra (334,000)
Largest cities: Sydney (4.3 million), Melbourne (3.8 million), Brisbane (1.8 million)

A Down Under

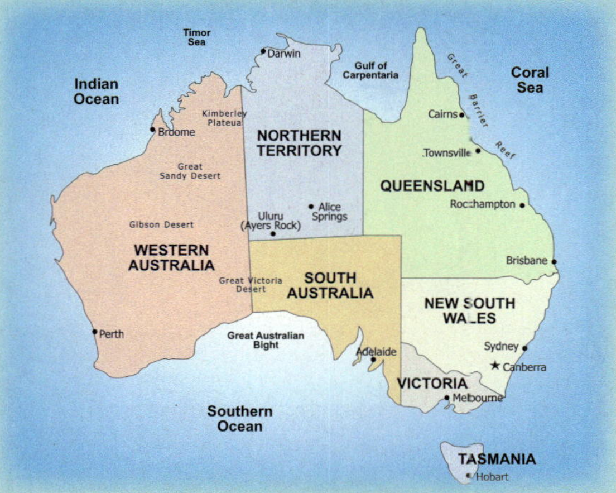

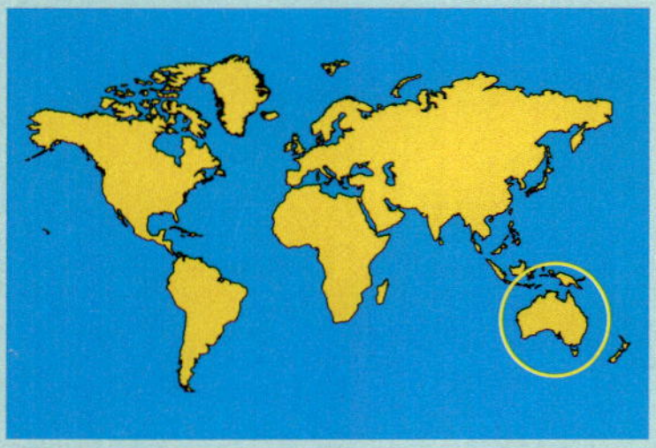

> – *Explain why Australia is often called 'Down Under'.*
> – *In which states are the three largest cities?*
> – *Use the map on the front inside cover to find out how wide Australia is at its widest point. Compare with Germany.*

B A short history of Australia

When the first Europeans came to Australia in the 16th century, between 300,000 and 1 million Aborigines already lived there. Many Aborigines were killed by the Europeans, while others died of the white people's diseases, until at the beginning of the 20th century there were only about 150,000. Today there are about 455,000 Aborigines in Australia.

The British king or queen is also the king or queen of Australia.

► WB 2–3 (pp. 2)

Ships from different countries came to Australia from around 1530 and in 1770 Captain James Cook claimed the world's largest island for Britain. In 1788 the British started a colony for convicts in Port Jackson (now Sydney). Over the next 80 years, Britain brought more than 160,000 convicts to Australia. Other immigrants arrived, and together with the former convicts they started colonies in different parts of the continent. The colonies became states, and in 1901 the Commonwealth of Australia was founded and became independent.

In the 20th century Australia kept its close links to Britain and fought with the British in both world wars. Since the 1970s Australia has done more and more business with Asia, and large numbers of immigrants now come to Australia from Asian countries.

> *Agree on four important facts of Australian history that your classmates should know.*

C Australia and the sun

Australians love to spend their time outdoors. But the sun down under is dangerous because of the hole in the ozone layer: more ultraviolet (UV) rays get through and burn people. The result is that skin cancer is more common in Australia than in any other country.

Some times of day are worse than others. The papers print the UV levels for the different hours of the day. When the levels are medium or higher, it's time to 'Slip! Slop! Slap!'

> *–What does the cartoon tell you to do? Why is it so important to 'Slip! Slop! Slap'?*
> *–What else is Cool Cat wearing that helps to protect him from the sun?*

D The natural sights of Australia

Australia's biggest tourist attractions are its natural sights. The country has everything from rainforests to deserts, and animals like the kangaroo, the koala and the emu are found only there.

One of Australia's most famous natural sights is the Great Barrier Reef. More than 2,000 km long, the reef is home to about 1,500 kinds of fish and 200 kinds of birds. Dolphins, whales, sea snakes and salt-water crocodiles can also be seen there.

Sadly, the reef is in danger. Corals die if the water temperature changes by more than a degree or two. And the oceans around Australia – like the rest of the world – are getting warmer.

> *Agree on three important facts about Australia's natural sights that your classmates should know.*

▸ Text File 3 (pp. 102–103) • WB 4 (p. 3)

2 Group puzzle (part 2)

a) *Each person in the group has a number (1, 2, 3, ...). Make new groups of four (A1, B1, C1, D1; A2, B2, ...). Tell the others in your new group the important information from your text. Take notes on the other texts.*

b) *Go back to your first group (A, B, C, D) and compare your information. Did you all understand the same things? If not, read the texts to check your information.*

▸ SF Taking notes (p. 128)

3 Population figures

STUDY SKILLS Understanding charts

The **title** of a chart tells you what it is about. Make sure you understand what the **figures** mean: are they percentages or numbers?

Bar charts (1 and 2 below) are often used to compare the number or size of two or more things. Use phrases like these to talk about bar charts:
- The bar chart is about ...
- It compares the size/number of ...
- ... has the largest/second largest/...
- ... is twice/three times/... as big as ...

Pie charts (3 below) help you to compare a percentage (e.g. Asians) with the whole pie (population of Australia). Use phrases like these to talk about the information in a pie chart:
- The pie chart shows the different ... in ...
- It is divided into ... slices which show ...
- A huge majority/small minority is ...
- ... per cent are ...
- There are more than/nearly twice as many ... as there are ...

a) *Partner A: Explain chart **1** to your partner.*
My chart compares the ... of four ...
*Partner B: Explain chart **2** to your partner.*
My chart compares the ... of four ...

b) *What do the two charts together tell you?*
... is very big, but the ... is very small. So it must be quite ... there.

1 Population in millions

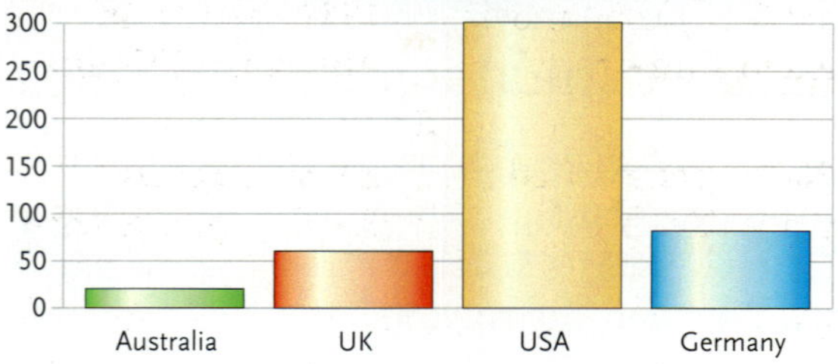

2 Land area in million sq km

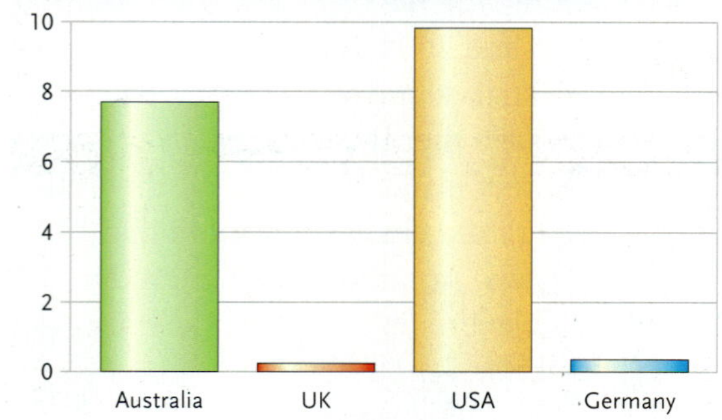

c) *Write about the pie chart below:*
- Say what the chart shows.
- Give details.
- Finish with a conclusion.

The pie chart shows the different ... There are ... main groups: The largest group is the ... They're about ... of the population. The next largest ... So, you can say ...

3 Ethnic groups in Australia

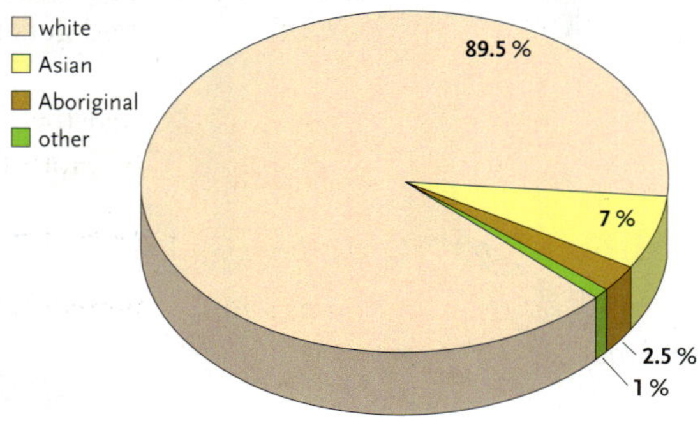

d) **Extra** *Why do you think Asians are the biggest ethnic minority in Australia?*

► *SF Understanding charts (p. 126)*

P1 REVISION Australian animals (Tenses: Simple present)

a) *Partner B: Look at p.92.*
Partner A: Write out these sentences about kangaroos. Use the correct form of the simple present.
There (is/are) 43 different kinds of kangaroo. Usually, kangaroos (lives/live) in groups. They (eats/eat) grass and leaves, but they (doesn't need/don't need) much water. Kangaroos (is/are) more active at night than during the day. If it's very hot, they just (sits/sit) under trees and bushes and (doesn't move/don't move). The biggest kangaroo – the Red Kangaroo – is about 1.8 metres tall. It (moves/move) at about 20–25 kph and (jumps/jump) two metres.

b) *Use these key words to complete the text.*
when kangaroo born, live in mother's pouch (kind of bag) for ten months / babies fed by mother until 18 months old, then can feed themselves / kangaroos not get very old, just 4 to 6 years.

c) *Read your text to your partner. Then listen to his/her text. Say one thing you found interesting about it.*

► *GF 1: Talking about the present (p. 145)*

P2 REVISION A famous Australian (Tenses: Simple past)

a) *Make a sentence in the simple past for each event in Nicole Kidman's life.*

1967: born in Hawaii, USA ► **1970**: takes first ballet lessons ► **1971**: family returns to Australia ► **1977**: starts drama lessons ► **1983**: appears in Australian TV series ► **1990**: makes first Hollywood movie and gets married to Tom Cruise ► **1994**: begins work with UNICEF ► **2001**: gets divorced ► **2003**: wins Oscar for her role in 'The Hours' ► **2006**: gets married to singer Keith Urban ► **2008**: daughter Sunday Rose is born

Nicole Kidman was born in Hawaii in the USA in 1967. She took …

b) **Extra** *Use linking words and your sentences from a) to write a text about Nicole Kidman. You can add more events if you like.*

► *GF 2: Talking about the past (pp. 146–147)*

P3 Extra STUDY SKILLS Understanding charts

Write a short text about the chart on the right. Explain in your text
– what the chart is about
– what it compares.

► *WB 5–7 (pp. 3–4)*

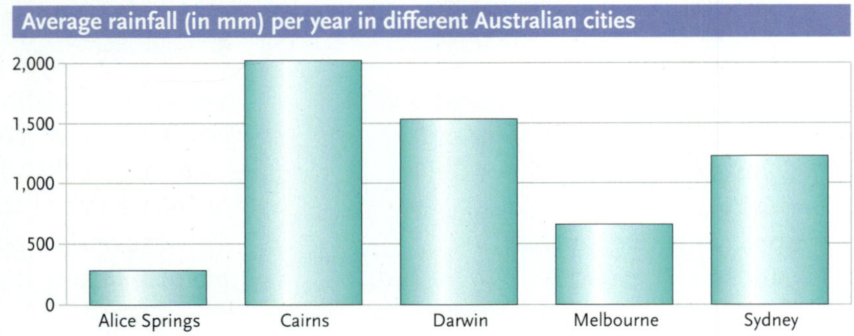

TWO AUSTRALIAN TEENAGERS

1 Jeannie – in the middle of nowhere

Hi Cath,
It was great to get your e-mail. Yes, I'd love to be your online friend, though I don't honestly think my life in western Queensland is as exciting as your life in Hong Kong.

My dad works here on a sheep station, so we live in the middle of nowhere. There are only twenty other people on the station but thousands and thousands of sheep. The nearest town is about 500 km away, so we don't have a local cinema, or doctor or even a school! But I still have school. My school is the Alice Springs School of the Air. It's cool! It comes to me through my computer. That means I don't have to sit in a classroom all day! (I can even take my laptop outside and do my work under a tree!) But I can talk to the teacher and class every day. Although Alice Springs is 800 miles away, my teachers are in a studio so I can even see them. A lot of our class have webcams, so we can see each other too. We're good friends even if we only meet about three times a year at one week courses.

You talk about your sports and hobbies – dragon boat racing, tennis and discos. Well, mine are a bit different! There's no one here at the station my age, so I have to do things on my own a lot. I ride every day – that's great. (I have my own horse, Sally.) And because we live in the middle of nowhere I'm allowed to ride a dirt bike – that's great fun.

I'm attaching some photos. Please mail again soon.
Your new online friend,
Jeannie

Describe what you see in the photos. Write a sentence as a caption for each.

▸ *SF Describing pictures (p. 121)*

2 Now you

Think: *What might be the advantages and disadvantages of the School of the Air?*
Pair: *Compare with a partner.*
Share: *Discuss with another pair.*
– It would be boring/fun/...
– I would miss/hate/...
– I think I could learn better because ...

3 Extra Royal Flying Doctor Service

Lonely sheep stations in the outback don't have local doctors, but people can call the Royal Flying Doctor Service (RFDS). Find out more about it (internet, books ...). How does it work?
Write two or three paragraphs. You can add photos or maps. Put your text in your DOSSIER.

▸ *SF Research (p. 124)*

4 Rob – sports-mad in Sydney

a) These are popular sports in Australia. Do you know other sports Australians like?

b) *Listen. Make a list of the sports Rob talks about. Which ones are not shown on this page?*

c) *Listen again. What are Rob's three favourite sports? Make notes so that you can give reasons for your opinion.*

► *SF Listening for detail (p. 127)*

d) *Which of the sports in your list interest you most? Why? Can you do them where you live?*

A: I'd love to surf because it seems to be exciting, but I couldn't do it here because we're 600 km from the sea.

B: Surfing is OK, but I'd really like to ...

5 Extra Game

Make two teams. Tell the other team about a sport (location, equipment, clothes), but don't say what it is. One point for each correct guess.

Team A: You play on a court, you need a racket and you wear shorts and a shirt!

Team B: Tennis!

► *SF Paraphrasing (p. 132)*

6 Now you

Think of differences between Jeannie's life and Rob's life. If you could visit one of them for a week, who would you choose? Why?

SPEAKING COURSE Part 1

P1 SPEAKING Good to meet you (Starting and continuing a conversation)

You want to talk to somebody you don't know: What should you do?
- find a way to start the conversation
- introduce yourself
- ask the person questions and answer his/hers
- ask the person for help if you need it or to repeat something if necessary
- end the conversation

a) *Match these phrases to the tips above.*

Sorry, I didn't get that. • Sorry, can you say that again, please?
Bye! • See you tomorrow.
By the way, my name's ... • How are you? • Good to meet you.
Hi! • Excuse me, ...
Have you ... before/yet? • Have you ever ...? • What about you?
Can you tell me ...? • Do you know where ... ?

start the conversation: Hi! / Excuse me, ...
introduce yourself: ...

b) *At the beach last week, Rob met Anna, an English tourist. Listen to their conversation and check the list you made in a).*

c) *ROLE PLAY*
With your partner act out a short conversation. Use the flow chart below and phrases from a).

Partner A:	**Partner B:**
– You want to sit down in a café. – You'd like to see the film 'Batman', but don't know where it's on.	– You're sitting alone at a table in a café. – You're reading a magazine with cinema tips.

Ask if you can sit at Partner B's table. → Answer Partner A. → Introduce yourselves. → Ask a few questions to get to know each other. → Ask Partner B if he/she knows where 'Batman' is on. → Help Partner A to find out where 'Batman' is on. → Ask Partner B if he/she would like to see the film with you. → Answer Partner A. → End the conversation.

d) **Extra** *ROLE PLAY*
In groups of three, act out a short conversation.
Situation:
Three students meet on a bush hike in Australia. A is German, B is Irish, C is American. Talk to each other about your holidays so far.

► SF Speaking Course (pp. 138–139) • WB 8 (p. 5)

P2 WORDS Tricky translations

Some German words have different English translations. Find the right translations for the words in brackets and complete the sentences.

1 (*tragen* – carry/wear) When Rob goes surfing in winter *he wears* a wetsuit. He loves the way the waves *carry* him to the beach.
2 (*bringen* – bring/take) ... me my paper please, and then could you ... this letter to the post office?
3 (*groß* – big/tall) The African elephant is between 3.5 and 4 metres ... and is known for its ... ears.
4 (*während* – during/while) We met some nice guys ... we were waiting for the train and chatted with them ... our journey to Melbourne.
5 (*brauchen*) The bus from the station to the airport ... about ten minutes. And it's free, so you don't ... a ticket.
6 (*machen*) What are you ... this evening? – Well, I have to ... dinner for my family.
7 (*fahren*) My mum can't ... a car, so she ... her bike to work. It if rains, she ... by bus.
8 (*vor*) I went to see a film two weeks ... . I met my friends ... the cinema.

▸ *SF Using a bilingual dictionary (p. 123)*

P3 Extra REVISION Rob couldn't go surfing (Past perfect)

Yesterday Rob and his friends in Sydney didn't do what they had planned. Why not?
Complete the sentences. Use the past perfect.

1 Rob couldn't go surfing because he *had hurt* (hurt) his knee.
2 Ryan couldn't go riding because his horse ... (run) away.
3 Holly didn't go swimming because two crocodiles ... (decide) to have a party on the beach.
4 Sheila didn't read her book because ...
5 Andy didn't meet his friend Nina because ...
6 Anna didn't go cycling because ...
7 Philip didn't fly to ...
8 Tom didn't ...

▸ *GF 2: Talking about the past (p. 146–147)*

P4 EVERYDAY ENGLISH WRITING Our lives (Writing an e-mail)

Look at pages 12 and 13 again. Write an e-mail to Jeannie or Rob.

– Tell them what you find interesting or surprising about their lives. → I was really interested to read/hear about ... • I think it's great that you can/have ... • I was really jealous when I read that you ...

– What else would you like to know about their lives? Ask some questions. → Are you allowed to ...? • What's your favourite ...? • Where/When/How often do you ...?

– Tell them something about your life, e.g. your school day, your favourite subject, the sports you enjoy, ... → My life in Germany is different from ... / like ... • For example, ...

▸ *SF Writing Course (pp. 134–135) • WB 9–10 (p. 6)*

THE ABORIGINAL PEOPLE OF AUSTRALIA

1 'Dreamtime'

The Aborigines had lived in Australia for over 40,000 years when the British started to settle there. Although there were 500 different groups of Aborigines with more than 200 languages, many traditions and beliefs united them. To this day, the Aborigines believe, for example, that the ancestors of everybody and everything once lived below the earth. In the 'Dreamtime', these Ancestors came out and made the mountains, valleys, rivers etc., and gave life to animals and people. Aborigines believe that the land, plants and animals are just as important as people. That's why people need to respect the plants, the land and the animals that live on it.

Do you think that land, plants and animals are as important as people? Why (not)?

2 Extra To Uluru-Kata Tjuta National Park: an imaginary journey

a) *Look closely at the photos from Uluru–Kata Tjuta National Park for two minutes. Then close your eyes and go there on an imaginary journey.*

Uluru rises from the flat desert

Cave at Uluru

An Aboriginal man plays the didger doo

Cave painting

b) *What was your strongest impression from your visit to Uluru? What did you see, smell or hear? Tell your group about it. Ask the others questions about their impressions.*

cave paintings • landscape • desert heat • sound of the didgeridoo

c) *Listen again. Give examples from the imaginary journey that show how Aborigines respect nature.*

▸ *SF Listening for detail (p. 127)*

3 The 'stolen generations'

Children were stolen for a racist ideal. Now a nation says sorry

Zita Wallace still remembers the day she was stolen from her Aboriginal family and taken to a home for orphans. The home was run by white nuns. She was seven years old.

At her house in Worita, Wallace spoke about her first night with the nuns. 'There were lots of children in one big room. We all had to sleep on hard mattresses on the floor. I was terrified.'

She told us that she had seen terrible things and would never forget those first hours. 'There was a 4-year-old girl who just cried and cried. It was so awful that I put my head under my blanket and cried too.'

Wallace belongs to the 'stolen generations', the thousands of mixed-race children with fair skin who were taken from their families. The government wanted them to forget their Aboriginal language and traditions and to grow up like white people. 'They hit us if we spoke our language,' Wallace told us.

The stealing of children ended after 60 years in 1970. In 1997 a government report said it was time to apologize to the stolen generations. Now, eleven years later, Australia is finally saying sorry.

Wallace and four other girls were tricked into leaving their homes. One day some nuns arrived at the door and said that the girls could go shopping with them. 'They put us in the back of a truck but we never went near a shop. They took us to a home hundreds of miles away.'

Zita Wallace with her aunt Aggie

Wallace said that she didn't care about getting money from the government. 'But I can't wait to hear that word tomorrow: sorry.'

> *Describe how Zita Wallace was stolen.*
> *When is the article from? What important event took place in that year?*

4 VIEWING Rabbit-proof fence

'Rabbit-proof fence' tells the true story of three Aboriginal girls who are 'stolen', escape and walk 1,900 km through the outback of western Australia to get home.

a) *Watch a scene from the film. Then answer:*

1 Do the girls know about the fence?
2 Does the mother know why the man in the car has come?
3 Does the worker help the children?

b) **Extra** *Watch again. Take notes on how the acting and the music help you to understand the mother's feelings and the children's feelings.*

– When the music gets louder you think ...
– The way the mother looks when the car arrives shows ...

▸ *SF Taking notes (p. 128)*

P1 Exploring language | Indirect speech

a) *The writer of the newspaper article reports what Zita Wallace said in the interview (p. 17):* She told us that she had seen terrible things and would never forget those first hours. *Study the chart below to learn how we report what someone said in the past.*

Direct speech	Indirect speech
'I don't care about getting money from the government.' ▸	Wallace said that she didn't care about getting money from the government.
'I saw terrible things.' ▸	She told us that she had seen terrible things.
'I'll never forget those first hours.' ▸	She said she would never forget those first hours.
'You can go shopping with us.' ▸	The nuns said that the girls could go shopping with them.

b) *Look again at the sentences in a). How do the verbs change?*

Direct speech	Indirect speech
simple present	simple past
simple past	...
will-future	... + infinitive
can	...

c) *Report these statements from another conversation with Zita Wallace.*

1 'A lot of Aborigines have no families.' ▸	Wallace said a lot of Aborigines ... no families.
2 'I can't understand why they didn't apologize sooner.' ▸	She told the reporter that she ... understand why they ... sooner.
3 'I found my mother later, but we never were close again.' ▸	She added that she ... her mother later, but they ... never ... close again.
4 'I'll be much happier after they apologize.' ▸	She said she ... much happier after they apologized.

▸ GF 4: Indirect speech I (p. 149)

P2 Samantha Harris, Aboriginal model (Indirect speech)

You've found an old interview with Aboriginal model Samantha Harris from March 2008.

1 'I'm 17 years old and 1.80 metres tall.'
2 'I live near Tweed Heads, New South Wales.'
3 'My dad is from Germany.'
4 'I have four brothers and one sister.'
5 'My friends call me Sam.'
6 'I like hip hop and reggae.'
7 'I have dark brown hair, and my shoe size is 41.'
8 'I can imagine travelling the world in ten years.'
9 'I don't make a lot of money with my modelling.'
10 'I want to be the first big Aboriginal model.'

Write down what Samantha Harris said about herself. Use words from the box below.

called • could imagine • didn't make • had (2x) • liked • lived • wanted • was (3x)

1 *Samantha said in 2008 that she was ...*
2 *She told the reporter that she ...*
3 *She added that her dad ...*

▸ WB 11 (p. 6)

P3 Nova Peris, Aboriginal sports star (Indirect speech)

You're doing research on Nova Peris, the first Aborigine who won gold in the Olympic Games (in 1996). You've marked these sentences from an interview. Put them in indirect speech for your report.

1 'I do lots of work in the area of Aboriginal health.'
Nova Peris said she did lots of work ...
2 'I teach parents about healthy food and exercise for their children.'
3 'I also give talks about the advantages of different cultures in the workplace.'
4 'I still do sports, but I don't take part in championships any more.'
5 'Having children was the most exciting thing in my life.'
6 'I'm sure my children will have an easier life.'
7 'I think the government will pay money to members of the stolen generations like my grandma.'

P4 How well do you know your classmates? (Indirect speech)

a) *Make groups of six. Each of you write sentences on a piece of paper:*
- one thing that makes you really happy
- the person you respect most
- a place you visited during the summer
- two things you hope will happen in the next six months

Write your name at the bottom of the page.

b) *Put all the pieces of paper in a box. Take one from the box. Tell your group what it says. Use indirect speech. Can the group guess who wrote the piece of paper? Then take turns.*

This girl wrote that winning at football made her really happy. She said she respected her sister most. She also wrote that ...

P5 ENGLISH FOR JOBS Basic telephone language

a) *Listen. What phrases can you find for:*
- Starting a phone call: *Hello. I'd like to ...*
- Saying what your call is about: *I'm calling ...*
- Asking about the job (pay, hours, ...): ...
- Ending the call: ...

Listen again and check.

b) *Think of more ways to ask about:*
- the kind of work someone is offering
- when the job starts and finishes
- how much money you would get
- where the job is

c) *Compare lists with a partner and add to your list if necessary.*

d) *A ROLE PLAY*
Partner B: Look at p. 92. Partner A: Look at the role cards below. Act out the two telephone dialogues.

1 Name: Jennifer Collins
- You're the owner of Adels Bush Hotel.
- You need someone to help in the kitchen: wash the dishes, clean vegetables etc.
- 7-month job: 1 March–30 Sept.
- Address: 12 Lawn Hill Road, Sydney
- $12–$15 per hour

2 You've seen a notice for a job on a farm. Call the farmer Philip Black to find out
- what kind of job it is
- what you would have to do
- how much you would earn
- where the farm is.

► WB 12–15 (pp. 7–9)

In the outback adapted from the novel 'A prayer for Blue Delaney' by Kirsty Murray

STUDY SKILLS **Reading stories**

When you read a story, the important thing is to understand the main ideas – you needn't understand every word.

If a word you don't know stops you from understanding the text, use the different ways you've learned to find out what that word means. If that doesn't help, use a dictionary.

► SF Reading stories (p. 129)

For the following text some important new words are explained at the bottom of each page.

The story so far

During the 1950s Australia wanted to add to its population, so orphans were sent from the United Kingdom to children's homes there. Colm is one of these British orphans. He is living in a home for boys, but the people at the home are very cruel and Colm decides to run away. He gets to know an old man, Bill, and his dog Rusty. When the police start to search for Colm, Bill offers to take him with him in Tin Annie – his old pickup truck[1] (ute) – as he travels through the Australian outback. Bill is hoping to get work on the Dog Fence which runs from south to north-eastern Australia.

As they drove out of Ceduna, Bill said, 'I heard from an old mate that there's work on the Dog Fence. Thought I might take it. No one will follow us in that lonely country.'

The Victoria Desert began to stretch out in front of them as they left town. They drove north towards the Dog Fence, through a wide, open landscape[2] of earth and sky.

It was slow and hot travelling along the Dog Fence. The more they drove inland, the hotter the air was until Colm felt he was breathing fire. He and Rusty hung their heads out the window, but it was worse than the burning heat[3] inside the car. The sandy air hurt Colm's skin and made his eyes sore. He pulled his head back inside. There was nothing to see except scrub[4] and tough little grasses in the rock and sand, and the fence that stretched[5] like a thin grey scar[6] across the landscape.

'What if we break down[7]?' asked Colm.

'Don't you worry about that. They used to do the fence on camel, but today they use jeeps. Tin Annie here, she's part camel, part jeep, so she'll be fine.'

'But what if we get lost[8]?'

Bill smiled. 'We'll follow the fence, mate. It's more than three thousand miles long and there's no way we can lose it.'

Bill stopped next to the fence where an emu had crashed into it. They both climbed out of the ute.

Bill shook his head. 'She's hit the fence very fast, this one. Seems she broke her neck[9].'

In the distance another emu was running across the desert. 'See, they get faster and faster.

[1] pickup truck ['pɪkʌp trʌk], ute [ju:t] *(AusE) kleiner Geländewagen mit offener Ladefläche* [2] landscape ['lændskeɪp] *Landschaft* [3] heat [hi:t] *Hitze* [4] scrub [skrʌb] *Gebüsch, Gestrüpp* [5] (to) stretch [stretʃ] *sich erstrecken* [6] scar [skɑ:] *Narbe* [7] (to) break down *eine Panne haben* [8] (to) get lost *sich verirren* [9] neck [nek] *Genick*

They run 30 miles an hour but they don't see the fence till they've hit it.'

Colm helped Bill as he looked for the tools he would need for the job and then climbed back into Tin Annie to wait while Bill repaired the fence. Later they stopped to fill in a hole made by a wombat. The day dragged on[1]. They drove so slowly that Colm got tired looking at the fence. When he closed his eyes he saw the endless fence as it passed them. Despite the flies and the heat, he fell asleep. When he woke up, it was to the sound of Bill repairing a fencepost.

Colm's shirt was wet[2] with sweat. He went round to the back of the ute and drank from the billycan[3]. The water was as warm as tea, but it was good to wet his throat. There were flies around his face and even if he tried to swat them away, they came back. Colm felt as if he was inside a strange and terrifying dream.

The days dragged on, long and boring. Colm's neck was sore from always turning his head one way to watch the fence. After a few days he started to fill the wombat holes while Bill repaired the holes in the fence. They filled up the billycans at every dam or tank, and ate tinned beef and tinned vegetables until Colm felt he couldn't take another mouthful of them. The nearest town was hundreds of miles away.

One morning, Rusty wasn't in camp when they woke up. Colm helped Bill to pack the breakfast stuff, and all the time he scanned the scrub and looked for a sign of movement.

'Where is that dog?' said Bill. He put two fingers in his mouth and whistled. Nothing moved.

'I'll find her,' said Colm. He walked out into the scrub. If he closed his eyes and willed[4] it, then he should be able to feel Rusty wherever she was. He was sure she was quite close.

When he opened his eyes he saw something move in the dust. Rusty was under a bush: she was shaking violently.

'Bill,' called Colm. 'Bill, here, I've found her! But something's wrong! Hurry!'

Bill knelt[5] beside the dog. When he touched her body, Rusty shook even more violently.

'What is it?' asked Colm.

'Snakebite[6], maybe, maybe not.'

Rusty started shaking uncontrollably, as if there was electricity running through her. Colm was cold with fear[7].

'What's wrong?' he cried, feeling tears in his eyes.

'I think she's eaten dingo bait. Poison[8]. It might be better for her if we killed her.'

Colm walked beside Bill as he carried Rusty over to the ute and put her on her blanket in the back. Bill picked up the knife he used to kill rabbits.

'No! What are you doing!' Colm grabbed Bill's hand. 'We have to save her.'

'Get out of my way,' said Bill. He pushed Colm away and held Rusty's head. Quickly he made cuts on the side of Rusty's ears. Blood poured down.

'Now go and fill the billycan.' Bill pushed it at Colm and then looked for something in the food bag.

When Colm returned, Bill threw lots of salt into the water. He took Rusty in his arms. 'Now I'll keep her mouth open. I want you to pour[9] the salty water straight down her throat.'

The salt water made Rusty throw up. When Bill put her down, she staggered around, vomiting[10] again and again. As soon as they could, they poured more water down her throat. Finally, when she'd finished, Bill put her on her old blanket under a bush. Bill and Colm knelt beside her and massaged her.

'Here, you need a break,' said Bill. 'Go get yourself a drink and sit in the car. I'll call you if I need you.'

'What are you going to do? You can't shoot[11] her, Bill. You can't.'

'I'm hoping it won't come to that.'

Colm walked back to Tin Annie, holding back tears.

The morning got hotter and hotter. Colm fell

---

[1] (to) drag on [ˌdræg‿ˈɒn] *sich hinziehen* [2] wet [wet] *nass* [3] billycan [ˈbɪlikæn] *Kochtopf, -geschirr* [4] (to) will sth. [wɪl] *etwas durch Willenskraft herbeiführen wollen* [5] (to) kneel [niːl], knelt, knelt [nelt] *knien, sich hinknien* [6] snakebite [ˈsneɪkbaɪt] *Schlangenbiss* [7] fear [fɪə] *Angst*
[8] poison [ˈpɔɪzn] *Gift* [9] (to) pour [pɔː] *schütten; strömen* [10] (to) vomit [ˈvɒmɪt] *sich übergeben* [11] (to) shoot [ʃuːt], shot, shot [ʃɒt] *erschießen*

asleep and then, when he woke, he prayed[1] as hard as he could. He was still praying when he heard the sound of Rusty's bark – a weak bark, but a bark. He ran across to where she lay.

'I prayed for her,' said Colm. 'Maybe it helped.'

'Maybe it did,' said Bill. 'Between your prayers and my hard work, she'll be better quite soon.'

****

After several adventures Bill finds work and shelter[2] for the three of them with an old friend at Tara Downs, a cattle station[3] up in the Northern Territory.

'C'mon. I've got a job to do. Can't just sit around and talk all day. A wild boar's[4] been making trouble just south a bit. They mess with the dams and the fences. Get in the ute and you can help.'

They drove out into the landscape where the old trees looked like burnt bones. Tin Annie struggled[5] over the dry creek[6] beds and Rusty put her head out the open window, watching the fine red dust fly up around the sides of the ute.

'This is the place. We'll look for the bugger on foot from here. You stay close by me.'

Colm followed Bill through the scrub. A hot, foul smell was in the air. As the smell got stronger, Rusty put her head down and walked in front, as if she was following something. She led[7] them to what was left of a steer. A cloud of flies flew up in the air.

Bill knelt down beside the dead steer. 'He's not long dead.'

They climbed up a nearby hill and scanned the countryside. Apart from a family of wallabies, they could see nothing.

'Damn, he's heard us. '

Bill turned to walk back to the steer. There was a noise in the scrub and the black boar was on them.

Colm jumped behind a rock as the boar hit Bill and sent him flying. It ran at the old man with its tusks[8], tearing[9] his boot and ripping open his leg. Bill let out a cry of pain.

Blood poured from Bill's leg as the boar attacked again, and the old man struggled free. Rusty sank her teeth into[10] the boar's leg, but it turned and tore her with its tusks. Rusty yelped and fell.

Colm jumped out from behind the rock. He had to do something.

Bill was afraid. 'Run, Colm, get out of here,' he shouted. 'Get help!'

Colm turned and ran down the path. He had nearly got to Tin Annie when he heard a terrible cry, more animal than human. Colm

---

1 (to) pray [preɪ] *beten* 2 shelter ['ʃeltə] *Unterkunft; Schutz* 3 cattle station *(AusE)* ['kætl ˌsteɪʃn] *Rinderfarm* 4 wild boar [ˌwaɪld 'bɔː] *Wildschwein* 5 (to) struggle over ... ['strʌgl] *sich über ... kämpfen, mühen* 6 creek *(AusE)* [kriːk] *Bach* 7 (to) lead [liːd], led, led [led] *führen* 8 tusk [tʌsk] *Hauer* 9 (to) tear [teə], tore [tɔː], torn [tɔːn] *(zer-, ein)reißen* 10 ... sank her teeth into ... [sæŋk] *... schlug ihre Zähne in ...*

stopped and turned. What if Bill was killed before he could get help? What should he do? Run to Tara Downs? Try to save Bill alone? Suddenly he knew there was only one answer and there was no time to lose.

He ran back to Bill. On the way he picked up a stick[1]. As he came over the hill, he ran at the boar, hitting it again and again. It turned to face Colm. There was blood on its tusks.

Bill tried to pull himself away, leaving a trail of blood behind him. Colm raised the stick high and brought it down on the boar's head. The boar snorted, but it didn't run at Colm, it turned back to Bill.

Colm threw the stick down and grabbed Bill's gun. He was shaking as he raised the gun to his shoulder. Colm knew that if he shot the animal in the back, it would only make it wild. He let out a scream, a long loud scream. The boar turned round. For a moment it stared at him. Then it lowered its head and ran towards him. Colm aimed[2] straight between the eyes.

The kickback from the gun made Colm stagger. He fell in the sand beside Rusty.

'Colm, my mate,' said Bill. He held out one bloodied hand and smiled. Then he lay back in the red dust and passed out[3].

Suddenly, everything was quiet. Blood soaked into the dry earth around Bill in a dark circle. Colm could see the bones of his leg where the boar had ripped open the flesh. He would have to stop the blood flow or Bill would bleed to death. Colm ran back to the ute and grabbed an old shirt to tie up the wound. Then he took off his own shirt and tore it up for Bill's hands. When he was sure the bleeding was slower, he sat back and tried to think. He had to get help, but how? The flies were gathering. He would have to get Bill into the car.

Colm took Bill's arms and put one over each of his shoulders and then tried to pull the old man up. It was almost impossible. He'd never be able to go a long way like this. He laid Bill down again and ran to Tin Annie. Colm took a deep breath and turned the key. Tin Annie started. He had no idea how to drive backwards, so he moved forward carefully, bringing the car as close to Bill as he could. Somehow he found the strength[4] to pull Bill back on his shoulders and put him into the car. Then he ran and picked Rusty up. He could just hear the dog's heartbeat and it gave him hope.

The dust flew up around the car as Colm raced[5] along the track. Every time they hit a stone Bill cried out with pain, but at least that meant he was still alive.

When they drove across a dry creek bed, Tin Annie first struggled, then stopped. Colm tried to start her up again. But even as his foot pushed to the floor, he knew it was a mistake. The old ute died completely.

They were just at the top of the hill and he could see Tara Downs, but there was still at least a mile to go. He tried to start the car again and again, but nothing happened. He would have to go on foot and leave Bill and Rusty in the car.

Colm wished the old man was conscious[6] and could tell him what to do next. Then he began the long run to Tara Down.

Colm's heart pounded and his head hurt, but the ground flew beneath him. He took the steps up to the house two at a time.

'It's Bill. An accident. He's bleeding, real bad. A boar ripped him up.'

Then Colm sank down on his knees. People appeared from nowhere. They ran, a car started up and strong arms helped Colm to his feet and took him into a bedroom. For a moment he struggled against them. 'I have to be with Bill.'

'It's all right.'

'Bill needs me,' said Colm.

'They're getting the Flying Doctor out here. We don't know if the old man will make it[7] if we have to drive him down to the hospital in Katherine. Best to fly him to Darwin.'

Colm felt the blood drain from his face[8]. 'He will make it. He has to make it.'

---

[1] stick [stɪk] *Stock* [2] (to) aim [eɪm] *zielen* [3] (to) pass out [ˌpɑːs‿ˈaʊt] *ohnmächtig werden* [4] strength [streŋθ] *Kraft* [5] (to) race *rasen, jagen* [6] conscious [ˈkɒnʃəs] *bei Bewusstsein* [7] (to) make it *es schaffen, durchkommen* [8] He felt the blood drain from his face. [dreɪn] *Er fühlte, wie ihm das Blut aus dem Gesicht wich.*

Working with the text

1 The story

a) *Look at this flow chart and retell the story.*

Bill and Colm drive into the Victoria Desert ... ► ... repair the Dog Fence where an emu ... ► ... fill holes made by ... ► Rusty disappears / something is wrong with the dog ...

▼

A black boar attacks Bill and Colm ... ◄ ... is badly hurt / ... has to help him ... ◄ ... takes Bill to the nearest cattle station ... ◄ ... the Flying Doctor has to help Bill ...

b) *What part of the story do you find most exciting? Why?*

► *GF 1: Talking about the present (p. 145)*

2 The characters

a) *Partner B: Go to p. 92.*
Partner A: Choose adjectives from the box below to describe Bill to your partner. Give reasons for your choice.

brave • clever • difficult • easy-going • friendly • helpful • honest • nervous • old • stupid • violent • young

Now listen to Partner B's description of Colm. Do you agree with it? Give reasons.

b) *What do you think Bill and Colm were thinking in these situations?*

a) 'Tin Annie here, she's part camel, part jeep. So she'll be fine.' (p. 20, ll. 36–37)
b) Bill picked up the knife he used to kill rabbits. (p. 21, ll. 122–123)
c) Colm aimed straight between the eyes. (p. 23, ll. 241–242)

c) **Extra** *Describe the relationship between Bill and Colm.*

3 Extra Wild Australian animals

a) *In the story you've read about a lot of typical Australian animals. Make a list and find more information on them.*

b) *Find out more about the Dog Fence.*

► *SF Research (p. 124)*

4 Extra The end of the story

a) *What do you think happened next?*
- *Did Bill survive?*
- *Did Colm try to follow Bill? Or did he go out into the bush alone? Or back to the children's home?*

Write an ending. Remember the steps of writing:
1. *Brainstorm your ideas. Make notes.*
2. *Write your text. Use linking words, adjectives and adverbs to make it more interesting.*
3. *Correct your text.*

b) *Make groups of 4–5. Read your texts to each other. Present the ones you like best to the class. You can put your text in your DOSSIER.*

► *SF Brainstorming (p. 132)* • *SF Writing Course (pp. 134–135)* • *WB 16 (p. 9)*

How am I doing?

a) *Find or choose the correct answers.* ► *SF Check yourself (p. 122)*

Facts about Australia

1 Name three important Australian cities.
2 Name three Australian animals.
3 Name two things Australians do to protect themselves from UV radiation.
4 Name three sports Australians like to do.
5 When it's spring in Germany, it's ... in Australia.
A spring B summer C autumn D winter
6 What other word do Australians use to talk about the bush?
A hinterland B outback C desert D Dreamland
7 The largest ethnic group in Australia is ...
A the Asians.
B the African-Australians.
C the Aborigines. D the Whites.
8 Aborigines of the 'stolen generations' ...
A were thieves.
B were taken away by Whites.
C lived before 1600.
D built the Dog Fence.

Grammar

9 Put these sentences in indirect speech.
a) Kim: 'I'll have a great time Down Under.' Kim said ...
b) Jess: 'I just love kangaroos.' Jess said ...
c) Tom: 'Frank visited Sydney in 2009.' Tom said ...
d) Lara: 'We can go again next year.' Lara said ...

Words

10 The 'former mayor' of a town is somebody who ... the town's mayor.
A was once B is now C wants to be D will soon be
11 'Common' is another word for ...
A difficult. B a community event.
C in the outback.
D done by many people.
12 When you need to do something, you ...
A are allowed to do it.
B are able to do it. C have to do it.
D want to do it.
13 If you want to send somebody a photo, you can always ... it to an e-mail.
A glue B attach C enter D send

Understanding charts

14 The chart on the right is a ... chart. It shows the ... of Australia's population that lives in big cities, near big cities and ... from the cities. More than ... thirds of Australians live in the cities, about ... live more or less ... the cities, and only ... far from the cities.

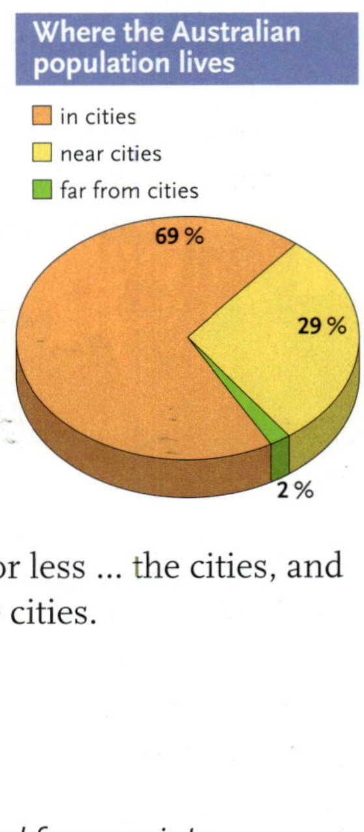

b) *Check your answers on p. 218 and add up your points.*

c) *If you had 27 or more points, well done! Maybe you can help students who had fewer points. If you had 26 points or fewer, it's a good idea to do some more work before you go on to the next unit. Where did you make mistakes? The chart below will tell you what you can do to improve your English.*

No.	Area	Find out more	Exercise(s)
1– 8	Facts about Australia	Parts A–C (pp. 8–19)	
9	Indirect speech	Exploring language (p. 18)	P 2–4 (pp. 18–19), WB 11–12 (pp. 6–7)
10–13	Words	Unit Vocabulary (pp. 156–161)	WB 9 (p. 6), 15 (p. 9)
14	Understanding charts	Part A (p. 10), SF (p. 126)	P 3 (p. 11), WB 7 (p. 4)

► **Skills check 1** *WB (pp. 10–15)*

1 WORDS Travelling

Fill in the right words to complete the sentences.
You're flying to Australia for a wonderful holiday. At the airport, you first (1) *check in*. Then you go to the (2) ... For your flight it's gate D21.

Now you're on the plane. The flight to Australia is very long and on the way you need to eat and drink. The flight attendant offers you a drink and a hot (3) ... There are lots of nice things on the menu today.

breakfast • (to) change planes • (to) check in • city centre • departure gate • key card • (to) land • meal • single ticket • suitcases • taxi • ticket machines

After you (4) ... at Singapore Airport, you finally (5) ... in Sydney. Of course, you hope that your (6) ... arrive too! If not, you'll have to go to the lost luggage office.

So how do you travel from the airport into the (7) ...? Well, the quickest and easiest way is to take a (8) ..., but it's also the most expensive one: it costs about 50 Australian dollars. So you decide to take a train instead. The (9) ... are easy to use and a (10) ... to the city is only 15 Australian dollars.

Now – tired but happy – you're at your hotel. The receptionist gives you the (11) ... to your room and tells you about the hotel – for example, the times when you can have (12) ... in the mornings.

2 Judy's job (Simple present and present progressive)

a) *Judy is the flight attendant who you can see in the photo above. Finish these sentences about her job. Use the* ***simple present*** *or the* ***present progressive****.*

1 Judy's job is exciting. She often ... (travel) to different countries.
2 Right now, she ... (fly) to Australia.
3 A typical day for Judy starts early. She usually ... (get up) at 5 o'clock. Then she ... (have) her breakfast and ... (drive) to the airport.
4 It is 10 o'clock now and Judy ... (work). She ... (bring) coffee and tea to the passengers on her plane.
5 Now it is 10 o'clock the next morning. Judy ... (just/arrive) at her hotel.
6 Judy always ... (stay) at a hotel when she is in another country. She ... (sleep) at the hotel – then the next day she ... (fly) home again.

b) *Write sentences about things that you often do and some things that you're doing right now.*
I often surf the internet. Right now, I'm chatting with my friends.

▸ *GF 1: Talking about the present (p. 145)*

3 Australia's most dangerous animals (Simple past and past progressive)

Read the text about Australia's most dangerous animals on the right, then complete the two stories below. Use the ***simple past*** *or* ***past progressive*** *of the verbs in brackets.*

> AUSTRALIA is home to some of the world's most dangerous animals. There are snakes, spiders and sometimes sharks. The most dangerous of all, however, are crocodiles. Two or three people die every year in crocodile attacks.

There's a crocodile in our tent!
In January 2005, two young Australians went camping near the Pentecost River in the north of Australia. At about 2 o'clock in the morning, they (1) *were sleeping* (sleep) when suddenly a crocodile (2) ... (come) into their tent. They (3) ... (run) to their car and (4) ... (climb) onto it. The next morning at 11 o'clock, they (5) ... (still/sit) on their car when some hunters (6) ... (arrive) and (7) ... (save) their lives.

Smile please!
In 2008, a tourist in Queensland was stupid – but lucky. He (8) ... (sit) in a boat on a river when a crocodile (9) ... (swim) towards the boat. The man's friend (10) ... (stand) on land. 'Put your hand in the water and play with the crocodile!' he (11) ... (shout). 'I'm going to take a photo.' Seconds later, the crocodile (12) ... (try) to bite the man's hand. 'It was a scary moment!', he (13) ... (say) afterwards.

▸ *GF 2: Talking about the past (pp. 146–147)*

4 WORDS It was scary! (Words that describe experiences)

a) *Look at the box. Find five pairs of adjectives that mean (almost) the same thing: good – ...*

b) *Find at least eight pairs of adjectives that mean opposite things: cool – boring; sad – ...*

c) *Write six sentences using adjectives from the box:*
1) Yesterday I played table tennis against my younger brother and lost 11–2. It was depressing!
2) ...

> amazing · awesome · awful · bad · boring · cool · crazy · dangerous · depressing · different · difficult · easy · excellent · exciting · fantastic · fine · funny · good · great · horrible · interesting · laughable · mad · nice · OK · sad · scary · silly · strange · surprising · terrible · unbelievable

5 WRITING One day last year ...

a) *Below is a very short story! Can you make it more interesting? Write the story again.*

> *Jake was riding his bike in the mountains. He fell off and broke his leg. He called for help with his mobile phone. Some people saved him. He went to hospital. He met Anne, a doctor. They fell in love. They got married.*

When?	one day last year, last September, first, then, next, after that, finally, ...
Who?	the man/woman/people who ...
How?	quickly, slowly, suddenly, ... (really) amazing/awful; (feel) happy/sad, ...
Linking words	because, but, so (that), although, when, while, ...

b) *Compare your story with a partner's.*

▸ *SF Writing Course (pp. 134–135)*

1 LISTENING Travelling to Australia

You are flying to Australia with your family.
- *Look at the questions below. You have 30 seconds.*
- *Listen to five announcements or short conversations that you hear on your journey. Note down the right answer – A, B or C.*
- *You will hear all the recordings* ***once****.*

1 At Heathrow Airport in London you hear this announcement: 'Flight Q201 to Sydney is now boarding at ...'

A GATE 7 B GATE 17 C GATE 70

2 On the plane from London to Sydney, the flight attendant is offering you ...

A an omelette or pasta.

B chicken with a salad or pork chops.

C chicken with a salad or pasta.

3 At Sydney Airport one of your suitcases is missing! The lost luggage office is ...

A just over there. B on the first floor. C next to the passport office.

4 A taxi from the airport into the city costs ...

A AU$ 50 B AU$ 52.50 C AU$ 55.20

5 Now you are at your hotel. Tomorrow breakfast is from ...

A 06:00–10:00 B 06:30–9:30 C 07:00–10:30

2 LISTENING Shark attack!

You are going to hear a radio news programme about how Jon Kerry, a young Australian, was attacked by a great white shark.
- *Look at the questions below for 30 seconds.*
- *Now listen and do the tasks. You will hear the news programme* ***twice****.*

a) *Which is right? Write down A, B, C or D.*

1 Jon was attacked near a beach in ...
A Queensland.
B South Australia.
C New South Wales.
D Western Australia.

2 When he was attacked, Jon was ...
A surfing.
B swimming.
C sunbathing.
D canoeing.

3 The shark bit into Jon's ...
A arm.
B foot.
C shoulder.
D leg.

4 It held him for around ...
A 3.5 seconds.
B 5 seconds.
C 40 seconds.
D 5 minutes.

5 After the attack ...
A a boat saved Jon in the water.
B the shark pulled Jon to the beach.
C Jon swam back to the beach.
D a big wave carried Jon to the beach.

6 Jon thought this was the ... part.
A most exciting
B easiest
C scariest
D most painful

b) *Finish the sentences.*

1 Jon's friends probably saved his life when they ... a rope[1] round his ... and stopped the bleeding.
2 Jon is lucky. He will always have a big scar[2] but he ...
3 Experts say that sharks don't normally ...
4 The experts also say that more people die in road accidents in Australia ... than from shark attacks ...
5 You should always swim ... so your friends can help you. And never swim ... or ... because that's when sharks usually feed.

[1] rope [rəʊp] *Seil* [2] scar [skɑː] *Narbe*

3 LISTENING Young Australians and the internet

Young Australians are among the world's biggest users of the internet. Six Australian students are discussing what they do online.

- *Look very carefully at the statements below for 30 seconds.*
- *Now listen and do the task.*
- *You will hear the recordings only **once**.*

Right or wrong? True or false? Note down 'T' or 'F'.

1. Student 1 thinks that she spends too much time online.
2. Student 2 never does just one thing at a time when he uses a computer.
3. Student 3 thinks her parents don't care about what she does online.
4. Student 4 thinks that young people know how to be safe online.
5. Student 5 tells a story about something that happened to her.
6. Student 6 thinks the internet is good for teenagers.

4 WRITING An online magazine for young Europeans

You often read an online magazine for young Europeans. This week, the magazine wants readers' ideas about the internet and it has a story competition.
Write about one of the two topics below. Write a text of about 150 words.

Topic 1: The internet and me
When and where do you usually use the internet? What do you do online? What things do you do most often online? Can the internet be bad for you?

Topic 2: A scary moment!
Finish this story in your own words.

It was a Saturday afternoon in September. I was bored, so I decided to go for a bike ride. After about an hour, I was on a small road in the country ...

How am I doing?

Check your answers to tasks 1–3 on page 218.

About the test

This test gave you the chance to try some of the kinds of tasks that you will have to do in your exam (*Abschlussprüfung*). If you found some tasks difficult, don't worry. You've got lots of time to practise. Remember: 'Practice makes perfect!'

Listening

The first three tasks in the test were listening tasks. The following questions will help you to think about how you did. Read the questions – which answer is right for you?

1 How hard or easy was each task?

	easy	OK	quite hard	very hard
Task 1				
Task 2				
Task 3				

2 What was difficult in the tasks?

a) People spoke too quickly.
b) I found the accents difficult.
c) There was a lot of information. I couldn't find the exact answers.
d) I didn't have time to finish all the tasks.
e) There were words and phrases that I just couldn't understand.

3 How did you do the tasks?

a) I read the tasks carefully first so I knew exactly what I had to listen for.
b) I looked quickly at the tasks first but only read them carefully while I was listening.
c) I wrote as many answers as I could the first time I heard the text and checked them (or filled in gaps) the second time.
d) There were lots of things I couldn't understand and I panicked.

▸ *SF Listening for detail (p. 127)* • *SF How to do well in a test (pp. 142–143)*

Writing

The fourth task in your test was a writing task. Work with a partner. Exchange the texts you've written and read your partner's text. Copy and fill in the assessment sheet[1] below. Remember: the idea is to help your partner with your feedback!

Assessment sheet	☹		😐		☺	
Name of partner ...	1	2	3	4	5	Comments
Did your partner ...						
1 ... write an interesting text/story?						
2 ... make grammar mistakes (with a tense, plural forms, etc.)?						
3 ... use interesting vocabulary?						
4 ... write longer sentences with linking words?						
5 ... write a text that is clear and easy to understand?						

▸ *SF Writing course (pp. 134–135)*

[1] assessment sheet *Beurteilungsbogen*

top jobs

Job information for young people

Welcome to the top jobs website.

Are you thinking about the future? Maybe you're not sure if you should stay at school or not. Do you need ideas about jobs or training? Do you want to find out about qualifications? Are you thinking about an apprenticeship? Then this is the website for you.

Abby, a chef on a ship

Alfie, a shop assistant in a shoe shop

Akeem, a mechanic in a garage

Binita, a police officer in an airport

Zach, a make-up artist for a film company

It's just the first step!

Your first job is an important decision for you but it doesn't have to be your job for life! Today some people change their jobs many times in their lives. You will learn important skills in every job you do – even in Saturday jobs or if you work as a volunteer. It's all good experience.

Ethan, a childcare assistant in a kindergarten

Poppy, a customer adviser in a bank

Amy, a fitness instructor in a sports centre

1 Top jobs?

a) *Choose your favourite and your least favourite job from the website. Make notes about*
- *what you like/don't like about the job*
- *why you would/wouldn't be good at it.*

b) *Make a double circle. Talk to different partners about jobs.*

A: What's your (least) favourite job? Why?

B: I would/wouldn't like a job as a ... because ...

... it looks fun/interesting/difficult/...

... you have to ...
work in a team/ with ...
work long hours/weekends/shifts
talk to/serve customers
meet/look after/advise people

... I'm (not) good at repairing things/...
... I'm (not) sporty/artistic/organized/calm/easy-going/hard-working/...

... I (don't) know a lot about cars/...
... I (don't) think you earn good money.

c) **Extra** *What's the most popular job in your class? And the least popular?*

2 What's the job really like?

a) *Listen to four of the people from the website.*
1. *Who is speaking?*
2. *Do they like their job?*
3. *Do they want to change jobs soon?*

b) *Listen again. Take notes.*
1. *Write down two good things and one bad thing that each person says about their job.*
2. *What plans for the future does each person have?*

3 Extra Now you

Ask a partner about his/her plans for the future.
When do you think you'll leave school?
What kind of job do you want to do?
Do you want to do an apprenticeship?

► *WB 1 (p. 16)* • **Text File 4** *(p. 104)*

PERSONALITY QUIZ

What's the right job for you?

Find out your personality type. Our quiz is just for fun, but it might give you some ideas for jobs.

1 You want to print your homework, but your dad says the printer isn't working. You say:

- A 'Stupid printer! I hate it!'
- B 'Don't worry, Dad. It's not important.'
- C 'I can see the problem. I know what to do.'
- D 'OK, I'll print it at school. And I'll phone a friend who can repair the printer.'

2 When you are asked to do jobs at home, …

- A you disappear!
- B you say OK. You don't mind helping. It's normal that everyone in the family helps.
- C you try to think of better ways to do the jobs.
- D you do the jobs quickly and then go on with more interesting things.

3 For a science project at school your group is designing a 'green' house that uses less energy. You say …

- A 'I'll do the presentation to the class.'
- B 'I'll choose the colours for the model and paint it. Is that OK?'
- C 'I'll do the internet research.'
- D 'OK, I've made the model. What's next?'

4 How would your teachers describe you?

- A 'Always late!'
- B 'A dreamer.'
- C 'A techie.'
- D 'An organized and reliable student.'

5 You're happy when …?

- A you're with a big group of friends.
- B you make someone smile.
- C you solve a difficult problem.
- D you finish everything on your to-do list.

6 Which is your favourite holiday?

7 If you were a fruit, what would you be?

- A A banana
- B A soft summer fruit, like a strawberry
- C A tomato. (Did you know they're a fruit, not a vegetable?)
- D But I'm not a fruit! I hate silly questions like this!

Count how many As, Bs, Cs and Ds you have.

THE RESULTS

Mostly A

Your personal qualities:

- **You're a confident, energetic and likeable person.**

You're artistic and you enjoy making things. But you get bored easily and you hate rules. You're good at starting things, but not so good at finishing them. You love an adventure. You want life to be fun and exciting.

Have you thought of a job as an actor or fitness instructor? Other ideas: a racing car driver, a waiter, a chef, …

Mostly B

Your personal qualities:

- **You're a calm, friendly, helpful and polite person.**

You're more interested in people than things. You love helping people and you're good at talking to them. You always try to do your best and you're good at working in a team. You want to change the world.

You might be interested in a job as a teacher or police officer. Other ideas: a vet's assistant, a dentist's assistant, …

Mostly C

Your personal qualities:

- **You're a hard-working and logical person.**

You're interested in everything around you – plants, animals, technology – and you want to understand how things work. You love information and you spend a lot of time on the internet. You're good at solving problems. You're more interested in ideas than people.

You could be a builder or a computer technician. Other ideas: a private detective, a truck driver, …

Mostly D

Your personal qualities:

- **You're a reliable, organized and punctual person.**

You're good at making decisions. You have a lot of fun with your friends, but you are serious about your work. You always finish what you've started. While everyone else is talking about it, you've done it! You think rules are important.

Your perfect job might be a bank clerk or a gardener. Other ideas: an office worker, a footballer, …

1 The quiz

a) *Do the quiz and read your results.*

b) *Talk about your results. Do you agree with the description of your personality type?*
- It says here that I'm/you're …
- I (don't) think that's true.
- I think I'm/you're a … person.

c) *What do you think of the jobs that the quiz suggests for you? What does your partner think?*
- I'd like/love/hate/ a job as a … because …
- … would be a good job for me/you because …
- Maybe you're right. / You're joking!

d) **Extra** *Suggest one more job for each personality type. Explain your choice to a partner.*

2 Personal qualities

a) Think: *Find adjectives and phrases on page 35 that match these jobs. Make lists.*

firefighter • make-up artist • mechanic • nurse

b) Pair: *With a partner agree on the four most important personal qualities for each job.*

c) Share: *Form a group with another pair. Compare your lists. Explain your choices.*

d) **Extra** *Choose two more jobs and list personal qualities that match them.*

P1 WORDS Jobs

a) Collect as many jobs as you can.

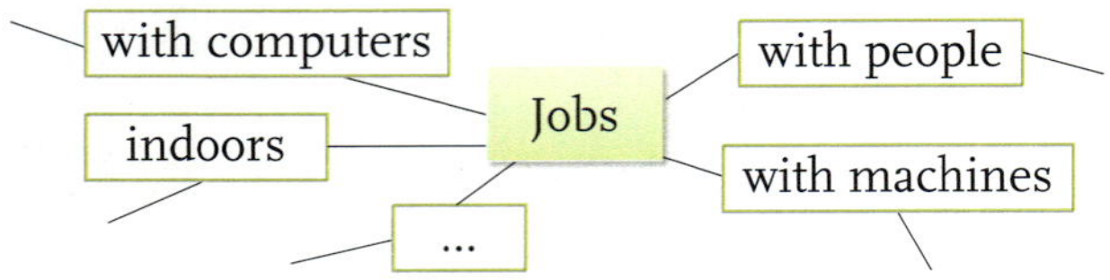

b) Think of a job. Describe it to a partner. Don't say the name! Can he/she guess the job?

In this job you ...

... sell things/work with .../repair ...

... have to be careful/reliable/calm/...

It's a job where ...

... you work in a workshop/shop/factory/...

Tip

If you can't find an exact English word for a job, you have to paraphrase it.

▸ *SF Paraphrasing (p. 132)*

P2 WORDS Job profiles

a) Read the job profile below. Match it to one of the jobs in the photos.

In this job you have to be very calm and confident. An important part of the job is checking equipment so you must be very careful. You have to like working in a team too. This is a great job because it's exciting and you can save people's lives. This isn't a good job if you don't like blood.

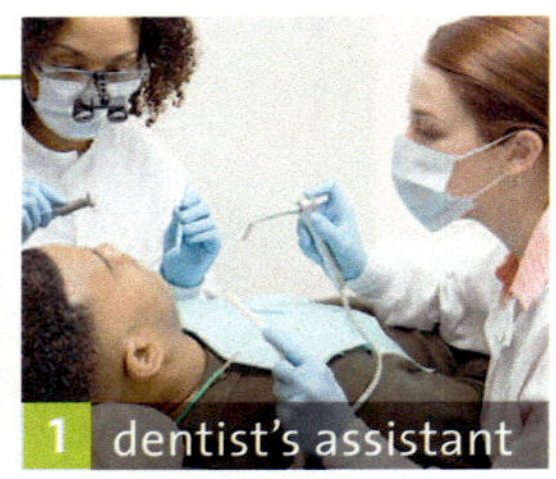
1 dentist's assistant

2 vet's assistant

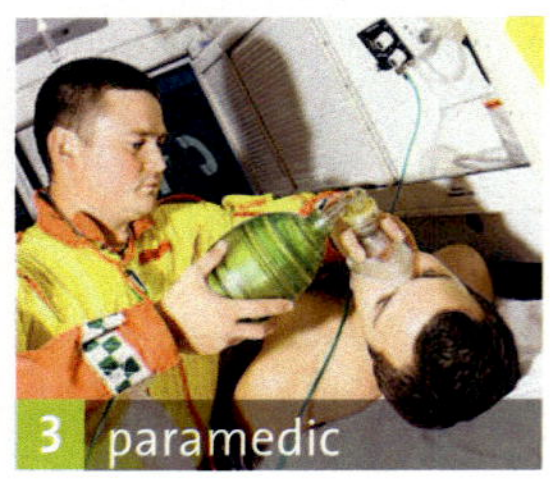
3 paramedic

b) Write another job profile. Find out about:
- what personal qualities you need and why
- what you have to do in the job
- what's good/difficult about the job

P3 WORDS Your profile

a) Make a chart for yourself like this. Use words and phrases from page 35.

personal qualities	*interests*	*possible jobs*
– confident *– good at solving problems* *...*	*– computers* *– like designing things* *– enjoy ...*	*– ...*

b) Use your chart to write a short personal profile. You can put it in your DOSSIER.

Personal qualities: I'm a confident person, but I can be shy with new people. I like working in a group, but I can work alone too. I ...

Interests: I have a lot of interests. I enjoy sport, for example ... And I'm also interested in ...

Possible jobs: I'm not sure what job I want to do. Maybe I'll be a ... That might be a good job for me because ... I'm also thinking about becoming a ...

▸ *WB 2–3 (pp. 16–17)*

P4 EVERYDAY ENGLISH MEDIATION Summer jobs in Britain

Partner B: Go to page 93.

a) *Partner A: You and your partner are looking for summer jobs in Britain next year. Tell your partner in German about this job. Say:*
- what you have to do in the job
- what sounds good/bad about the job

b) *Your partner will tell you about another job. Listen carefully and take notes.*

c) *Which job do you like best? Why?*

BJ'S BURGERS

BJ'S BURGER RESTAURANT

Summer work for energetic people!

We are looking for good people to join our team. You will be the face of BJ's, so you need to be friendly, polite and good at smiling. You also need to be quick and helpful. **We need people to serve customers, prepare and cook food and to clean the restaurant.**
Experience useful, but full training will be given.

Download an application form here and send it to us, or bring it to our restaurant.

P5 EVERYDAY ENGLISH WRITING Filling in a job application form

a) *Fill in a copy of the form for yourself.*

b) *Check your partner's form.*
- Did your partner write clearly and use a black pen?
- Is the form neat? Are there any spelling mistakes?

BJ'S BURGERS

Job application form for BJ'S BURGERS

Personal details (Please write clearly and use a black pen.)

First name(s): Jade Louise Last name: Hunter

Address: 3 Oakwood Close, Cambridge CB1 7LY

Tel no (home): 01223 456238 Tel no (mobile): 07938 575593

Email address: jlhunter@mvmail.com

Your work experience

Company	From	To	What did you do?
Sugar'n' Spice Café	July 2008	Sept 2008	Prepared food, served customers and cleaned the kitchen in a busy café

Your education

School	From	To	Subjects
Cambridge High School	2005	to date	GCSEs in Maths, English, French, Art, Technology

More about you

Look at these pairs of statements. Which statement describes you best?
For each pair of statements, choose A or B. Example:

	A		B	
	I like working in a team.	X	I like working on my own.	
1	I am organized.	X	I work quickly.	
2	I do what I am asked to do.		I volunteer for work.	X
3	I work best on my own.		I work best with others.	X
4	I think the customer is always right.	X	I think the customer is often wrong.	
5	I like to be part of a group.	X	I like to do my own thing.	

▸ WB 4–7 (pp. 17–19)

APPLYING FOR A JOB

1 Writing a CV

The Coffee Pot

Waiter/waitress for busy town centre café (weekends). Be part of a friendly team, listen to cool music all day, wear jeans! Apply with CV to: The Coffee Pot, High Street, Hertford SG14 3SY

a) *James wants to apply for this job. Look at his CV. Which of the things in the box are on it?*

address • age • date of birth • last name • nationality • postcode • sex • telephone number

b) **Extra** *What things are usually on a German CV? What's different on this CV?*

► *SF Writing a CV (p. 136)*

Jamie Williams
12 Bluebell Court, Old Hall Green, Hertfordshire SG11 1DS
Telephone: 01920 462233 | Email: jwilliams29@aol.com

Personal statement	I am a hard-working, reliable student. I like working in a team. I am looking forward to getting more experience in the workplace.
Education	
2006 to date	The Chauncy School, Ware (secondary school)
1999–2006	Little Hadham School (primary school)
Qualifications	
Studying for GCSEs in	English, Maths, Geography, Science, Music, French, History, Art
Other skills	First-aid certificate, moped licence, basic computer skills
Work experience	Two weeks in a hotel; babysitting job at weekends
Hobbies and interests	I play table tennis and basketball in after-school clubs. I am a member of the school camera club and Ware Youth Club.
References	Mrs K Smith, Manager, Hertford House Hotel ksmith@herthousehotel.co.uk

12 Bluebell Court
Old Hall Green
Hertfordshire SG11 1DS

The Coffee Pot
High St
Hertford SG14 3SY

30 November 2010

Dear Sir/Madam

I am writing about your ... in the Herts Gazette of 28th November for a job as a ... in your café. I would like to ... for the job. My ... is enclosed.

I am a friendly, ... person and I enjoy meeting new people. As you can see from my CV, I did work experience in a ... I worked in the kitchen. I also served ... in the restaurant. The hotel manager will be happy to give me a ... Her contact ... are in my CV. I am available for an interview at any time.

I look forward to hearing from you.
Yours faithfully

Jamie Williams

Jamie Williams

2 A letter of application

Complete Jamie's letter of application to the café with words from the box.

advertisement • apply • CV • customers • details • helpful • hotel • reference • waiter

STUDY SKILLS Formal letters

This kind of letter is a formal letter, so use formal style, e.g. **I am**, not **I'm**, **advertisement**, not **ad**.
If you don't know the name of the person you're writing to, start with **Dear Sir/Madam** and end with **Yours faithfully**.
If you know the name of the person (e.g. **Dear Mrs Smith**), end with **Yours sincerely**.

► *SF Writing formal letters (p. 137)* • **Text File 5** *(pp. 105–107)*

P1 STUDY SKILLS CVs

a) *Look at the job advert below. What kind of person are they looking for? What do you have to do in the job? Take notes.*

You must be – friendly, ... You have to – help on ...

Meadows Home Farm

We are looking for a reliable person with lots of energy to help us this summer on the farm and in our farm shop. Great job for foreign students who want to practise their English.

If you like living in the country and don't mind working at weekends, send your CV and letter of application to Jane Hall, Meadows Home Farm Shop, Harston, Cambridge CB22 4BE, Great Britain or jh@homefarm.co.uk

b) *Partner B: Go to page 93.*
Partner A: Tell your partner about this candidate.
I've got the CV of someone called ...
She's got these qualifications: ...
She has done some work experience in ...
She's interested in ...
Then listen to your partner. He/She will tell you about another candidate.

CURRICULUM VITAE

Lena Dickhaus
Rosenstrasse 12, 42857 Remscheid, Germany
Telephone: 0049 202 334 84
Email: ldickhaus@email-rs.de

Education
2004–2010 Albert-Schweitzer-Realschule (secondary school), Remscheid, Germany

2000–2004 Eisenstein Primary School, Remscheid, Germany

Qualifications
Studying for *Fachoberschulreife* (similar to GCSEs)
Languages: English (6 years), French (4 years)
European Computer Driving Licence (ECDL)

Work experience
Work experience in a zoo shop (3 weeks)

Hobbies and interests
My hobbies are cycling and badminton. I am very interested in nature and animals.

References
Mrs Schwede (manager of zoo shop),
Zoo Wuppertal, Hubertusallee 30, 42117
Wuppertal, Germany

c) *Look back at your notes from a). Which candidate should get the job ? Why? Discuss.*

P2 STUDY SKILLS Writing a letter of application

a) *Improve this letter. Rewrite the underlined parts with words and phrases from the box.*

advertisement • apply for • customers • I am • I do not • I enclose • I look forward to hearing from you • similar to • team • the experience • will be happy to

b) *Imagine you want a summer job in Britain. Read the ad below and write your own CV and letter of application.*

PARKVILLE HOTEL

Looking for a summer job?
Hard-working person needed to help in the kitchen of our busy hotel restaurant. Must be happy to do evening and weekend work. Free meals, uniform and use of our sauna.

Interested? Email your CV and letter of application to Paul Robinson, Parkville Hotel
jobs@parkvillehotel.co.uk

Dear Ms Hall

I am writing about your ad in the Cambridge News and I would like to have the job. Here is my CV. I'm 17 years old and I will leave school at the end of June with the Fachoberschulreife, which is a bit like GCSEs in Britain.

I am a friendly, helpful person and I enjoy working in a group of people. I am very reliable and I don't mind working at weekends. I have studied English for six years and my level is quite good. This year I worked in a zoo for three weeks. I did office work and served people in the zoo shop. I really enjoyed what I did there. The manager can give me a reference.

Write back soon.

Yours sincerely

Lena Dickhaus

Lena Dickhaus

► WB 8–9 (p. 20)

THE BUSINESS: A REALITY TV SHOW

1 Top tips for interviews

Saturday 6.30 pm

THE BUSINESS

On this week's show the big boss is Rita McQueen from the fashion company RMQ.
The prize is two weeks' work experience as Rita's assistant. The candidates Lucy and Mani have to impress Rita in an interview. They got some tips from adviser Simon Gubbins.

'Big boss' Rita McQueen. Who will she choose?

Listen carefully to the questions!

Don't talk too quickly.

Relax! Before an interview listen to music or do yoga.

Smile in the interview!

Dress suitably. Don't wear bright colours or too much make-up.

Show your interest in the company.

Don't talk too much.

Prepare answers to questions like 'What are your strengths and weaknesses?'

Which three tips do you think are the most important?

2 VIEWING The interviews

a) Watch the interviews. Give points to Mani and Lucy on a copy of this chart.

b) Which candidate should win?

c) Watch the results. What do you think about Rita's decision?

Assessment sheet	☹		😐		☺	
The candidate	**1**	**2**	**3**	**4**	**5**	**Comments**
1 was relaxed and friendly				✓		*smiled a lot*
2 dressed suitably						
3 listened carefully						
4 talked well (not too much/too little)						
5 was well prepared						

3 Internet forum ▶ TV talk ▶ The Business

Max1234 (2 days ago) Did you see the show last night? I loved the part when Mani told Rita that he was the best. The look on Rita's face!! What was your favourite 'Mani moment'?

Flipper (2 days ago) For me, the best part was when they went shopping. Simon told Mani and Lucy to look for clothes for the interview. Simon asked Mani to choose a tie. I laughed so much when I saw the tie that Mani bought!

AliceW (1 day ago) Yeah! That tie was crazy! The adviser told them not to be shy – not a problem for Mani!

EJ (1 day ago) He was so cheeky in the interview! Rita asked him what he knew about her business. And he clearly didn't know much. Then Rita asked him if he had any weaknesses. And Mani said no! And then he asked her when he could start!! Rita chose the wrong one!

Which parts of the show did these people like best? Describe the part you liked best to a partner.

P1 SPEAKING How would you describe yourself? (Having a job interview)

a) *Read this interview for a weekend job in a computer shop. Decide how you would answer the interviewer's questions.*

Interviewer Hello, I'm Jack Bond.
You A Hi. B Hello, nice to meet you.
Interviewer Did you have a good trip here?
You A Fine thanks. B No, but I'm here now.
Interviewer Good. Thanks for your application. Can I ask why you want to work for us?
You A Well, my mum saw your advert and she told me to apply.
B Well, I'm really interested in the things that you sell and I know I'd be good at this kind of work.
Interviewer How would you describe yourself?
You A I'm hard-working and reliable. I'm also interested in new technology.
B I have a lot of friends and I'm interested in computer games and music.
Interviewer Have you got any experience?
You A No, not really. We did work experience at school. I worked in a hotel but that wasn't real work.
B I did three weeks' work experience in a hotel. I really enjoyed talking to the guests.
Interviewer What are your weaknesses?
You A I'm not great at Maths.
B My marks in Maths weren't great last year, but my marks are better this year.
Interviewer Now, do you have any questions about the job?
You A Yes. Could you tell me what hours I'd have to work?
B Yes. Could you tell me how long the breaks are?
Interviewer You have to work from 8.30 to 3 o'clock and you get two 20-minute breaks. – OK? Well, that's it for today. We'll make our decision and will let you know soon.
You A OK. Thanks very much. B Can't you tell me right now? Oh well, goodbye.
Interviewer Thanks for coming. Goodbye.
You A Goodbye and thank you very much. B See you later.

b) *Practise the interview with a partner.*

c) *You're going to take part in an interview. Partner A is the candidate. Partner B will ask the questions. Partner C will assess the candidate.*
Partner B: Go to page 94.
Partner C: Go to page 96.
Partner A: Read the role card on the right.

ROLE CARD Partner A:

You're going to an interview for this job:

Local football club is looking for **friendly students** to work in club shop on match days.
You will get necessary training.
Candidates should live near the stadium. **Apply now!**

HORNBY F.C.

Be ready to tell the interviewer about:
- your personal qualities
- your interests
- why you're interested in the job

Prepare some questions, e.g. about the pay, what you have to do, etc.

d) *Discuss the assessment. Then swap roles.*

▸ *SF Speaking Course (pp. 138–139) • WB 10 (p. 21)*

P 2 REVISION Talking to a teacher (Indirect speech)

Steve had an interview. Complete the text. Use the verbs in the box.

could • did • had • had been • had worked • liked • wanted • was • were • would get

(1) I'm a confident person.

(2) I can work in a team.

(3) I have lots of ideas.

(4) I like working with children.

(5) I sometimes do babysitting.

(6) I worked in a summer camp in the holidays.

(7) I was a group leader.

(8) I hope I'll get an apprenticeship.

Steve told his teacher that he *was* a confident person. He said that he (2) work in a team. He added that he (3) lots of ideas. He also said that he (4) working with children and that he sometimes (5) babysitting. He told the teacher that he (6) in a summer camp in the holidays. He also said that he (7) a group leader. He added that he hoped he (8) an apprenticeship.

P 3 Exploring language Indirect speech: commands, requests and questions

a) *In the internet forum (p. 40) people report what Simon told Mani and Lucy to do. Compare the sentences on the right with what Simon said.*

Look for clothes for the interview.

Mani, please choose a new tie.

Don't be shy!

Simon told Mani and Lucy to look for clothes for the interview.
Simon asked Mani to choose a new tie.
He told Mani and Lucy not to be shy.

b) *Report these sentences.*

1 'Listen carefully to the questions, Mani.' – Simon told Mani to ...
2 'Lucy, please talk more.' – Simon asked Lucy to ...
3 'Mani, don't talk too much.' – He told Mani ...
4 'Say thank you at the end.' – He told them both ...

c) *Now look at these direct questions. Compare them with the indirect questions. What's the same? What's different? What does 'if' mean here?*

1 'What do you know about my business?'
2 'Do you have any weaknesses?'

1 Rita asked him what he knew about her business.
2 Rita asked him if he had any weaknesses.

► GF 5: Indirect speech II (p. 150)

P 4 Before the interview (Indirect speech: commands and requests)

Grace is going to her first job interview. Her dad has some tips for her. Write down what he said.

1 'Clean your teeth before the interview.'
Grace's dad told her to ...
2 'Don't wear too much make-up.'
He told her not to ...
3 'Please wear a nice jacket.'
He asked her to ...
4 'Be polite and friendly.'
5 'Don't talk too quickly.'
6 'Please don't eat anything in the interview!'
7 'Smile!'
8 'Don't be nervous.'
9 'Please send me a text at the end.'

► WB 11–12 (pp. 21–22)

P5 At the travel agent's (Indirect speech: questions)

a) *Adam applied to Sunshine Travel Agent's for a job. He had his interview with the owner, Mrs Tay. Later Adam's friend Katy wants to know what questions Mrs Tay asked. What does Adam tell Katy? Change the tense.*

1 Mrs Tay asked me what kind of person I was.
2 She wanted to know what my favourite …

b) Extra *Ask each other some of Mrs Tay's questions.*

P6 I asked her if I could get a cheap holiday (Indirect speech: questions)

Adam also told Katy about the questions he asked Mrs Tay. What did he tell Katy? Change the tense.

1 'Can I get a cheap holiday?'
I asked her if I could …
2 'Can I wear jeans to work?'
3 'Do you close for lunch?'
4 'Do I have to work on Saturdays?'
5 'Is the office busy on Saturdays?'
6 'Will you give me some training?'
7 'Will I get the job?'

P7 ENGLISH FOR JOBS Calling about an interview

a) *Listen to the phone call. Complete the message.*

Message for
Mr White

Message
… … called.
He wanted to check …
– tomorrow …
His phone no. is 07786 … …

b) *Listen to the next call. Complete Jemma's notes.*

Interview time: - …
Place - … Street …
big … building
Ask for … at the … desk

▸ WB 13–16 (pp. 22–24)

HOME NEWS MUSIC SPORT SCIENCE BUSINESS

BUSINESS

How to be a teenage millionaire

Before you read the text, talk about these questions:
- How do teenagers usually earn money?
- Do you know anybody who has their own business?

She hasn't got a rich family. She hasn't won the lottery. But at 17, Ashley Qualls, a computer geek from Detroit, is a millionaire. She's a successful businesswoman with her own company and she has bought a house for $250,000. But she's still too young to vote!

Ashley's idea was very simple. Her website, whateverlife.com, offers free designs that teenagers can use for their myspace.com pages.

Ashley, who is known as "AshBo" to her friends, has been working with websites since she was about nine years old. While other children were watching TV or playing outside, she was teaching herself HTML. She loved working with colours and designs for myspace.com layouts.

In 2004, she borrowed $8 from her mother to buy the whateverlife.com domain name. She didn't want to start a business. She just wanted a website to show her layouts to her friends.

More and more people started to visit the website and download Ashley's designs. Within a few weeks, she had 100 visitors. Then 5,000. Now her website has over 3,000 designs and gets over 7 million visitors a month. "I used to be excited when there were two people on the site and one was me!" says Ashley.

Advertisers started to get interested in advertising on her site and in September 2005 Ashley received her first cheque from the big

Ashley with some of her friends

advertising company, Value Click Media. It was for $2,700. "It was more than I made in a month," her mother says. That was just the start. The next cheque was for $5,000, the third was for $10,000.

When the first money arrived, her mother couldn't believe it. She wasn't sure if it was really possible to make money from a website. But Ashley was confident. She told her mother: "No, I really trust this. I think it's really gonna happen."

Although she was an excellent student at her high school, Ashley found it difficult to go to school and run a company. In January 2006, six months before her 16th birthday, she left school. She decided to continue studying from home so that she would have more time for the business. It was a big decision, so how did people react? "Everybody was shocked," she says. "They asked, 'Are you sure you know what you're doing?' But I had this crazy chance to do something different."

Most websites for teenagers are designed by adults. When you go to Ashley's site, it is clearly something that has been made by a teenager. This gives Ashley a big advantage because she understands what teenagers want. "They look at me and think, 'She's my age, she must know what I like.' "

The business now brings in about $70,000 a month. (The designs are still free. The money comes from advertising.) Ashley is learning how to be the "big boss". Her mother now works for her as a manager and she has a business adviser who helps her too. She also pays some of her friends to work for her after school and at weekends.

It's not easy to be someone's boss and their friend. Last year one of Ashley's friends was helping her, but Ashley thought she wasn't working hard enough. Ashley says that things were difficult between them for a while, but they are friends again now. Now she has a set of rules for everyone who works for her. "I tell them they have to give me at least 25 layouts a week to get paid," Ashley says. "It's just business."

Ashley had the right idea at the right time, and some people would say she was just lucky. But she clearly is very ambitious and determined and she works hard to make her business a success. "You have to believe in yourself and believe in what you're doing," says Ashley. "These have been the best few years of my life, and also the most stressful ... If people think running **WhateverLife** has always been easy, they are wrong," she adds.

Sometimes Ashley misses the normal life of a teenager. More than once she has returned to her old school, Lincoln Park High School, just for the day. Her friends will finish school soon. "I miss the fact that I won't graduate with my friends. They're all getting excited and it's sad to know I won't be a part of that exact moment."

And the future? Ashley hasn't got any definite plans. She wants to go to college, and she's thinking of going to design school in New York, which she calls her "dream city".

Working with the text

1 The story

a) *Match the sentence halves about Ashley.*

1 Ashley Qualls is only 17 years old, but ...
2 Teenagers can download Ashley's designs ...
3 When she was nine, Ashley began to ...
4 Ashley's website became popular very quickly and ...
5 Ashley started to earn money when ...
6 Ashley's website is popular with teenagers because ...
7 Ashley's relationship with her friends is special because ...
8 Ashley is not sure about her future, but ...

a from her website.
b it now gets over seven million visits a month.
c advertising companies got interested in her website.
d she wants to go to design school in New York City.
e she's already got her own internet company.
f she's their boss.
g she knows what they like.
h teach herself HTML.

b) *All these sentences are true, but which of them sums up the article best?*

1 Ashley's family isn't rich and her mum works for her.
2 Ashley left school when she was 15 because she wanted more time for her business.
3 Ashley's business started as a hobby, but she worked hard and now she's very successful.
4 Ashley's web designs are free and her website is popular with teenagers.

2 The person

a) *How would you describe Ashley? Use at least three words from the box. Find examples in the text to support your answer.*

ambitious • hard-working • easy-going • a geek • artistic • difficult • fun • greedy

I think she is hard-working because in the text it says that she started when she was nine years old.

b) *Find four or more facts that show the positive and negative side of Ashley's success. Take notes.*

c) *What do you think of Ashley's story? Would you like her life? Tell a partner what you think.*

I'd like to... / But I wouldn't want to ...
... study at home / earn lots of money
... pay my friends or my mum to work for me
... be the boss
... work so hard / have no time to relax ...
So to sum up I would/wouldn't like Ashley's life.

3 Extra Your comment

Write a comment about Ashley Qualls' story for this internet forum.

Today at 13:32 Chris wrote:
Ashley's story is very interesting. She's a role model for young people.

By Lea at 14:01: I don't agree. I don't think she's a role model. She's just a lucky person. We only read about her because she has lots of money. There are lots of young people who are much better role models. I'd like to read about young people who are trying to help other people.

By Maria at 14:24: I disagree with Lea. It wasn't luck. She is determined and works hard. Well done Ashley! She's a role model for me.

► *WB 17 (p. 24)*

How am I doing?

a) *Find or choose the correct answers.*

Describing personal qualities

Instead of the underlined words use a word from the box. There are more words than you need.

ambitious • calm • cheeky • greedy • logical • popular • punctual • reliable • sporty •

1 I'm not really someone who likes sport.
2 Sue is liked by everyone.
3 She's a person who does what she promises.
4 He's a little bit rude, but in a funny way.
5 I'm someone who wants to be successful.
6 They're never late for anything.

Complete the sentences with the two adjectives that go together best.

7 I'd say that I'm a ... and ... person.
A calm B greedy C organized
8 In this job you have to be ... and ...
A informal B punctual C reliable
9 He's successful because he's ... and ...
A ambitious B cheeky C confident

Grammar

10 Ms Hall phoned Lena Dickhaus. Put her words in indirect speech.
a) 'Please come for an interview next week.' – Ms Hall asked Lena ...
b) 'Don't worry if next week isn't possible.' – Ms Hall told Lena ...
c) 'Can you come in two weeks?' – Ms Hall asked ...
d) 'Do you need directions for getting here?' – Ms Hall asked ...

Words

What's the name for a person who ...
11 helps doctors and sick people in a hospital?
12 repairs cars in a garage?
13 sells holidays to people?
14 looks after very young children?
15 helps bank customers decide how to save their money?
16 teaches people how to do exercises?
17 helps a vet in an animal clinic?

CVs

18 Name four headings you can use in a CV.

Letters of application

19 Start a letter of application with ... *Dear Sir or Madam* when
A you know B you don't know
the name of the person you're writing to.
20 Say where you found out about the job ...
A at the beginning of the letter.
B at the end of the letter.
21 When you're writing, it's better to use ...
A short verb forms (*I'm, I don't*, etc.).
B long verb forms (*I am, I do not*, etc.).
22 Saying something about your personal qualities is ...
A usually a good idea.
B something you should never do.
23 Always enclose ...
A your CV.
B photos of you and your family.
24 When you know the name of the person you're writing to, end the letter with ...
A Yours faithfully ... B Yours sincerely ...

b) *Check your answers on p. 219 and add up your points.*

c) *If you had 27 or more points, well done! Maybe you can help students who had fewer points. If you had 26 points or fewer, it's a good idea to do some more work before you go on to the next unit. Where did you make mistakes? The chart below will tell you what you can do to improve your English.*

No.	Area	Find out more	Exercise(s)
1– 9	Personal qualities	pp. 32–35	P 3, p. 36; WB 2–3 (pp. 16–17)
10	Indirect speech	Exploring language (p. 42)	P 4–6, pp. 42–43; WB 11–14 (pp. 21–33)
11–17	Words	pp. 32–35	P 1–2, p. 36; WB 1 (p. 16), 15 (p. 23)
18–24	CV, Letter of Application	Part B (p. 38), SF (pp. 136–137)	P 1–2, p. 39; WB 8–9 (p. 20)

▸ *Self-evaluation 1–2 WB (p. 25)* • **Skills check 2** *WB (pp. 26–31)*

WORLDWIDE

LIVE ► | STARS ► | MEDIA ► | POLITICS ► | JOBS ►

Sunday, 2.05 pm

In this week's WORLDWIDE teenagers from around the world talk about their lives.

Hannah Tilling, Derby, UK

Hannah Tilling, 15

Let me tell you a bit about my lifestyle. First there's shopping. That's what I think about all the time. Shopping for important stuff: glitter, colour, clothes, shoes and accessories.
Then there's talking. I can talk about nothing for hours, especially on the phone.
I've always found it easy to make new friends. With girls I just say 'Do you want to come shopping with me?'
With boys it's easy too. If I fancy a boy, I go up to him, smile and just talk about anything that comes into my head. You have to do all the talking with boys – they're so shy.

Craig Carter, Auckland, New Zealand

Craig Carter, 16

I'm the head boy at our school in Auckland and I'm mad about sport – especially rugby. I'm one of the little white boys in our 1st XV – most of the other guys are Maori or Pacific Islanders. I'd like to have a career in sport one day and I am already making some money from it. I'm a surf lifesaver and work at an Auckland beach in the summer. My parents are worried that I won't be good enough for a sports career. So they make sure I work hard at school too.

1 Six teenagers

a) *Read about Craig, Hannah and Lina. Take notes under these headings.*

Interests/Fun	Work/School
Friends/Family	Future plans

b) *Listen to Tyler, Elin and Chia-Wen. Do they speak about all four topics? Take notes under your headings.*

c) *Compare your notes. Say what you find interesting about the six teenagers.*

Elin Nieminen, Eno, Finland

Chia-Wen Lin, Kuala Pilah, Malaysia

Tyler Ford, Eugene, Oregon, USA

Lina Ejogo, Ife, Nigeria

Lina Ejogo, 17

I get up at 5 am and do my chores at home and then I walk to school. It takes nearly an hour. My favourite subjects are physics and chemistry and I'm top of my school in them.

I and my six brothers and sisters all go to school. But my parents have no money for books, so I have to share them with my classmates. But it is the same for many of my class. There are 60 in our class and we have about 30 books. But at least we all have chairs. When I get back home in the evening, I do my homework. It's dark then and in Ife we don't often have electricity. But we have candles, so I can work.

In my free time I do extra physics classes and help my mother in the market. My parents sell second-hand clothes there.

Go here for our interviews with Tyler, Elin and Chia-Wen.

2 Now you

a) *Which of the teenagers would you most like to meet? Decide what you would tell him/her about yourself. Make notes under the headings from 1a or other headings that fit you better.*

b) *Use your notes to write down what you would tell the teenager. Explain how your life is similar to/different from his/hers. You can put your text in your DOSSIER.* ► *WB 1 (p. 32)*

MOBILE

1 Mobile life

a) *Ask your teacher for a copy of the following questionnaire and answer the questions.*

1 What do you do most with your mobile?

a) make calls ☐
b) send text messages ☐
c) play games ☐
d) take photos ☐
e) …

For questions 2–12 choose the best answer for you:

a) **Sure!**
b) **No way!**
c) **I'm not sure.**

2 Is it OK to send a text message while you're talking to somebody?

3 Is it OK to talk on a mobile in a café or restaurant?

4 Is it OK to send or receive text messages during lessons at school?

5 Is it all right to secretly film someone or take a photo of them with your mobile?

6 Would you read or write text messages if you were at a funeral?

7 Are you allowed to stay out later if you have your mobile with you?

8 Do you let your parents look at the messages and pictures on your mobile?

9 Is it OK to invite someone on a date by text message?

10 Is it OK to end a relationship by text message?

11 Is it OK to dodge calls from your parents?

12 Would you feel unwanted if a whole day went by and your mobile phone didn't ring?

b) **Extra** *Questions 2–12 in a) are about 'rules' for using mobiles. Think of another rule and make a question about it. Choose the two best questions from your class and answer them.*

c) *With a partner, compare all your answers.*
– How did you answer question 1/2/…?
– Oh, I had the same answer as you./ My answer was different. I …
– I think it's OK to … I've done it once/a few times/often. What about you?
– I agree/don't agree. I've never …

d) *Collect all the class's answers in a survey.*

2 What do you think?

a) *Divide the class into two groups – A and B.*
Group A students:
Think of arguments why you should be allowed to use your mobile phone at school. Write them down.
Group B students:
Think of arguments why you should not be allowed to use your mobile at school. Write them down.

b) *Exchange your arguments in a double circle – Group A students on the inside, Group B on the outside. Change partners three or four times.*

P1 STUDY SKILLS Outline and written discussion

a) *Using an outline to structure your text*
Think of more arguments for and against the statement on the right. Complete this outline.

STUDY SKILLS Outline

An outline helps you to structure a written discussion before you start writing.
Here's an example:

1 Introduction
2 First point of view
  2.1 First argument
  2.2 Second argument
  2.3 ...
3 Opposite point of view
  3.1 First argument
  3.2 ...
4 Conclusion

1 Introduction
2 Students should not be allowed
  2.1. can get help from outside in tests
  2.2. lessons are interrupted
  ...

ASAP = as soon as possible

b) *A written discussion*

1 **Introduction**
First introduce the topic. Start with a personal experience or a general question.

2 **Present the first point of view**
Present one point of view. It's often better to start with the view you disagree with. Explain the arguments and give examples for them.

3 **Present the opposite point of view**
Then present the arguments for the other point of view. Begin this part with a sentence that links it to the first point of view.

4 **Conclusion**
In the conclusion present your own point of view. Don't present new arguments.

Add arguments to the text and complete it.

Nearly all students have mobiles. But should they be allowed to take them to school?

Some people say that students really need mobiles. First, they might have to call their parents after school, for example when they miss the bus. Second, parents might want to contact them, for example when students don't go home right after school.
...

However, other people are against mobiles at school because they think that students might use them to get help from outside, for example in tests. Another argument against mobiles is that lessons are interrupted, for example when a phone rings.
...

After looking at both sides I think that mobiles should not be allowed at schools because there are more disadvantages than advantages. I think it's just unfair when some students use them to do better in a test.

c) *Find arguments for and against this statement:*
'School students should rate their teachers on the internet.'

Make an outline. Then discuss the topic in writing. You can also use the phrases on the right.

In my opinion • Other people disagree. • So ... • That's why ... • To sum up, ...

► *SF Outline and written discussion (p. 140) • WB 2 (p. 32)*

P2 WORDS Tricky translations (False friends)

a) *Find the correct word.*

German	English	English	German
bekommen	?	become	?
streng	?	strong	?
brav	?	brave	?
Meinung	?	meaning	?
Chef	?	chef	?
Keks	?	cake	?
(der) See	?	sea	?
Flur	?	floor	?
Rock	?	rock	?
Mörder	?	murder	?

b) *What's the English for the German words?*

1 Where did you *bekommen* that blue Rock?
2 Everyone thinks our new Maths teacher is very *streng*. What's your *Meinung*?
3 The police photographer took pictures of the *Mörder*.
4 After lunch, we walked around the *See*.
5 I'd like to *werden* a member of the club.
6 The telephone is outside in the *Flur*.
7 Would you like a *Keks* or some *Kuchen* with your tea?
8 We sat on a *Felsen* and looked at the *Meer*.
9 Be *brav* while I'm out!

▸ *SF Using a bilingual dictionary (p. 123)*

P3 EVERYDAY ENGLISH You and your mobile

a) *Complete the dialogue.*

A: Hey, that (number/ringtone) sounds great. Where did you get it?
B: I (called/downloaded) it from this cool website.
A: Have you got the website address?
B: No, not here. At home.
A: (Call/Text) me the address when you get home. Anyway, so who is the (letter/text message) from?
B: From Chloe. Oh, no, she's waiting at the wrong place.
A: Well, (call/check your mailbox) her and tell her to come here.
B: I've got no money on my phone.
A: Oh, right. I think I've (saved her number/missed a call) in my (calendar/contacts) – yes, here it is. I'll (call/download) her right now. Oh, wait, it says here that I've (missed a call/taken a picture) – I'll just (check my mailbox/check the time) to see who it was.
B: Who was it?
A: My mum. I'll call her back later. OK, so I'll tell Chloe to meet us here at – I'll just (check the time/save her number) – at 5:45, OK?
A: Right.

b) **Extra** *Your grandfather has just got his first mobile phone. He asks you to tell him what he can do with it. Write a dialogue between your grandfather and you and act it out.*

YOU WERE TALKING TO YOURSELF? – GOOD, FOR A MOMENT I THOUGHT YOU HAD ONE OF THOSE DREADFUL MOBILE PHONE THINGS!

c) **Extra** *Why is your mobile phone important to you? Talk to a partner.*

▸ *GF 3: Talking about the present (p. 145) • WB 3–4 (p. 33)*

P4 ENGLISH FOR JOBS Useful phrases

a) Listen to the three dialogues on the CD. Match them to the jobs below.

A shop assistant in a mobile shop

A customer adviser in a bank

A waiter in a restaurant

b) Listen again. Who uses these phrases? – Which phrases could you use in any of these jobs?

- A The +exchange rate is €1 ... to the pound.
- B Do you want to pay +cash or by +credit card?
- C What would you like to drink?
- D There's your +receipt.
- E Of course you can – if the phone isn't blocked.
- F Would you like anything else?
- G Can you enter your PIN please?
- H Are you ready to +order?
- I That's 15 euros, please.
- J How can I help you?
- K What can I do for you?
- L How do you want your money? Is a 20-euro +note OK?

c) Choose two of the situations below and prepare dialogues. Then act them out.

Partner A: You're a shop assistant.
Partner B: You want to buy a cheap mobile phone in a mobile shop.

Partner B: You're the waiter/waitress.
Partner A: You want to order two pieces of apple cake and two hot chocolates in a café.

Partner B: You're a customer adviser at a bank.
Partner A: You want to change some euros into Australian dollars (2 AUS dollar = 1 euro).

P5 WRITING My mobile life

Imagine what your mobile would say if it could talk to you. What would it tell you about you? About your funniest, saddest, most interesting calls? What did it do today? Did it help you? How? What was the most exciting thing that happened – and the most boring? Write your mobile's story.

► WB 5 (p. 34)

TEENS IN TROUBLE

1 ASBO boy

By Jeremy Armstrong

Once he was a trouble-maker. For years, Shane Preston, from Darlington in the north-east of England, kicked footballs against his neighbours' houses and cars, rode motorbikes on pavements and attacked other teenagers. Then the courts gave him a four-year anti-social behaviour order (ASBO).

At just 14 he was banned from some areas of his hometown. He was not allowed to leave home between 9 pm and 7 am and the police sent photos of him to hundreds of people living in the area.

It was hard punishment – but the surprising thing is that it has worked. Now 17, Shane has volunteered with the YMCA and helped to build a children's play area. He has trained as a builder and he's looking for work. He hopes he will be able to find his first real job soon.

Shane believes the ASBO helped him to straighten up his life. 'I've grown up, I think. The ASBO has helped me because it has kept me out of trouble. It was terrible when posters showing my picture appeared around the town. I used to hang out with other kids in front of the shops. But I've got different friends now. And in the end it's got nothing to do with others – it's up to me.'

ASBOs: What happens?

An ASBO tells you what you are not allowed to do, for example:

- go out at night
- go to particular places in your area
- go into particular shops or bars or cinemas
- have particular things with you, like alcohol
- meet more than one or two other people in public places

If you break your ASBO, you can go to prison.

ASBOs: What for?

Courts can give anti-social behaviour orders (ASBOs) to people who

- spray or write graffiti
- use racist language
- make too much noise late at night
- are drunk in the streets
- smoke or drink under age
- deal drugs
- use violence
- break windows or vandalize cars, gardens or parks

Every year about 1800 people get an ASBO. But many people think they don't work.

a) *What did Shane do wrong? How was he punished?*

b) *Why does Shane think the ASBO was good for him? How has his life changed since he got the ASBO?*

c) *What was the worst thing about the ASBO in Shane's opinion? What do you think was the worst thing?*

d) *Do you think ASBOs would be a good idea in Germany?*

► **Text File 6** *(pp. 108–110)*

2 Gallery walk: your opinion

a) *Make six groups, one for each statement. In your group, write your statement on a piece of paper. Hang your paper on the classroom wall.*

b) *Discuss your statement. Write down your arguments for and against it. Move to the next statement, discuss it and add your arguments.*

c) *At the end, go back to your own statement. Are you for or against it? Discuss. Then read out the best three arguments to the class.*

1 Local newspapers should have photos of teenagers who cause trouble.
2 15-year-olds have to be home before 9 pm.
3 We should put violent teenagers in prison.
4 Teenagers who cause trouble need help instead of punishment.
5 People under 21 years old should not be allowed to drink alcohol.
6 If teenagers commit a crime, we should punish their parents and teachers.

3 VIEWING High school boot camp

'High school boot camp' is a film about the 'Eagle Academy', a military-style school in Florida. Teenagers in trouble volunteer to go there for six months – no one makes them go. Here is what one of them, Dave Murray, said before he went to the camp:

> Right now I'm screwing up, erm, not listening to no one. What I expect to get out of this camp is to get bigger, stronger and straighten up my life.

a) *What do you think might happen at a boot camp? Brainstorm ideas in a group.*

b) *Watch part 1 of the DVD about the teenagers' first day at the camp. How do you feel about what happens there? Is it different from what you expected?*

– It's really shocking/funny/stupid/scary/...
– I think the boys were really scared/shocked/ ...
– The drill instructors are loud/crazy/scary/...
– ...

c) *Watch part 1 again. Take notes on what happens. Then make a list in your group. Choose one interesting thing about the boot camp from your list. Explain why you think it happens there.*

d) *Watch part 2 of the DVD about the teenagers' last day at the camp. Do they feel good or bad about their time there? Give as many of their reasons as you can.*

e) *Look back at what Dave Murray said before he went to boot camp. Do you think boot camps really help people like him to 'straighten up' their lives? Give reasons. Here are some ideas:*

– Yes, because they learn discipline.
– No, because they'll forget everything after they leave.
– Discipline doesn't change a person.
– You need discipline. You have to learn to follow the rules if you want to do well.
– People have to learn how to think for themselves, not learn how to follow rules.
– I'm sure you get really fit at boot camp. That's good.
– You don't have to go to boot camp to get fit.

▸ WB 6 (p. 34)

P1 SPEAKING Boot camps (Having a discussion)

a) *Collect as many arguments for and against boot camps as you can.*

FOR	AGAINST
– boot camp helps people to learn discipline – ...	– kids soon forget about boot camp and get in trouble again – ...

b) *Look at the five steps in the discussion process. Then match the phrases in the box to the steps.*

... because ... • Could you say that again? • First ... /Second ... /And finally ... • For example ... • I agree (with you). • I don't think you can say ... • I see what you mean but ... • I think/I feel ... • In my opinion ... • Let me explain ... • No, that's not right. • Sorry, I don't agree with you. • Sorry, but I don't understand what you mean. • That's a good point. • That's why ... • Yes, but ... • You're right.

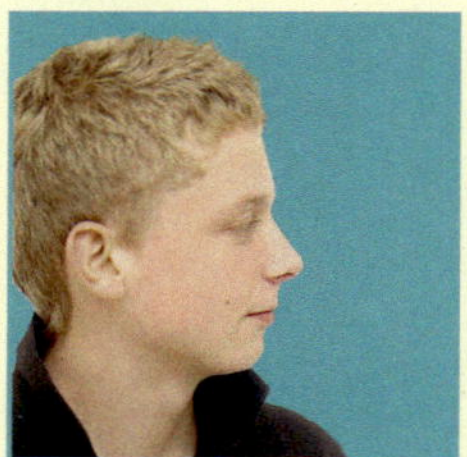

1 Expressing an opinion

2 Giving reasons and examples

3 Asking for clarification

4 Agreeing

5 Disagreeing

c) *Listen to the CD. Which of the phrases from b) can you hear in the discussion about boot camps?*

d) *Use your arguments from a) and the phrases from b) to continue the discussion you've just heard. One of you should argue FOR, one AGAINST.*

e) **Extra** *Choose one of the statements below and brainstorm arguments for and against it. Then have a short discussion about it.*

- We should ban music with violent lyrics.
- Teenagers should not be allowed to drive a car.

► *SF Speaking Course (pp. 138–139) • WB 7–8 (pp. 35–36)*

P2 WORDS Teenage trouble

Choose the right answer. Then read the correct sentence out loud.

1 If you **vandalize** something,
- A you break it.
- B you steal it.

2 If you **stay out of trouble**,
- A you break the rules.
- B you follow the rules.

3 If you **commit a crime**,
- A you act legally.
- B you act illegally.

4 If you are **a troublemaker**,
- A you stay out of trouble.
- B you cause trouble.

5 If you **are banned** from a place,
- A you are not allowed to stay there.
- B you have to stay there.

6 If something **worries** you,
- A it makes you nervous or afraid.
- B it makes you happy.

P3 WORDS First ASBO

Complete the text with the correct words.

Kelly was a clever girl who usually found school ... (bored/boring), so nobody was really ... (surprised/surprising) that she often got into trouble there. Her mother, a single, ... (hard-working/time-wasting) shop assistant, didn't usually get home till late in the evening. Kelly felt a bit ... (unwanted/wanted) and didn't know where her life was taking her. When a ... (broken/closed) window was found in a classroom one day, everyone blamed Kelly. That's when she decided she wasn't (interested/interesting) in going to school any more. She started to hang out with a group of ... (music-loving/graffiti-spraying) youths in a park behind the station. Her mother felt Kelly was a ... (changed/well-behaved) person, but didn't know what to do about it. What Kelly really needed was a ... (good-looking/warm-hearted) teacher or social worker to give her a ... (helping/shaking) hand. But instead she spent her time with her ... (trouble-free/trouble-making) friends who were taking her down the path to her first ASBO.

P4 Additional information Posters showing his picture (Understanding participle clauses)

a) *Read sentences 1 to 5. Choose the correct meaning for each one (a or b) and write it down.*

1 Shane saw posters showing his picture.
- A Shane was showing his picture when he saw posters.
- B Shane saw posters which showed his picture.

2 Most kids breaking the law get into trouble.
- A Most kids break the law and get into trouble.
- B Most kids who break the law get into trouble.

3 The people living here are afraid of crime.
- A The people who live here are afraid of crime.
- B The people live here because they're afraid of crime.

4 Kids growing up in the 1960s had problems too.
- A Kids who grew up in the 1960s had problems too.
- B Kids who grow up in the 1960s have problems too.

5 The police saw a girl spraying graffiti.
- A The police saw a girl who was spraying graffiti.
- B The police saw a girl while they were spraying graffiti.

b) *Look again at your five sentences from a). Which of these statements is correct?*

6 All the sentences are in the same tense.

7 All the sentences use a relative clause.

► *GF 6: Participles (p. 151) • WB 9–11 (pp. 36–37)*

GET INVOLVED

1 Club blogs

Volunteer Manatee

ABOUT US | PRODUCTS & SERVICES | PARTNERS | NEWS

PROGRAMS

ManaTEEN Projects

The ManaTEEN Club in Florida is one of the nation's largest teen volunteer programs with over 10,000 teen members. They do more than 1.7 million hours of volunteer work.

Springs Clean-up

Along with some of my ManaTEEN friends, I went to the ManaTEEN SOS project at Weeki Wachee Springs. What an experience it was! We snorkeled through the crystal clear water and collected trash, like bottles, glass, and plastic. So much trash is thrown into the springs. It's such a shame! I pulled up a huge piece of clear glass that was hard to see. People can easily cut themselves on something like that. We had a competition to see who could pick up the most trash. I was beaten by my best friend Zach.

After a break for some pizza, we all jumped back into the water and continued our work. Of course trash isn't the only thing that is found at Weeki Wachee Springs. There are lots of beautiful fish and I even saw a turtle. This was my favorite ManaTEEN Club project! – Patrick

YOUTUBE | BLOG | GALLERY | SCHOLARSHIPS | CONTACT US

hickoryrecord.com

Powered by: Hickory Daily Record — FOR YOU. ABOUT YOU. EVERY DAY. 24 HOURS A DAY.

Hickory Soup Kitchen

This summer, we've been raising money for the Hickory Soup Kitchen, so others can have something to eat. We both like helping and wanted to get more involved because something must be done to help people in need.

To raise money we have been to two churches. Lots of people have donated. During vacation Bible school, all the kids had a competition to see who could bring in the most money, so a lot of coins and dollar bills have been donated. Altogether we've raised $427.

Today we got the food. We decided to spend half our money on meat, because the kitchen doesn't get a lot of meat – it costs so much. And we got ketchup and canned vegetables because the soup kitchen often doesn't have enough of that kind of thing. We've taken all the food to one of the churches, where it can be stored overnight. It will be given to the Hickory Soup Kitchen tomorrow.
– Alex & Andrew

▷ *Describe what kind of community service the American students did.*
– Find reasons they give for their volunteering. Why do they think it's a good idea?

▷ *What do you think they have learned from their experience?*

2 Community service – US style

Volunteering for community service is an important tradition in the US. Many young people get involved because they want to – but many others do community service because they have to. Their parents think it will be good for them or it's part of their school work, as this school website shows:

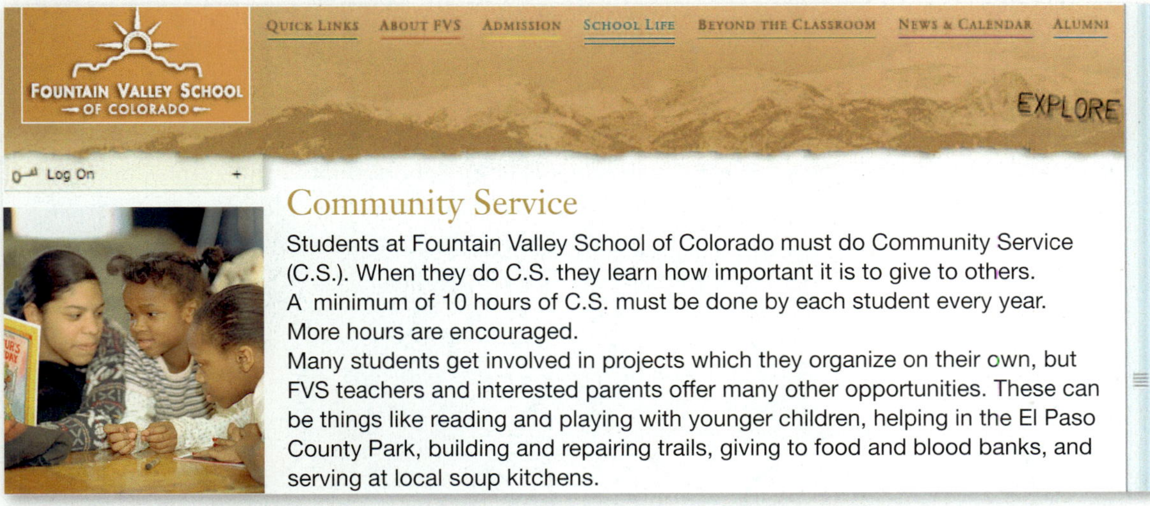

Community Service

Students at Fountain Valley School of Colorado must do Community Service (C.S.). When they do C.S. they learn how important it is to give to others.
A minimum of 10 hours of C.S. must be done by each student every year.
More hours are encouraged.
Many students get involved in projects which they organize on their own, but FVS teachers and interested parents offer many other opportunities. These can be things like reading and playing with younger children, helping in the El Paso County Park, building and repairing trails, giving to food and blood banks, and serving at local soup kitchens.

a) *Why do students at this American school have to volunteer for community service? What kind of things can they do?*

b) **Extra** *Imagine why you might need help from students who do community service when you're old or ill. Discuss with a partner.*

c) **Extra** *Think of arguments for and against:* 'German school students should have to do ten hours of community service every year.'
Discuss your arguments and agree on the best one for and the best one against.
Do the same again with another pair.

3 Now you

a) *Have you ever volunteered for community service? What did you do and why? If you haven't volunteered, explain which kind of community service you would/wouldn't like doing.*

b) *What kind of service would help your town/area most? Use a placemat to find the best ideas in your group. Explain how you could help.*

P1 REVISION Quiz (The passive: simple present / simple past)

Choose an answer to each question and write it down.

1 On July 4th, Independence Day ... (is celebrated/is celebrating)
A in France. B in Canada. C in the US.

On July 4th, Independence Day is celebrated ...

2 English and French ... (are speaking/are spoken)
A in Australia. B in Canada. C in the US.

The Dog Fence in Australia ... (was building/was built)
A in the 1880s. B in the 1980s. C in the 1990s.

3 The Star Wars films ... (make) by
A George Luca. B Woody Allen. C David Yate.

4 High School Boot Camp ... (produce) in
A California. B Florida. C Georgia.

5 The Commonwealth of Australia ... (found)
A in 1530. B in 1778. C in 1901.

P2 Police report (The passive: present perfect)

a) *Look at this sentence from p. 58:*
A lot of coins and dollar bills have been donated.
Now complete these sentences:
A lot of money has ... stolen from the bank.
Four TVs ... been stolen from a shop.

b) *Complete the policeman's report about what has happened during the week.*

1 a statue • (steal) • from the museum
A statue has been stolen from the museum.
2 two shop windows • (break) • in High Street
3 the station wall • (spray) • with graffiti
4 a young teenager • (injure) • by a truck
5 a student • (attack) • on the way to school
6 four mobiles • (steal) • at Oldham School

c) *Write a short report on anti-social behaviour at your school. Start like the example below.*
So far this year there's been some anti-social behaviour at ...
Quite a few / Some bikes have been ...

P3 Exploring language The passive with must, can and will ...

Compare the active sentences on the left with the passive sentences on the right.

1 We must do something to help people. — Something must be done to help people.
2 We can store the food at the church. — The food can be stored at the church.
3 We'll give it to the kitchen tomorrow. — It will be given to the kitchen tomorrow.

Complete the rule.
- In active sentences we use ..., ... or will with an infinitive
- In passive sentences we use must be, ... or ... with a past particple.

▸ GF 7: The passive (p. 152) • WB 12–13 (p. 37)

P4 Youth club rules (The passive with must, can, ...)

Complete the rules.

1 Bikes must not be ... (bring) into the building.
Bikes must not be brought ...
2 No alcohol can be ... (bring) into the club.
3 Valuables can be ... (leave) in the safe.
4 All rooms must be ... (keep) clean.
5 Rubbish must be ... (put) in bins.
6 All club equipment ... (must – share).
7 The games room ... (must – tidy) daily.
8 Food ... (can – prepare) in the kitchen.
9 Food... (must – not eat) in the games room.
10 The toilets ... (must – clean) every week.
11 Lights ... (should – turn off) when you leave.

P5 When will the furniture be moved? (The passive with will)

Partner B: Go to page 94.
Partner A: You're a youth club manager. A company is going to do some work at the club next week. You phone the company to find out when the jobs will be done. Ask like this:
When will the furniture be moved ...?
Change roles after number 5.

1	move furniture to garage	...	6	repair showers	Wed
2	repair windows	...	7	install new toilet	Thu
3	paint windows	...	8	paint games room	Thu
4	build new cupboards	...	9	put up bookshelves	Fri
5	install new lights	...	10	move furniture back	Fri

▸ GF 3: Talking about the future (p. 148)

P6 MEDIATION Volunteering in Germany

You're thinking of doing a Freiwilliges Soziales Jahr. *You've found an online brochure. Write to an American e-friend and tell him/her:*

- *what kind of jobs you can do*
- *where you can do your community service*
- *how it will help you in the future*

Ein Beitrag für sich und die Gesellschaft

Aus freien Stücken anderen helfen. Behinderte Menschen im Alltag unterstützen. Im Naturschutzpark Nistkästen anbringen und Fußwege sauberhalten. Im Jugendklub eine Disco organisieren oder einen Musik-Workshop vorbereiten. Mit alten Menschen mal einen Spaziergang unternehmen. In Russland in einem Kinderheim arbeiten. Im Sportverein Kids das Dribbeln beibringen. Sportspiele im Schulhort organisieren. Oder auf der Open-Air-Bühne mit Kindern Griffe auf der Rockgitarre üben – das und vieles mehr ist möglich im Freiwilligen Sozialen Jahr (FSJ) – oder im Freiwilligen Ökologischen Jahr (FÖJ). Dem freiwilligen Engagement sind keine Grenzen gesetzt, und auch im Ausland gibt es zahlreiche Möglichkeiten.
Wer sich dafür entscheidet, zwischen Schule und Ausbildung einen Freiwilligendienst zu absolvieren, bekommt oft mehr als nur eine berufliche Orientierung. Erste Fachkenntnisse und die erworbenen sozialen Kompetenzen machen junge Menschen fit für den Berufseinstieg und erhöhen ihre Beschäftigungschancen. Zugleich tut es gut, sich für andere einzusetzen und Verantwortung zu übernehmen. Manch einer sammelt dabei die ersten Auslandserfahrungen. Von dem Engagement profitieren also beide Seiten: die jungen Freiwilligen und die Gesellschaft.

Quelle: Bundesministerium für Familie, Senioren, Frauen und Jugend

▸ WB 14–15 (p. 38)

The caller by Robert D. San Souci (adapted)

Some important new words in this text are explained at the bottom of each page.

► *SF Reading stories (p. 129)*

It was hot at Aunt Margaret's funeral. Lindsay Walters had to stand in the burning sun in her black dress, while the minister said the prayers[1].

Lindsay was angry because she should be at Missy's, should be helping her best friend get ready for a party.

A cell phone rang. Lindsay knew from the ringtone that it was her father's. He went red. At least she knew enough to turn hers off at a funeral. Her father pulled his phone out and shut it off. He checked his watch.

At the end of the funeral, Lindsay went behind a tree, took out her own cell phone, and called Missy's number. It was busy[2]. Probably her friend was making plans with Noelle or Candice for the party. She made a face at her phone, turned, and walked straight into her father, who was talking into his phone.

She went back to her mother, who introduced her to some boring old ladies. She had to nod and look sad as they talked about her aunt. When her father returned, Lindsay asked, "Can we go now?"

"I just have to make one more call," her father said.

When the last old lady and the minister had gone, Lindsay said to her mother, "Please, please, please make Daddy get off the phone so we can go!"

"Stop whining[3]," her mother said, and told Lindsay and her brothers, Darren and David, to go to the car. Then she went over to where Mr. Walters was still talking on the phone. She made him end his call. Now both of them were angry. Mr. Walters put his cell phone into his pocket. "All right, let's go," he said.

Some people from the funeral had stopped by the house. Lindsay's sad-looking parents and their guests drank coffee and talked about how nice Aunt Margaret had been.

"As long as you didn't make her angry," said Mr. Walters with a laugh. "I remember as a kid she could be terrible if she thought someone had been rude or was lying[4] or cruel." Lindsay knew what he was talking about. Lindsay thought of her aunt in heaven – she would terrorize the angels for not being holy[5] enough.

But the guests finally left. Lindsay ran to her room to change so that her father could drive her to Missy's party. When she was ready she took out Aunt Margaret's gold ring with real diamonds. She had always loved it, and Aunt Margaret had promised it to her before she died. Her mother told her to only wear the ring at special times. Well, showing off[6] to Missy and Noelle and Candice and the others was special!

Her cell phone rang.

There was a strange noise, then whispers sounding like a crowd. Finally a tired, dry, old voice said, "Lindsay, this is Aunt Margaret."

"Right! Very funny, Missy. Guys – see you in a few minutes." Lindsay hung up[7] and put her phone into her party bag. She put her ring in her jeans pocket so her parents wouldn't see and ran down the stairs two at a time.

"Where's Dad? He said he would drive me to Missy's."

"He's looking for his cell phone in the car," her mother said. "It fell out of his pocket."

Lindsay went and helped her father, but they couldn't find the phone. He was angry. She was glad[8] she was staying at Missy's after the party.

At Missy's party, all the girls were jealous of the real diamonds on Lindsay's finger. She forgot all about their phone joke.

"I hated to go to that old folk's home," Lindsay told them. "I just said I wanted to go, because I wanted this ring."

Her cell phone rang.

Lots of noise, more whispers, the same dry voice saying, "Lindsay, this is Aunt Margaret. I must talk to you."

Clearly it wasn't her friends trying to trick her. It must be Darren and David. She whispered to her friends, "It's my creepy[9]

---

[1] prayer [preə] *Gebet* [2] busy *besetzt* [3] (to) whine [waɪn] *jammern* [4] (to) lie [laɪ] *lügen* [5] holy ['həʊli] *heilig* [6] (to) show off *angeben* [7] (to) hang up *auflegen* [8] glad [glæd] *froh* [9] creepy ['kri:pi] hier: *nervig*

brothers. They want me to think it's my aunt's ghost[1]." The others rolled their eyes.

"Is it really you, Aunt Margaret?" asked Lindsay. She tried to sound scared.

"Yes. I just wanted to hear your voice again. You were my favorite. You loved me best."

Lindsay held up the ring as she talked. "Well, it was really your ring I loved. I hated going to that place where you stayed. And all that stuff you told me about when you were young was boring. So thanks for the ring and goodbye, Aunt Margaret!" Lindsay ended the call.

She pushed *69 and saw that her brothers were calling from her father's cell phone.

"They're using my dad's phone that he lost. They must have found it in the car. They are going to get so busted[2] for this when I get home."

When the party ended and the other girls left, Missy's parents said they were going out. When they were gone, the girls went upstairs to Missy's room to call their friends. They lay on Missy's bed and chatted into their cell phones.

Lindsay was just going to call her boyfriend of the week when her phone rang.

"Lindsay, I am very disappointed[3] in you." The same voice. "I don't think you deserve[4] my ring. I'm coming to get it back."

"Get real[5]!" She ended the call. It had come from her father's cell phone. She called the number but the phone just rang and rang. She hung up and called home. Her mother answered.

"Mom," she said, "Darren and David found Dad's phone. They're using it to call me and bug[6] me. They just did it again."

"That's not possible," said her mother. "They've been watching TV for the last hour. And your father is sure he dropped his phone at the funeral this afternoon." Her mother sounded worried. "Perhaps it's a crank caller[7]."

"The calls are coming from Dad's cell phone," Lindsay explained. "But –"

There was a loud noise. The phone went dead. Missy looked up as her phone went dead, too. The lights in the house went out.

"Blackout[8]," said Missy. All the other houses in the neighborhood were dark.

"I don't think that would shut off our phones," said Lindsay.

"Well, it did," said Missy. "Anyway, this is cool. We can tell ghost stories."

"I don't want to," said Lindsay. She wished she was at home, not in a house without lights.

"Chicken[9]!" her friend said.

There was a knock downstairs at the front door. Thump. Thump. Thump.

Missy got up to answer it.

"Don't!" cried Lindsay. She couldn't say why she was scared, but she was.

"You are so stupid," said Missy. "My folks[10] forgot their keys. Probably the doorbell doesn't work in the blackout."

"Please, don't go!"

"Stay here if you're so scared," said Missy and shook her head. "What a baby!" She left.

Lindsay closed the bedroom door and locked it. She heard the front door open and close a moment later. She thought she heard a soft sound. Then quiet.

Her cell phone rang.

She grabbed it. She hoped it was her mother.

"Lindsay, I've come for my ring, you unhappy child. I'm at the bottom of the stairs right now. Let's play that game I played when you were a little girl. The one your father told me not to play, because it scared you so? But you loved it – you loved being scared. Don't you like being scared anymore?"

"Missy? This isn't funny."

But Missy's phone was still on her bed.

"One step, two – I'm coming for you," said the voice on the phone.

Thump, thump on the stairs.

"Three steps, four – better lock the door. Five steps, six – say your prayers quick."

If the phone was working, Lindsay thought, she could call for help. She hung up and called home. It was answered on the third ring.

"Seven steps, eight – not long to wait," said her mother's voice.

She hung up and called 911.

---

1 ghost [gəʊst] *Geist* 2 (to) get so busted ['bʌstɪd] etwa: *zur Schnecke gemacht werden* 3 disappointed [ˌdɪsə'pɔɪntɪd] *enttäuscht*
4 (to) deserve [dɪ'zɜːv] *verdienen* 5 Get real! etwa: *Hör auf mit dem Quatsch!* 6 (to) bug sb. [bʌg] *jn. ärgern, nerven*
7 crank caller [kræŋk] *Juxanrufer/in* 8 blackout ['blækaʊt] *Stromausfall* 9 chicken hier: *Angsthase* 10 folks [fəʊks] *Familienmitglieder*

"Nine steps, ten –we're near the end," said a man's voice.

She hung up and threw the phone onto the bed next to Missy's.

"Eleven, twelve, and one step more – too late for you, I'm at the door!" It was Aunt Margaret's angry voice.

Someone knocked loudly.

THUMP! THUMP! THUMP!

"Go away! Leave me alone! I didn't mean what I said!" Lindsay started to cry.

"Gotcha[1]!" cried Missy through the door. "You're crying! This is better than telling ghost stories! Wait till Noelle and Candice hear I made you cry. You and that stupid ring you think is so cool."

Lindsay, angry at her friend's trick, wiped away her tears and opened the door. "I never want to talk to you again!" she shouted.

But it wasn't Missy holding Lindsay's father's phone in a muddy[2] hand as the lights came on[3].

Working with the text

1 The story

a) *Whose 'muddy hand' do you think it is at the end of the story?*

b) *Finish these sentences about the story:*

1 Lindsay gets a diamond ring from ...
2 Before Lindsay goes to Missy's house, she gets a call from someone who says ...
3 Lindsay doesn't believe that the caller ...
4 At Missy's house, Lindsay gets another call ...
5 While Lindsay is speaking to her mom ...
6 When everything is dark, the girls hear ...
7 Missy wants to ... but Lindsay ...
8 When Lindsay opens the door, she thinks ...

2 Creating suspense

In line 63, the writer starts to create suspense.
'Lindsay, this is Aunt Margaret.'

Copy and complete the graph. The numbers on the left show the level of suspense. At the bottom you can enter line numbers from the text. Continue the red line to show where the suspense rises and falls. Where is the climax of the story?

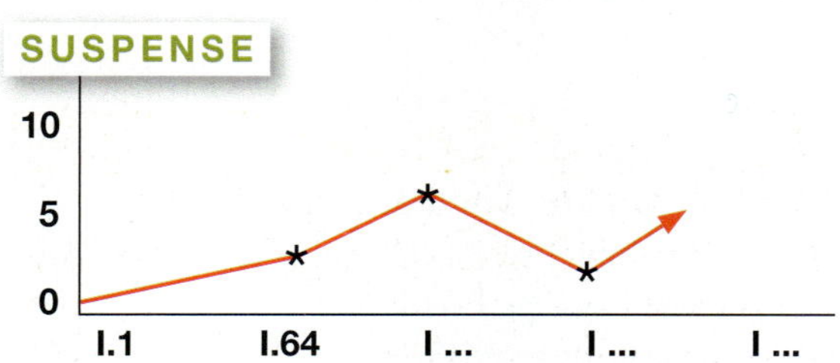

3 Lindsay's character

a) *Check the lines in the text. Then choose an ending for each statement. Explain your choice.*

ll. 13–18:
Lindsay tries to phone Missy because she ...
A wants to tell her about the funeral.
B wants to talk about the party.

ll. 22–24:
Lindsay looks sad because she ...
A knows the old ladies expect it.
B misses her aunt.

ll. 56–59:
Lindsay thinks it's special to show her friends the ring because ...
A they're interested in jewellery.
B she hopes they will be jealous.

ll. 193–194:
Lindsay says she didn't mean what she said ...
A because she's sorry she hurt her aunt.
B because she's afraid.

b) *Would you like to be Lindsay's friend? Give some reasons for your answer.*
I wouldn't like to be Lindsay's friend. She only visited her aunt because ...
I'd like to be Lindsay's friend because ...

Do you feel sorry for Lindsay at the end of the story? What would you say to her when she's alone in the bedroom?

▸ **Text File 7** *(pp. 111–117)* • *WB 16 (p. 39)*

---

[1] Gotcha = Got you! *Hab dich! / Reingelegt!* [2] muddy ['mʌdi] *schmutzig, schlammverschmiert* [3] (to) come on hier: *angehen*

How am I doing?

a) *Find or choose the correct answers.*

Teen world

1 UK teenagers can get ASBOs for ...
A good school work. B bad school work.
C anti-social behaviour.
D success at sport.

2 ASBOs are given by ...
A the courts. B the police.
C the church. D the government.

3 The ManaTEEN club is a volunteer programme for teenagers who ...
A like cleaning. B have been given an ASBO. C want to help others.
D like water sports.

Words

4 Can I change a ten-pound ... into two fives?
A cash B money C note D receipt

5 I'll just enter your phone number in my ...
A mailbox. B contacts. C text.
D ringtone.

6 Instead of the words in bold print, use one of these verbs: ***donate***, ***order***, ***receive***, ***store***.
a) **keep** milk in the fridge
b) **give** money to charity
c) **ask for** a hamburger and coke
d) **get** a text message

7 Complete the sentences with one of these verbs: ***commit***, ***get***, ***move***, ***train***.
a) I'll have to ... these books to another shelf.
b) If you ... a crime, you will be punished.
c) Jo has started to ... as a shop assistant.
d) Don't ... in trouble with the police again!

8 Choose words to complete each sentence.
A Scotland and Norway are ... countries. (English-speaking/oil-producing)
B What a ... dog! (well-behaved/well-paid)
C We had some delicious ... soup. (home-made/warm-hearted)

9 Complete the sentences with one of these prepositions: ***along with***, ***by***, ***instead of***, ***up to***.
a) Let's cycle ... going by bus.
b) Pay ... credit card if you have no cash!
c) She walked ... him and kissed his cheek.
d) We stood in the queue ... hundreds of other people.

Grammar

10 The girl helping the old lady was a volunteer. Which is correct: a, b or c?
A The old lady was a volunteer.
B The girl was helping a volunteer.
C The girl was helping an old lady.

11 Complete the sentences. Use the passive.
a) A boy who vandalized a park ... (take) to the police station, where the police are interviewing him.
b) His name ... (can – not print) in the newspapers because he is under 16.
c) He ... (take) to court tomorrow morning.
d) I think he (must – punish).

Study Skills

12 In a written discussion, you use examples to support your ...

13 Write one phrase from Unit 3 to ...
a) express an opinion.
b) agree with an opinion.
c) disagree with an opinion.
d) ask for clarification.

b) *Check your answers on p. 220 and add up your points.*

c) *If you had 26 or more points, well done! Maybe you can help students who had fewer points. If you had 25 points or fewer, it's a good idea to do some more work before you go on to the next unit.*

No.	Area	Find out more	Exercise(s)
1– 3	Teen world	Part B (pp. 54–55), Part C, p. 58	WB 4 (p. 33), 6 (p. 34), 12 (p. 37), 15 (p. 38)
4– 9	Words	Unit vocabulary (pp. 167–171)	P 2–3 (p. 56), WB 3 (p. 33), 6 (p. 34), 8–10 (p. 36)
10–11	Grammar	Exploring language (p. 60), GF 6–7 (pp. 151–152)	P 4 (p. 57), P 2–5 (pp. 60–61) WB 12–14 (p. 37–38)
12–14	Skills	Part A, p. 51, SF (p. 140)	P 1 (p. 51), WB 2 (p. 32)

1 WORDS Free-time activities

a) Work with a partner. How many free-time activities can you add to the list below?

horse riding • drawing and painting • listening to music • playing a musical instrument • watching TV or DVDs • playing basketball • playing football • cycling • using a computer • reading books or magazines • relaxing • meeting friends • ...

b) Look at your list and put the activities into groups.

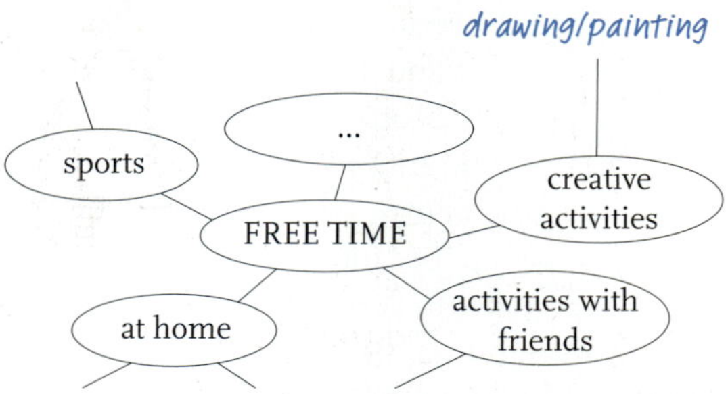

c) Talk about the free-time activities from b). Tell each other why you like/don't like doing them.

A: I often go horse riding. I love horses and I think it's great to be with them every day.

B: Well, maybe, but it sounds like a lot of work. But I enjoy listening to music ...

2 WORDS Talking about films

You see this film review on a movie website. Put in the correct form of the words and phrases in the box to complete the text.

(to) act • actor • drama • famous • main character • star • (to) take part in • talent • (to) tell the story • true events

Take the Lead *****

'Ballroom dancing meets New York's gangs'

The (1) *drama* *Take the Lead* (2) ... of Pierre Dulaine, a ballroom dance teacher, who goes to work in one of New York's most difficult inner city schools full of problem kids. *Take the Lead* is actually based on (3) ..., and Pierre Dulaine is, in fact, a real person. He still works with American teenagers around the USA and became quite (4) ... since the film came out.

The (5) ... of the film is the Spanish American (6) ... Antonio Banderas. He plays the (7) ... Pierre Dulaine. When Dulaine first arrives in the school, the kids all think he is crazy. They are into hip hop, not classical dance. However, after Dulaine shows them a tango with another professional dancer, the kids start to get interested. The film ends when they all (8) ... a national ballroom competition.

The kids are all 'normal' American teenagers and had never (9) ... before. But they are all natural acting (10) ... and some of them are amazing hip hop dancers.

In 2006, *Take the Lead* won an award for 'Best Teen Movie.'

3 I'd love to be a movie star (Conditional sentences type 2)

Finish these sentences about being a famous movie star. All the sentences are conditional sentences type 2.

1 If a famous director chose (choose) me for one of his films, I'd / would be (be) famous too.
2 I ... (go) to Hollywood if I ... (become) a famous actor.
3 I ... (not live) here if I ... (be) rich.
4 If I ... (act) in a movie, all my friends ... (come) to see me.
5 If I ... (have) lots of money, I ... (buy) a yacht.
6 If I ... (play) a part in a movie, I ... (meet) famous actors every day on the film set.
7 But the problem is, if I ... (be) a movie star, I ... (not see) my family very often.
8 Perhaps I ... (not be) so happy if I ... (be) a film star!

► *GF 8.1: Conditional sentences 2 (Revision) (p. 153)*

4 SPEAKING Having a conversation

Talk to your partner for about two minutes about something that interests you – films, magazines, music, what you did last weekend, the town where you live, ... The phrases below will help you.

starting a conversation	Hello. / Hi. / My name's ... / What's your name? / ...
likes and dislikes	I like / don't like ... / What about you? / And you? / ...
showing interest	Really? / Oh, that's interesting! / Sounds great! / Wow! / ...
agreeing and disagreeing	Yes, me too. / That's right! / Oh, I don't. / Sorry, I don't agree. / ...
asking questions	So when did you ...? / Why ...? / How long ...? / Where ...? / Sorry, can you say that again please? / ...
ending the conversation	See you soon. / Bye!

► *SF Speaking Course (pp. 138–139)*

5 WORDS Jim and Kate (Words that describe feelings)

a) *Complete these sentences with words or phrases from the box on the right.*

angry • be afraid • be mad about sb./sth. • bored • confused • cool • different • excited • great • happy • independent • jealous • lonely • (to) look forward to sth. • nervous • proud • relaxed • responsible (for) • sad • safe • scared • silly • strange • surprised • terrible • tired • shy

1 Jim and Kate have been together for a month now and they ... still ... each other.
2 Kate was ... when Jim asked her if she'd like to date him. She thought he liked Laura.
3 Jim is usually very ..., so he wasn't even nervous on their first date.
4 But when Kate left his MP3 player on the bus last week, he was very ... with her.
5 Sometimes Kate is ... when Jim tries to be funny – his jokes are very strange!
6 At first she didn't want to meet Jim's parents as she always feels a bit ... with new people.
7 When Kate met her old boyfriend Pete at a party, Jim was a bit ... at first – until he saw that she wasn't interested in Pete any more.
8 They're ... the summer holidays this year: they're going to Canada for three weeks!

b) *Write six sentences like these with words you haven't used in a).*

1 READING Choosing a book

These American high school students are in their English literature class. They have to choose a book to read. To help them, their English teacher has written short summaries of some books.

Look at the profiles of the five students and the seven book summaries below. Choose the best book for each student.

Answer: Student A – Book ...

Student A : Conrad

Conrad doesn't really enjoy reading short stories or novels, but he reads magazines. He loves sport and is also interested in music and skateboarding.

Student B : Brittany

Brittany has her own blog where she writes her thoughts. She is fascinated by young people, their loves and fears, their relationships, and their problems.

Student C : Jeanette

Jeanette loves reading stories. For her, a 'good book' is one where the characters have lots of real life adventures. She doesn't like fantasy or horror stories.

Student D : John Paul

John Paul is interested in football but the thing he likes best is computer games. He particularly loves fantasy games where 'anything is possible'.

Student E : Ricki

Ricki's family came to the US from Puerto Rico. Now, as a teenager, he is interested in politics and wants to help people from ethnic minorities.

BOOK SUMMARIES

Fiction

1 **Dark Universe** Three teenage friends fall through a 'time hole' and find themselves in a parallel world where amazing and fantastic things happen. Can they survive – and will they ever return to their old lives?

2 **Something** Something is 'out there'. Waiting. Watching. Looking for you! VERY scary!

3 **Lola and the Detective Agency** When Lola and her friends discover a crime, nobody believes them. They have to set up their own detective agency to catch the criminals. Lots of action right up to the last page!

Non-fiction

4 **Voices from the fields** Fascinating interviews with migrant workers from Mexico who talk about their lives in the fields of California where they pick fruit.

5 **Strategies for teens** Being a teenager is not always easy but this book is full of great advice about families, boy/girlfriends and many other aspects of teen life.

6 **The Journey West** The book uses diaries, letters and old photos to tell the fascinating story of the long journeys to the West in America's history.

7 **Babe** Babe Ruth was probably the greatest baseball player who has ever lived. This biography tells the true story of his life. Wonderful descriptions of exciting games!

2 MEDIATION A note to your friend

Your American friend is staying with you in Germany at the moment. Your friend would like to know about some interesting things to do.

Read the brochure below and write a short note in English to your friend. Give the main points about the tour. Use the example on the right to help you.

Hi!
Hope you slept well. You wanted to know about some interesting things to do while I'm at school. I found out about some guided cycle tours that sound great. Here are the main points:
–
–

Erleben Sie die Stadt per Rad

Fahrrad-Stadtrundfahrten

Fahrrad-Rundfahrten durch die Stadt – für Gruppen von 10–15 Personen – begleitet von erfahrenen Stadtführern.

Sehen Sie unsere Stadt und ihre Attraktionen vom Fahrrad aus. Wir machen Halt an interessanten Punkten. Dort werden Sie Informationen über die Geschichte der Stadt und touristische Highlights erhalten.

Dauer
Unsere abwechslungsreiche Tour führt durchs Stadtzentrum und verschiedene Stadtteile und dauert ca. 120 Minuten, in denen wir etwa 12 km zurücklegen.

Abfahrt
März – September
täglich 10:00 und 14:00 Uhr.

Treffpunkt ist vor dem Informationszentrum neben der Liebfrauenkirche im Stadtzentrum (bei schlechtem Wetter im Informationszentrum).

Preise
€ 29,– pro Person inkl. Fahrradmiete
(Bei angemeldeten Gruppen mit mehr als 25 Teilnehmern € 22,50 pro Person.)

3 READING Dev Patel

This text is from an online British movie magazine. Read the whole article through first, then do the two tasks on page 71.

Meet Dev Patel, teenage movie star

The hit movie *Slumdog Millionaire* tells the story of 17-year-old Jamal, one of the millions of extremely poor people (the 'slumdogs') who live in the slums[1] of India's largest city, Mumbai. Jamal goes on the Indian TV gameshow *Who Wants to Be a Millionaire?*, answers all the questions correctly, wins the top prize – and finds the girl he loves. In 2009, the movie won eight Oscars. Its star was the young English actor Dev Patel …

When Dev Patel arrived in Mumbai to film Slumdog Millionaire, it was only his second visit to India. In fact, learning the Mumbai accent was, he says, one of the hardest things he had to do. He wasn't a famous actor, either. He had liked drama very much at school in England, and he had played a small part in a British TV series, but that was all. So how did he become Jamal and what was it like when he was suddenly an international movie star?

Dev was born near London in 1993. His parents are Indians who had moved to England when they were young. His dad is a computer technician, his mum a carer[2].

Dev went to a 'typical' English secondary school. His first hobby was martial arts – karate then tae-kwon-do. He was excellent at both and even took part in the Youth Olympics. But after a role in a school play, Dev found that what he really loved was acting.

His mum wanted to encourage him, and when Dev was 14, she showed him a small advertisement in a newspaper. A TV company wanted people for a series called *Skins*, about a group of teenage friends. Dev wrote a reply – and got a part.

Three years later – Dev was 17 – the successful British film director Danny Boyle was looking for someone to play Jamal in *Slumdog Millionaire*. Mumbai is the home of the huge Indian movie industry. People sometimes call it Bollywood: Bombay (the old name for Mumbai) plus Hollywood. The problem was that young, male Bollywood actors are all very strong and handsome. Boyle wanted a young man who looked more like a 'slumdog'. It was Boyle's daughter who told her dad about Dev – she often watched *Skins*. Dev had five auditions[3] ('I was crying at the end because I didn't think I'd get the part', he says) but then he was Jamal.

For Dev, the next five months were like a dream. He was in Mumbai and on a movie set. With him were a world-famous director, some of the best known older Bollywood stars, real kids from the slums of Mumbai, and the beautiful young actress who is his girlfriend in the movie. 'I grew up five years in those five months,' Dev says.

What did the real people from Mumbai's slums think? Dev was amazed by them. They were so proud that they were in the movie. 'Don't tell people we're poor,' they said to Dev and Boyle. 'Tell them we're happy. We aren't poor because we're happy.'

---

[1] slum [slʌm] *Slum, Elendsviertel* [2] carer ['keərə] *(Alten-)Pfleger/in* [3] audition [ɔː'dɪʃn] *Sprechprobe*

Questions on the text

a) *Choose the correct answer – A, B, C or D.*

1 What do you learn most about in this article?
A the Indian movie industry.
B the film *Slumdog Millionaire.*
C the young English actor Dev Patel.
D the life of the poor people in the slums of Mumbai.

2 The article says Dev Patel got the lead role in *Slumdog Millionaire* because ...
A he was strong and handsome.
B he knew Danny Boyle's daughter.
C he really loved acting.
D he looked a bit like a 'slumdog'.

3 In the movie, Dev plays the role of a young Indian man who ...
A wins an Oscar.
B becomes a millionaire.
C moves to Mumbai.
D tells a story.

4 Before he acted in the film *Slumdog Millionaire*, Dev ...
A was already a famous actor.
B had lived for a long time in Mumbai.
C had only played a small role in a TV series.
D could speak with a Mumbai accent.

5 Dev ...
A has Indian parents but grew up in England.
B has English parents and grew up in England.
C has Indian parents and moved to England when he was small.
D has English parents but grew up in India.

6 Which activity interested Dev most when he was at school?
A tae kwon do
B acting
C the Youth Olympics
D karate

7 How did Dev get the part in *Skins*?
A His dad helped him.
B A TV company wrote to him.
C He often watched it on TV.
D He replied to a newspaper advertisement.

b) *Finish the sentences with information from the text.*

1 Danny Boyle, the director of *Slumdog Millionaire*, chose Dev for the part of Jamal and not a young, male Bollywood actor because Dev ...
2 Mr Boyle found out about Dev from ...
3 At the end of his auditions, Dev was crying because ...
4 Filming *Slumdog Millionaire* in Mumbai changed Dev a lot. He describes this change when he tells us that ...
5 Dev expected the people who lived in the slums of Mumbai to be really sad. In fact, he found that although they are poor, ...

4 SPEAKING Talking about a picture

Partner A

Describe to your partner what you can see in the photo on the right.
(Partner B: just listen).
Speak for around one minute.

- *Who are the people in the photo? Where are they? What are they doing?*
- *Describe their feelings.*
- *Would you like to be one of the people in the photo? Why (not)?*

Partner B

Now it's your turn. Describe to your partner what you can see in the photo on the right.
(Partner A: just listen).
Speak for around one minute.

- *Who are the people in the photo? Where are they? What are they doing?*
- *Describe their feelings.*
- *Would you like to be one of the people in the photo? Why (not)?*

5 SPEAKING Hobbies and interests

Now talk to your partner. Tell each other about your hobbies and interests.
Talk together for about three minutes. Here are some ideas:

- What do you like doing in your free time? Why?
- Where, when and how often do you do those things?
- Do you do them alone, with your family or with friends?
- Describe the last time you did one of the activities.
- Is there one thing you hate doing?

How am I doing?

Check your answers to tasks 1 and 3 on p. 220.

About the test

This second test gave you another chance to try some of the kinds of tasks that you will do one day in your exam (*Abschlussprüfung*). This time, the tasks tested your reading, mediation and speaking skills. If you found some tasks difficult, don't worry. You've got lots of time to practise. Remember: 'Practice makes perfect!'

Reading

Task 1 and task 3 in the test were reading tasks. The following three questions will help you to think about how you did. Read the questions – which answer is right for you?

1 How hard or easy was each task?

	easy	OK	quite hard	very hard
Task 1				
Task 3				

▸ *SF Reading Course (pp. 130–131)*

2 What was difficult in the tasks?

a) The texts were quite long and complicated.
b) There were words and phrases that I just couldn't understand.
c) There was a lot of information.I couldn't find the exact answers.
d) The tasks weren't like the tasks that we do in class.

3 How did you do the tasks?

a) I read each task carefully so that I knew what to look for in the texts.
b) I tried to understand the main ideas of the text first. That helped me to guess words that I wasn't sure about.
c) If there was a task that I wasn't sure about, I left it out and came back to it later.
d) I scanned the text when I looked for a special piece of information.
e) I checked my answers at the end to make sure I hadn't made a 'silly' mistake.

▸ *SF How to do well in a test (pp. 142–143)*

Speaking

1 Copy and fill in the assessment sheet below about your partner's description in the fourth task (Talking about a picture).

Assessment sheet	☹		😐		☺	
Name of partner ...	1	2	3	4	5	Comments
Did your partner ...						
1 ... speak clearly and loudly enough?						
2 ... say enough?						
3 ... answer all the questions?						
4 ... use interesting vocabulary?						
5 ... explain his/her ideas well?						

2 Now look at the checklist on the right and talk about how well you did in the fifth task, the dialogue about your hobbies and interests.

a) We listened to each other.
b) We only gave short answers.
c) We showed interest in each other.
d) There was a good flow in our dialogue.[1]

▸ *SF Speaking course (pp. 138–139)*

[1] There was a good flow in our dialogue. *Unser Gespräch verlief flüssig.*

Unit 4 Big city life

JOHANNESBURG

1 Now you

a) *Look at the photos of Johannesburg, Mumbai and Berlin. What do you feel when you look at them? Write down at least one sentence for each photo.*

When I look at the photo of the ..., I feel angry/excited/...

dusty road • graffiti • polluted river • shiny skyscrapers • slums • street café • ...

b) *Compare with a partner. Discuss why you feel the way you do.*

mumbai

Berlin

2 Living in a big city

a) *Brainstorm and make notes on the advantages and disadvantages of living in a big city.*

advantages	disadvantages
lots to do	crowded
shiny skyscrapers	slums

b) *Report to the class.*

c) **Extra** *Write a short text about a big city you would like to visit.*

▸ WB 1 (p. 40)

MUMBAI

1 A lover's embrace
Adapted from 'Mumbai' by Suketu Mehta

Look at the photo. What might the text be about? Why might it be called 'A lover's embrace'?

The manager of Mumbai's railway system was recently asked when its five million daily passengers would be able to move around the city comfortably. 'Not in my lifetime,' he answered.

If you take a train into Mumbai today, you find out about the temperature of the human body as it presses against you from all sides. A lover's embrace couldn't be closer.

One morning I took a rush hour train. There were so many passengers I couldn't get all the way into the carriage. As the train got faster, I held on to the top of the open door. I was afraid I would be pushed out, but someone said: 'Don't worry, if they push you out, they'll also pull you in.'

If you are late for work in Mumbai, and get to the station just as the train is leaving, you can run up to the crowded carriages and you will find that many hands reach out to pull you on board. As you run along next to the train you will be picked up, and a small space will be made for your feet in the open door. The rest is up to you; you will probably have to hold on to the door with your fingers and be careful not to lean out too far.

But just think about what has happened: the other passengers have stood like this for hours, their shirts are wet with sweat, but they can still feel with you, know that your boss might shout at you or pay you less if you miss this train. So they have made space where there is no space to take one more person with them. And at the moment of contact, they do not know if the hand that is reaching for theirs belongs to a Hindu or Muslim or Christian or if you were born in this city or arrived only this morning or if you're from Mumbai or New York. All they know is that you're trying to get to the city of gold, and that's enough. Come on board, they say. We'll make space for you.

a) *Were your ideas correct? Why is travelling in the Mumbai train like 'a lover's embrace'?*

b) *Is the writer surprised that passengers help others onto the train? Why (not)? What can happen if people are late for work?*

c) *Do differences between people count on the train to Mumbai? What examples does the writer give?*

2 Extra One of a crowd

a) *Collect ideas about crowded places and how you feel about them.*

b) *Write about 80 words on your experience of being in crowds.*

Crowded places	Positive feelings	Negative feelings
station in rush hour	excited	nervous
football stadium	...	...
...		

3 City fact file: Mumbai

Facts and figures

Name: The city was called Bombay until 1996.
Population: 13.9 million. Mumbai is India's biggest city, but not the capital of the country (that's New Delhi).
Population per sq km: 8,170
Number of tourists per year: 1 million

Present

Today Mumbai is the biggest, richest, fastest city in India. It may soon be the biggest city in the world. Mumbai is India's financial centre and home to 'Bollywood', the biggest film industry in the world.

Past

Bombay became a British possession in 1661 and for centuries was a centre of British power in India.

In the 20th century, Bombay played a big role in the fight for India's independence from Britain. Mahatma Gandhi, father of non-violent protest, started the *Quit India* movement in a park there. India became independent in 1947.

Language in Mumbai

The Indian language Marathi is the most common language in Mumbai; the other main languages are Hindi, Gujarati and English. English is the main language of the city's office workers. If you want to succeed, you have to speak English.

मुंबई भारत का वित्तकेन्द्र
और बॉलीवुड की मातृभूमि है

> *Why was Mumbai important in the past? Why is it important today?*

4 VIEWING Mumbai

a) *Watch the first video clip about Mumbai. What is similar to a big city in Germany? What's different? Find examples.*

b) *Now watch the second video clip. It's about public transport in Mumbai. Match the sentence halves.*

1 The four main kinds of public transport are	*a* an adventure.
2 Buses and trains are	*b* good for short trips outside city areas.
3 The best way for visitors to travel is	*c* buses, trains, taxis and auto-rickshaws.
4 The black and yellow taxis are	*d* very cheap, but also very crowded.
5 The auto-rickshaws are	*e* cheaper than the ones with air conditioning.
6 Crossing the street is	*f* by taxi.

5 Bollywood

world cinema guide
BOLLYWOOD

What is Bollywood?

Bollywood is the name for the Hindi language film industry – it's a play on the word Hollywood: The B is from Bombay, where most of the studios were built.

Bollywood is the largest film industry in the world. It makes about 1,000 films a year – twice as many as Hollywood. India has a huge cinema audience with about 3,000 million cinema visits a year, twice as many as in the US. Bollywood films are also very popular outside India, especially in countries with a big ethnic Indian population, like the UK.

What's a typical Bollywood film like?

In the past traditional Bollywood films have been epics – stories from Indian history and legends with colourful costumes, comedy scenes and lots of song and dance numbers. The story is often about young lovers whose families are against their relationship. Usually there's a happy ending.

Today Bollywood films are moving into a more modern world. But, although there's lots of passion, kissing on screen is still taboo.

And of course India's growing television industry has created a lot of new jobs for Bollywood film people. Slowly the Indian soap opera is taking large audiences away from the movies.

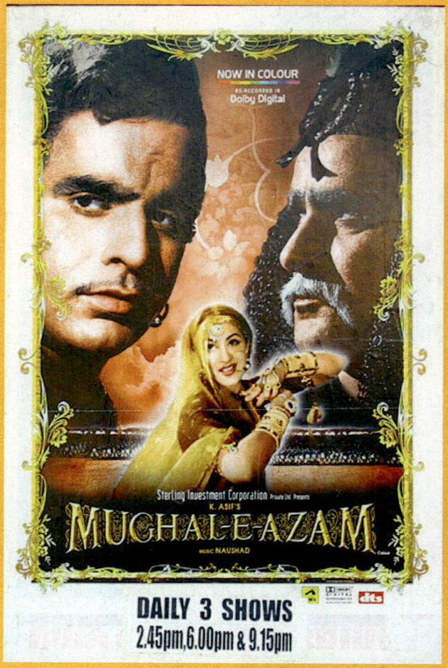

In what ways is Bollywood changing? What reasons could there be for this?

▸ WB 2–3 (pp. 40–41)

P1 WORDS City life

a) *For each noun find at least two adjectives that go with it.*
– airport: modern, busy ... – businessmen: ambitious, successful ...

Nouns
air • airport • businessmen • +commuters • concerts • factories • financial centre • +motorway • skyscrapers • sport events • stadium • +suburbs • tourists • traffic • underground • water • zoo

Adjectives
ambitious • busy • crowded • dangerous • dirty • exciting • expensive • +fashionable • fresh • international • huge • local • modern • noisy • open-air • polluted • quiet • shiny • +stressed • successful • trendy • ...

b) *Make ten sentences with nouns from a):*
Modern airports all look the same.
To succeed, businessmen have to be ambitious.

c) **Extra** *Compare your sentences.*

P2 REVISION Conditional sentences (types I and II)

Remember

Conditional sentences
Type 1: *If it doesn't rain, we'll play football tomorrow.*
simple present *will / can / may ...*
Type 2: *If it didn't rain so much, we would play football more often.*
simple past *would / could / might ...*

a) *You're planning a holiday in Mumbai. Complete the conditional sentences (type 1).*

1 If I go there from late September, there ... (not be) too much rain.
2 I'll stay at a nice hotel if it ... (not be) too expensive.
3 If I have enough time, I ... (can visit) the Bollywood studios.
4 If it ... (not cost) too much, I ... (have) at least one meal at a top restaurant.
5 I ... (take) an elephant ride outside the city if I ... (find) a guide.
6 If it ... (be) really as great as they say, maybe I ... (not want) to come back home!

b) *Complete the sentences (type 2).*

1 If I had more money, I would/wouldn't ...
2 If there was no internet, ...
3 If I didn't live in Germany, I'd like to live ...
4 If I didn't have to go to school, I'd ...
5 If I was an adult now, I could ...
6 If we didn't have laws, people would ...

c) *Make appointments. Interview your partners about their ideas for b). Take notes.*
What would you do if you had more money?
What would life be like if there was no internet?
Where would you like to live if ...

d) *Report to the class on what you learned about your classmates.*
If Jan had more money, he'd support a charity.

► GF 8.1: Conditional sentences (I, II) (p. 153) • WB 4 (p. 41)

JOHANNESBURG

1 The Y Generation

A new generation is bringing life to South Africa's largest city.

It's lunchtime at The Zone, an American-style shopping mall in Johannesburg's Rosebank neighbourhood. There was a time when only whites could come here.

Today black teenagers, mobiles to ears, are walking up and down the mall, wearing the baggy jeans and trainers that are the uniform of American hip hop.

But they're wearing it with a bit of African style: floppy hats that they pull down over their eyes so that they look like local gangsters, and T-shirts by trendy local fashion designers. Some of the shirts have political slogans from South Africa's past; one has a picture of Nelson Mandela's jail cell on it.

A popular place in the mall is outside the YShoppe and YFM Studio. YFM is the Joburg youth music radio station that first brought kwaito to the people. South Africa's hip hop, a mixture of Western dance tracks and lyrics in the many languages of Soweto street slang, became popular after Mandela's election in 1994.

Today YFM's audience is almost 2 million, Joburg's youth is known as the Y Generation and kwaito's biggest stars, who were once poor township kids, are millionaires with their own TV shows, fashion labels and record companies.

Not far from the mall is Melville, an area with lots of cafés and clubs. At one of them, the 'Colour Bar', most of the barmen are white. Half the customers are white, half are black. Mixed-race couples are normal here: the Colour Bar is colour-blind.

Adapted from 'Johannesburg Travel and Leisure', Go2SouthAfrica.com

a) *What is South Africa's Y Generation? What are its members like?*

b) *Make a list of adjectives that describe the city.*
young, multi-cultural, ...

c) *Agree on three adjectives that make the city seem interesting for young tourists.*

d) **Extra** *Use the adjectives you chose in c) to make a simple poster or a logo for Johannesburg. Show all the posters and logos in class. Choose the one you think would 'sell' Johannesburg best.*

2 City fact file: JOHANNESBURG

Facts and figures

Population: 3.9 million. Johannesburg is South Africa's biggest city, but not the capital, which is Pretoria.
Population per sq km: 2,365
Number of tourists per year: 4.5 million

Past

Johannesburg was founded when gold was discovered in the area in 1886. By 1900 it had a mixed population of 100,000 people: Britons living in the British colonies in South Africa; Boers whose Dutch ancestors had come in the 17th century; and Africans working in the growing city.

In 1910, the British and the Boers, who had fought each other in two wars, came together to form one white government for South Africa. Discrimation against blacks, already bad, got worse. After 1948, under new apartheid laws, racial segregation became even stricter. Blacks had to live in separate townships like Johannesburg's Soweto (South West Township). They could not vote until the end of apartheid. Then, in 1994, they elected Nelson Mandela, South Africa's first black president.

Present

Johannesburg is South Africa's most important economic centre. Banks and other big companies have their main offices there. Many people are rich, but a lot more are still poor and the crime rate is high. Another problem, not just in Johannesburg, is AIDS: 34% of South Africans between 25 and 29 have HIV.

In 2010 hundreds of thousands of tourists came to South Africa for the FIFA World Cup. The first and last matches were played in Johannesburg.

Language in Johannesburg

There are eleven official languages in South Africa: English, Afrikaans (similar to Dutch) and nine African languages. English is the most important language in public life.

> *What did the apartheid laws mean for black South Africans? What is Johannesburg known for today?*

▸ *WB 5 (p. 42)*

3 A tour of Soweto (adapted from the novel 'Many Stones', by Carolyn Coman)

Berry is a high school student from the US. Her parents are divorced and she lives with her mother. When her older sister Laura is murdered in South Africa, their father wants to visit the school where she had worked as a volunteer. Berry decides to go with him. They have just arrived in Johannesburg when her father tells her they're taking a tour of Soweto.

I have never been surrounded by so many black people in all my life – all black people, because not one white person lives in Soweto. Mr Joseph Otambo, a big black man in a brightly coloured shirt, is driving us around the neighbourhoods of Soweto in his car.

▸▸

He tells us that in the huge hospital we drive past, one third of the babies are born with AIDS. In a neighbourhood of bigger, nicer homes, he stops and points to a house. 'This is the home of Desmond Tutu, winner of the Nobel Peace Prize.' A little while later he shows us the home where Nelson Mandela once lived. 'Also a Nobel Peace Prize winner.' Mr Otambo turns and looks at my father and me and holds up two fingers. 'The only neighbourhood in the world with two winners!' And he laughs.

I don't feel embarrassed any more about being here and doing what we are doing, because Mr Otambo doesn't seem to be. He points to places and tells us things, laughs a lot.

We drive past a small school and he tells us, 'This is where the schoolchildren were shot during the uprising in 1976.'

At the first squatter village we come to – miles of tents and shacks that were put together with cardboard and metal and pieces of wood – he points to an outhouse and says, 'This is a toilet the people here use.'

I sit quietly in the car and look at what he has shown us: an outhouse, falling apart. It reminds me of the latrine we had at summer camp, but the one at camp was a lot better.

'Now you can see the inside of the toilet,' he says, at another broken outhouse without a door. 'There are not enough for all the people who live here.'

Mr Otambo invites us to go inside one of the shacks. It is part of the tour. If I had known that, I would have stayed at the hotel. Mr Otambo tells us it's all right with the woman who lives there, that people in the village want visitors to see with their own eyes what it is like for some of the people who live here in Soweto.

I don't know if anybody can see I'm scared. My father goes first. We leave the car and enter the shack closest to the road. There is a woman there, she's sitting on a small bed. She says her name is Mary and we all shake hands and then we are silent inside the dark tent. There is a picture from a magazine on the wall, but the wall is a piece of cardboard. A towel hangs and divides the space into rooms, but the whole place is no bigger than the playhouse Laura and I had behind our old home. When my father asks, Mary tells us she has six children.

Six kids, six. In this place where I am standing, crowded together with just her and my father. I wish she hadn't told us. I don't want to know that she's a mom. Suddenly I can't stand it that Mary, this woman, is a mom, just like my mom is a mom. I want her to be so different that the way she lives could somehow be OK. But how can it be OK? It can't.

Working with the text

1 Understanding the story

a) *Make a chart of places Mr Otambo shows Berry and her father. What information does he give at each one?*

Place	Information
hospital	1/3 of babies born with AIDS
1st house	...

b) *Why do people in Soweto want tourists to come?*

c) *What does Berry say about her feelings in ll. 23–24, 52 and 68–73? Why do you think she feels like this? Would you feel the same?*

2 Background research

a) *Mr Otambo says something about the following topics. Find out more about one of them.*

- AIDS in South Africa
- Desmond Tutu
- Nelson Mandela
- Soweto Uprising (1976)

b) *Report to your group what you have learned. Ask your classmates if you want to know more about their topics.*

▸ SF Research (p. 124) • WB 6 (p. 42)

P1 Apartheid in South Africa

a) *Partner B: Go to p. 95.*
Partner A: Read the text below and find answers to the questions.

1 What advantages did white people have in South Africa during apartheid?
2 What disadvantages did black schools have?
3 Why did black students protest in 1976?
4 How has the school system changed since the end of apartheid?

b) *Ask Partner B about the following:*
– how the apartheid laws divided people up
– why South African football is a good example of the apartheid system
– why South Africa was thrown out of FIFA
– what happened when apartheid ended
Then answer Partner B's questions.

▸ *SF Taking notes (p. 128)*

c) **Extra** *Write a short text about apartheid.*

Apartheid and schools

Under South Africa's apartheid system, whites (less than 20 % of the population) had big advantages over other ethnic groups. About 87 % of the land in South Africa was in white hands. And only whites could be in the government.

From the 1950s South Africa had separate education systems for the different 'races'. Much more money was spent on the schools for whites. From an early age, blacks were victims of discrimination. Black students had less equipment in their schools, fewer classrooms and fewer school books. The government did not want blacks to have a good education, because it knew that they would then want more rights.

When the government tried to make black teachers use Afrikaans in their lessons, the language of the majority of white people, black students in Soweto protested on 16 June, 1976. The protests became violent ('Soweto Uprising'), and hundreds of young people were killed.

Apartheid ended in the early 1990s. Today there is one state school system with no segregation. Every year on 16 June, South Africa remembers the Soweto Uprising and the students who were killed in 1976.

P2 WORDS Tricky translations (German 'machen')

You can't always use ***make*** *when you translate German phrases with the word* ***machen*** *into English. Complete the sentences below. Only one of the English phrases has the word* ***make****. You can use the dictionary at the back of the book if necessary.*

▸ SF Using a bilingual dictionary (p. 123)

1 If you're tired we'll ... now. *(Pause machen)*
   take a break
2 Do you want to ... of the city? *(Fotos machen)*
3 Sit down and ... *(es sich bequem machen)*
4 Where did you ... last summer? *(Ferien machen)*
5 Our teacher wants us to ... on South Africa. *(ein Projekt machen)*
6 I'll have to ... for school now. *(sich fertig machen)*
7 Let's ... on the big wheel! *(eine Fahrt machen)*
8 Does your company ... Japan? *(Geschäfte machen mit)*
9 Let's ... now. *(einen Spaziergang machen)*
10 Where can I learn to ...? *(Judo machen)*

P3 Exploring language | Additional information | Conditional sentences type III

a) *Find the following sentence in the text on p. 82 (ll. 45–46).*
If I had known that, I would have stayed at the hotel.

Find the correct answers.
The sentence tells us that the writer ...
a) **knew** / **didn't know** something.
b) **stayed** / **didn't stay** at the hotel.

b) *You were at a party you didn't enjoy very much. Choose the best ending for each of the sentences.*

1 I would have eaten more ...
2 I would have enjoyed the music ...
3 I would have asked somebody to dance ...
4 I wouldn't have left the party early ...

if I hadn't felt so nervous.
if it had been more fun.
if they had turned it up a bit.
if the food had been better.

▸ GF 8.2: Conditional sentences (III) (p. 153)

P4 I would have taken the bus

What would you have done differently? Make short dialogues like the one in the photo.

1 A: Jo was late for our date, so I went home.
   B: (wait for him) *I would have ...*
2 A: I just wore jeans to my job interview.
   B: (wear a suit) *I would have ...*
3 A: I stayed at a hotel in London.
   B: *Hotels are expensive. I ...* (Bed & Breakfast)

Now change roles.

4 B: A man climbed through our neigbour's window yesterday, but I didn't do anything.
   A: *I would have ...* (phone the police)
5 B: I bought a pink T-shirt last Saturday.
   A: (buy a blue one) *I would have ...*
6 B: I watched football on TV yesterday.
   A: *Football's boring. I ...* (a film)

▸ WB 7–9 (pp. 43–44)

P5 ENGLISH FOR JOBS (Writing a letter of enquiry)

a) *Read the following letter of enquiry. What shows you that it is a formal letter?*

Remember

In a formal letter you use formal style, e.g. *I am*, not *I'm*.

▸ *SF Writing formal letters (p. 137)*

Blombach Travel Agency
Denglerallee 68
28199 Bremen
Germany

12 May 2011

The Hiker's Store
15 Nelson Street
6571 Knysna
South Africa

Enquiry about hiking tours

Dear Sir/Madam

I have seen an internet advertisement for your shop and I am writing to ask if your company could help us with organizing hiking tours in your area.

At Blombach Travel Agency we offer our German customers hiking and cycling tours all over the world. I would be interested to know if you could find local tour guides for us and if our customers could rent equipment from your shop.

Thank you very much for your help. I look forward to hearing from you.

Yours faithfully

Andrea Ulrich
Programme manager

In the **subject line** and the **first paragraph** you let the reader know what your enquiry is about.
I am writing to ask if / enquire about ...
Please send me ...

In the **second paragraph** you describe your enquiry in more detail.
I would be interested to know ...
I would especially like to ...

In the **last paragraph** you thank the reader and add a friendly phrase.
I look forward to hearing from you.

b) *Imagine you work at Blombach Travel Agency. Write a letter like the one in a) to the*
Bay Hotel
16 Gordon Street
6571 Knysna
You're looking for 10 double rooms on 27 and 28 October and would like to know about prices and services.

▸ *WB 10 (p. 44)*

BERLIN

1 English connects

Listen to Part 1 on the CD.
Who are the people in the photos?
Where are they from?

1

2 The next morning ...

3

4

2 The photostory

a) *Choose one picture from the story and explain how it shows that English connects.*

b) *Look at photo number 7 and read the speech bubbles again. Who is more polite, Leena or Pedro? Explain.*

c) *Listen to parts 1 and 2 on the CD. What more do you learn about the characters? Who did you find easiest to understand?*

3 City fact file: Berlin

Facts and figures

Population: 3.4 million
Berlin is Germany's capital and largest city.
Population per sq km: 3,840
Number of tourists per year: 7.58 million

Past

Berlin was founded in 1237. It became the capital of Brandenburg in the 15th century, later of Prussia and, in 1871, of Germany.

After World War II Berlin, like Germany, was divided. Berlin had four sectors: French, British and American (West Berlin), and the Russian sector (East Berlin). In 1949, East Berlin became the capital of a separate state, the German Democratic Republic (GDR). West Germany's capital was Bonn.

Until 1961 people could leave the GDR through West Berlin. To prevent this, the GDR built a wall between the two parts of the city. East Germans could not travel west any more, and West Berlin was now cut off from its hinterland and from the rest of the city.

In November 1989 the Berlin Wall fell and the two Germanies were reunified in 1990. In 1999 the German parliament moved from Bonn to Berlin.

Present

Berlin is an important cultural centre, especially for youth culture. The city's clubs attract young people from all over Europe.

Language

Although German is the main language in Berlin, English is used in a lot of big companies and research institutions. It is the main language of tourism, important in hotels, restaurants and shops.

14% of the city's population are foreign, so many other languages are also spoken.

4 A Berlin presentation (1)

At the end of Part C, you will give a presentation.

Step 1 *Decide on a topic, for example:*
- Comparing Berlin, Mumbai, Johannesburg
- East/West Berlin in the days of the Wall
- The fashion/club scene in Berlin
- Sights in Berlin tourists don't usually see

Step 2 *Do research on your topic.*

Remember

Always use more than one source. Try to use some sources in English.

▸ SF Research (p. 124)

Step 3 *Decide on a form for your presentation:*
- poster / overhead transparencies + talk
- computer + projector + talk

Step 4 *Prepare your presentation:*
- Give your talk a clear structure (a beginning, a middle, an end).
- Prepare note cards with key words.
- Prepare visual materials for your talk.

STUDY SKILLS **Using visual materials**

Visual materials (pictures, posters, transparencies, maps, timelines, charts, etc.) make your talk easier to understand.

▸ SF Using visual materials (p. 125)

Step 5 *Practise your presentation.*
- Do it at least once, for example in front of an audience or a mirror.
- Use ideas from the Speaking Course on p. 90.

▸ SF Giving a presentation (p. 125)

P1 WORDS Adjectives

a) *Try to work out the meaning of the adjectives on the right. Then check in a dictionary.*
bloody – blutig
colourful – ...

bloody • colourful • fruity • hairy • icy • impressive • juicy • meaty • painful • unforgettable • unforgiveable • useless

b) *Match the adjectives and nouns. Write down twelve pairs:* a bloody civil war, ...

1	bloody • colourful • icy • unforgiveable	bird • civil war • mistake • roads
2	fruity • hairy • impressive • painful	building • drink • experience • monster
3	juicy • unforgettable • meaty • useless	moment • stew • rubbish • oranges

c) **Extra** *Write sentences with adjective/noun pairs from b).*
The Reichstag is Berlin's most impressive ...

P2 EVERYDAY ENGLISH Staying at a hostel

a) *Look at the sentences. Guess who says them:*
- the receptionist
- the tourist

b) *Try to match the sentences to these situations:*
- getting information
- checking in
- checking out

c) *Listen to the three dialogues and check.*

d) *Prepare and practise two dialogues like the ones you've just heard.*

What time is breakfast?
Here's your key card.
When are you planning to arrive?
I'd like to book a room.
Single or double? Or dormitory room?
I hope you enjoyed your stay.
How would you like to pay?
Does the price include breakfast?
How much do the rooms cost per night?
I have a reservation for a single room.

P3 STUDY SKILLS Using visual materials

a) *Make two bar charts to compare the population figures and the population per sq km of Mumbai, Johannesburg and Berlin:*
- Mumbai: 19.2 million/8,170 per sq km
- Johannesburg: 7.15 million/1,960 per sq km
- Berlin: 3.4 million/3,840 per sq km

b) *Make a timeline for Berlin. Use the dates in the City fact file on p. 88 and add these dates:*
1701: capital of Prussia
1791: Brandenburg Gate finished
1945: World War II ends, rebuilding the city begins

▸ *WB 11–16 (pp. 45–47)*

SPEAKING COURSE Part 4

P4 SPEAKING A Berlin presentation (2) (Giving a presentation)

► *SF Giving a presentation (p. 125)*

a) *Where do these steps belong: to the beginning of your presentation, the middle or the end?*

A: Make clear when you are starting a new section of your talk.

B: Sum up your main points and make it clear that you've finished.

C: Give an outline of your presentation.

D: Introduce your topic.

E: Ask if anybody has questions or would like to comment on anything you've said.

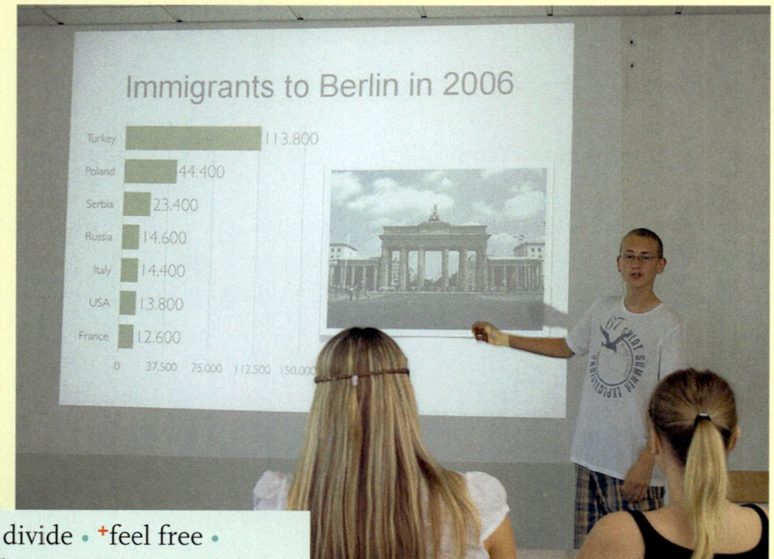

b) *Try to complete the sentences below with the phrases in the box. Then listen to the talk on Berlin and check.*

+draw your attention to • divide • +feel free • First • look at • present • pie chart • sections • +slide • sum up • have a look • topic

1 The ... of my talk today is 'Berlin: past, present and future'.

2 I'm going to ... this talk into four ...

3 ..., I'll give you some general facts about the city of Berlin.

4 Next I'll ... the history of Berlin.

5 Finally, I'll ... some interesting highlights of Berlin's culture.

6 Now please ... at the population of Berlin.

7 On the next ... you'll see a ... of the ethnic groups in the city.

8 Those were the basic facts. Now I'd like to ... the history of Berlin.

9 To ... my talk, I think we have seen that Berlin is a pretty exciting place to visit.

10 Please ... to ask questions or comment on anything I've said.

c) *Use the phrases you have learned to give your presentation.* ► *SF Speaking Course (pp. 138–139)*

Remember

- Don't just read out loud. Use cards with key words to help you to speak freely.
- Wait until your audience is ready before starting.
- Look at your listeners during your talk.
- Explain visual materials as you use them.
- At the end, thank your audience for listening.

► *WB 17–18 (p. 48)*

How am I doing?

a) *Find or choose the correct answers.*

City facts

1 Mumbai was once a(n) ... possession.
A Chinese B British C American

2 Which of the following is not typical of traditional Bollywood films?
A gun fights B songs C dancing
D colourful costumes E love stories

3 Johannesburg ...
A is the capital of South Africa.
B has the biggest harbour in the country.
C is South Africa's main business centre.

4 How many official languages does South Africa have?
A one B two C eleven
D twenty-nine

5 Berlin became a divided city after ...

6 The German parliament moved to Berlin nine years after German ...

Grammar

7 In which of these sentences is the test already over?
A If you had done all the homework, you would have done better in the test.
B If you do all the homework, you'll do well in the test.
C If you did all the homework, you would do well in the test.

8 Choose the right ending for this sentence: If I had scored one more goal, ...
A we would win the match.
B we'll win the match.
C we would have won the match.

Words

9 Find a word to match these definitions:
a) another word for trendy: f__________
b) a short time ago: r__________
c) part of a city outside the centre: s________
d) ask for information: e________

10 Complete the sentences with these prepositions: **in**, **of**, **on**, **to**.
a) Does anyone want to comment ... the film we've just seen?
b) Life is quieter if you live ... the suburbs.
c) I prefer small towns ... huge cities.
d) Hot summers are typical ... South Africa.

11 Complete the sentences with the opposite of one of these words: **check in**, **dry**, **outside**, **war**.
a) I don't want to fight. I want to live in ...
b) It isn't raining now, but the ground is ...
c) The cabin had small windows and the ... was very dark.
d) You have to ... of the hotel before 11 am.

12 For each group of nouns choose one which can form an adjective ending with **-al**.
a) cloud – culture – danger – fog
b) colour – health – race – stress
c) crowd – office – success – storm

Writing a letter of enquiry

13 Describe the details of your enquiry in ...
A the second paragraph.
B the subject line. C the first sentence.
D the last sentence.

b) *Check your answers on p. 221 and add up your points.*

c) *If you had 21 or more points, well done! Maybe you can help students who had fewer points. If you had 20 points or fewer, it's a good idea to do some more work before you go on to the next unit. The chart below will tell you what you can do to improve your English.*

No.	Area	Find out more	Exercise(s)
1– 6	City facts	Parts A–C (pp. 74–88)	
7– 8	if-clauses	Exploring language (p. 84)	P 4 (p. 84), WB 4 (p. 41), 9 (p. 44)
9–10	Words	Unit vocabulary (pp. 172–176)	P 1 (p. 79), WB 2 (p. 40), 8 (p. 43), 11 (p. 45), 13–14 (p. 46)
13	Letters of enquiry	P 5 (p. 85); Skills File (p. 137)	WB 10 (p. 44)

▸ *Self-evaluation WB (p. 49)*

Unit 1 **Part B**

P1 REVISION Australian animals (Tenses: Simple present)

▸ p. 11

a) *Write out these sentences about koalas. Use the correct form of the simple present.*
Koalas (is/are found) only in parts of Australia. Although they (looks/look) like bears, they (doesn't belong/don't belong) to the bear family. They only (eats/eat) the leaves of eucalyptus trees. The leaves (contains/contain) so much water that the koalas (doesn't have to drink/don't have to drink). Koalas (doesn't sleep/don't sleep) at night – that's when they (moves/move) around.

b) *Use these key words to complete the text.*
when baby born, move into mother's pouch, kind of bag, fed by mother / after ten months too big for pouch, mother carry baby on her back until 1 year old / koalas live 10 to 12 years

c) *Listen to your partner's text. Say one thing you found interesting about it. Then read your text to him/her.*

Unit 1 **Part C**

P5 ENGLISH FOR JOBS I'm looking for a job (Basic telephone language)

▸ p. 19

d) *A ROLE PLAY*
Look at the role cards below. Act out the two telephone dialogues.

1 You've seen a notice for a job in a hotel. Call the owner Jennifer Collins to find out
- what kind of job it is
- what you would have to do
- how much you would earn
- where the hotel is.

2 Name: Philip Black
- You're a farmer.
- You need 4–6 workers to pick oranges from January to June.
- Address: 480 Humber Road, Forster, New South Wales
- $13 – $18 per hour

Unit 1 **Part D**

2 Bill and Colm

▸ p. 24

a) *Do you agree with Partner A's description of Bill? Give reasons.*
Then choose adjectives from the box below to describe Colm to your partner.
Give reasons for your choice.

brave • clever • difficult • easy-going • friendly • helpful • honest • nervous • old • stupid • violent • young

Unit 2 **Part A**

P4 EVERYDAY ENGLISH MEDIATION Summer jobs in Britain ▸ p. 37

a) *You and your partner are looking for summer jobs in Britain next year. Your partner will tell you about a job. Listen carefully and take notes.*

b) *Tell your partner in German about the job on the right. Say:*
- what you have to do in the job
- what sounds good/bad about the job

c) *Which job do you like best? Why?*

Assistant for Gino's ice cream vans

Spend your summer in the park!
Must be able to speak good English and be good at maths. You will sell ice creams, cold drinks and snacks. Great job for students looking for summer work! Jobs for 6 people.

Please contact Maria on **07978-569-0897**

Unit 2 **Part B**

P1 STUDY SKILL CVs ▸ p. 39

b) *Listen to your partner. He/She will tell you about a candidate for the job. Then tell your partner about this candidate.*
I've got the CV of someone called …
He's got these qualifications: …
He has done some work experience in …
He's interested in …

c) *Look back at your notes from a). Which candidate should get the job ? Why? Discuss.*

Arda Demir
Kantstrasse 65, 24943 Flensburg, Germany
Telephone: 0049 122 39 09 090
E-mail: arda.demir@flensmail.de

Personal statement
I am a hard-working person. I am good at working as part of a team, or on my own. I am interested in solving technical problems and working with machines.

Education
2008 to date Eckener-Schule-Flensburg (technical college)
2002-2008 Realschule-West (secondary school), Flensburg
1998-2002 Eickum Primary School

Qualifications
2008 *Fachoberschulreife* (GCSE)
Driving licences: tractor licence since 2008, car licence since 2010

Languages
English (8 years), Danish (3 years)

Work experience
Apprenticeship as mechanic

Hobbies and interests
Computers, repairing cars and bikes, football, helping on uncle's farm

References
Mr Altermann (manager, engineering company), Boge GmbH, Lister Rund 12, 24943 Flensburg, Germany

Unit 2 **Part C**

P1 SPEAKING How would you describe yourself? (Having a job interview) ► p. 41

c) ***Partner B**: You have to interview Partner A for a job. Read the role card to prepare for the interview.*

Partner B: Role card

You're going to interview Partner A for this job ►

Welcome the candidate. Be friendly!

- Ask the candidate
  - about his/her personal qualities
  - about his/her interests
  - why he/she's interested in the job
- At the end ask the candidate if he/she has any questions.
- Here's some extra information about the job:
  Workers have to sell soft drinks and fast food, clean the shop, work for about 5 hours
  Pay: £5.52 per hour
  They can watch the matches!
- Thank the candidate and say goodbye.

Local football club is looking for **friendly students** to work in club shop on match days. You will get necessary training. Candidates should live near the stadium. **Apply now!**

HORNBY F.C.

Unit 3 **Part B**

P5 When will the furniture be moved? (The passive with will) ► p. 61

Partner B: You work for the company that is going to do some work for a youth club next week. The club phones to ask when the jobs will be done. Answer like this:

The furniture will be moved …

Change roles after number 5.

1 move furniture to garage	Mon	6 repair showers	…
2 repair windows	Mon	7 install new toilet	…
3 paint windows	Tues	8 paint games room	…
4 build new cupboards	Tues	9 put up bookshelves	…
5 install new lights	Wed	10 move furniture back	…

Unit 4 **Part B**

P1 Apartheid in South Africa ▸ p. 83

a) *Partner B: Read the text below and find answers to the questions.*

1 How did apartheid laws divide people up in South Africa?
2 How did the apartheid system show itself in South African football?
3 During apartheid, was the South African football team successful in international competitions? Why (not)?
4 What happened when apartheid ended?

b) *Answer Partner A's questions. Then ask about the following:*

- *which advantages whites in South Africa had over other ethnic groups*
- *who had disadvantages in education*
- *why students in Soweto protested in 1976*
- *how the education system has changed since the end of apartheid*

c) **Extra** *Write a short text about apartheid. You can put it in your DOSSIER.*

Apartheid and football

South Africa's apartheid laws (1949–1991) divided people into four 'races': whites, Bantu (black Africans), coloured (mixed race) and Asian (Indian or Pakistani).

Like everything in South Africa, football was divided by race. There were four football associations, one for each 'race'. The white association, FASA, chose the players for South Africa's all-white national team.FASA had difficult relations with FIFA, the international football association, which was against apartheid.

In 1976 the South African police killed hundreds of young black protesters in the township of Soweto. From then on FASA was not allowed to take part in the World Cup any more. In other sports too, the country was banned from international competitions.

When apartheid ended in the early 1990s, South Africa's four football associations came together and formed one association for South Africans of every colour: the South African Football Association (SAFA). In 1992, SAFA became a member of FIFA.

Unit 2 Part C

P1 SPEAKING How would you describe yourself? (Having a job interview)

***Partner C**: Partner B will interview Partner A for this job.* ▼

Local football club is looking for **friendly students** to work in club shop on match days.
You will get necessary training.
Candidates should live near the stadium. **Apply now!**

HORNBY
F.C.

You have to watch the interview and assess the candidate. Copy the assessment sheet below to prepare for the interview.

Assessment sheet	☹		😐		☺	
The candidate	**1**	**2**	**3**	**4**	**5**	**Comments**
1 was relaxed and friendly				✓		*smiled a lot*
2 dressed suitably						
3 listened carefully						
4 talked well (not too much/too little)						
5 was well prepared						

When the interview is finished, tell the candidate how he/she did in the interview. Use the assessment sheet. The phrases below will help you.

- You were very relaxed/ ...
- That was good. I gave you 5/4 points for that.
- You didn't talk very much./ ...
- That wasn't so good. I gave you 2/1 points for that.
- Your final score was ...

TF 1–10		Inhalt	Seite	

TF 1 PROJECT: What's so special about Australia?

What's so special about Australia that about four million people visit it every year? Why is the rest of the world fascinated by the place? Doing a project about different aspects of the world's largest island may help you to understand.

Divide the class into groups. Each group chooses one of the following topics (or another topic about Australia). Do the project in your group. Present your topic to the class.

Topic 1 The geography of Australia

Australia has lots of different landscapes, from desert to rainforest. You could do your project on the different regions. Or on the island of Tasmania. Find out what these places are like, who or what lives there, how they survive, ...

The Great Barrier Reef

The Daintree Rainforest

Topic 2 The cities of Australia

You could find out more about the most important cities of Australia. Where are they located? Why there? What are the different cities famous for? What can visitors do in each place? ...

A famous Sydney landmark

Project work

1 **Choose a topic**
In your group, brainstorm and decide: What topic will you do? Who will do what and by when? When can you meet?

2 **Research and take notes**
Collect information on your topic. Choose the best information and take notes.
▸ *SF Research (p. 124)* · *SF Marking up a text (p. 128)*

3 **Decide how to present the information**
Do you want to do a computer presentation or prepare a poster, a booklet, a video or a slide show? Collect suitable materials like photos, film clips, etc.

4 **Prepare your presentation**
Structure the notes and materials you have collected. Write notes and practise the presentation with your group.
▸ *SF Giving a presentation (p. 125)*

Topic 3 The animals of Australia

Everyone has heard of the kangaroo, and everybody loves koalas. But Australia has lots of other fascinating animals. You might want to find out which ones are dangerous. Which ones can only be found in Australia? Are any of them threatened? What's the worry about rabbits? ...

A 'Tasmanian Devil'

A platypus

A salt-water crocodile, or 'salty'

Topic 4 The first people of Australia

Perhaps you'd like to learn more about the Aborigines. How do they live in modern Australia? Are their lives different to those of white Australians? What can you find out about their beliefs and legends? Or about their art and music? ...

Aborigine painting

Topic 5 The sports of Australia

What sports are Aussies especially good at? Who are their famous sports stars? What's different about Australian rules football, and how did the game get started? ...

Aussie rules football

TF 2 Australian signs

1 Sign language

a) *Make groups of five. Each person describes one of the signs 1–5. You can use a dictionary.*

– On sign ... you can see ...
– It says that ...

b) *Discuss in your group what you think each sign means. Where can each one be seen?*

– I think sign ... means that you have to be careful because ... / that it's dangerous to ...
– You'll probably find this sign by the road/...

c) *What have you learned from the signs about Australia? Make notes and report to the class.*

2 Role play

You and your partner want to go swimming, but you see sign 3 or 4.

Partner A: *You still want to swim.*

Partner B: *You don't want to go into the water because of the sign.*

Make a dialogue. You can start like this:

A: Let's go swimming/surfing.
B: Are you mad? Look at the sign – there are sharks[1] here.
A: ...

[1] shark [ʃɑːk] *Hai*

3 Funny signs

a) *What do you think the sign on the right is trying to say?*

b) *Draw a sign of your own – it can be serious or funny.*

c) *What does your partner think your sign means?*

5

TF 3 Ecosystems[1] in Australia

1 Food chains[2]

Plants and animals need energy, which they get from food. Plants can make their own food, so they are called ***producers****. Animals must get their food by eating plants or other animals, so they are called* ***consumers****.*

a) *Is a tree a producer or a consumer? Why?*

b) *Complete the food chain in diagram A. Use the words in the box.*

insects • crocodiles • plants • frogs

Diagram A: A food chain

Producers	→	Primary consumers	→	Secondary consumers	→	Tertiary consumers[3]
...	are eaten by	...	are eaten by	...	are eaten by	...

2 Food webs

A food web is a lot of food chains put together, like these food chains from the food web below:

grass > kangaroos > dingos
grass > grasshoppers > frogs > kookaburras

a) *Find four more food chains in the food web in diagram B and describe them.*

b) *How many different kinds of food do snakes eat?*

Diagram B: A food web

If the population of a part of the food web increases[4] or decreases[5], the populations of other parts of the food web will also increase or decrease. Some animals will eat more of another animal or plant. Some animals will not have enough food and they will die.

c) *What will happen if the population of an animal in the food web increases or decreases? Talk about what will happen to the populations of the other animals in the web.*

If the population of	snakes frogs dingos ...	increases/ decreases,	then the population of	snakes frogs dingos ...	will increase/ decrease.

[1] ecosystem ['i:kəʊsɪstəm] *Ökosystem* [2] food chain ['fu:d tʃeɪn] *Nahrungskette* [3] primary/secondary/tertiary consumer ['praɪməri kən,sju:mə, 'sekəndri, 'tɜ:ʃəri] *Primär-/Sekundär-/Tertiärkonsument* [4] (to) increase [ɪn'kri:s] *anwachsen, zunehmen* [5] (to) decrease [dɪ'kri:s] *zurückgehen, abnehmen, sinken*

3 An ecosystem in disorder[1]

TOADZILLA!

27 March 2009

A toad[2] as big as a small dog was found in Australia this week. The cane toad was 20 cm long – twice as big as most cane toads.

In 1935, farmers in Queensland brought 102 cane toads to Australia because they had problems with insects in their fields. They wanted the cane toads to eat the insects.

Unfortunately that was a really bad idea! Today there are about 200 million cane toads and native Australian animals are in danger.

The government is now asking people to hunt cane toads and kill them. So, why is the situation so bad for the native animals of Australia?

The main reason is the fact that cane toads are poisonous[3]. Animals (like crocodiles, snakes, lizards and birds) that try to eat the cane toad, or its eggs, die from the poison.

Another problem is that cane toads eat almost anything that moves, like native snakes, frogs, lizards and birds.

Now scientists are searching for a way to control the cane toad population in Australia ... before it's too late.

Fast facts: Cane toads

From: South America

Scientific name: Bufo marinus

Size: About 10 to 15 cm long.

What do they eat? Almost anything: insects, lizards, frogs and small snakes, even cat and dog food.

What are they eaten by? Snakes, lizards, crocodiles, birds (but most of them die from the toad's poison!)

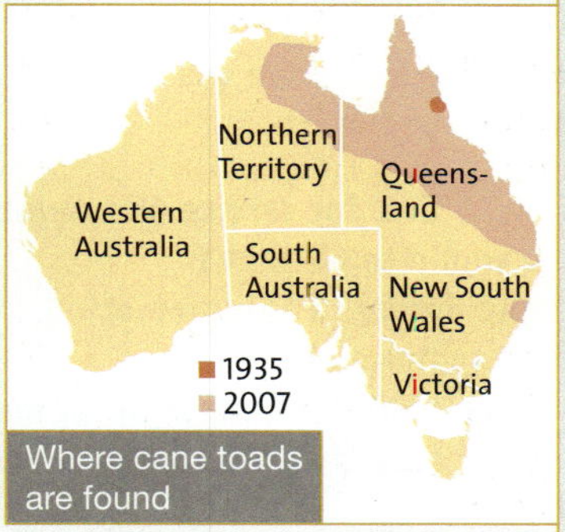

Where cane toads are found

Reproduction: Cane toads have about 8,000 to 35,000 eggs twice a year.

a) *Answer the questions about the article.*

1 How did cane toads arrive in Australia?
2 What does the Australian government want people to do about cane toads?
3 Why are cane toads a problem for native animals? Give two reasons.

b) *Look at the photos, the map and the fast facts box. Describe what they show.* ▸▸

Activate your English
- The photo/map/fast facts box shows/gives information about ...
- It says that .../It shows ...
- This is a photo/map of ...
- In 1935 cane toads were found in ... In 2007 they were found in ...

c) *Look at the food web on p. 102 again. What will happen if the cane toad arrives in this place?*

d) *Do you think that it would be a good idea to bring a new animal to Australia that could eat the cane toad? Why (not)?*
I think it might make the situation better/worse because the new animal might ...

4 Rabbits in Australia

Find out how rabbits arrived in Australia and write a short text. Where did they come from and when were they brought to Australia? Include a fast facts box, a map and/or a diagram. You can put your text in your DOSSIER.

[1] in disorder [dɪsˈɔːdə] *in Unordnung; (funktions)gestört* [2] toad [təʊd] *Kröte* [3] poisonous [ˈpɔɪzənəs] *giftig*

TF 4 Nine to five by Dolly Parton

Listen to the song. What sort of job does the woman do? Does she like her job? Does she like her boss?

Tumble outta bed and I stumble to the kitchen
Pour myself a cup of ambition
Yawnin', stretchin', try to come to life
Jump in the shower and the blood starts pumpin'
Out on the streets the traffic starts jumpin'
And folks like me on the job from nine to five

Chorus:
Workin' nine to five
What a way to make a livin'
Barely gettin' by
It's all takin' and no givin'
They just use your mind
And they never give you credit
It's enough to drive you
Crazy if you let it

Nine to five, for service and devotion
You would think that I
Would deserve a fair promotion
Want to move ahead
But the boss won't seem to let me
I swear sometimes that man is out to get me
Mmmmm ...

(...)

Nine to five, yeah
They got you where they want you
There's a better life
And you think about it, don't you?
It's a rich man's game
No matter what they call it
And you spend your life
Puttin' money in his wallet

1 Understanding the song

What do these phrases from the song mean?

1 'It's all takin' and no givin'' (l. 10)
- A The boss only takes and doesn't give anything back.
- B The worker only takes and doesn't give anything back.

2 'you spend your life / Puttin' money in his wallet' (ll. 28–29)
- A You work hard and your boss gets rich.
- B You give your boss money.

2 Men and women at work

a) *Can you think of any jobs that were traditionally only for men or only for women? Make two lists. What's the situation today?*

b) *What does the chart below tell you about pay for men and women who do the same job?*

Job	Weekly pay in 2007 ($)	
	Men	Woman
Care assistant	435	350
Nurses	420	383
Waiter/waitress	399	327
Shop assistant	380	313
Cook	356	319

c) *In groups of three to five, write a short comment on each of these statements.*
- There are jobs that only men can do.
- Men and women should earn the same if they do the same job.
- An interesting job is more important than earning lots of money.

TF 5 Diary of a teenage job hunter by Ewan Denham, 17, Swindon, Wiltshire

What would be your dream summer job? Why? How would you find a summer job?

Diary of a teenage job hunter

Day 1

Yay! Summer's nearly here! And summer means money! It's time to start looking for my dream summer job. I've only got one rule for summer work: I will NOT work in a café.
I worked in our neighbour's café once. It was OK, but I don't want to spend another summer serving customers who tell me that the tea's too hot, or the ice cream's too cold!

I bet I would be a good receptionist. I'm friendly and I hear it's good money for sitting at a desk all day. Yeah. I could definitely do that. Well, now that I've decided that, I think I've done enough for today. Tomorrow, I'll apply for some jobs.

Day 2

Today I will find my job. I can just feel it. Jobs4u.co.uk has a good selection, so I'll start there.
This will be so easy. I put in 'receptionist' as my keyword and I choose the 'office work' section. I find 7 great possibilities straightaway. I apply for each of them. In my application I am confident, but not too confident. I say that my CV is attached. It's a very nice CV. It's got a personal statement and it tells you everything you need to know about me. I quickly check the email before I send it. No spelling mistakes, it looks great. I expect I will get the phone calls about the interviews by the end of the week.

Day 3

No one has called yet. The companies have probably had a lot of applications. No problem. Jobs4u has lots of new opportunities today. I sent yesterday's email to 18 new companies.
Mum says why don't I go next-door and ask Sandra if she needs any help in the café. I tell her the perfect job is out there waiting for me. I just need to find it.

Day 4

Hum. Still no calls. Also, I realize that none of the 18 emails I sent yesterday had my CV attached. Oops! That's OK. I sent out another 12 emails today (with CVs). The interviews should start very soon.

Day 7

No replies! Nix, nothing, nada! How is that possible? I have sent out 37 applications! Maybe I need to change my keywords. I start looking in the 'tourism' and 'general' sections of Jobs4u. I also look at giveusajob.co.uk. I'm starting to think that Jobs4u is some kind of joke. Perhaps there aren't any real jobs on there at all. (Maybe I'm getting a bit paranoid?)

Day 12

Yes! I've got an interview! At last! It's a customer service job where I'll earn £600 a week. That's really good money. I don't mind serving customers for £600 a week! But my interview is in less than 2 hours, so I need to get ready.

Day 12, later

That job seemed just a little bit strange. After the interview, I think I know less about the job than when I went in. This is what happened in the interview:

Interviewer – – Hi, Ewan. I'm Carla. Did you have any problem getting here today?

Me – – No, no problems, thank you.

Interviewer – – Well, we are happy to have you in our team, Ewan.

Me – – Huh. I've got the job?

Interviewer – – (Laughs) I mean if you get the job ... Now, as you know, the money's good. Do you have any questions?

Me – – Um ...What exactly do I have to do in this job?

Interviewer – – You will work with a fantastic product and deliver a great customer experience. Anything else?

Me – – Um, er, no, I don't think so.

Interviewer – – Well, that's great! I think you're perfect for the job.

Me – – I am?

Interviewer – – Come in tomorrow, at 9 am.

Day 13

I arrive at the office at 9 and Carla is there with a small group of people.

Carla – – Hello and welcome everyone! Please sit down.

(I find a chair.)

Carla – – You are all here today because you have been chosen for a very important and exciting job.

(Sounds good)

Carla – – You are hard-working, reliable people who want to be part of a great team.

(That's me!)

Carla – – That's why you have been chosen to be part of this amazing opportunity.

(Great!)

Carla – – For just £200 we can show you the easy way to earn £600 a week. For this small price we will give you everything you need to start ...

(Huh? I have to pay them?)

I'm out of here!

Day 14

Back to the hunt.

Day 15

Mum says why don't I contact some temp agencies. Brilliant! Why didn't I think of that? I need a temporary job. Temp agencies give people temporary jobs. We were made for each other. I contact 6 of them.

Day 16

One of the agencies has called me! They don't actually have a job right now, but they want me to come in for an interview. This sounds good.

Day 17

That interview went a lot better than the last one. They haven't got a job for me right now, but they think they'll have a suitable job soon. And I don't have to pay them money first.

Day 21

I give up. I can't do it anymore. I've heard nothing from the temp agency. I don't want to waste anymore time looking at Jobs4u. It's time to break the rules!

Day 23

I've done it! I've finally got a job. I will spend my summer working at Sandra's café. It's a great job and the money's OK! It's good to know that dreams can come true, isn't it?

1 Understanding the text

Are these sentences true or false? Explain.

1 In the beginning, Ewan doesn't want to work in a café.
2 He doesn't want to work as a receptionist.
3 He checks his CV for spelling mistakes.
4 On Day 7 Ewan tries another website.
5 At the job interview on Day 12, Ewan finds out all about the customer service job.
6 On Day 13 Ewan leaves because he doesn't want to give Carla £200.
7 Ewan gets a job with a temp agency.
8 In the end, Ewan still doesn't want to work in a café.

2 Tips for job hunters

a) *What did Ewan do right? What did he do wrong?*

b) *Write three tips for people who want a summer job.*

3 Ewan's Diary

Write Ewan's diary entry at the end of his first week at Sandra's café.

4 Now You

Write about your own experience of looking for a part-time job.

– What kind of job did you want?
– What did you do to find a job?
– What kind of job did you get?
– What did you have to do?

TF 6 A different kind of justice[1]

1 Crime in England and Wales: some facts and figures

a) *Look at the chart and describe what it shows.*

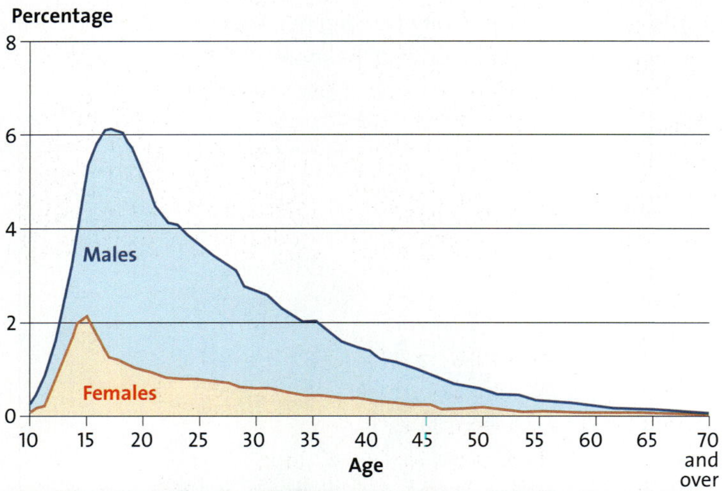

Offenders[2] as a percentage of the population: by age, 2006, England and Wales

Activate your English
- The chart shows us ...
- From the chart we can see that ...
- It gives us the figures/percentages/numbers/... for ...
- With the facts and figures we can compare ...
- The percentage of ... is/rises/drops between (the age of) ... and ...

b) *Discuss the other facts and figures with your partner.*
- In **2006**, **1.42** million offenders were found guilty[3] of crimes or warned in England and Wales.
- **80 per cent** of these offenders were male.
- **7** per cent were aged under 18.
- In June **2006** there were **10,230** young offenders aged **15–20** in prison.
- **Four** out of every **10** young offenders commits another crime in the first year after leaving prison.

2 Bus attack (Part 1)

Now read this case study of two young offenders in England.

Over a period of time two boys had been throwing stones at the Number 67 bus as it went past Gateway School. The bus wasn't hit but some passengers were frightened[4].

One day a stone came through the bus window next to the seat of 71-year-old Margaret Wilson. Mrs Wilson was shocked and had a mild heart attack.

The bus driver, Phil Saunders, stopped the bus and called an ambulance. Mrs Wilson was taken to hospital.

Mr Saunders had never experienced anything like this in his fifteen years as a bus driver and was shaken up by the attack. His bus company contacted the police.

[1] justice ['dʒʌstɪs] *Gerechtigkeit* [2] offender [ə'fendə] *Straftäter/in* [3] (to) find sb. guilty ['gɪlti] *jn. schuldig sprechen, für schuldig befinden*
[4] frightened ['fraɪtənd] *verängstigt*

Sergeant Brian Yates, a police officer who worked with schools, went to Gateway School. He held an assembly[1] in which he told the students about the attack and asked them to put a note in a box if they knew who the stone-throwers were.

The notes in the box named two 15-year-old boys, Luke H. and Reece B. After Sergeant Yates spoke to them, Luke and Reece admitted[2] that they were guilty.

a) *Match the sentence halves correctly.*

1 Two boys sometimes threw stones
2 One day a stone
3 It shocked
4 She had
5 She was taken
6 A police officer held
7 He asked students to write notes
8 Two boys, Luke H and Reece B,

a) a mild heart attack.
b) an assembly at Gateway School.
c) an old lady.
d) at the Number 67 bus.
e) if they knew who the stone-throwers were.
f) to hospital.
g) went through the bus window.
h) were named.

b) *Why do you think Luke and Reece threw stones at the bus? Collect ideas in class.*
fed up with school, to look big[3], ...

c) *What do you think will happen next?*

Luke and Reece will	go to court get an ASBO ...

d) **Extra** *What would happen to them if they were students at your school? Discuss.*
see the head teacher, have to apologize, ...

"Here's my report Dad.
I got an A, an S, a B and an O."

3 Bus attack (Part 2)

Sergeant Yates didn't want Luke and Reece to be prosecuted[4] and get a criminal record[5]. He said the boys were still young and they had never been in trouble with the police before. So he suggested a restorative justice conference[6] where the two boys would meet the people they had harmed[7] face to face.

Next, Yates visited the boys' families. Luke lived with his grandparents. They were terribly upset by the case, especially by what had happened to the victim, Margaret Wilson.

At first Luke and Reece were not sorry about what they had done – only about

[1] assembly [əˈsembli] *Versammlung* [2] (to) admit [ədˈmɪt] *zugeben* [3] (to) look big *groß tun, sich wichtig machen* [4] prosecuted [ˈprɒsɪkjuːtɪd] *strafrechtlich verfolgt* [5] criminal record [ˌkrɪmɪnl ˈrekɔːd] *Vorstrafe* [6] restorative justice conference [rɪˌstɔːrətɪv ˈdʒʌstɪs ˌkɒnfərəns] *ein außergerichtliches Treffen von Täter/in, Opfer und Vermittler/in mit dem Ziel des Täter-Opfer-Ausgleichs* [7] (to) harm [hɑːm] *schaden, schädigen*

getting caught. So Brian Yates and some teachers at the school spent a lot of time with them before the conference. They wanted to help them understand what harm they had done.

At the conference, Luke and Reece sat face to face with people from the police and the bus company. And with the bus driver and Ms. Wilson's daughter.

The conference had a very big effect on Luke and Reece.

'I'm sure Mum would be sad to see how upset the boys are,' Mrs Wilson's daughter told the conference. 'And she'll be happy to hear that they've promised to make up for[1] what they've done.'

In the end, the agreement was that Luke and Reece would go to the bus company every Saturday for six months to clean the buses. And they did. Their families reported that it had changed their behaviour.

But Luke and Reece still didn't understand why other students had 'grassed'[2] on them. So Sergeant Yates arranged another assembly at school. Here, a number of children explained why they had named Luke and Reece. They said it had given Gateway School a bad reputation[3] and that someone could have been badly hurt.

Luke and Reece were respected more at school for cleaning the buses. The other students thought it showed they were sorry. The two boys felt they had made up for what they had done and this made a big difference to them.

a) *Were you surprised by what happened in the case after the boys threw stones at the bus? Why (not)?*

b) *Give a short summary of the case.*

Activate your English
- This is a case study of a crime in ...
- The crime was committed by ...
- They admitted they were ...
- The victim of the crime was ...
- The boys were not prosecuted ...
- They went to a restorative justice conference.
- They made up for their crime by ...

4 Discussing the case

Discuss the case in your group. The following questions might help you. Present your ideas to the class.
- Should the bus company or the victim have prosecuted Luke and Reece? Why/Why not?
- Was the restorative justice conference a good idea in their case? Give reasons.
- Do you think the agreement at the conference was fair? Or would some time in prison or an ASBO have been better? Explain your opinion.
- Was it right of other students to 'grass on' Luke and Reece? Give reasons.

► *SF Speaking Course (pp. 138–139)*

SOCIAL STUDY SKILLS | Case study

You usually look at a case from the outside. Then think about:
- **the people**: who was involved in the case and what did they do?
- **the case**: what happened exactly?
- the possible **solutions** and the **consequences** (e.g. for the offenders)
- what you can **learn from** the case.

You can also try to look at the case from the **inside**. Consider:
- how the people who were involved might have felt.
- what you would have done in their position.

[1] (to) make up for sth. *etwas wieder gutmachen* [2] (to) grass on sb. [grɑːs] *(infml) jn. verpfeifen* [3] a bad reputation [ˌrepjuˈteɪʃn] *ein schlechter Ruf, ein schlechtes Ansehen*

TF 7 **Famous** (abridged and adapted from *Totally over you* by Mark Ravenhill)

Before you read

What makes someone famous? Brainstorm a few ideas with a partner and write them down. Now read the play.

CAST (all aged 14 to 16)	
Kitty	Jake
Rochelle	Dan
Hannah	Tyson
Sinita	Framji
Victor	
Michael	
Rubin	

An empty stage.
Kitty and Jake enter. Kitty is carrying a bag.

Kitty — Don't laugh, Jake, don't laugh at me.
Jake — I'm sorry, Kit. But when you talk about celebrity[1], when you tell me that you and Roche and H and Sin are going to be famous –––
Kitty — We are.
Jake — – I have to laugh.
Kitty — Because …?
Jake — Because … In six months – six months when I thought we'd told each other all our secrets – six months and you've never told me that –
Kitty — And when I do you laugh at me.
Jake — I'm sorry, Kit.
Kitty — I choose to share my dream with you and you laugh.
Jake — I shouldn't but – I just never knew. Tell me. Tell me what you dream about.
Kitty — You mustn't laugh.
Jake — I won't.
Kitty — Even a little laugh and I'll stop.
Jake — I promise. I want to understand girls. I want to understand what goes on in their heads. I want to know what you talk about. You and Roche and H and Sin. Tell me. Tell me about your dream.
Kitty — OK. We're going to be celebrities. Pretty soon, you're going to see us everywhere. Huge billboards[2] with our faces on. TV screens with us talking, moving, dancing, laughing. The front pages will tell you what we're up to[3] every day. You go to buy a can of coke – they'll have our faces on the side. Lots of Japanese kids are going to dress like us. Your screensaver, your desktop, your mobile's welcome screen – all of them will be me and Roche and H and Sin.

Pause. Then Jake laughs.

Kitty — Oh piss off[4], Jake. Just piss off.
Jake — I'm sorry, Kit. I just … You know.
Kitty — What?
Jake — Look at us. This town, this school. It just seems such a fantasy.
Kitty — An ambition. That's the trouble with you, Jake. You don't want anything.
Jake — I want –––
Kitty — I am so fed up with you.
Jake — I'm sorry, I'll –––
Kitty — I don't want to see you any more.
Jake — What, you're …?
Kitty — I'm ending this relationship[5]. Here. Now. Goodbye.
Jake — No. Kit. Wait. You can't just walk away.
Kitty — Why not?
Jake — Because I love you.
Kitty — That's nice.
Jake — And you love me.
Kitty — Do I? Do I really, Jay? I don't think so. No. I think I used to. But I'm growing up fast. Six months ago I was a kid and now …
Jake — Now you're a celebrity.

---

[1] celebrity [sə'lebrəti] *berühmte Persönlichkeit* [2] billboard ['bɪlbɔːd] *Reklametafel* [3] what we're up to *was wir machen, was wir so treiben*
[4] Piss off. [ˌpɪs‿'ɒf] *(Slang, vulgär) Hau ab!* [5] relationship [rɪ'leɪʃnʃɪp] *Beziehung*

Kitty Now I'm ready to be a celebrity. And I don't need you any more.

Jake Kitty, please.

Kitty You're a nice guy. You're quite good-looking. You have a sense of humour[1]. Someone else will go out with you.

Jake No.

Kitty Goodbye. I'm not your girlfriend any more.

Jake I've still got the photo of you up beside my bed. The photo I put up the day I asked you out and you said yes.

Kitty You have to go now. Rochelle's on her way here and we've got a lot to talk about.

Jake Plans for the future?

Kitty Sort of.

Jake So what now? Talk to your stylists? Talk to your PR[2] people? Sort out a few photo-shoots[3]? A few interviews?

Kitty Piss off, Jake.

Jake Or maybe you're just going to sit here with your magazines like *Heat* and *Hello* ---

Kitty No, actually, no.

Jake --- sit here and waste your time with pointless[4], pointless dreams?

Rochelle enters.

Rochelle Hi, guys.

Jake What are you going to be?

Kitty How do you mean?

Jake In five years, ten years, twenty years. What are you going to be?

Kitty I told you, Jacob. Celebrities.

Rochelle That's right.

Jake Are you going to be in a band?

Kitty Maybe. I don't know.

Jake Or act?

Kitty Yeah. Could do.

Jake Or model or present on MTV or –?

Kitty Yeah, yeah, Jake ---

Jake Well – which one? What's going to make you famous?

Kitty I don't know. I don't care. It doesn't matter.

Jake You've got to have a talent.

Kitty Of course, yeah.

Jake And I hate to tell you this, girls, but you can't sing, you can't act, you're OK-looking but you're not models ---

Kitty We'll find a way.

Jake You're dreaming, the pair of you.

Kitty OK. You want to know? You want to know what's going to make us famous?

Jake Yes. I want to know.

Kitty OK. We're going to date celebrities.

Rochelle That's right.

Kitty By the end of the day I'm going to be dating a celeb.

Rochelle That's right

Jake That's a promise?

Kitty That's a promise.

Jake Ha. Ha. Ha.

Jake exits[5].

Kitty Loser. We're going to show him.

Rochelle Maybe he's right, Kit. Maybe we're never going to make it.

Kitty No. You know what that horoscope said.

Rochelle I know.

Kitty "Finish old relationships and prepare to live your dreams." And that's exactly what we've got to do. Did you do it?

Rochelle Yeah. I did it just like you said. Only ...

Kitty I need you with me, Rochelle. We've got to stick together[6]. Everybody else in this stupid school, this stupid town, is going to laugh at us, but you and me and H and Sin, we've got to be there for each other. OK?

Rochelle OK. Just ...

Kitty Yeah?

---

[1] sense of humour [ˌsens‿əv ˈhjuːmə] *(Sinn für) Humor* [2] PR (Public Relations) *Öffentlichkeitsarbeit; Werbung* [3] photo-shoot *Fototermin, Fotoshooting* [4] pointless [ˈpɔɪntləs] *sinnlos* [5] (to) exit [ˈeksɪt] *hinausgehen; von der Bühne abgehen* [6] (to) stick together *(infml) zusammenhalten*

Rochelle Dan cried. When I said, “I don’t want to be your girlfriend any more,” he started to cry. With great big tears. And I wanted to say, “Dan, Dan. Stop. I didn’t mean it. I still love you.”

Kitty But you didn’t.

Rochelle No, Kit. I didn’t.

Kitty You had to do it, Roche. Dan’s a nice guy –

Rochelle He’s a really nice guy.

Kitty – but can you imagine him with David Beckham or Sting or the Queen?

Rochelle No. No, I can’t.

Kitty He’d say all the wrong things.

Hannah enters.

Hannah Oh God. I feel like such a bitch[1]. “Tyson, this is the end.” He just kept on repeating in this really miserable voice: “Why? Why” Why?” Over and over again. “Why? Why? Why?” And now he wants back everything he ever gave me: CDs, videos, T-shirts. Everything. I’m going to miss them so much. This better be worth it, Kit.

Kitty Worth it? H, what’s Tyson when you are going to have your pick[2] of film stars, singers, footballers, models? You want Brad Pitt?

Hannah I’d love Brad Pitt but –––

Kitty Then work it, girl. We’re going to be so famous he won’t resist[3].

Hannah But isn’t he with –––?

Kitty You’ll be all over the papers for days. Your PR people will have to work so hard. “I’m sorry about all the hurt I’ve caused,” you’ll say. “But Brad and I are so happy together.”

Hannah Yes. A quiet wedding. Brad. Our families. And a few friends.

Kitty That’s it. And where’s Tyson going to be? The supermarket? The call centre?

Hannah Car-park attendant[4] maybe.

Kitty Let him read about it in the papers.

Hannah Brad and I are going to meditate together for an hour every morning.

Sinita enters, crying.

Sinita I hate you, Kitty. Why did you make me do that? I love Framji, I do. And now. I finished with him. *(She cries.)*

Rochelle Come on, babe.

Sinita He says he never wants to see me again. Or walk down the same street as me. Or take the same bus as me. Or use the same search engine as me. Totally – gone. Forever. And what am I going to do without him?

Kitty Do without him? Do without him? You know what you’re going to do without him. Same as me without Jay, same as Roche without Dan, same as H without Ty. Be a celebrity.

Sinita And are you sure about that, Kit?

Kitty Yes of course. Totally sure. Aren’t you?

Sinita Well ...

Kitty Sin. You can’t give up this easily. I know this is hard. But think of the reward[5]. Think of waking up in this totally fantastic house next to your totally fantastic boyfriend.

Rochelle And there’s a TV crew already there as you open your eyes. They’re making a documentary about you 24/7[6]. There’s a whole channel that shows it all totally live.

Hannah And then you exercise with your personal trainer.

Kitty Make some calls to Japan as you eat your breakfast – they’re planning this Barbie-type doll[7] of you for markets all around the world.

Rochelle The morning: photo-shoots – a calendar. Some measurements[8] for your wedding dress. *Hello* is sponsoring your wedding. Only fourteen months to go.

---

[1] bitch [bɪtʃ] *(Slang, abwertend) Schlampe, Miststück* [2] the pick of *der/die/das Beste von, die Besten von* [3] (to) resist [rɪˈzɪst] *widerstehen*
[4] car-park attendant [əˈtendənt] *Parkplatzwächter/in* [5] reward [rɪˈwɔːd] *Belohnung* [6] 24/7 *rund um die Uhr (24 Stunden, 7 Tage die Woche* •
[7] doll [dɒl] *Puppe* [8] measurement [ˈmeʒəmənt] *Maße*

Hannah Lunch with Beyoncé and Madonna. Chatter[1], chatter. You debate: is hatha yoga now out? Then cameras: flash, flash, flash.

Kitty The afternoon: a massage and a meeting with a team from LA who want to turn you into a cartoon series for TV. You tell them: nice idea but you want to see what happens with the movie rights first.

Rochelle Then off to a gallery. You've done a painting for charity. Just a fun thing. "I'm no artist," you tell the reporters. "But I do care about sick children and I just wanted to do what I could to help."

Hannah And then up the red carpet[2] at a film première. "Is it true that they're making you into a musical?" "No comment." Then party, party. "Hi, Nicole! Hi, Ewan! Hallo, Uma!"

Kitty And as you fall into your bed you say: "I did it. This is me. My dream, my hope, my destiny[3]. Celebrity." Today was hard. I know that, girls. "Finish old relationships"; that's hard. But now it's time, time to live your dreams. Are you going to do that, Sin?

Sinita Will I have a stalker[4]?

Kitty Maybe.

Sinita I'd like a stalker. Someone who fills their house with pictures of me. Goes through my bins. Names all their children after me. Who can't get me out of their head.

Kitty Of course you'll have a stalker.

Sinita And says he'll shoot himself if I don't return his calls.

Kitty Yes. Absolutely.

Sinita Oh wow.

Kitty Are we sticking together, girls? Are we sistas?

Rochelle
Hannah
Sinita *(together)* Yeah.

Kitty Then come on. New *OK* out today. New *Sugar*. See what our horoscopes say today.

Kitty takes magazines from her bag and hands them round.

Kitty OK. Horoscope time. Oh my God. Oh my God. Look at this. "A stranger will show you the way to future happiness today." What does that mean? Keep your eyes open for a stranger, girls.

Kitty, Rochelle, Hannah and Sinita exit. Jake and Victor enter.

Jake Victor. Will you stop following me? I want to be alone.

Victor But we said we'd go to a movie.

Jake Yeah. Well, I've changed my mind.

Victor There's a sci-fi thing. Which sounds good. Or an action thing. Which sounds OK. Or a comedy. Which sounds really funny. Which do you fancy[5]?

Jake None of them.

Victor I've got some DVDs if you want to ---

Jake No.

Victor Or games. My mum left pizza and some oven chips ---

Jake Vic. I want to be by myself. Please.

Victor But – why?

Jake Kit finished with me.

Victor No way.

Jake Yeah. She chucked[6] me. So ---

Victor I'm sorry.

Jake And I just want to go into my room and be alone.

Victor But surely a movie would ---

Jake No, Vic. I'm sorry.

Victor Or a pizza or just hanging out at Burger King.

Jake Victor. No.

Victor But I'm your friend.

Jake I know and ---

Victor All the things we've done together. Things I've done for you.

---

[1] (to) chatter ['tʃætə] *plappern, schwätzen* [2] carpet ['kɑ pɪt] *Teppich* [3] destiny ['destəni] *Schicksal* [4] stalker ['stɔːkə] *jd., der eine andere Person (meist eine/n Prominente/n) verfolgt und belästigt* [5] (to) fancy sth. ['fænsi] *Lust auf etwas haben* [6] (to) chuck sb. [tʃʌk] *mit jm. Schluss machen*

Jake But Vic – you're a dork[1]. You've never been out with a girl.

Victor I'd like to.

Jake And I don't want to talk to someone who doesn't know anything about girls.

Victor You know Letitia?

Jake If you haven't been out with a girl you're a child, Vic.

Victor She did the Nurse in that scene from Romeo and Juliet.

Jake That's the difference between us, Vic.

Victor I like Letitia. I keep on having dreams about her. I want to ask her out.

Jake You're a child and I'm a man.

Dan enters.

Dan I don't believe it. I just don't believe it. Roche finished with me.

Jake She chucked you?

Dan Just sat down and said: "I don't want to see you any more. We're finished. Over." She wants to be a celebrity, Jay.

Jake Oh my God.

Tyson enters.

Tyson Bitch. Bitch. Bitch.

Jake What's that, Ty?

Tyson Hannah. What a freaking[2] bitch. Chucked me. I've never been chucked. Never.

Jake Did she say she wanted to be –––?

Tyson A celebrity. Can you believe that? I told her: no freaking way, baby. And then she got mad at me and chucked me. I'm just so angry.

Victor Maybe going to a movie would help?

Tyson What's he doing here? What are you doing here?

Victor There's a sci-fi movie –––

Tyson Shut up, Victor, shut up.

Framji enters.

Framji Guys. You'll never guess. Sin finished with me.

Jake We know. Same for all of us, Fram. Me and Kit. Dan and Roche. H and Ty. You and Sin. We've all been chucked.

Dan On the same day.

Tyson At the same time.

Framji But – they must have planned this.

Jake That's right.

Framji I don't believe it. What a bitch.

Tyson Yeah. Total bitches. All of them.

Kitty, Rochelle, Hannah and Sinita enter.

Kitty Oh, hi. We didn't know you were here.

Jake Yeah. That's right. We're here.

Hannah We're looking for a stranger. To show the way to future happiness.

Tyson Right.

Rochelle Like it says here. You seen a stranger?

Dan No. Don't think so. No.

Kitty Come on, girls. They're not going to help us.

Kitty, Rochelle, Hannah and Sinita exit.

Framji Did you see that? Didn't even look at me.

Jake We need to show them, guys.

Tyson Yeah. We need to punish them.

Dan We need to hurt them.

Framji To teach them a lesson[3].

Jake To show them how stupid they are.

Dan But how?

Victor Maybe if I –––?

Dan What's the best way to make them suffer[4]?

Victor Can I –––? I've got an idea.

Tyson Victor. You don't know anything about girls. You go off to the library and let us figure this thing out[5].

Framji They're coming back. They're coming this way.

Dan Run.

Jake Stay.

Tyson Hide.

---

[1] dork [dɔːk] *(infml) Trottel, Langweiler* [2] freaking ['friːkɪŋ] *(infml) verdammte(r, s)* [3] (to) teach sb. a lesson *jm. eine Lektion erteilen*
[4] (to) suffer ['sʌfə] *leiden* [5] (to) figure sth. out [ˌfɪgər‿'aʊt] *etwas herausfinden*

Victor Guys. I'm going to show you ... Can I show you? Guys.

Jack, Dan, Tyson and Framji hide. Kitty, Rochelle, Hannah and Sinita enter. Victor covers his face.

Victor The future. The future. I see the future.

Rochelle Ugh. Look. A loony[1].

Sinita A loony homeless person.

Hannah Ugh. Gross[2]. They don't wash. And they really smell.

Sinita And they get really aggressive if you don't give them money.

Rochelle Well, I'm not giving him anything.

Kitty Girls. Listen for a moment. Just listen to what he's saying.

Victor The mortal[3] man walks backward
His face toward what's gone
The future is a mystery
But still he travels on.

Sinita It's like mad person's talk.

Kitty No. It makes sense[4] if you listen.

Victor But I am not as other men
Who only see what's done
My brain[5] is burnt with future lives
I see the world to come[6].
The future. The future. I see the future.

Kitty Who are you?

Hannah Kit, I think we ought to be going now.

Kitty No, no. We've got to talk to him. Find out ---

Rochelle He's really creepy[7], Kit.

Sinita Yeah. I think he may be dangerous.

Kitty But girls – if he sees the future ---

Victor I know you. I know you. I know you. I know you.

Sinita Oh my God. He's going completely mental[8].

Rochelle I want another Diet Coke. Let's all go and buy another Diet Coke.

Sinita Yeah, Roche. Good idea.

Kitty Girls. We've got to ask him. We've got to make him tell us. What happens to us? How do we get to be celebrities?

Hannah There's no point asking him. He's a loony.

Kitty Stick together, girls. We've got to stick together.

Victor I know you. I know you. I know you. I know you.

Kitty Me?

Victor Everybody knows you.

Kitty In the future.

Victor You are famous in the future.

Kitty Oh my God. That's amazing.

Victor Your picture is everywhere in the future. A hotel in Bangkok, an IMAX in New Mexico, a hologram in Times Square – it's you.

Kitty I knew it. I knew I was right.

Victor You are a line of clothes, a cola drink, a fitness video, a salad dressing, a doll, a video game, a mouse pad, a car sticker, a newspaper column, a talkshow, the most hits in a day on AOL, a remix, beauty tips, a diet plan, a chain of restaurants, a sex symbol, role-model superstar. You are live action, animation[9], computer-generated, holographic, CD ROM, exclusive pictures, pay-to-view. All of them are you and you are all of them. Oh, yes, I know you. In the future I know you. In the future everybody knows you.

Kitty And Roche and H and Sin as well?

Victor And Roche and H and Sin as well.

Rochelle Oh, my God.

Hannah Oh, my God.

Sinita Amazing.

Victor The bedrooms that you live in now will be museums – a place for all your fans to come. Coaches[10] will stop outside your school: "That's the place. That's where she studied."

Rochelle That is so cool.

---

1 loony ['lu:ni] *Verrückte(r)* 2 gross [grəʊs] *(infml) ekelhaft* 3 mortal ['mɔ:tl] *sterblich* 4 (to) make sense *(einen) Sinn ergeben*
5 brain [breɪn] *Gehirn* 6 the world to come *die Welt von morgen (die Zukunft)* 7 creepy ['kri:pi] *unheimlich* 8 mental ['mentl] *verrückt* •
9 animation [ˌænɪ'meɪʃn] *(Computer-)Animation* 10 coach *Reisebus*

Victor Everybody who ever knew you will sell everything you gave them. "This item[1] personally touched by Kitty." And everything bought – instantly[2].

Sinita What will we be famous for?

Victor Do you know the band "Awesome"?

Sinita No.

Victor Four boys. The finest voices, best dance routines. Best songs. The four most famous faces of the future.

Kitty And we're ...

Victor You date them. And they bring you fame.

Hannah And when do we meet them? Where do we meet them?

Victor You've already met them.

Kitty We have?

Victor They are here in your town, your school right now. "Awesome" are amongst you. The four most famous faces of the future, the biggest celebrities the world has ever known are Jake and Dan and Ty and Framji.

Sinita But we just ... Oh no ...

Victor Yes?

Rochelle We just chucked them.

Victor You ...? Oh no. Then you must unchuck them fast. You can't meddle[3] with the future. You have to date them or the future's empty: blank[4] videos, blank ads, blank T-shirts, blank covers on the magazines. Without your faces, there is nothing. Quick, quick. Find your friends. Oh God. It's hurting. When time is bent[5] like this it hurts me. Ugh. Ugh. Put the future right. Go out with Jake and Dan and Ty and Fram. Date "Awesome"! Agh! Agh!

Kitty Oh my God!

Victor Before it's too late! Aaaaaaggh!

Kitty, Rochelle, Hannah, Sinita exit.

Working with the text

1 Understanding the play

a) *What is the play about? What is its message? Write down five ideas on five cards.*

b) *Compare your ideas in a group and choose the three best ones. Present your ideas to the class.*

2 Understanding the details

a) *Answer these questions:*

1 What dream does Kitty share with Jake on page 111?

2 What reasons does Kitty give for finishing with Jake? Find as many reasons as you can.

3 How do Kitty and her friends plan to become celebrities?

b) *Write five more questions about the play. Collect the ten best questions on the board and try to answer them in class.*

3 Your reactions to the play

Which of the adjectives in the box describe what you think of the play? Explain your reactions.

annoying • boring • clever • funny • interesting • realistic • sad • silly • uninteresting • unrealistic

---

[1] item ['aɪtəm] *Gegenstand* [2] instantly ['ɪnstəntli] *sofort* [3] (to) meddle with ['medl] *herumspielen mit, sich einmischen in*
[4] blank [blæŋk] *leer, unbespielt* [5] (to) be bent [bent] *gekrümmt, gebogen, verbogen sein*

TF 8 Mumbai slums[1]

Mumbai is home to more than 6 million squatters[2] – people who have nowhere to live so they have to occupy[3] private or public land and build their communities there. Sanjay Gandhi Nagar is such a squatters' town.

It was Alice in Wonderland in reverse[4]: a rabbit hole in the ceiling[5]. That's how I entered my room in Sanjay Gandhi Nagar: having walked into my landlord's[6] shop, I step around the guys making clothes, climb the ladder in the corner and pull myself through the opening.

Home was a bare[7] concrete[8] cell, perhaps 10 by 14 feet, with grey walls and two small windows. My landlord, kindly, had given me a bed, two chairs and a ceiling fan[9] – the smallest and noisiest fan I had ever seen. I moved the bed under the fan, hoping to escape from the mosquitoes at night.

Made mostly of concrete, Sanjay Gandhi Nagar could be called an upper-class squatter community. This neighborhood of 300 families was about an hour from downtown Mumbai by train. Sanjay Gandhi Nagar had electricity. My room had no water, but the community did have water within a few feet of almost every doorway. However, the water only came on between 2:00 and 5:00 in the mornings, so when anyone needed to fill their buckets[10], they had to wake up in the middle of the night. I saw some of my neighbors only at 3 a.m., when we were filling our water buckets.

Sanjay Gandhi Nagar had two shared toilet blocks: 10 toilets each, five for women and five for men. It sounds like a lot, but during the morning rush, you sometimes had to wait for 15 minutes or so, with your bucket of water (poor Indians don't use toilet paper).

Most people bathe outside. They sit in a large bucket, pour[11] water over themselves, and wash. Men bathe in their underwear; women bathe wearing saris.

I paid 1,000 rupees a month for my room: about $ 22. This was a fair price, but it also made my room too expensive for many squatters in Mumbai.

Abridged and adapted from 'Shadow cities', by Robert Neuwirth

a) *Read the report carefully. Take notes. What do you find most shocking, interesting, surprising? Tell your partner. Does he/she agree?*

b) *Use the chart and explain how people in Mumbai's slums cope with[12] their everyday problems.*

problems	*what people do*
mosquitoes	*they use a ceiling fan*
...	...

[1] slum [slʌm] *Slum, Elendsviertel* [2] squatter ['skwɒtə] *Land-, Hausbesetzer/in* [3] (to) occupy ['ɒkjupaɪ] *besetzen* [4] in reverse [rɪ'vɜːs] *umgekehrt* [5] ceiling ['siːlɪŋ] *(Zimmer-)Decke* [6] landlord ['lændlɔːd] *Vermieter* [7] bare [beə] *leer, kahl, bloß* [8] concrete ['kɒŋkriːt] *Beton-* [9] fan *Ventilator* [10] bucket ['bʌkɪt] *Eimer* [11] (to) pour [pɔː] *gießen, schütten* [12] (to) cope (with) [kəʊp] *zurechtkommen (mit)*

TF 9 Shooting Jozi

In July 2007, one hundred people in some of the poorest areas of Johannesburg were given disposable cameras[1] to help them to document their lives. These are some of the pictures they took.

A

C

D

B

E

F

1 The photos

a) *Make groups of four. Each of you chooses one of the photos A–F. Make notes and tell the others what you think ...*

- *the photo shows.*
- *the photo says about how people live in the slums of Johannesburg.*
- *the photo says about their feelings.*

▸ *SF Describing pictures (p. 121)*

b) *Why do you think the photographer chose to take these pictures? Discuss in your group.*

I think the photographer of C was proud of ...
Maybe he/she wanted to show how ...
He/She probably thought he/she could ...

2 Now you

Take photos of six aspects of your life. Use your photos to make a poster. Add English captions and a few sentences about each photo. Display your poster.

---

[1] disposable camera [dɪ'spəʊzəbl] *Wegwerfkamera*

Skills File – Inhalt

Im **Skills File** findest du Hinweise zu Arbeits- und Lerntechniken. Was du in den Skills-Kästen der Units gelernt hast, wird hier näher erläutert.

Was du bereits aus Band 4 von English G 21 kennst, ist mit **REVISION** gekennzeichnet, z. B.
– **REVISION Describing pictures**, Seite 121
– **REVISION Giving a presentation**, Seite 125.

Viele neue Hinweise helfen dir bei der Arbeit mit Hör- und Lesetexten, beim Sprechen, beim Schreiben von eigenen Texten, bei der Sprachmittlung und beim Lernen von Methoden.

Manchmal gibt es auch Aufgaben dazu.

STUDY AND LANGUAGE SKILLS

SF REVISION Learning words

Worauf solltest du beim Lernen und Wiederholen von Vokabeln achten?

- Lerne immer 7–10 Vokabeln auf einmal.
- Lerne neue und wiederhole alte Vokabeln regelmäßig – am besten jeden Tag 5–10 Minuten.
- Lerne mit jemandem zusammen. Fragt euch gegenseitig ab.
- Schreib die neuen Wörter auch auf und überprüfe die Schreibweise mithilfe des *Dictionary* oder *Vocabulary*.

Wie kannst du Wörter besser behalten?

Wörter kannst du besser behalten, wenn du sie in Wortgruppen sammelst und ordnest:

- **Gegensatzpaare** sammeln, z. B. alive ◂▸ dead, majority ◂▸ minority, forget ◂▸ remember
- Wörter mit **gleicher Bedeutung** sammeln, z. B. (to) train – (to) practise
- Wörter in **Wortfamilien** sammeln, z. B. friend, boyfriend, girlfriend, friendly, unfriendly, make friends, ...
- Wörter in **Wortnetzen** (*networks*) sammeln und ordnen.

SF REVISION Describing pictures

Wie kann ich Bilder beschreiben?

- Um zu sagen, wo auf einem Bild etwas abgebildet ist, benutze:
  at the top/bottom • in the foreground/background • in the middle • on the left/right
- Diese Präpositionen sind auch hilfreich:
  behind • between • in front of • next to • under
- Um zu beschreiben, was die Personen auf dem Bild tun, benutze das **present progressive**.
  Jeannie is riding her horse.

Wie kann ich beschreiben, was die Personen fühlen?

Oft sollst du dich in eine Person auf einem Foto hineinversetzen und beschreiben, was sie fühlt oder denkt. Schau dir das Foto genau an und nimm dir Zeit, dir die Situation vorzustellen. Beim Formulieren helfen dir phrases wie:
Maybe the woman/man in the photo is thinking about ... •
I think he/she feels/wants to ...

SF REVISION Check yourself

How am I doing?

Damit du weißt, in welchen Bereichen des Englischen du noch Schwächen hast und welche du schon beherrschst, solltest du dich immer wieder selbst überprüfen. Das kannst du auf unterschiedlichen Wegen tun. Eine Reihe von Tipps kennst du vermutlich schon.
Du kannst dich auch nach jeder Unit mithilfe der *How am I doing*-Seiten selbst überprüfen. Dabei gehst du wie folgt vor:

1. Du machst die einzelnen Aufgaben und überprüfst deine Ergebnisse.
2. Dann schaust du dir die Bereiche, in denen du Fehler gemacht hast, nochmal an. Halte dich dabei an die Hinweise in der Spalte *Find out more*.
3. Nun übst du gezielt diese Bereiche. Dazu schaust du in der Spalte *Exercises* nach, wo du im Englischbuch und Workbook Übungen dazu findest.
4. Nach einiger Zeit machst du die Aufgaben in *How am I doing?* noch einmal und vergleichst die Lösungen mit deinen Ergebnissen vom ersten Mal.

Die Arbeit mit einem persönlichen Fehlerheft

Ein weiterer, sehr hilfreicher Weg ist das Anlegen eines Fehlerheftes.
Dafür legst du dir ein DIN-A4 oder DIN-A5 Heft an. Dieses unterteilst du z. B. nach folgenden Schwerpunkten:

1. Drittel: Words 2. Drittel: Grammar 3. Drittel: Spelling

Dann untersuchst du deine Klassenarbeiten und andere schriftliche Arbeiten auf deine Fehlerquellen hin. Dein/e Englischlehrer/in zeigt durch Abkürzungen am Rand, was für eine Art Fehler du gemacht hast.

WORDS

Wrong	Correct	REMEMBER
He goes to school ~~with the~~ bus.	He goes to school by bus.	mit dem Bus fahren – go by bus
We've got a ~~strong~~ teacher.	We've got a strict teacher.	Nicht verwechseln: streng – strict / strong – stark
I climbed ~~on~~ a tree.	I climbed a tree.	auf einen Baum klettern – climb a tree

Tipp

- Ergänze das Heft jedes Mal, wenn du eine Klassenarbeit oder einen Text von deinem Lehrer/deiner Lehrerin zurückbekommen oder wenn du eine „*How am I doing*“-Seite bearbeitet hast.
- Überprüfe, ob du bestimmte Fehler immer wieder machst. Wenn ja, such dafür Übungen in deinem Englischbuch, deinem Workbook, deinem *e-Workbook* oder frag deinen Lehrer/deine Lehrerin nach Übungen.
- Schau dir vor jeder Klassenarbeit die Fehler an, die du oft machst.
- Mach dir mithilfe des Grammatikteils die Regeln noch einmal bewusst, die dir besonders schwerfallen..

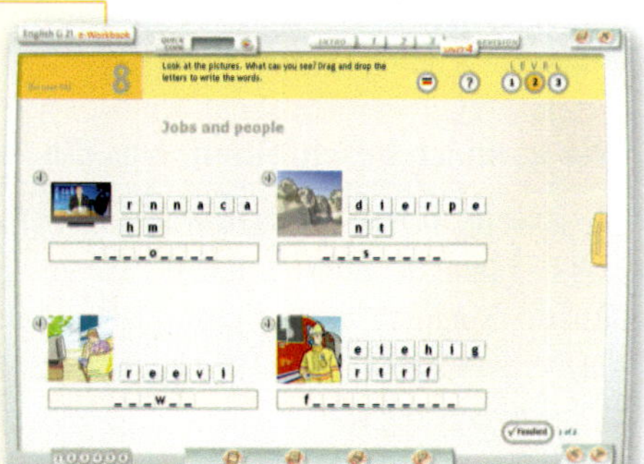

SF REVISION Using a bilingual dictionary

Wann brauche ich ein zweisprachiges Wörterbuch?

Du verstehst einen Text nicht, weil er zu viele Wörter enthält, die dir unbekannt sind, und die Worterschließungstechniken (▸ *SF Working out the meaning of words, p. 130*) helfen dir nicht weiter?
Du sollst einen Text auf Englisch schreiben, und dir fehlt das eine oder andere Wort, um deine Ideen auszudrücken? Du willst z. B. sagen, die Geschichte *In the Outback* (Seite 20–24) dreht sich um Bill und Colm und Bills Hund Rusty, aber du kennst das englische Wort für „drehen" nicht?
In solchen Fällen hilft dir ein zweisprachiges Wörterbuch.

Wie benutze ich ein zweisprachiges Wörterbuch?

- Die **Leitwörter** *(running heads)* oben auf der Seite helfen dir, schneller zu finden, was du suchst. Auf der linken Seite steht das erste Stichwort, auf der rechten Seite das letzte Stichwort der Doppelseite.
- **drehen** ist das **Stichwort** *(headword)*. Alle Stichwörter sind alphabetisch geordnet: **d** vor **e**, **da** vor **de** und **dre** vor **dri** usw.
- Die **kursiv gedruckten** Hinweise helfen dir, die für deinen Text passende Bedeutung zu finden.
- Die **Ziffern 1.**, **2.** usw. zeigen, dass ein Stichwort mehrere ganz verschiedene Bedeutungen hat.
- Dem Stichwort sind **Beispielsätze** und **Redewendungen** zugeordnet. In den Beispielsätzen und Redewendungen ersetzt eine **Tilde** (~) das Stichwort.
- Im englisch-deutschen Teil der meisten Wörterbücher findest du außerdem Hinweise auf **unregelmäßige Verbformen**, auf die **Steigerungsformen der Adjektive** und Ähnliches.
- Die **Lautschrift** gibt Auskunft darüber, wie das Wort ausgesprochen und betont wird.
- Bei kniffligen Wörtern gibt es in vielen Wörterbüchern **Info-Boxes**, in denen dir mehr Hilfen und Hinweise gegeben werden, hier z. B. für das deutsche Wort „bringen".

Dr.

Dr. (*Abk. für* ***Doktor***) Dr., Doctor
Drache dragon
Drachen *Papierdrachen* kite; *Fluggerät* hang glider

Drehbuch screenplay, script
drehen 1 *Verb mit Obj* turn; *Film* shoot*; *Zigarette* roll **2**: ***sich ~*** turn; *schnell* spin*; ***sich ~ um*** *übertragen* be* about
Drehkreuz turnstile; **Drehorgel** barrel organ ['ɔːɡən]; **Drehort** location; **Drehstuhl** swivel chair; **Drehtür** revolving door
Drehung turn; *um eine Achse* rotation
Drehzahl (number of) revolutions *Pl od.* revs *Pl*
Drehzahlmesser rev counter
drei three
Drei three; *Note etwa* C; ***ich habe eine ~ geschrieben*** I got a C
dreidimensional 1 *Adj* three-dimensional **2** *Adv*: ***etwas ~ darstellen*** depict sth. three-dimensionally; **Dreieck** triangle ['traɪæŋɡl]; **dreieckig** triangular [traɪ'æŋɡjʊlə]

bringen

bring (**herbringen; mitbringen**) wird nur verwendet, wenn jemand oder etwas zum Ort des Sprechers oder Hörers gebracht wird:

Schön, dass du zu meiner Party … | I'm glad you can come to my party. Can …

take (**weg-, hinbringen; mitnehmen**) wird verwendet, wenn jemand oder etwas woanders hingebracht oder mitgenommen wird:

Kannst du morgen deinen Bruder zur Schule bringen? | Can you take your brother to school tomorrow?

Welche englische Entsprechung von **drehen** brauchst du in diesen Sätzen?
1. She's a good dancer, she loves to ... round and round as fast as she can.
2. Lots of Hollywood stars come to Berlin to ... their films here.

Tipp

- Nimm nicht einfach die erste Übersetzung, die dir angeboten wird! Lies den Wörterbucheintrag, bis du die richtige Übersetzung gefunden hast.
- Wenn du unsicher bist, ob du die richtige Übersetzung gefunden hast, schau dir den Eintrag zu dieser Übersetzung an. Wenn du z.B. überprüfen willst, ob „spin" im zweiten Satz oben die richtige Übersetzung für „drehen" ist, such einen Eintrag unter „spin" und lies ihn dir durch.

SF REVISION Research

Wo kann ich Informationen finden?

Find some information about the Flying Doctor Service in Australia – so oder so ähnlich lauten Aufgaben, die dir oft als Hausaufgabe gestellt werden.
Wenn du nach Informationen suchst, solltest du immer **mehrere Quellen** verwenden. Du kannst im Internet, in einem Lexikon, Atlas, Wörterbuch oder Schulbuch nachschlagen. Benutze auch möglichst einige englische Quellen, z. B. Websites (s. u.), CDs und DVDs.

- Internet/Lexikon für alle Wissensgebiete, wichtige Personen und Ereignisse
- Atlas: geografische und politische Übersichten, Städte, Flüsse
- Wörterbücher: Rechtschreibung und Bedeutung von Wörtern
- Schulbücher: verschiedene Wissensgebiete

Wie kann ich das Internet zur Recherche nutzen?

Eine wichtige Informationsquelle ist das Internet. Aber manchmal findest du dort so viele Informationen, dass du schnell den Überblick verlierst. Diese Tipps sollen dir dabei helfen, nicht im *world wide web* verloren zu gehen.

- Fertige eine Liste mit Schlüsselwörtern *(keywords)* zu deinem Thema an: *Australia, flying, doctor, service, ...*
- Überlege, welches Schlüsselwort oder welche Kombination von Schlüsselwörtern am besten sein kann. *„Flying Doctor Service"+Australia* oder *Australia+flying+doctor+service*
- Wenn du dir zunächst einen Überblick verschaffen willst, kannst du auch ein Nachschlagewerk im Internet anklicken, wie z. B.
  www.infoplease.com
  www.en.wikipedia.org
- Manchmal gibt es dort auch Links, die dir weiterhelfen können.
- Suchmaschinen wie z. B. *Google, Altavista* oder *Yahoo* helfen dir, mithilfe deiner Schlüsselwörter Websites zu deinem Thema zu finden. Verwende eine Suchmaschine und gib deine Schlüsselwörter in die Suche ein.
- Wenn die angezeigten Websites dir nicht helfen oder du zu viele Websites angezeigt bekommst, versuch es noch einmal, indem du deine Schlüsselwörter präzisierst.

mit **allen** Wörtern	Australia	10 Ergebnisse
mit der **genauen Wortgruppe**	"Flying Doctor Service"	
mit **irgendeinem** der Wörter		
ohne die Wörter		

Tipp

- Verwende immer mehrere Quellen, um sicherzugehen, dass die Informationen stimmen.
- Suche Antworten auf die 5 Ws (**who**, **what**, **when**, **where**, **why**).
- Bei englischen Quellen brauchst du nicht alles zu verstehen. Konzentrier dich auf das Wesentliche (▸ *Reading Course, p. 130*).
- Schreib die Quellen nicht wortwörtlich ab, sondern mach dir Notizen. Notier dir auch, wo du die Informationen jeweils her hast.

SF REVISION Giving a presentation

Wie mache ich eine gute Präsentation?

Vorbereitung
- Schreib die wichtigsten Gedanken als Notizen auf, z.B. auf nummerierte Karteikarten oder in der Mindmap.
- Übe deine Präsentation zu Hause vor einem Spiegel. Sprich laut, deutlich und langsam und mach Pausen an geeigneten Stellen.

Folien oder Poster
- Overhead-Folien oder Poster sind gut, um
  - zu zeigen, wie dein Vortrag aufgebaut ist
  - Tabellen, Diagramme usw. für alle lesbar zu präsentieren
  - die wichtigsten Punkte zusammenzufassen.
- Schreib groß und für alle gut lesbar.

Durchführung
- Bevor du beginnst, sortiere deine Vortragskarten.
- Häng das Poster auf bzw. leg deine Folie auf den ausgeschalteten Projektor oder bereite den Beamer vor.
- Warte, bis es ruhig ist. Schau die Zuhörer an.
- Erkläre zu Anfang, worüber du sprechen wirst. Lies nicht von deinen Karten ab, sondern sprich frei.

Schluss
- Beende deinen Präsentation mit einem abschließenden Satz.
- Frag die Zuhörenden, ob sie Fragen haben. Bedanke dich fürs Zuhören.

My presentation is about ... First, I'd like to talk about ... Second, ...

This picture/photo/ ... shows ...

That's the end of my presentation. Have you got any questions?

Ausführlichere sprachliche Hilfen für Präsentationen findest du unter:
▸ *Giving a presentation – useful phrases (p. 139)*

SF Using visual materials with a presentation ▸ *Unit 4, Part C (p. 88)*

Wofür sind visuelle Materialen gut?

Deine Zuhörer/innen werden deinem Vortrag mit mehr Aufmerksamkeit folgen. Sie können sich viel mehr merken, wenn du nicht nur sprichst, sondern ihnen auch etwas zum Anschauen bietest (Visualisierungen). Das können z.B. Fotos, Cartoons, Landkarten, Zeitleisten, Diagramme, Poster oder Filmausschnitte sein.

Was muss ich bei visuellen Materialen beachten?

Vorbereitung
- Das Gerüst deines Vortrags sollte stehen, bevor du anfängst, dir darüber Gedanken zu machen, welche Visualisierungen gut passen könnten.
- Diagramme und Tabellen sind gut, um Zahlen zu verdeutlichen; Zeitleisten sind gut, um eine Entwicklung zu zeigen; Fotos und Cartoons sind gut, wenn man seinen Vortrag auflockern will.

Durchführung
- Bezieh deine visuellen Materialien in deinen Vortrag ein, um etwas zu veranschaulichen, aber lies nicht einfach von der Folie etc. ab.

SF Understanding charts ▸ Unit 1, Part A (p. 10)

Welche Informationen kann ich Diagrammen (charts) entnehmen?

Diagramme stellen statistische Vergleiche zwischen mindestens zwei Dingen dar. Sie können dabei recht unterschiedlich sein (s.u.). Das richtet sich danach, ob man Zahlen oder Prozentsätze miteinander vergleichen will.

Welche unterschiedlichen Formen von Diagrammen gibt es?

- **Bar charts (*Säulendiagramme*)** beschreiben häufig die Anzahl oder Größe von zwei oder mehr Dingen:
- **Pie charts (*Kreis-/Tortendiagramme*)** geben einen schnellen Überblick über die prozentuale Verteilung.
- **Charts (*Tabellen*)** ermöglichen den Vergleich unterschiedlicher Daten anhand von Zahlen und Prozentsätzen.
- **Line graphs (*Kurvendiagramme*)** stellen den Zusammenhang zwischen zwei Parametern dar.

Wie kann ich beschreiben, was die Diagramme darstellen?

Um ein Diagramm zu beschreiben solltest du folgende Fragen beantworten:

- **What is the graph/chart/table about?**
  The bar/pie... chart is about ... • The line graph deals with ... • It is taken from ...
- **What does the graph/chart/table compare?**
  The graph/chart/table compares the size/number of ... •
  It shows the different ... • The pie chart is divided into ... slices that show ...
- **What does the chart tell you? What information does it give you?**
  ... has the largest/second largest • ... is twice/three times/... as big as ... •
  There are more than/almost twice as many ... as there are ... •
  A large majority/small minority/ ... • ... per cent of ...

Manchmal kann es hilfreich sein, wenn du auch noch Aussagen über den Zeitraum der Statistik und/oder die Form der Darstellung machst:
The chart is about the years ...

Tipp

Benutze das **simple past**, wenn du dich auf einen Zeitpunkt in der Vergangenheit beziehst: The rainfall was 1992 mm in Cairns in 2008.

Benutze das **simple present** bei allgemeingültigen Aussagen: The average rainfall in Cairns is 2215 mm per year. Benutze das simple present auch, wenn du deine Schlussfolgerungen wiedergibst. Cairns is a city with lots of rain per year.

Benutze das **present perfect**, wenn du dich auf einen Zeitraum beziehst, der von der Vergangenheit bis heute reicht: Over 400,000 Asians have immigrated to Australia since 2000.

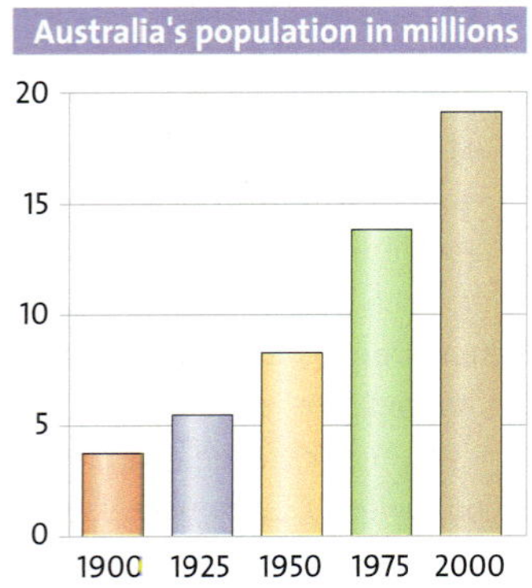

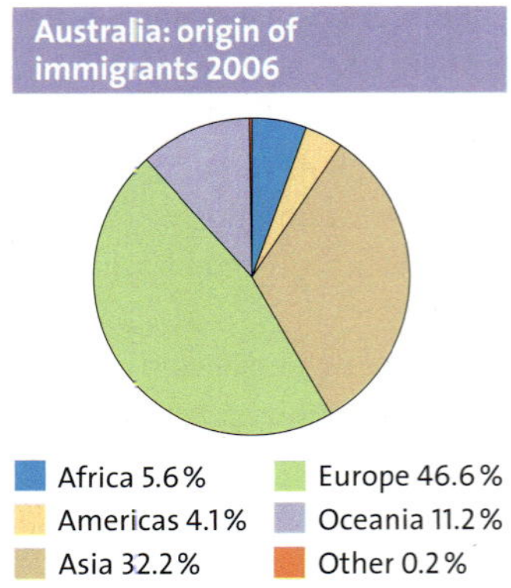

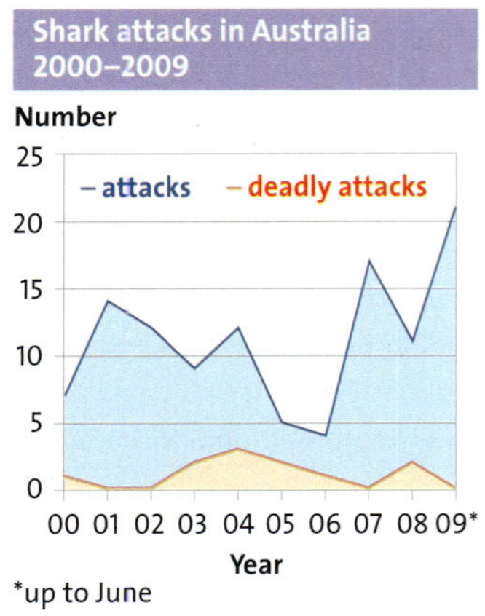

LISTENING AND READING SKILLS

SF REVISION Listening for detail

Was muss ich allgemein beim *Listening* beachten?

Vor dem Hören:
- Lies dir die Fragen durch. So weißt du, worauf du beim Hören achten musst.
- Nutze Überschriften oder Bilder um zu erahnen, um was es geht.
- Bereite dich darauf vor, Notizen zu machen. Leg z. B. eine Tabelle oder Liste an.

Beim Hören:
- Achte auf Geräusche, unterschiedliche Stimmen und wie Leute sprechen.
- Mach nur kurze Notizen, z. B. Symbole oder Stichworte, keine ganzen Sätze.
- Lass dich nicht verunsichern, wenn du mal einen Satz nicht verstehst.

Nach dem Hören:
- Vervollständige deine Notizen sofort.
- Achte beim zweiten Hören auf das, was du zuerst nicht gut verstanden hast.

Wie kann ich Einzelheiten (details) heraushören?

1. Mach dir bewusst, welche Einzelheiten du heraushören sollst bzw. willst. Lass dich von anderen Einzelheiten nicht ablenken.
2. Manche Signalwörter machen es dir leichter, den Hörtext zu verstehen:
   Aufzählung: **and**, **another**, **too**
   Gegensatz: **although**, **but**
   Grund, Folge: **because**, **so**, **so that**
   Vergleich: **larger/older/... than**, **more**, **most**
   Reihenfolge: **before**, **after**, **then**, **next**, **later**, **when**, **at last**, **at the same time**
3. Unterteile Telefonnummern beim Aufschreiben : **0171 572 45 89**.

SF REVISION Interactive listening

Beim Hören von Telefonansagen fehlt dir der Blickkontakt. Aber wenn du dich gut auf die Ansage oder Durchsage vorbereitest, kann dir nichts passieren.

Vor dem Hören:
- Überlege dir vorher, welche Informationen du suchst und auf welche Schlüsselwörter du dafür achten solltest. Schreibe sie auf.
- Geh zum Telefonieren möglichst an einen ruhigen Ort.

Beim Hören:
- Bleib ruhig! Du kannst eine Telefonansage mehrmals hören.
- Achte besonders darauf, ob du für deine Information eine Zahl drücken musst. Zahlen sagen dir, wie du die Ansage fortsetzen kannst. Oft werden sie auch wiederholt.
- Höre besonders genau zu, wenn deine Schlüsselworter genannt werden und mach dir Notizen zu ihnen.

Nach dem Hören:
- Geh das Gehörte noch mal in Gedanken durch. Hast du alles richtig verstanden und hast du alle Informationen? Wenn du nicht sicher bist, ruf einfach noch mal an. Es läuft ein Band und du störst niemanden.

SF REVISION Taking notes

Worum geht es beim Notizenmachen?

Wenn du beim Lesen oder Zuhören Notizen machst, kannst du dich später besser an das Gehörte oder Gelesene erinnern, wenn du etwas vortragen, nacherzählen oder einen Bericht schreiben sollst.

Wie mache ich Notizen?

In Texten oder Gesprächen gibt es immer wichtige und unwichtige Wörter. Die wichtigen Wörter werden Schlüsselwörter **(key words)** genannt und nur die solltest du notieren. Meist sind das Substantive und Verben, manchmal auch Adjektive oder Zahlen.

Tipp

- Verwende Ziffern (z. B. „7" statt „seven").
- Verwende Symbole und Abkürzungen, z. B. ✔ (für Ja) und + (für und) oder US für United States, C. für Caitlin.
  Du kannst auch eigene Symbole erfinden.
- Verwende not oder ✕ statt „doesn't" oder „don't".

SF REVISION Marking up a text

Wann sollte ich einen Text markieren?

Du hast einen Text mit vielen Fakten vor dir liegen und sollst später über bestimmte Dinge berichten. Dann wird es dir helfen, die für die Aufgabenstellung wichtigen Informationen im Text zu markieren.

Wie gehe ich am besten vor?

Lies den Text und markiere nur die für dein Thema wichtigen Informationen. Nicht jeder Satz enthält für deine Aufgabe wichtige Wörter, und oft reicht es aus, nur ein oder zwei Wörter in einem Satz zu markieren.

- Du kannst wichtige Wörter einkreisen.
- Du kannst sie unterstreichen.
- Du kannst sie mit einem Textmarker hervorheben.

ABER:
Markiere nur auf Fotokopien von Texten oder in Büchern, die dir gehören.

Sydney Opera House
The Sydney Opera House is one of the most famous buildings in the world. It houses the large Concert Hall (2,678 seats), the Opera Theatre (1,507 seats), other smaller theatres and a place for open-air events.

Sydney Opera House
The Sydney Opera House is <u>one of the most famous buildings in the world</u>. It houses the large Concert Hall (2,678 seats), the Opera Theatre (1,507 seats), other smaller theatres and a place for open-air events.

Sydney Opera House
The Sydney Opera House is one of the most famous buildings in the world. It houses the large Concert Hall (2,678 seats), the Opera Theatre (1,507 seats), other smaller theatres and a place for open-air events.

SF Reading stories ▸ *Unit 1, Part D (p. 20)*

Was ist das Besondere beim Lesen von längeren Geschichten auf Englisch?

Geschichten lesen macht Spaß. Du tauchst in eine andere Welt ein, lernst Menschen kennen, die du im wirklichen Leben nie treffen würdest (wie z.B. Colm im Outback Australiens) und erhältst Einblicke in ihr Leben, erfährst, was sie denken, was sie fühlen.
Dabei ist es nicht so wichtig, dass du beim Lesen jedes Wort verstehst. Lass dich einfach von der Handlung durch die Geschichte tragen.

Hier nun ein paar Tipps, die es dir erleichtern, eine längere Geschichte auf Englisch zu lesen.

Vor dem Lesen

1. Lies die **Einführung** und die **Überschrift**(en) und sieh dir die **Bilder** zum Text an. Sie geben dir erste Informationen über das, was dich erwartet. Stell dir vor, worum es in der Geschichte gehen könnte.
2. Bei Lektüren oder Romanen gibt es hinten auf dem Buchumschlag meist einen kurzen **Klappentext** mit einer kleinen Zusammenfassung der Handlung – natürlich ohne, dass das Ende verraten wird.

Während des Lesens

1. Tauche ein in die Geschichte. Lies zügig! Kümmere dich nicht um einzelne Wörter, die du nicht kennst oder nicht verstehst. Lies einfach weiter! Das Wichtigste ist, dass du im Großen und Ganzen die Handlung verstehst.
2. Wenn du merkst, dass du der Handlung nicht mehr folgen kannst, weil du zu viele Wörter nicht verstehst oder wenn du denkst, dass bestimmte unbekannte Wörter sehr wichtig sind, dann nutze alle dir bekannten Techniken, um die Bedeutung zu erschließen:
   - Sieh dir noch einmal die Bilder an.
   - Beachte den Textzusammenhang.
   - Kennst du ähnliche englische oder deutsche Wörter?
   - Vielleicht kennst du Teile der unbekannten Wörter?
     (▸ *SF Working out the meaning of words, p. 130*).
3. Wenn das alles nicht hilft und du immer noch das Gefühl hast, dass ein bestimmtes Wort für das Verständnis des Fortgangs der Handlung wichtig ist, schlag es im Wörterbuch nach. (▸ *SF Using a bilingual dictionary, p. 123*).
4. Um der Handlung besser folgen zu können, kann es helfen, wenn du nicht die ganze Geschichte hintereinander liest. Hör ab und zu auf zu lesen, schließ das Buch und denk darüber nach, was du bis dahin gelesen hast. Erzähl jemandem, was bisher geschah und was du noch nicht verstanden hast. Oft klären sich manche Fragen im Gespräch. Dann lies weiter.
5. Mach ruhig auch mal eine Lesepause, das ist bei Lektüren besonders wichtig. Wenn du nach 20–30 Minuten Lesen 5 Minuten Pause machst, kannst du dir die Einzelheiten der Geschichte besser merken.

Tipp

Beim Lesen von englischen Lektüren oder Büchern kann dir eine Lesetagebuch (*reading log*), wie du es sicher aus dem Deutschunterricht kennst, das Verstehen und Behalten erleichtern.

REVISION READING COURSE – Zusammenfassung

Working out the meaning of words

Das Nachschlagen unbekannter Wörter im Wörterbuch kostet Zeit und nimmt auf Dauer den Spaß am Lesen. Oft geht es auch ohne Wörterbuch!

Was hilft mir, unbekannte Wörter zu verstehen?

1. Bilder zeigen oft die Dinge, die du im Text nicht verstehst. Schau sie dir deshalb vor dem Lesen genau an.
2. Oft hilft dir der Textzusammenhang, z. B.
   When we *reached* the station, Judy went to the ticket machine to buy our tickets.
3. Zu manchen englischen Wörtern fallen dir vielleicht deutsche, französische oder lateinische Wörter ein, die ähnlich geschrieben oder ausgesprochen werden, z. B.
   excellent, **millionaire**, **nation**, **reality**.
4. Manchmal stecken in unbekannten Wörtern bekannte Teile, z. B.
   friendliness, **helpless**, **understandable**, **gardener**, **tea bag**, **waiting room**.

Skimming and Scanning

Skimming: Lesen, um sich einen Überblick zu verschaffen

Beim **Skimming** überfliegst du einen Text schnell, um dir einen ersten Eindruck zu verschaffen, worum es geht. Das hilft dir herauszufinden, ob ein Text, den du im Internet oder einem Buch gefunden hast, überhaupt die Informationen enthält, nach denen du (z. B. für ein Referat) suchst. Achte dabei auf

– die **Überschrift**
– die **Zwischenüberschriften** und **hervorgehobene** Wörter oder Sätze
– die **Bilder** und **Bildunterschriften**
– den **ersten** und den **letzten Satz** jedes Absatzes
– **Grafiken**, **Statistiken** und die **Quelle** des Textes

Scanning: Lesen, um nach bestimmten Informationen zu suchen

Beim **Scanning** suchst du einen Text nach Schlüsselwörtern *(key words)* ab und liest nur dort genauer, wo du sie findest. Das hilft dir, wenn dich nur bestimmte Aspekte eines Themas interessieren. Geh dabei so vor:

Schritt 1: Denk an das Schlüsselwort, nach dem du suchst, oder schreib es auf.

Schritt 2: Geh mit deinen Augen und dem Finger schnell durch den Text, in breiten Schlingen wie bei einem „S“ oder „Z“ oder von oben nach unten wie bei einem „U“. Dabei hast du das Schriftbild oder das Bild der Wörter, nach denen du suchst, vor Augen. Die gesuchten Wörter werden dir sofort „ins Auge springen“.

Schritt 3: Wenn das Schlüsselwort, nach dem du suchst, im Text nicht vorkommt, überlege dir, welche anderen Wörter mit den benötigten Informationen zu tun haben, und such nach diesen.

Finding the main ideas of a text

Wenn du Texte wie Zeitungsartikel, Berichte oder Kommentare richtig verstehen willst, ist es gut, wenn du ihre Hauptaussagen erkennst und nachvollziehst, wie sie zusammenhängen. Dabei hilft dir ein Blick auf die Struktur dieser Texte.

Wie finde ich die Hauptaussagen eines Textes?

1. Jeder Text dreht sich um ein Thema oder hat eine Hauptaussage, z. B.
   This summer we've been raising money for the Hickery Soup Kitchen.
   Diese Hauptaussage findest du oft im **ersten Absatz**. Lies ihn deshalb besonders gründlich durch (vgl. den Text auf S. 58 unten)..
2. Die Hauptaussage wird in der Regel durch weitere Aussagen bzw. Gedanken unterstützt, z. B.
   To raise money we've been to two churches.
   Du findest sie oft im ersten oder letzten Satz der nachfolgenden Absätze.
3. Diese weiteren Aussagen bzw. Gedanken werden oft durch Beispiele und Begründungen ergänzt, z. B.
   Lots of people have donated ... Altogether we've raised $427.

Tipp

Die folgenden Wörter oder Ausdrücke werden oft im Zusammenhang mit Begründungen oder Beispielen verwendet:
and so • because • e.g. • etc. • for example • for lots of reasons • this shows that • that's why • ... % of ... are ...

Drawing conclusions

Wenn du bei einer Arbeit Fragen zu einem Text beantworten sollst oder bei einer Recherche Informationen zu einer bestimmten Frage in einem Text suchst, kann es gut sein, dass du an mehreren Stellen schauen musst oder dass die Antwort nicht 1:1 im Text steht.

Wie funktioniert schlussfolgerndes Lesen?

1. Die einfachste Form des schlussfolgernden Lesens besteht darin, die Informationen aus verschiedenen Textstellen zusammenzuführen. Beim Text auf S. 17 z. B. sollst du beschreiben, wie Zita Wallace gestohlen wurde. Dazu musst du dir mehrere Textstellen ansehen.
2. Manchmal steht die Antwort auf eine Frage nicht direkt im Text. Dann musst du sie dir erschließen. Du fragst dich z.B., ob die Kinder der „stolen generations" lange auf eine Entschuldigung der australischen Regierung warten mussten. Dafür musst du Fakten im Text finden, die etwas mit der Frage zu tun haben:

FACTS: – stealing of mixed-race children ended in 1970
– Australian government apologized in 2008
CONCLUSION: the Australian government apologized 38 years later – that's a very long time.

SPEAKING AND WRITING SKILLS

SF REVISION Paraphrasing

Worum geht es beim Paraphrasing?

Paraphrasing bedeutet, etwas mit anderen Worten zu erklären. Das ist hilfreich, wenn dir ein bestimmtes Wort nicht einfällt oder wenn dein Gegenüber dich nicht verstanden hat (siehe auch ▸ *SF Mediation, p. 141*).

Wie gehe ich beim Paraphrasing vor?

- Man kann mit einem Wort umschreiben, das dieselbe Bedeutung hat:
  'to wonder' is the same as 'to ask yourself'
  Oder man sagt das Gegenteil.
  'alive' is the opposite of 'dead'
- Manchmal braucht man mehrere Wörter, z. B. wenn man etwas beschreibt oder erklären will, wie man es verwendet. Dabei benutzt man ein allgemeines Wort (**general word**) und nennt weitere Eigenschaften.
  A racing car is a very fast car.
- Oder du umschreibst das Wort mit **... is/are like ...**
  A chef is like a cook, he or she is the main cook in a restaurant.
- Du kannst auch einen Relativsatz (**relative clause**) verwenden:
  A garage is a place where cars are checked and repaired.
  A nurse is a person who looks after people who are ill, usually in a hospital.

SF REVISION Brainstorming

Wofür ist Brainstorming gut?

Bei vielen Aufgaben ist es nützlich, wenn du im ersten Schritt möglichst viele Ideen zum Thema sammelst. Dabei helfen dir die folgenden Techniken.

Drei verschiedene Brainstorming-Techniken

Technik 1: Making a list
Schreib die Ideen so auf, wie sie dir einfallen, und zwar für jede Idee eine neue Zeile. Lies im zweiten Schritt alle deine Ideen durch. Überlege, welche Ideen davon für dein Thema sinnvoll sind und wie du sie zusammenfassen kannst.

Technik 2: Making a mindmap
Leg eine Mind map an.
- Überlege dafür, welche Oberbegriffe zu deinem Thema passen. Verwende unterschiedliche Farben für jeden Oberbegriff.
- Ergänze jede Idee, die zu einem Oberbegriff passt, auf einem Nebenast. Nimm dafür nur wichtige Schlüsselwörter. Du kannst statt Wörtern auch Symbole verwenden und Bilder ergänzen.

Technik 3: The 5 Ws
Schreib die 5 W-Fragen **Who? What? When? Where? Why?** in eine Tabelle. Die Ideen, die dir zu der jeweiligen Frage kommen, werden darunter geschrieben.

SF REVISION Summary writing

Wenn du einen Text zusammenfasst, gibst du die wichtigen Informationen oder Ereignisse in kürzerer Form wieder.

Wie gehe ich beim *summary writing* vor?

1. Lies den Text einmal ganz durch, damit du verstehst, worum es geht. Mach dir noch keine Notizen.
2. Lies den Text noch einmal gründlich, Satz für Satz, durch und mach dir Notizen zu den 5 Ws:

Who?	Who is the text about?
What?	What happens?/What does somebody do?
When?	When does something happen?
Where?	Where does it happen?
Why?	Why does somebody do something?

Was auf diese Fragen Antwort gibt, ist wichtig. Auslassen kannst du dagegen Beispiele, Vergleiche, Zitate, direkte Rede, ausschmückende Adjektive und andere Textteile, die der Beschreibung dienen.

3. Leg den Text nun beiseite und schreib die *summary* mithilfe deiner Notizen.

– Erklär in den ersten ein oder zwei Sätzen, worum es in dem Text geht.

• Vergleiche diese drei Anfänge einer *summary* von *In the outback* (S. 20–23). Welcher gibt am besten das Thema der Geschichte wieder?

IN THE OUTBACK is a story about Australia.

IN THE OUTBACK is a story about Bill and Colm.

IN THE OUTBACK is a story about Bill and Colm's journey along the Dog Fence.

Du kannst für deine einleitenden Sätze die folgenden phrases verwenden:
The story is about ... • **The text describes ...** • **The article shows ...** • **In the story we get to know ...**

– Im Hauptteil solltest du die wichtigen Ereignisse der Geschichte oder die Hauptpunkte des Artikels wiedergeben.
  - Verwende dafür deine Notizen zu den 5 Ws.
  - Schreib den Text nicht ab, sondern benutze deine eigenen Worte.

They're getting the Flying Doctor out here. We don't know if the old man will make it if we have to drive him down to the hospital in Katherine. Best to fly him to Darwin.

→ *They call the Flying Doctor Service to fly Bill to the hospital in Darwin.*

– Schreib die summary im **simple present**, auch wenn die Geschichte oder der Artikel in der Vergangenheit spielt. Nicht vergessen: im **simple present** wird in der 3. Person Singular **-s** angehängt: **He/She thinks...**

REVISION WRITING COURSE – Zusammenfassung

The steps of writing

1. Brainstorming – Ideen sammeln (s. S.132).
2. Schreiben. Dabei achte darauf,
   - deine Sätze zu verbinden und auszubauen (*Writing better sentences*)
   - deinen Text gut zu strukturieren (*Using paragraphs*)
   - bei einem Bericht die 5 Ws abzudecken (*Writing a report*)
3. Deinen Text inhaltlich und sprachlich überprüfen (*Correcting your text*)

Writing better sentences

Linking words

Eine Geschichte klingt interessanter, wenn man die Sätze mit **linking words** miteinander verbindet. Dabei gibt es mehrere Möglichkeiten:

- **Time phrases** wie at 7 o'clock, every morning, in the afternoons, a few minutes later, suddenly, then, next ...
- **Konjunktionen** wie although, because, but, so ... that, that, when, while
- **Relativpronomen** wie that und who

Adjektive und Adverbien

- Mit Adjektiven kannst du eine Person, einen Ort, einen Gegenstand oder ein Erlebnis genauer und interessanter beschreiben. Vergleiche:
  The man looked into the room. ► The young man looked into the empty room.
- Mit Adverbien kannst du beschreiben, **wie** jemand etwas macht:
  The young man looked nervously into the empty room.

Using paragraphs

Structuring a text

Ein längerer Text ist besser zu verstehen, wenn er mehrere Absätze enthält:

- eine Einleitung (**beginning**) – hier schreibst du, worum es geht
- einen Hauptteil (**middle**) – hier schreibst du mehr über dein Thema
- einen Schluss (**end**) – hier bringst du den Text zu einem interessanten Ende.

Topic sentences

Am Anfang eines Absatzes sind kurze, einleitende Sätze (**topic sentences**) gut, weil sie den Lesern sofort sagen, worum es geht, z. B.

1. Orte: My trip to ... was fantastic. / ... is famous for ... / ... is a great place.
2. Personen: ... is funny/interesting/clever ...
3. Aktivitäten: ... is good fun. / Lots of people ... every day.

Wie kann ich meine Absätze interessant gestalten?

- Beginne mit einem interessanten Einstiegssatz:
  You'll never guess what happened to me today! / Did I tell you that ...?
- Fang für jeden neuen Aspekt einen neuen Absatz an.
- Beende deinen Text mit einer Zusammenfassung oder etwas Persönlichem.

Writing a report – structuring information

Worauf kommt es bei einem Bericht an?

- Gib dem Leser **eine schnelle Orientierung**, was passiert ist.
- Beginne mit **wichtigen Informationen** und gib erst dann Detailinformationen.
- Ein Bericht gibt immer Antworten auf die **5 Ws**:
  Who? What? When? Where? Why? und manchmal auch auf **How?**
- Verwende das *simple past*.

Correcting your text

Ein Text ist noch nicht „fertig", wenn du ihn zu Ende geschrieben hast. Du solltest ihn immer mehr als einmal durchlesen:

- einmal, um zu sehen, ob er vollständig und gut verständlich ist
- noch einmal, um ihn auf Fehler zu überprüfen, z. B. **Rechtschreibfehler *(spelling mistakes)*** oder **Grammatikfehler *(grammar mistakes)***.

tomato [tə'mɑːtəʊ], *pl* **tomatoes** Tomate II

wife [waɪf], *pl* **wives** [waɪvz] Ehefrau II

drop (**-pp-**) [drɒp] fallen lassen I

forget (**-tt-**) [fə'get] vergessen I

Spelling mistakes

Lies deinen Text langsam, Wort für Wort, Buchstabe für Buchstabe. Wenn du unsicher bist, hilft dir ein Wörterbuch. Beachte folgende Regeln:

Tipp

- Manche Wörter haben Buchstaben, die man nicht spricht, aber schreibt, z. B. **autumn**, **climb**.
- Manchmal ändert sich die Schreibweise, wenn ein Wort eine Endung erhält,
  z. B. **take** → **taking**, **terrible** → **terribly**, **lucky** → **luckily**,
  try → **tries** (**aber** **stay** → **stays**), **run** → **running**, **drop** → **dropped**.
- Beim Plural tritt manchmal noch ein **-e** zum **-s**, z. B. **church** → **churches**.

Grammar mistakes

Diese Tipps helfen dir, typische Fehler zu vermeiden:

Tipp

- Im **simple present** wird in der 3. Person Singular **-s** angehängt: **she knows**
- **Unregelmäßige Verben:** Manche Verben bilden die Formen des *simple past* und des Partizip Perfekt *(past participle)* unregelmäßig. Die unregelmäßigen Formen musst du lernen. Die Liste steht auf S. 214–215.
  go – went – gone; buy – bought – bought
- **Verneinung:** Im *simple present* werden Vollverben mit **don't/doesn't** verneint, im *simple past* mit **didn't**.
- **Satzstellung**: Im Englischen gilt immer (auch im Nebensatz):
  a) subject – verb – object (SVO) ... when **I saw my brother.**
  als **ich meinen Bruder sah.**
  b) Orts- vor Zeitangabe **I bought a nice book in the city yesterday.**

SF Writing a CV

▸ *Unit 2, Part B (p. 38)*

Was ist ein CV?

„CV“ bedeutet „Lebenslauf“. Ein CV ist eine Zusammenfassung deiner bisherigen Ausbildung, deiner Fähigkeiten und deiner Interessen. Du brauchst einen CV, wenn du dich um eine berufliche Anstellung bewirbst. Die Amerikaner nutzen statt „CV“ das Wort „résumé“.

Oliver Schäfer
Tulpenweg 34 32051 Herford, Germany
Telephone: 00 49 5221 978036
Email: oliver.schaefer@email-hf.de

Education
2003-2009 Gutenberg-Realschule (secondary school), Herford, Germany
1999-2003 Regenbogen Grundschule (primary school), Herford, Germany

Qualifications
Studying for Fachoberschulreife (equivalent of GCSEs)
Languages: English (6 years), French (4 years)
Driving Licence since 2008

Work experience
Work experience at a garage (3 weeks)

Hobbies and interests
My hobbies are cycling, doing workouts, repairing all kinds of machines. I am very interested in technical things and computers.

References
Available on request

Geburtsdatum und – ort werden in einem britischen CV **oft nicht** genannt.

Gib bei deiner Telefonnummer auch die **internationale Vorwahl** mit an.

Fettgedruckte Überschriften und eine **klare Gliederung** erleichtern das Lesen.

GCSEs gibt es nur in Großbritannien, in den USA entspricht das dem **US highschool diploma**.

An dieser Stelle kann auch eine **konkrete Person** als **Referenz** genannt werden wie im CV auf S. 38. Selbstverständlich musst du ihn oder sie vorher fragen!

Im CV auf S. 38 findest du auch die Abschnitte **Personal statement** und **Other skills** – diese Abschnitte sind möglich, aber nicht zwingend notwendig für einen CV.

Tipp

Bevor du deinen CV losschickst, geh folgende Checkliste durch:
- Habe ich weißes A4-Papier benutzt? Ist das Blatt sauber und ordentlich?
- Habe ich den CV mit einem Computer geschrieben?
- Ist die Seite klar gegliedert und gut lesbar?
- Habe ich alle zentralen Bereiche abgedeckt: meine Erfahrungen, meine Interessen, meine Fähigeiten und persönlichen Eigenschaften?
- Habe ich auch wirklich keine sprachlichen Fehler in meinem Schreiben?

SF Writing formal letters ▸ *Unit 2, Part B (p. 38)*

Beim Briefeschreiben musst du unterschiedliche Regeln beachten, je nachdem ob du einen förmlichen Brief (*formal letter*) an unbekannte Personen, Behörden, Zeitschriften usw. schreibst oder einen persönlichen, informellen Brief (*informal letter*) an Freunde oder Verwandte.

Worauf kommt es bei förmlichen Briefen an? (Formal letter)

1. Schreibe deine Adresse (ohne Namen) und das Datum in die rechte obere Ecke. Verwende keine typisch deutschen Buchstaben wie z.B. ß, ä, ö, oder ü.
2. Die Anschrift steht links.
3. Die Anrede lautet *Dear Sir or Madam*. Wenn du den Namen des Adressaten kennst, beginne deinen Brief mit *Dear Mr/Mrs/Ms* ...
4. Verwende Langformen (*I am, I would like* statt *I'm, I'd like* etc.).
5. Nenne zu Beginn den Grund deines Briefes.
6. Bedanke dich bei Bitten und Anfragen im Voraus (*We look forward to hearing from you. Thank you.*).
7. Beende den Brief mit *Yours faithfully*, wenn du den Adressaten nicht kennst. Hast du den Adressaten am Anfang des Briefes mit Namen angeredet, dann schreibe *Yours sincerely*.
8. Unterschreibe den Brief und tippe zusätzlich deinen Namen.

Example for a letter of application

(1) Schillerstr. 17
37067 Goettingen
Germany

(2) Jane Hall
Meadows Home Farm Shop
Harston
Cambridge CB22 4BE
Great Britain

4 May 2010

(3) Dear Ms Hall

(5) I am (4) writing to you about the advertisement from April 21st in the Cambridge Weekly News. I would love to work for (4) you at Meadows Home Farm this summer.

I am 16 years old and I have a good level of English but would like to improve my speaking skills. I am hard-working, friendly and a fast learner. At home I look after two horses so farm work is not new to me. I have also worked in a sports shop so I have experience in serving people and working in a team. My hobbies are horse riding, playing volleyball and hiking. Please find my CV with this letter.

Thank you for your time. I look forward to hearing from you. (6)

(7) Yours sincerely

(8) *Tamara Wille*
Tamara Wille

Tipp

Beachte, was du zum Schreiben von Texten gelernt hast:
- Vor dem Schreiben: Ideen sammeln, dann sortieren.
- Während des Schreibens: Sätze verbinden und ausbauen; strukturieren.
- Nach dem Schreiben: Überprüfe deinen Brief inhaltlich und sprachlich.

▸ *SF Writing Course, pp. 134–135*

Was ist bei persönlichen Briefen anders? (Informal letter)

Hier sind die Regeln nicht ganz so streng. Aber beachte folgendes:
- Schreibe deine Adresse (ohne Namen) und das Datum in die rechte obere Ecke.
- Verwende keine typisch deutschen Buchstaben wie z.B. ß, ä, ö, oder ü.
- Du benötigst keine Anschrift.
- Du kannst deinen Brief mit *Dear/Hello/Hi* ... beginnen.
- Nenne zu Beginn den Grund deines Briefes, stelle auch Fragen.
- Beende den Brief mit einem freundlichen Gruß/Ausblick/Erwartungen/...
- Schließe deinen Brief mit *Yours/Best wishes/Love/*... ab.

SPEAKING COURSE – Zusammenfassung

Starting and continuing a conversation ▸ *Unit 1, Part A (p. 14)*

Ein Gespräch beginnen

Ein Gespräch auf Englisch zu beginnen ist einfacher, als du vielleicht denkst. Es gibt immer mehrere Möglichkeiten:

– **wenn du etwas erfragen willst** *(z.B. den Weg oder die Uhrzeit)*
  Excuse me, do you know ... • Excuse me, can you tell me ...
– **wenn du jemanden begrüßen möchtest oder kennen lernst**
  Hi • Hello oder Good morning • Good evening (bei Erwachsenen) ...
  Oft kann man das Gespräch dann mit einer allgemeinen Bemerkung weiterführen: Great day today! • Fantastic concert, isn't it? • ...
– **wenn du jemanden wieder triffst**
  Hi, ..., how are things? • Hi, how is it going? • Hi, ... Good to see/meet you. • Fine weather today, isn't it?

Ein Gespräch führen

Für den weiteren Verlauf des Gesprächs sind diese Wendungen nützlich:

– **sich vorstellen:** By the way, my name's ... • I'm ... • Nice to meet you.
– **sich kennen lernen:** Have you ... before? • Have you ever ...? • What about you?
– **sich verabschieden:** See you tomorrow/next week. • Bye!

Und wenn du etwas nicht verstanden hast, kannst du immer nachfragen:
Sorry, I didn't get that. • Sorry, can you say that again, please?

Tipp
- Oft hört man zur Begrüßung auch How are you? oder How do you do? Das sind einfache Begrüßungsformeln. Es wird nicht erwartet, dass man darauf eine Antwort gibt.
- Am besten sagst du einfach Fine, thanks. How about you?

Having a job interview ▸ *Unit 2, Part C (p. 41)*

Sich vorbereiten

Auf ein Vorstellungsgespräch musst du dich unbedingt vorbereiten. Du solltest Fragen zu den folgenden Bereichen beantworten können:

– deine Eigenschaften (**personal qualities**), Stärken (**strengths**) und Schwächen (**weaknesses**)
– deine Interessen (**interests**) und Arbeitserfahrungen (**work experience**)
– was dich an dem Jobangebot reizt (**why you're interested in the job**).

Überleg dir auch eigene Fragen, zum Beispiel zu deinem Tätigkeitsbereich (**what you have to do**) oder zur Bezahlung (**the pay**).

Im Vorstellungsgespräch

Im Vorstellungsgespräch ist es wichtig, dass du freundlich bist und dich als positiver und interessierter Mensch präsentierst.

– **bei der Begrüßung:** Hello, nice to meet you. • Good morning.
– **warum du dich beworben hast:** Well, I'm really interested in what you do / ...
– **wenn es um deine Joberfahrungen geht:** I really enjoyed working with ...
– **bei der Verabschiedung:** Goodbye and thank you very much.

Tipp
- Hör gut zu, wenn du etwas gefragt wirst.
- Sprich nicht zu viel, aber auch nicht zu wenig.
- Sprich nicht zu schnell.

Having a discussion

▸ Unit 3, Part B (p. 56)

Seine Meinung zum Ausdruck bringen und erklären

1. **Expressing an opinion:** In einer Diskussion ist es gut, wenn du möglichst klar und deutlich sagst, was du zu einer bestimmten Frage denkst:
   I think ... • I feel ... • In my opinion ...

2. **Giving reasons and examples:** Es ist aber noch wichtiger, dass du Beispiele und Argumente nennst, die deine Meinung unterstützen – schließlich willst du deine Gesprächspartner von deinem Standpunkt überzeugen!
   because ... • First ... / Second ... • For example ... • Let me explain ... • That's why ... ?

Auf andere in einer Diskussion reagieren

Asking for clarification: Manchmal ist es notwendig nachzuhaken, weil man ein Argument nicht verstanden hat:
Could you say that again? • Sorry, but I don't understand what you mean.

Agreeing with someone: Wenn du die Meinung eines anderen unterstützen willst, kannst du das so zum Ausdruck bringen:
I agree (with you/...) • That's a good point. • You're right.

3. **Disagreeing with someone:** Oft widerspricht man nicht direkt, sondern leitet seine Reaktion mit **Sorry, ...** oder **I don't think** ... ein. Zeig immer Respekt für die Meinung des oder der anderen.
   I don' t think you can say ... • I see what you mean but ... • No, that's not right. • Sorry, I don't agree with you • Yes, but ...

▸ *Classroom phrases (pp. 222–223)*

Giving a presentation – useful phrases

▸ Unit 4, Part C (p. 90)

Einleitung

Nenne am Beginn deines Vortrags dein Thema und gib einen kurzen Überblick darüber, worum es in deinem Vortrag geht:
The topic of my talk today is ... • I'm going to divide this talk into four sections. • First, I'll give you some general facts about ... • Next I'll look at ... • Finally I'll ...

Während der Präsentation

Mach deutlich, wenn du einen neuen Abschnitt in deinem Vortrag beginnst.
Now please have a look at ... • Now I'd like to draw your attention to ... • As you can see in ...

Schluss

Am Ende deines Vortrags fass die wichtigsten Punkte zusammen. Frag deine Zuhörer, ob sie etwas nachfragen oder kommentieren möchten.
To sum up my talk I ... • Please feel free to ask questions or comment on anything I've said.
Ausführlichere Hinweise zur Vorbereitung und Durchführung einer Präsentation findest du unter: ▸ *Giving a presentation (p. 125)*

SF From outline to written discussion ▸ *Unit 3, Part A (p. 51)*

Worum geht es bei einem *Outline*?

Immer wieder sollst du zu strittigen Fragen wie z.B. **Students should not be allowed to take mobiles to school** schriftlich Stellung nehmen und deine Position überzeugend darlegen. Dabei sollst du zeigen, dass du dich intensiv mit dem Thema auseinandergesetzt und Pro und Contra abgewogen hast. Dafür ist es hilfreich, wenn du erst Argumente sammelst und sie dann **noch vor** dem Schreiben des Textes gliederst. Diese Gliederung nennt man *Outline*. Es erleichtert dir das anschließende Schreiben.

Wie gehe ich bei einem *Outline* vor?

1. Collecting ideas
Hierbei kannst du unterschiedliche Techniken nutzen. Dabei ist es sinnvoll, wenn du neben den Argumenten auch konkrete Beispiele notierst, die deine Aussage verdeutlichen.

▸ *SF Brainstorming (p. 132)*

2. Outlining
Mit Hilfe des *Outline* strukturierst du dann die Ideen, die du zuvor gesammelt hast. Überleg dir, welche Meinung du zu der gestellten Frage hast. Führ im *Outline* erst die Argumente auf, die gegen deine Meinung sprechen. Stell erst danach die Argumente und Beispiele vor, die deine Meinung stützen.
Eine Erörterung besteht aus vier Teilen. Ordne deine Ideen stichwortartig nach dem Schema rechts.

1 Introduction
2 Arguments against
  2.1 First argument
  2.2 Second argument
  2.3 ...
3 Arguments for
  3.1 First argument
  3.2 Second argument
  3.3 ...
4 Conclusion

Wie mache ich aus dem *Outline* eine Erörterung?

1. Introduction
In der Einleitung stellst du das Thema vor und beschreibst, worum es geht. Dabei kannst du von einer persönlichen Erfahrung oder einem allgemein bekannten Problem ausgehen.
Lots of people think ... • It is generally believed that ... • I once ... • You often hear people say that • , ... so the questions is: should ... or not?

2. Present the first point of view
Zunächst führst du die Argumente an, die gegen deine Überzeugung sprechen.
First ...; second ...; • another argument for/against ... is ... • For example, ... • It might also be argued that ... • One could well say that ... • Finally ... • So ... • That's why

3. Present the opposite point of view
Präsentiere dann die Argumente, die deine Meinung stützen. Wichtig ist, dass du eine Überleitung schreibst und deine Argumente mit Beispielen (z.B. aus deiner eigenen Erfahrung) anreicherst.
However, lots of people feel ... • Other people disagree. They think that ... • It's also important to remember ... • It is only partly true that ...

4. Conclusion
Am Schluss wägst du das Für und Wider nochmal ab und nennst deine Meinung. Nenn keine neuen Argumente mehr.
To sum up, I would say that ... • After looking at both sides I think ...

MEDIATION SKILLS

SF REVISION Mediation

REVISION Wann muss ich zwischen zwei Sprachen vermitteln?

Manchmal musst du zwischen zwei Sprachen vermitteln; das nennt man *mediation*.

1. Du gibst englische Informationen auf Deutsch weiter:
   Du fährst z.B. mit deiner Familie in die USA und deine Eltern oder Geschwister wollen wissen, was jemand in einem Café gesagt hat oder was an einer Informationstafel steht.
2. Du gibst deutsche Informationen auf Englisch weiter:
   Vielleicht ist bei dir zu Hause eine Austauschschülerin aus den USA oder Dänemark zu Gast, die kein Deutsch spricht und Hilfe braucht.
3. In schriftlichen Prüfungen musst du manchmal in einem englischen Text gezielt nach Informationen suchen und diese auf Deutsch wiedergeben.

REVISION Worauf muss ich bei mediation achten?

- Übersetze nicht alles wörtlich.
- Gib nur das Wesentliche weiter, lass Unwichtiges weg.
- Verwende kurze und einfache Sätze.
- Wenn du ein Wort nicht kennst, umschreibe es oder ersetze es durch ein anderes Wort.

Was kann ich tun, wenn ich ein wichtiges Wort nicht kenne?

Vielleicht findest du es manchmal schwer, mündliche Aussagen oder schriftliche Textvorlagen in die andere Sprache zu übertragen, z.B. weil:
- dein Wortschatz nicht ausreicht
- dir bekannte Wörter „im Stress" nicht einfallen
- spezielle Fachbegriffe auftauchen.

Manche Wörter kannst du umschreiben, z.B. mithilfe von Relativsätzen wie:
It's somebody/a person who ...
It's something that you use to ...
It's an animal that ...
It's a place where ...

▸ *SF Paraphrasing, p. 132*

EXAM SKILLS

SF REVISION How to do well in a test

Countdown zum Testerfolg

Ein Test ist angekündigt? Kein Grund zur Panik. Wichtig ist, dass du weißt, worauf du dich vorbereiten musst. Im Zweifelsfall frag deine Lehrerin oder deinen Lehrer. Der Countdown kann beginnen!

Eine Woche vor dem Test

1. Lies noch einmal die **Texte** der zuletzt durchgenommenen Unit (vor allem Lead-in, A-Section und Text, eventuell auch das Background File). Fasse mündlich oder schriftlich zusammen, worum es ging.

2. Wiederhole den **Wortschatz** der Unit mithilfe des Vocabulary, des Wordmaster oder des *English Coach*. Schreibe dir die Wörter und Wortverbindungen, die du immer wieder vergisst, auf ein Blatt Papier. Eine Mindmap oder ein Wortfeld helfen beim Behalten.

3. Geh auch noch mal die neue **Grammatik** durch. Aufgaben zur Selbstüberprüfung und zum Üben findest du im *Practice*-Teil, auf der Seite „How am I doing?", im *Grammar File*, in deinem *Workbook* und im e-*Workbook*. (▸ *SF Check yourself, p. 122*)

Zwei oder drei Tage vor dem Test

1. Wiederhole den **Wortschatz**. Manche Wörter sitzen noch nicht? Schreibe einen kurzen Text, in dem du sie verwendest.

2. Lies die **Schülerbuch-Texte** ein weiteres Mal.

3. Erkläre einem Freund oder einer Freundin die neue **Grammatik**. Klappt nicht richtig? Dann lies nochmal im Grammar File nach.

Am Abend vor dem Test

1. Entspanne dich. Du kannst lesen, dich in die Badewanne legen, Musik hören, fernsehen, ...

2. Geh zur gewohnten Zeit ins Bett.

Am Morgen des Tests

1. Steh rechtzeitig auf, damit du nicht hetzen musst.

2. Lies etwas „zum Aufwärmen", aber schau nicht mehr in dein Schülerbuch.

Während des Tests

1. Denk daran: Du hast dich gut vorbereitet. Es gibt keinen Grund, nervös zu sein.

2. Konzentriere dich auf den Test, lass dich nicht ablenken.

3. Lies dir die Aufgaben genau durch. Dann löse zuerst die Aufgaben, die dir einfach scheinen. Wende dich erst danach den schwereren Aufgaben zu.

4. Aufgaben, die du bearbeitet hast, hakst du ab. So siehst du, wie du vorankommst, und behältst den Überblick.

5. Schau ab und zu auf die Uhr. Du solltest dir für den Schluss noch Zeit einplanen, um deine Antworten nochmal durchzulesen und zu korrigieren.

Good luck!

Aufgabenstellungen verstehen

Bevor du damit anfängst, die Aufgaben zu bearbeiten, stell sicher, dass du genau weißt, was du machen sollst. Lies die Aufgabenstellung Wort für Wort langsam und gründlich und von Anfang bis Ende durch. Sollst du z. B. ganze Sätze schreiben oder dir nur Notizen machen? Du kannst besonders wichtige Dinge der Aufgabenstellung unterstreichen und die Aufgabe, wenn nötig, für dich in einzelne Schritte unterteilen.

Worauf sollte ich bei Multiple-Choice-Aufgaben achten?

- Lies die Frage oder den Satz sehr genau durch.
- Bevor du dir die Lösungsangebote anschaust, deck sie mit Papier ab. Überleg dir, was die richtige Antwort sein könnte. Wenn das dann auch als eine Lösungsmöglichkeit angeboten wird, ist es meistens richtig.
- Lies immer alle vorgegebenen Lösungen, bevor du dich entscheidest.
- Achte darauf, dass du nur **eine** der Antworten ankreuzt – es sei denn, dass in der Aufgabenstellung ausdrücklich gesagt wird, dass mehrere Antworten richtig sein können.
- Mach erst alle Aufgaben so gut du kannst. Lass keine Aufgabe aus, aber geh zum Schluss zu den Fragen zurück, bei denen du unsicher bist.
- Wenn das alles nicht hilft, such nicht mehr nach der richtigen Antwort, sondern nach den falschen Antworten. Weil drei Antwortmöglichkeiten falsch sein müssen, kannst du erschließen, dass die vierte Antwort richtig ist. Hier ist ein Beispiel. Stell dir vor, du hörst folgenden Dialog.

  Boy *Wow, that was great, Dad. Thanks. Can we do it again next weekend?*
  Dad *Sure, Greg – if the weather's nice. But let's find an easier tour next time – I'm a bit tired.*

Dazu wird dir die multiple-choice Frage hier rechts gestellt.
Greg und sein Vater müssen etwas im Freien gemacht haben, denn Gregs Dad spricht über das Wetter. Also sind die Antworten **B** und **C** falsch. Man schwimmt keine Touren, also ist **A** auch falsch. Daher muss **D** die richtige Antwort sein.

1. Greg and his dad have just
A been swimming.
B been to a fitness club.
C seen a movie.
D been on a bike ride.

Grammar File – Inhalt

Im **Grammar File** (S. 144–155) wird zusammengefasst, was du in diesem Band **über die englische Sprache** lernst.

In der **linken Spalte** findest du **Beispielsätze** und **Übersichten**.

Indirect speech (reporting verb: simple past)

Zita Wallace said **that** she had seen terrible things. She added **that** she would never forget those first hours.

He said his name was Paul.
Er sagte, dass er Paul heißt.

Veränderungen der Zeitformen bei einleitende

	Direct speech
present ▸ **past**	'I don't care about money.'

Additional information

So gekennzeichnete Abschnitte enthalten Grammatik, die du nicht selbst zu verwenden brauchst. Du solltest aber verstehen, was dort erklärt wird, damit du keine Schwierigkeiten mit Texten hast, in denen diese Grammatik vorkommt.

In der **rechten Spalte** stehen **Erklärungen** und nützliche **Hinweise**.

Das **rote Ausrufezeichen** (**!**) macht dich auf besondere Fehlerquellen aufmerksam.

Hinweise wie ▸ *Unit 1, Part C: P 1–4 (pp. 18–19)* geben an, welche Übungen zu einem **Grammar-File**-Abschnitt gehören.

Die **grammatischen Fachbegriffe** (*grammatical terms*) kannst du auf den Seiten 154–155 nachschlagen.

Am Ende der Abschnitte stehen wieder kleine Aufgaben zur Selbstkontrolle. Schreib die Lösungen in dein Heft. Überprüfe sie dann auf Seite 155.

GF 1 Talking about the present Über die Gegenwart sprechen

Du möchtest ausdrücken,

– dass etwas **regelmäßig** geschieht ▸ *The simple present: GF 1.1*	→	Hanna **gets up** at 7 o'clock every morning. Hanna steht jeden Morgen um 7 Uhr auf.
– dass etwas **gerade jetzt** geschieht ▸ *The present progressive: GF 1.2*	→	It's 7 o'clock. Hanna **is getting up**. Es ist 7 Uhr. Hanna steht (gerade) auf.

1.1 The simple present

Dave Wilson **usually** gets the bus to school.
On Mondays his mother takes him in the car.
He **never** cycles to school because it's too far.

Das ***simple present*** wird verwendet,

◂ um über Handlungen und Ereignisse zu sprechen, die **wiederholt, regelmäßig, immer** oder **nie** geschehen (oft mit Zeitangaben wie *always, never, usually, sometimes, often, every week, on Mondays* usw.).

Dave and his family live in Manchester.
He plays hockey and collects models of old cars.
His dad works for a building company.

◂ um über **Dauerzustände**, **Hobbys** und **Berufe** zu sprechen.

! *He, she, it* – das „s" muss mit.

Verneinte Sätze	I don't cycle to school.	Dave doesn't walk to school.
Fragen	Do you go to school by bus? **Where** do the Wilsons live?	Does your mother take you in the car? **When** does Dave's mother take him in the car?

1.2 The present progressive

What's Dave doing? – **Just now** he's cleaning his bike.

Dave (on the phone) I can't talk right now, Jack. I'm cleaning my bike.

Das ***present progressive*** wird verwendet,

◂ um über Handlungen und Ereignisse zu sprechen, die **jetzt gerade im Gange** sind (oft mit Angaben wie *at the moment, now, just*).

! Die Handlung, um die es geht, kann für einen Augenblick unterbrochen sein, z.B. durch ein Telefonat. Wichtig ist, dass sie noch nicht abgeschlossen ist.

This week Dave's grandma is staying at the Wilsons' because Dave's mum is ill.

◂ um über **vorübergehende Zustände** zu sprechen (begrenzter Zeitraum: *this week*).

Verneinte Sätze	The Wilsons aren't working.	Dave isn't watching TV.
Fragen	Are you watching TV? **What** are you doing?	Is Dave cleaning his bike? **Who** is Dave talking to?

Dave's dad works for a building company. Look, he's working at his desk at the moment.

GF 2 Talking about the past Über die Vergangenheit sprechen

Du möchtest ausdrücken,

– dass etwas in der Vergangenheit **geschah**; das Geschehen ist **abgeschlossen** und **vorbei** ▸ *The simple past: GF 2.1*	→	Emma **left** school in 2007. Emma ging im Jahr 2007 von der Schule ab.
– dass etwas in der Vergangenheit **gerade im Gange (noch nicht abgeschlossen) war** ▸ *The past progressive: GF 2.2*	→	We **were leaving** the building when we heard the explosion. Wir waren gerade dabei, das Gebäude zu verlassen, ...
– dass etwas **vor etwas anderem** in der Vergangenheit stattgefunden hatte ▸ *The past perfect: GF 2.3*	→	Connor **had** already **left** when we arrived. Connor war schon gegangen, als wir ankamen.
– dass etwas **irgendwann** geschehen ist, oft mit **Auswirkungen auf die Gegenwart**	→	Jane **has left** her purse at home, so she can't pay for her bus ticket. Jane hat ihre Geldbörse zu Hause gelassen, ...
– dass ein Zustand **in der Vergangenheit begonnen** hat und **noch andauert** ▸ *The present perfect: GF 2.4*	→	We**'ve had** our dog for three years now – since 2007. Wir haben unseren Hund jetzt seit drei Jahren ...

2.1 The simple past

Last Friday Katie's family flew to Spain.
Letzten Freitag ist Katies Familie nach Spanien geflogen / flog Katies Familie nach Spanien.
Two years ago the Websters moved to Bath.
Vor zwei Jahren sind die Websters nach Bath gezogen.

Wenn man über Vergangenes berichtet, benutzt man überwiegend das ***simple past***. Man beschreibt damit Handlungen, Ereignisse und Zustände, die zu einer bestimmten Zeit in der Vergangenheit *(yesterday, last Friday, two years ago, in 2003, between 2005 and 2008, ...)* stattfanden.

! Im Deutschen wird in diesen Fällen oft das Perfekt verwendet, im Englischen jedoch nicht.

Verneinte Sätze	They didn't fly to France.	Katie didn't want to go at first.
Fragen	Did you go on holiday last year? **Where** did you go?	Did Katie like it? **When** did the Websters move to Bath?

2.2 The past progressive

What were you doing yesterday at 3.30? –
I was waiting for my sister at the school doors.
She was still talking to our Maths teacher.

Angela was just crossing the road when she saw her boyfriend.
Angela war gerade dabei, die Straße zu überqueren, ...

Das ***past progressive*** wird verwendet,

◂ um über Handlungen und Ereignisse zu sprechen, die zu einer bestimmten Zeit in der Vergangenheit noch im Gange, also noch nicht abgeschlossen waren.

◂ wenn man beschreiben will, was gerade vor sich ging *(she was just crossing the road)*, als etwas anderes passierte *(she saw her boyfriend)*.

Verneinte Sätze	You weren't listening.	It wasn't snowing when we left the house.
Fragen	Were you watching TV? **What** were they doing?	Was she crossing the road when it happened? **What** was she doing?

2.3 The past perfect

When Emma arrived home, her parents had already eaten.
Als Emma zu Hause eintraf, hatten ihre Eltern bereits gegessen.

Wenn man sagen will, dass etwas noch vor etwas anderem in der Vergangenheit stattgefunden hatte, dann benutzt man das ***past perfect***.

Verneinte Sätze	They hadn't gone to bed.	Emma hadn't eaten anything all day.
Fragen	Had you seen that film before? **What** had they done?	Had Emma eaten when she came home? **Where** had she been all day?

2.4 The present perfect

! Das ***present perfect*** hat mit der **Vergangenheit und mit der Gegenwart** zu tun. Es wird verwendet,

Will Smith is great. I've seen most of his films.
Luke has **already** done his Maths homework, but he has**n't** started his French **yet**.
Have you **ever** been to Paris?
– No, I haven't. But I've **always** wanted to go.

Mel has lost her mobile. Her dad is very angry.

◄ wenn man sagen will, **dass** jemand etwas getan hat oder **dass** etwas geschehen ist. Dabei ist nicht wichtig, wann es geschehen ist – ein genauer Zeitpunkt wird nicht genannt. Das *present perfect* steht oft mit Adverbien der unbestimmten Zeit wie *already, just, never, ever, not ... yet*.
Oft hat die Handlung Auswirkungen auf die Gegenwart (Mels Vater ist wütend, weil sie ihr Handy verloren hat).

We've had our new car **since April**.
Wir haben unser neues Auto seit April.

since **+ Zeitpunkt**

We've had our new car **for three months**.
Wir haben unser neues Auto seit drei Monaten.

for **+ Zeitraum**

◄ für **Zustände**, die in der Vergangenheit begonnen haben und jetzt noch andauern (oft mit ***since*** bzw. ***for***).

! Im Deutschen steht in diesen Fällen meist das Präsens, im Englischen muss das *present perfect* stehen.

Verneinte Sätze	I haven't been to Paris yet.	Luke hasn't done his French homework.
Fragen	Have you been to Paris? **What** have you done?	Has Mel found her mobile yet? **Which** of these films have you seen already?

Additional information

2.5 The present perfect progressive

I've **been writing** e-mails all day.
Ich **schreibe** (schon) den ganzen Tag E-Mails.

We've **been learning** French for four years.
Wir **lernen** seit vier Jahren Französisch.

Auch das ***present perfect progressive*** hat mit der Vergangenheit und mit der Gegenwart zu tun. Es wird verwendet für **Vorgänge** und **Handlungen**, die in der Vergangenheit begonnen haben und jetzt noch andauern (oft mit ***since*** bzw. ***for***).

! Auch hier steht im Deutschen meist das Präsens – aber im Englischen das *present perfect progressive*.

GF 3 Talking about the future Über die Zukunft sprechen

Du möchtest ausdrücken,		
– dass etwas für die Zukunft **geplant** ist ▸ *The going to-future: GF 3.1*	→	I'm **going to watch** the new Bond film tonight. Ich sehe mir heute Abend den neuen Bond-Film an.
– wie etwas in der Zukunft **sein wird** (**Vorhersagen, Vermutungen**) ▸ *The will-future: GF 3.2*	→	It **will be** warm and sunny in Spain. I'm sure you'**ll like** it there. Es wird warm und sonnig sein in Spanien. Ich bin sicher, dass es dir dort gefallen wird.
– dass etwas für die Zukunft **fest verabredet** ist (es steht schon im Kalender) ▸ *The present progressive: GF 3.3*	→	We'**re having** a party on Saturday. Would you like to come? Wir geben nächsten Samstag eine Party. ...

3.1 The *going to*-future

My boyfriend says he's going to be an engineer.
Mein Freund sagt, er will Ingenieur werden.

Look at those clouds. There's going to be a storm.
... Es wird ein Gewitter geben.

Das **Futur mit *going to*** wird verwendet,

◂ wenn man über **Vorhaben, Pläne, Absichten** für die Zukunft sprechen will.

◂ um auszudrücken, dass etwas **wahrscheinlich gleich geschehen wird** – es gibt bereits deutliche **Anzeichen** dafür (*hier:* die Wolken am Himmel).

3.2 The *will*-future

It will be cold and windy, and we will get some rain in the afternoon.
I'll be 15 next October.

I expect Ella will be late again as usual.
Ich nehme an, Ella kommt wie üblich wieder zu spät.

Just a moment. I'll open the door for you.
Moment. Ich mache Ihnen die Tür auf.
I won't tell anyone what's happened. I promise.
Ich sage niemandem, was passiert ist. ...

Das **Futur mit *will*** wird verwendet,

◂ um **Vorhersagen** über die Zukunft zu äußern. Oft geht es dabei um Dinge, die man nicht beeinflussen kann, z.B. das Wetter.

◂ um eine **Vermutung** auszudrücken (oft eingeleitet mit *I think, I'm sure, I expect, maybe*).

◂ wenn man sich **spontan** – also ohne es im Voraus geplant zu haben – zu etwas **entschließt**. Oft geht es dabei um **Hilfsangebote** oder **Versprechen**.

3.3 The present progressive (future meaning)

We're driving to Scotland next Friday to visit my grandparents.
I'm meeting a friend in town tonight.

Das ***present progressive*** wird verwendet, wenn etwas **für die Zukunft fest geplant** oder **fest verabredet** ist (manchmal spricht man vom *diary future*). Durch eine Zeitangabe wie *tonight* oder aus dem Zusammenhang muss klar sein, dass es um etwas Zukünftiges geht.

Additional information

3.4 The simple present (future meaning)

The next train to Bath **goes** in ten minutes.
The next drawing class **starts** on 2 September.

Das ***simple present*** wird verwendet, wenn ein **zukünftiges Geschehen** durch einen **Fahrplan**, ein **Programm** oder Ähnliches festgelegt ist (manchmal spricht man vom *timetable future*). Verben wie *arrive, leave, go, open, close, start, stop* werden häufig so verwendet.

Unit 1

GF 4 Indirect speech (I) Die indirekte Rede (I)

Direct speech

Zita Wallace says, 'I **saw** terrible things. I'**ll** never **forget** those first hours.'

◄ In der **direkten Rede** wird **wörtlich** wiedergegeben, was jemand sagt oder gesagt hat. Direkte Rede steht in Anführungszeichen (deutsch: „...“; englisch: '...').

Indirect speech (reporting verb: simple present)

Zita Wallace says **that** she **saw** terrible things and **that** she **will** never **forget** those first hours.

◄ In der **indirekten Rede** (*indirect* oder *reported speech*) wird berichtet, was jemand sagt oder gesagt hat. Die indirekte Rede wird mit Verben wie *say, tell sb., add, answer, explain, write* eingeleitet.

Indirect speech (reporting verb: simple past)

Zita Wallace said **that** she had seen terrible things. She added **that** she would never forget those first hours.

◄ Wenn das **einleitende Verb im *simple past*** steht (*she said/told us/explained/answered* usw.), dann werden die Zeitformen der direkten Rede meist verändert: Sie werden um eine Zeitstufe in die Vergangenheit „zurückverschoben“ *(backshift of tenses)*.

He said his name was Paul.
Er sagte, dass er Paul heißt.

! Im Englischen steht vor der indirekten Rede kein Komma und das Wort *that* wird oft weggelassen.

Veränderungen der Zeitformen bei einleitendem Verb im *simple past*

	Direct speech	Indirect speech
present ▸ past	'I don't care about money.' 'Australia is saying sorry.'	Zita **said** she didn't care about money. The report **said** Australia was saying sorry.
past ▸ past perfect	'I saw terrible things.'	Zita **told** us she had seen terrible things.
can* ▸ *could	'You can go shopping with us.'	The nuns **said** that the girls could go shopping with them.
***will*-future ▸ *would* + infinitive**	'I'll never forget those days.'	Zita **said** she would never forget those days.
***going to*-future ▸ *was/were going to* + infinitive**	'The government is going to apologize.'	They **said** the government was going to apologize.
present perfect ▸ past perfect	'I haven't forgotten that evening.'	Zita **added** that she hadn't forgotten that evening.

Verben im *past perfect* bleiben unverändert, da man sie nicht weiter „zurückverschieben“ kann.

▸ *Unit 1, Part C: P 1–4 (pp. 18–19)*

Berichte, was Ella ihrer Freundin Lucy am Telefon erzählt hat. Schreib die Sätze in indirekter Rede in dein Heft.

1 'My mom is still at work.'	Ella **said** her mom ...
2 'She has to work late.'	She **told** Lucy that her mom ...
3 'Mom won't be home till nine.'	She **added** that her mom ...
4 'Dad will probably want a pizza.'	She also **said** her dad ...
5 'I'll call again later.'	She **told** Lucy she ...

Unit 2

GF 5 Indirect speech (II) Die indirekte Rede (II)

5.1 Commands and requests

Aufforderungen und Bitten

Simon Look for clothes for the interview.
And don't be shy.

Simon told them to look for clothes for the interview. And he told them not to be shy.
Simon sagte ihnen, sie sollten sich nach Kleidung für das Interview umsehen. Und er sagte ihnen, dass sie nicht schüchtern sein sollten.

◄ **Aufforderungen, Anordnungen** und **Ratschläge** werden in der indirekten Rede meist mit ***tell sb. to do sth.*** (bzw. ***tell sb. not to do sth.***) wiedergegeben.

Simon Mani, please choose a new tie.

Simon asked Mani to choose a new tie.
Simon bat Mani, eine neue Krawatte zu wählen.

◄ Eine **Bitte** wird meist mit ***ask sb. to do sth.*** (bzw. ***ask sb. not to do sth.***) wiedergegeben.

▸ *Unit 2, Part C: P 3a–b, P 4 (p. 42)*

Berichte, was die Lehrerin gesagt hat. Verwende told ... *oder* asked ...

1 'Emily, please don't argue with Jacob.' — The teacher asked Emily not to ...
2 'Jacob and Emily, discuss your opinions quietly.' — She told Jacob and Emily ...
3 'Emily, don't use bad language in my classroom.' — She ...
4 'Jacob, please revise your essay.' — She ...

5.2 Questions

Fragen

Auch bei Fragen in der indirekten Rede werden die Zeitformen in die Vergangenheit „zurückverschoben", wenn das einleitende Verb im *simple past* steht.

Direct question (with question word)	What do you know about my business?
Indirect question	Rita asked Mani **what** he knew about her business.

◄ Wenn die direkte **Frage mit einem Fragewort** beginnt (*what, when, where, why, how* usw.), dann wird das Fragewort in der indirekten Frage beibehalten.

Direct question (yes/no question)	Do you have any weaknesses?
Indirect question	Rita asked him **if** he had any weaknesses.

◄ Handelt es sich bei der direkten Frage um eine **Frage ohne Fragewort** *(yes/no question)*, dann wird die indirekte Frage mit ***if*** („ob") eingeleitet.

▸ *Unit 2, Part C: P 3c, P 5–6 (pp. 42–43)*

Olivia war in London. Im Englischunterricht stellen ihre Mitschüler/innen Fragen. Berichte.

1 'Did you go to Camden Lock Market?' — Mike asked if Olivia ...
2 'Where did you stay?' — Sophie asked ...
3 'Are London restaurants expensive?' — Jessie wanted to know ...
4 'Can you buy cheap clothes and CDs in London?' — Antonia wanted to know ...

Unit 3

GF 6 Participles Partizipien

6.1 REVISION Participle forms

Formen des Partizips

Present participle (-ing):

play	→	**playing**	try	→	**trying**
phone	→	**phoning**	plan	→	**planning**

◂ Das **Partizip Präsens** *(present participle)* bildet man durch Anhängen von ***-ing*** an den Infinitiv. Beachte die Besonderheiten bei der Schreibung.

Past participle, regular verbs (-ed):

play	→	**played**	try	→	**tried**
phone	→	**phoned**	plan	→	**planned**

◂ Das **Partizip Perfekt** *(past participle)* eines regelmäßigen Verbs wird durch Anhängen von ***-ed*** an den Infinitiv gebildet. Beachte auch hier die Besonderheiten bei der Schreibung.

Past participle, irregular verbs:

go	→	**gone**	make	→	**made**
take	→	**taken**	write	→	**written**

Bedenke, dass unregelmäßige Verben eigene 3. Formen haben, die man einzeln lernen muss.

▸ *Unregelmäßige Verben (pp. 214–215)*

Additional information

6.2 Participle clauses instead of relative clauses

Partizipialsätze anstelle von Relativsätzen

Partizipialsätze können Relativsätze ersetzen.

1 Shane saw posters **showing his picture.**
... Poster, die sein Bild zeigten.

2 Now Shane is a reliable young man **looking for work.**
... zuverlässiger junger Mann, der Arbeit sucht.

3 The photos **sent to people in his area** showed a 14-year-old trouble-maker.
... die Fotos, die den Leuten in seiner Gegend geschickt wurden, ...

▸ *Unit 3, Part B: P 4 (p. 57)*

◂ Partizipialsätze mit ***present participle*** (Sätze **1** und **2**) entsprechen Relativsätzen im **Aktiv**:

1 ... ***showing*** *his picture* = ... ***which showed*** *his picture*

2 ... ***looking*** *for work* = ... ***who is looking*** *for work*

◂ Partizipialsätze mit ***past participle*** (Satz **3**) entsprechen Relativsätzen im **Passiv**:

3 ... ***sent*** *to people in his area* = ... ***that were sent*** *to people ...*

GF 7 The passive Das Passiv

7.1 REVISION Active and passive

Active: **The ManaTEEN friends** found bottles and glass in the springs.
Die ManaTEEN-Freunde fanden Flaschen und Glas in den Quellen.

Passive: **Bottles and glass** were found in the springs.
Flaschen und Glas wurden ... gefunden.

A lot of trash is thrown into the springs. But of course trash is not the only thing that is found at Weeki Wachee Springs.

I **was beaten** by my best friend.
Ich wurde von meinem besten Freund besiegt.

Aktiv und Passiv

◄ Ein **Aktivsatz** beschreibt, **wer oder was etwas tut**. Der Aktivsatz links handelt von den ManaTEEN-Freunden und ihren Aktivitäten.

◄ Ein **Passivsatz** beschreibt, **mit wem oder womit etwas geschieht**. Der Passivsatz links handelt von dem Müll, der in den Quellen gefunden wurde.

In **Passivsätzen** steht nicht, wer die Handlung ausführt. Oft ist das unwichtig oder nicht bekannt. Das Passiv wird oft in Nachrichten, in Zeitungsartikeln, in technischen Beschreibungen und auf Schildern verwendet, wenn man den „Täter" oder „Verursacher" nicht nennen kann oder nicht nennen will.

! Wenn in einem Passivsatz der „Täter" oder „Verursacher" doch genannt werden soll, dann verwendet man ***by ...*** .

7.2 Form

Form

Das Passiv bildet man mit einer **Form von *be*** und der 3. Form des Verbs (Partizip Perfekt, *past participle*).

The passive

Simple present: ***am/are/is*** + past participle	So much trash is thrown into the springs. So viel Müll wird in die Quellen geworfen.
Simple past: ***was/were*** + past participle	I was beaten by my best friend. Ich wurde von meinem besten Freund besiegt.
Present perfect: ***have/has been*** + past participle	A lot of coins and bills have been donated. Eine Menge Münzen und Noten sind gespendet worden.
will*-future:** ***will be + past participle	The food will be given to the Soup Kitchen tomorrow. Morgen werden die Lebensmittel der Suppenküche übergeben (werden).
Modal auxiliaries: ***can/must/should/... be*** + past participle	The food can be stored there overnight. Die Lebensmittel können dort über Nacht gelagert werden. Something must be done / should be done to help people in need. Es muss / sollte etwas getan werden, ...

► *Unit 3, Part C: P 1–5 (pp. 60–61)*

Vervollständige die Passivsätze. Achte auf die richtige Zeitform.

1 Every week bottles and trash ... (throw) into our garden, or graffiti ... (spray) on our wall.
2 Last week three bikes ... (steal) from the school yard.
3 This week so far two mobiles ... (steal) from kids in my class – and it's only Wednesday.
4 I expect a few windows ... (break) in our school before the end of the month.
5 A lot more ... (must / do) to stop thieves, bullies and vandalism.

Unit 4

GF 8 Conditional sentences Bedingungssätze

8.1 **REVISION Type 1 and type 2**

If you run, you'll catch the bus.
Wenn du rennst, kriegst du den Bus noch.

If you miss the bus, you can take / should take / must take a taxi.
Wenn du den Bus verpasst, kannst/sollst/musst du ein Taxi nehmen.

Typ 1 und Typ 2

◄ **Typ 1** („**Was ist, wenn …**"-**Sätze**)
Diese Bedingungssätze beziehen sich auf die **Gegenwart** oder die **Zukunft**.
Sie drücken aus, was unter bestimmten Bedingungen **geschieht** oder **geschehen kann/soll** usw.

***if*-Satz (Bedingung)**	**Hauptsatz (Folge)**
If you run,	*you'll catch the bus.*
If you miss the bus,	*you can take a taxi.*
simple present	**– *will-future* – *can/should/must* + Infinitiv**

If you ran, you would catch the bus.
Wenn du rennen würdest, würdest du den Bus noch kriegen.

If you caught the bus, you could be home in time for dinner.
Wenn du den Bus kriegen würdest, könntest du rechtzeitig zum Abendessen daheim sein.

▸ *Unit 4, Part A: P 2 (p. 79)*

◄ **Typ 2** („**Was wäre, wenn …**"-**Sätze**)
Diese Bedingungssätze beziehen sich auch auf die **Gegenwart** oder die **Zukunft**.
Sie drücken aus, was unter bestimmten Bedingungen **geschehen würde** oder **könnte**.

***if*-Satz (Bedingung)**	**Hauptsatz (Folge)**
If you ran,	*you would catch/could catch/might catch the bus.*
simple past	***would/could/might* + Infinitiv**

Additional information

8.2 **Type 3**

If you had run, you would have caught the bus.
Wenn du gerannt wärst, hättest du den Bus noch gekriegt.

If you had caught the bus, you could have had dinner with us.
Wenn du den Bus gekriegt hättest, hättest du mit uns Abendbrot essen können.

▸ *Unit 4, Part B: P 3 (p. 84)*

Typ 3

◄ **Typ 3** („**Was wäre gewesen, wenn …**"-**Sätze**)
Diese Bedingungssätze beziehen sich auf die **Vergangenheit**.
Sie drücken aus, was unter bestimmten Bedingungen **geschehen wäre** oder **hätte geschehen können**.
Der Sprecher stellt sich nur vor, was geschehen wäre, aber in Wirklichkeit nicht geschehen ist:
Wenn du gerannt wärst, hättest du den Bus erwischt – aber da du nicht gerannt bist …

***if*-Satz (Bedingung)**	**Hauptsatz (Folge)**
If you had run,	*you would have caught/could have caught the bus.*
past perfect	***would/could* + *have* + Partizip Perfekt**

Grammatical terms (Grammatische Fachbegriffe)

active ['æktɪv]	Aktiv	*Beckham **scored** the final goal.*
adjective ['ædʒɪktɪv]	Adjektiv	*good, red, new, boring*
adverb ['ædvɜ:b]	Adverb	*always, badly, here, really, today*
adverb of frequency ['fri:kwənsi]	Häufigkeitsadverb	*always, often, never*
adverb of indefinite time [ɪnˌdefɪnət 'taɪm]	Adverb der unbestimmten Zeit	*already, ever, just, never*
adverb of manner ['mænə]	Adverb der Art und Weise	*badly, happily, quietly, well*
article ['ɑ:tɪkl]	Artikel	*the, a/an*
auxiliary [ɔ:g'zɪliəri]	Hilfsverb	*be, have, do; will, can, must*
backshift of tenses ['bækʃɪft]	Verschiebung der Zeitformen *(bei der indirekten Rede)*	*'I'**m** sorry.'* ► *Sam said he **was** sorry.*
command [kə'mɑ:nd]	Befehl, Aufforderungssatz	*Open your books. Don't talk.*
comparison [kəm'pærɪsn]	Steigerung	*old – older – oldest*
conditional sentence [kənˌdɪʃənl 'sentəns]	Bedingungssatz	*I'd call him if I knew his number.*
conjunction [kən'dʒʌŋkʃn]	Konjunktion	*and, or, but; because, before*
contact clause ['kɒntækt klɔ:z]	Relativsatz ohne Relativpronomen	*She's the girl **I love**.*
countable noun ['kaʊntəbl]	zählbares Nomen	*girl – girls, pound – pounds*
definite article ['defɪnət]	bestimmter Artikel	*the*
direct speech [ˌdaɪrekt 'spi:tʃ]	direkte Rede, wörtliche Rede	***'I'm sorry**.'*
gerund ['dʒerənd]	Gerundium	*I like **dancing**. **Dancing** is fun.*
***going to*-future**	Futur mit *going to*	***I'm going to watch** TV tonight.*
***if*-clause** ['ɪf klɔ:z]	*if*-Satz, Nebensatz mit *if*	***If I see Jack**, I'll tell him.*
imperative [ɪm'perətɪv]	Imperativ (Befehlsform)	*Open your books. Don't talk.*
indirect speech [ˌɪndərekt 'spi:tʃ]	indirekte Rede	*Sam said **(that) he was sorry**.*
infinitive [ɪn'fɪnətɪv]	Infinitiv (Grundform des Verbs)	*(to) open, (to) see, (to) read*
irregular verb [ɪˌregjələ 'vɜ:b]	unregelmäßiges Verb	*(to) go – went – gone*
main clause	Hauptsatz	***I like Scruffy** because I like dogs.*
modal, modal auxiliary [ˌməʊdl‿ɔ:g'zɪliəri]	modales Hilfsverb, Modalverb	*can, could, may, must*
negative statement [ˌnegətɪv 'steɪtmənt]	verneinter Aussagesatz	*I don't like bananas.*
noun [naʊn]	Nomen, Substantiv	*Sophie, girl, brother, time*
object ['ɒbdʒɪkt]	Objekt	*My sister is writing **a letter**.*
object form ['ɒbdʒɪkt fɔ:m]	Objektform (der Personalpronomen)	*me, you, him, her, it, us, them*
participle ['pɑ:tɪsɪpl]	Partizip	*planning, taking; planned, taken*
participle clause [ˌpɑ:tɪsɪpl 'klɔ:z]	Partizipialsatz	*I saw a boy **playing in the street**.*
passive ['pæsɪv]	Passiv	*The goal **was scored** by Beckham.*
past participle [ˌpɑ:st 'pɑ:tɪsɪpl]	Partizip Perfekt	*cleaned, planned, gone, taken*
past perfect [ˌpɑ:st 'pɜ:fɪkt]	Plusquamperfekt, Vorvergangenheit	*He cried – he **had hurt** his knee.*
past progressive [ˌpɑ:st prə'gresɪv]	Verlaufsform der Vergangenheit	*At 7.30 I **was having** dinner.*
personal pronoun [ˌpɜ:sənl 'prəʊnaʊn]	Personalpronomen (persönliches Fürwort)	*I, you, he, she, it, we, they; me, you, him, her, it, us, them*
plural ['plʊərəl]	Plural, Mehrzahl	
positive statement [ˌpɒzətɪv 'steɪtmənt]	bejahter Aussagesatz	*I like oranges.*
possessive determiner [pəˌzesɪv dɪ'tɜ:mɪnə]	Possessivbegleiter (besitzanzeigender Begleiter)	*my, your, his, her, its, our, their*
possessive form [pəˌzesɪv fɔ:m]	*s*-Genitiv	*Jo's brother; my sister's room*
possessive pronoun [pəˌzesɪv 'prəʊnaʊn]	Possessivpronomen	*mine, yours, his, hers, ours, theirs*
preposition [ˌprepə'zɪʃn]	Präposition	*after, at, in, next to, under*
present participle [ˌpreznt 'pɑ:tɪsɪpl]	Partizip Präsens	*cleaning, planning, going, taking*
present perfect [ˌpreznt 'pɜ:fɪkt]	*present perfect*	*We**'ve made** a cake for you.*
present perfect progressive [ˌpreznt ˌpɜ:fɪkt prə'gresɪv]	Verlaufsform des *present perfect*	*We**'ve been waiting** for an hour.*

present progressive [ˌpreznt prəˈgresɪv]	Verlaufsform der Gegenwart	*The Hansons **are having** lunch.*
pronoun [ˈprəʊnaʊn]	Pronomen, Fürwort	
quantifier [ˈkwɒntɪfaɪə]	Mengenangabe	*some, a lot of, many, much*
question tag [ˈkwestʃən tæg]	Frageanhängsel	*This place is great, **isn't it?***
question word [ˈkwestʃən wɜːd]	Fragewort	*what?, when?, where?, how?*
reflexive pronoun [rɪˌfleksɪv ˈprəʊnaʊn]	Reflexivpronomen	*myself, yourself, themselves*
regular verb [ˌregjələ ˈvɜːb]	regelmäßiges Verb	*(to) help – helped – helped*
relative clause [ˌrelətɪv ˈklɔːz]	Relativsatz	*There's the girl **who helped me**.*
relative pronoun [ˌrelətɪv ˈprəʊnaʊn]	Relativpronomen	*who, that, which, whose*
reported speech [rɪˌpɔːtɪd ˈspiːtʃ]	indirekte Rede	*Sam said **(that) he was sorry**.*
request [rɪˈkwest]	Bitte	*Can you help me with this?*
short answer [ˌʃɔːt_ˈɑːnsə]	Kurzantwort	*Yes, I am. / No, I don't.*
simple past [ˌsɪmpl ˈpɑːst]	einfache Form der Vergangenheit	*Jo **wrote** two letters yesterday.*
simple present [ˌsɪmpl ˈpreznt]	einfache Form der Gegenwart	*I always **go** to school by bike.*
singular [ˈsɪŋgjələ]	Singular, Einzahl	
statement [ˈsteɪtmənt]	Aussagesatz	
subject [ˈsʌbdʒɪkt]	Subjekt	***My sister** is writing a letter.*
subject form [ˈsʌbdʒɪkt fɔːm]	Subjektform (der Personalpronomen)	*I, you, he, she, it, we, they*
subordinate clause [səˌbɔːdɪnət ˈklɔːz]	Nebensatz	*I like Scruffy **because I like dogs**.*
tense [tens]	Zeitform	
uncountable noun [ʌnˈkaʊntəbl]	nicht zählbares Nomen	*bread, milk, money, news, work*
verb [vɜːb]	Verb	*hear, open, help, go*
***will*-future**	Futur mit *will*	*I think it **will be** cold tonight.*
word order [ˈwɜːd_ɔːdə]	Wortstellung	
yes/no question	Entscheidungsfrage	*Are you 13? Do you like comics?*

Lösungen der Grammar-File-Aufgaben

p.149
1 Ella said her mom was still at work.
2 She told Lucy that her mom had to work late.
3 She added that her mom wouldn't be home till nine.
4 She also said her dad would probably want a pizza.
5 She told Lucy she would call again later.

p.150/1
1 The teacher asked Emily not to argue with Jacob.
2 She told Jacob and Emily to discuss their opinions quietly.
3 She told Emily not to use bad language in her classroom.
4 She asked Jacob to revise his essay.

p.150/2
1 Mike asked if Olivia had gone to Camden Lock Market.
2 Sophie asked where Olivia had stayed.
3 Jessie wanted to know if London restaurants were expensive.
4 Antonia wanted to know if you could buy cheap clothes and CDs in London.

p.152
1 Every week bottles and trash are thrown into our garden, or graffiti is sprayed on our wall.
2 Last week three bikes were stolen from the school yard.
3 This week so far two mobiles have been stolen from kids in my class – and it's only Wednesday.
4 I expect a few windows will be broken in our school before the end of the month.
5 A lot more must be done to stop thieves, bullies and vandalism.

Das **Vocabulary** (S.156–176) enthält alle neuen Wörter und Wendungen aus Band 5, die du lernen musst. Sie stehen in der Reihenfolge, in der sie in den Units vorkommen.

Das **Dictionary** (S.177–212) enthält den Wortschatz der Bände 1 bis 5 in alphabetischer Reihenfolge. Dort kannst du nachschlagen, was ein Wort bedeutet, wie man es ausspricht oder wie es genau geschrieben wird.

So ist das Vocabulary aufgebaut:

- Hier siehst du, wo die Wörter vorkommen.
  p.10 = Seite 10
  p.11/P 2 = Seite 11, Übung 2
- Die Lautschrift zeigt dir, wie ein Wort ausgesprochen und betont wird.
- Eingerückte Wörter lernst du am besten zusammen mit dem vorausgehenden Wort, weil die beiden zusammengehören.
- Die blauen Kästen solltest du dir besonders gut ansehen.

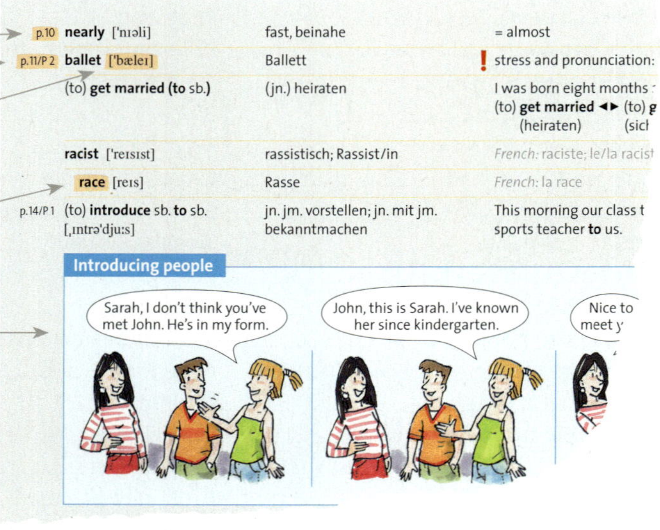

p.10	**nearly** ['nɪəli]	fast, beinahe	= almost
p.11/P 2	**ballet** ['bæleɪ]	Ballett	! stress and pronunciation:
	(to) **get married (to** sb.)	(jn.) heiraten	I was born eight months … (to) **get married** ◄► (to) g… (heiraten) (sic…
	racist ['reɪsɪst]	rassistisch; Rassist/in	*French:* raciste; le/la racist…
	race [reɪs]	Rasse	*French:* la race
p.14/P 1	(to) **introduce** sb. **to** sb. [ˌɪntrə'djuːs]	jn. jm. vorstellen; jn. mit jm. bekanntmachen	This morning our class t… sports teacher **to** us.

Tipps zum Wörterlernen findest du im Skills File auf Seite 121.

Abkürzungen:

n = *noun*	*v* = *verb*
adj = *adjective*	*adv* = *adverb*
prep = *preposition*	*conj* = *conjunction*
pl = *plural*	*no pl* = *no plural*
p. = page	pp. = pages
sb. = somebody	sth. = something
jn. = jemanden	jm. = jemandem
AE = *American English*	*BE* = *British English*
infml = *informal* (umgangssprachlich, informell)	

Symbole:

! Hier stehen Hinweise auf Besonderheiten, bei denen man leicht Fehler machen kann.

◄► ist das „Gegenteil"-Zeichen:
(to) **get married** ◄► (to) **get divorced**

~ Die **Tilde** in den Beispielsätzen steht für das neue Wort. Beispiel:
area – Germany has an ~ of about 357,000 sq km.

Unit 1: Australia

p.6	**shock** [ʃɒk]	Schock, Schreck	Germany got a ~ when England beat them 5–1.
	magical ['mædʒɪkl]	zauberhaft, wundervoll	*French:* magique
	the bush [bʊʃ]	der Busch *(unkultiviertes, „wildes" Land in Australien, Afrika)*	
	bush [bʊʃ]	Busch, Strauch	
	(to) **be about to do** sth.	im Begriff sein, etwas zu tun; kurz davor sein, etwas zu tun	I **was ~ to** go to bed when the doorbell rang.
	sleeping bag ['sliːpɪŋ bæg]	Schlafsack	a **sleeping bag**

wave [weɪv]	Welle	You need big **~s** to go surfing.
(to) **carry** ['kæri]	tragen	! • He's **carrying** a suitcase. (Er trägt einen Koffer.) • He's **wearing** jeans and a red shirt. (Er trägt Jeans und ein rotes Hemd.)
barbecue ['bɑ:bɪkju:]	Grillfest, Grillparty	
alcohol ['ælkəhɒl]	Alkohol	*French:* l'alcool *(m)*
common ['kɒmən]	weit verbreitet, häufig	It's a ~ mistake to say 'England' when you mean 'the UK'.
at someone's place	bei jemandem zu Hause	Are we going to meet at the pub or **at your ~**?
gallery ['gæləri]	(Bilder-)Galerie	! stress: **<u>gal</u>lery** ['gæləri] *French:* la galerie
the outback ['aʊtbæk]	*(Australien)* das Hinterland	

PART A Australia – facts and figures

p.8	**figure** ['fɪgə]	Zahl, Ziffer	The **~s** aren't 100 per cent correct. Please check them again. ! stress: **<u>fig</u>ure** ['fɪgə]
	area ['eəriə]	Fläche	Germany has an ~ of about 357,000 sq km.
	Aborigine [ˌæbə'rɪdʒəni]	*Ureinwohner/in Australiens*	noun: **Aborigine** – adjective: **Aboriginal** [ˌæbə'rɪdʒənl]
	disease [dɪ'zi:z]	Krankheit	
	colony ['kɒləni]	Kolonie	! stress: **<u>col</u>ony** ['kɒləni] Australia was once a British ~. *French:* la colonie
	convict ['kɒnvɪkt]	Sträfling, Strafgefangene(r)	
	former ['fɔ:mə]	ehemalige(r, s), frühere(r, s)	Bonn is the ~ German capital.
	continent ['kɒntɪnənt]	Kontinent, Erdteil	! stress: **<u>con</u>tinent** ['kɒntɪnənt] *French:* le continent
	independent [ˌɪndɪ'pendənt]	unabhängig	Australia became ~ from Britain in 1901. *French:* indépendant, e
	close [kləʊs]	eng	Australia kept its ~ links to Britain after 1901. We've been ~ friends since we went to school together.
	(to) **do business with** ['bɪznəs]	Handel treiben mit; Geschäfte machen mit	Germany **does** a lot of ~ **with** Russia and China. Does your company **do** much ~ **with** China?
p.9	**because of** [bɪ'kɒz‿əv]	wegen	

because – because of

• before a <u>clause</u>: **because** *(conj)*	We stayed inside **because** <u>it was raining</u>.	... **weil** <u>es regnete</u>.
• before a <u>noun</u>: **because of** *(prep)*	We stayed inside **because of** <u>the rain</u>.	... **wegen** <u>des Regens</u>.

ozone layer ['əʊzəʊn leɪə]	Ozonschicht	

	ultraviolet rays [ˌʌltrəˌvaɪələt ˈreɪz]	ultraviolette Strahlen	
	cancer [ˈkænsə]	Krebs *(Krankheit)*	*French:* le cancer
	sunscreen [ˈsʌnskriːn]	Sonnenschutzmittel	Remember to put on ~ before you go out in the sun.
	desert [ˈdezət]	Wüste	*French:* le désert
	emu [ˈiːmjuː]	Emu	an **emu** 
	reef [riːf]	Riff	
	dolphin [ˈdɒlfɪn]	Delfin	! stress: **dolphin** [ˈdɒlfɪn]  
	whale [weɪl]	Wal(fisch)	
	by two degrees/ten per cent	um zwei Grad / zehn Prozent	House prices fell ~ eight per cent last year.
p.10	**percentage** [pəˈsentɪdʒ]	Prozentsatz, prozentualer Anteil	A pretty high ~ of people go to work by bike. *French:* le pourcentage
	bar chart [ˈbɑː tʃɑːt]	Balkendiagramm	 a **bar chart** a **pie chart**
	pie chart [ˈpaɪ tʃɑːt]	Tortendiagramm	
	e.g. [ˌiːˈdʒiː] *(from Latin:* exempli gratia*)*	z.B. (zum Beispiel)	! you write: **e.g.** – farm animals, **e.g.** cows you say: **for example** – ..., **for example** cows
	(to) **divide** sth. **(into)** [dɪˈvaɪd]	etwas (auf)teilen (in)	The teacher **~d** the class **into** six groups. *French:* diviser
	slice [slaɪs]	Scheibe; (Kuchen-)Stück	 a **slice** of ... bread orange pizza
	nearly [ˈnɪəli]	fast, beinahe	= almost
p.11/P 1	**leaf** [liːf], *pl* **leaves** [liːvz]	Blatt *(an Pflanzen)*	
	back	Rücken; Rückseite	
p.11/P 2	**ballet** [ˈbæleɪ]	Ballett	! stress and pronunciation: **ballet** [ˈbæleɪ]
	(to) **get married (to** sb.**)**	(jn.) heiraten	I was born eight months after my parents **got ~**. (to) **get married** ◄► (to) **get divorced** (heiraten) (sich scheiden lassen)

PART B Two Australian teenagers

p.12	**nowhere** ['nəʊweə]	nirgendwo(hin)	It's the only hotel. There's ~ else to stay. Jeannie lives miles away from the nearest town <u>in the middle of ~</u>. (*etwa:* ... am Ende der Welt)
	though [ðəʊ]	obwohl	= although
	honest ['ɒnɪst]	ehrlich	Be ~. Say what you think. *French:* honnête I **~ly** think ... = Ich glaube, ehrlich gesagt, dass ...
	sheep station	*(Australien)* Schaffarm	
	still	trotzdem, dennoch	**!** **still** = **1.** (immer) noch – Look, it's **still** raining. **2.** trotzdem – It was cold, but I **still** went out.
	dirt bike ['dɜːt baɪk]	Geländemotorrad	a **dirt bike**
	dirt [dɜːt]	Schmutz, Dreck	noun: **dirt** – adjective: **dirty**

	(to) **attach (to)** [ə'tætʃ]	anhängen, anheften (an) *(an Brief, Mail)*	You can ~ the photos and mail them to me. I'**m ~ing** some photos of Ashley's party. *French:* attacher (à)
p.13	**skydiving** ['skaɪdaɪvɪŋ]	Fallschirmspringen	
	Aussie ['ɒzi] *(infml)*	Australier/in; australisch	**!** pronunciation: **Aussie** ['ɒzi]
p.14/P 1	(to) **continue** [kən'tɪnjuː]	fortsetzen; weitermachen (mit)	(to) **continue (with)** a lesson = (to) **go on with** a lesson *French:* continuer
	conversation [ˌkɒnvə'seɪʃn]	Gespräch, Unterhaltung	*French:* la conversation
	(to) **introduce** sb. **to** sb. [ˌɪntrə'djuːs]	jn. jm. vorstellen; jn. mit jm. bekanntmachen	This morning our class teacher **~d** our new sports teacher **to** us.

Introducing people

	(to) **repeat** sth. [rɪ'piːt]	etwas wiederholen	(to) say or write sth. again *French:* répéter
	I didn't get that. *(infml)*	Das habe ich nicht mitbekommen. / Ich habe das nicht verstanden.	**I didn't ~ that.** Could you repeat that, please? John told me a joke, but **I didn't ~ it**.
p.15/P 2	**tricky** ['trɪki]	verzwickt, heikel	a **tricky** situation/problem/question
	wetsuit ['wetsuːt]	Surfanzug, Taucheranzug	

PART C The Aboriginal people of Australia

p.16	(to) **settle** ['setl]	sich niederlassen, siedeln; besiedeln	Millions of immigrants **~d** in the US in the 19th century. North America **was** first **~d** by the English in the 16th century.
	belief [bɪ'li:f]	Glaube, Überzeugung	verb: (to) **believe** – noun: **belief**
	(to) **unite** [ju'naɪt]	vereinen, vereinigen, verbinden	the **United** Nations (die Vereinten Nationen) the **United** States (die Vereinigten Staaten) *French:* unir
	to this day	bis heute, bis zum heutigen Tag	Grandma has always loved the Beatles – they're her favourite band **to this ~**.
	ancestor ['ænsestə]	Vorfahre/Vorfahrin	Grandpa says one of our **~s** was a pirate.
	(to) **need to do** sth.	etwas tun müssen; etwas zu tun brauchen	(to) have to do sth.

'need' als Hilfsverb – 'need' als Vollverb

Hilfsverb

Du kennst bereits das **Hilfsverb *need***. Es kommt nur im *simple present* vor und hauptsächlich in verneinter Form.

You **needn't** wait for him.
*Du **brauchst nicht** auf ihn zu warten.*

Vollverb

Das **Vollverb** *(to)* ***need to*** *do sth.* kannst du auch in anderen Zeiten verwenden, und es kommt auch in bejahten Sätzen und in Fragen vor.

You **don't need to** wait for him.
*Du **brauchst nicht** auf ihn zu warten.*

I **didn't need to** tell her. She knew it already.
*Ich **musste** es ihr **nicht** erzählen. ...*

! (to) **need to do** sth.: Verneinung und Fragebildung wie bei allen Vollverben mit einer Form von *do*.

Everybody **needs to** sleep, eat and drink.
*Jeder **muss** schlafen, essen und trinken.*

Do we **need to** book a table?
***Müssen** wir einen Tisch buchen?*

	(to) **respect** [rɪ'spekt]	achten, respektieren	(to) **respect** other people's rights/opinions/views *French:* respecter
p.17	**generation** [ˌdʒenə'reɪʃn]	Generation	! stress: **generation** [ˌdʒenə'reɪʃn] *French:* la génération
	racist ['reɪsɪst]	rassistisch; Rassist/in	*French:* raciste; le/la raciste
	race [reɪs]	Rasse	*French:* la race
	ideal [aɪ'di:əl]	Ideal, Idealvorstellung	! stress and pronunciation: **ideal** [aɪ'di:əl] *French:* l'idéal *(m)*
	orphan ['ɔ:fn]	Waise, Waisenkind	a child without living parents
	(to) **run** sth.	etwas leiten *(Hotel, Firma usw.)*	My aunt **~s** a home for orphans.
	nun [nʌn]	Nonne	
	mattress ['mætrəs]	Matratze	! stress: **mattress** ['mætrəs]
	fair [feə]	hell *(Haut; Haare)*	

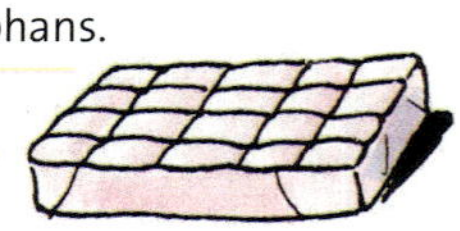

(to) **apologize (to** sb. **for** sth.) [ə'pɒlədʒaɪz]	sich (bei jm. für etwas) entschuldigen	(to) say sorry He **~d for** not writing sooner.
finally ['faɪnəli]	schließlich, endlich	We had to wait hours before our plane ~ left. And ~, the first prize goes to Sarah Atkinson. *French:* finalement
(to) **trick** sb. **into** doing sth. [trɪk]	jn. mit einer List / einem Trick dazu bringen, etwas zu tun	The thief **~ed** the girl **into** opening the door. Dad **was ~ed into** buying a second-hand watch that didn't work.
(to) **trick** sb.	jn. reinlegen	I saw he had **~ed** me and I felt so stupid.
truck [trʌk]	Last(kraft)wagen, LKW	 a **truck**
rabbit-**proof** ['ræbɪt pruːf]	kaninchen-sicher, kaninchen-fest	! Common words with **-proof**: a **weatherproof/windproof/rainproof** jacket; a **waterproof** watch; a **fireproof** door; a **childproof** bottle
p.19/P 5 **basic** ['beɪsɪk]	grundlegend; Grund-, Haupt-	**basic** computer skills; the **basic** idea/problem/question/facts
pay [peɪ]	Bezahlung, Lohn	verb: (to) **pay** – noun: **pay**
owner ['əʊnə]	Besitzer/in	
(to) **wash the dishes** ['dɪʃɪz]	das Geschirr abwaschen	  (to) **wash the dishes** a **dishwasher**
address [ə'dres]	Adresse	! spelling: *English* **a<u>dd</u>ress** – *German* **Adresse** *French:* l'adresse *(f)*
notice ['nəʊtɪs]	Mitteilung, Aushang	You can put your ~ on the notice board.
(to) **earn** [ɜːn]	verdienen *(Geld, Respekt usw.)*	

Unit 2: The world of work

pp.32/33 **training** ['treɪnɪŋ]	*(berufliche)* Ausbildung	He had to do special ~ to become a paramedic. He finished his ~ in 2008.
qualification [ˌkwɒlɪfɪ'keɪʃn]	Abschluss, Qualifikation	! stress: **qualifi<u>ca</u>tion** [ˌkwɒlɪfɪ'keɪʃn] *French:* la qualification
apprenticeship [ə'prentɪʃɪp]	Lehre, Ausbildung	She began her ~ as a hairdresser in 2007.
apprentice [ə'prentɪs]	Auszubildende(r), Lehrling	When you start work as an ~, you don't earn very much.
decision [dɪ'sɪʒn]	Entscheidung	verb: (to) **decide** [dɪ'saɪd] – noun: **decision** ! (to) **<u>make</u> a decision** = eine Entscheidung fällen *French:* la décision
chef [ʃef]	Koch, Köchin *(Berufsbezeichnung)*	! English **chef** = German „Koch/Köchin" English **boss** = German „Chef/Chefin" 
childcare assistant ['tʃaɪldkeər‿əˌsɪstənt]	Kinderpfleger/in; Erzieher/in	
mechanic [mə'kænɪk]	Mechaniker/in	*French:* le/la mécanicien/ne

garage ['gærɑːʒ]	Autowerkstatt *(oft mit Tankstelle)*	
customer adviser [əd'vaɪzə]	Kundenbetreuer/in, -berater/in	
(to) **advise** sb. [əd'vaɪz]	jn. beraten	! (to) **advise** sb. **to do** sth. = jm. raten, etwas zu tun
advice *(no pl)* [əd'vaɪs]	Rat, Ratschlag, Ratschläge	Take my ~: go and see a doctor. (Hör auf meinen Rat: ...) ! She gave me **some** / **lots of** / **a piece of** advice. *Never:* She gave me ~~an advice~~ / lots of ~~advices~~.
make-up artist ['ɑːtɪst]	Maskenbildner/in	
fitness instructor ['fɪtnəs‿ɪnˌstrʌktə]	Fitnesstrainer/in	
(to) **work long hours**	lange arbeiten	
(to) **serve** [sɜːv]	bedienen *(Kunden)*	I waited for ten minutes before the shop assistant **~d** me. *French:* servir
(to) **repair** [rɪ'peə]	reparieren	*French:* réparer
sporty ['spɔːti]	sportlich	
artistic [ɑː'tɪstɪk]	künstlerisch	! He's **artistic.** = Er ist künstlerisch begabt. nouns: **art** (Kunst), **artist** (Künstler/in) – adjective: **artistic** *French:* artistique
organized ['ɔːgənaɪzd]	(gut) organisiert	~ crime (das organisierte Verbrechen); an ~ person (eine gut organisierte Person) ! stress: **organized** ['ɔːgənaɪzd] *French:* organisé, e
calm [kɑːm]	ruhig, still	quiet; not nervous: a ~ person, a ~ sea *French:* calme

PART A Personality quiz

p.34 **personality** [ˌpɜːsə'næləti]	Persönlichkeit	*French:* la personnalité
I don't mind helping/ working/...	Es macht mir nichts aus zu helfen / zu arbeiten / ...	

(to) mind

I **don't mind helping** in our shop, but I hate having to get up so early.	Es macht mir nichts aus, ...
I'd like to ask you a few questions, **if you don't mind**.	..., wenn Sie nichts dagegen haben.
Do you mind if I open the window?	Stört es Sie, ...
Would you mind waiting outside, please?	Würden Sie bitte draußen warten?

reliable [rɪ'laɪəbl]	zuverlässig, verlässlich	Our car ist not very ~. There's always something wrong with it.
(to) **make** sb. **do** sth.	jn. dazu bringen, etwas zu tun	Funny films ~ me laugh, and sad films ~ me cry.

	(to) **solve** [sɒlv]	lösen; aufklären	(to) ~ a problem / a puzzle / a crime / a case
p. 35	**mostly** ['məʊstli]	hauptsächlich, überwiegend	Tomorrow will be cold and ~ cloudy.
	confident ['kɒnfɪdənt]	selbstbewusst, (selbst)sicher	I'm very shy, and I feel nervous when I'm with other people. I'd like to be more ~.
	energetic [ˌenə'dʒetɪk]	dynamisch, tatkräftig, energisch	I'm an active, ~ person who loves sports. *French:* énergique
	racing car ['reɪsɪŋ kɑː]	Rennwagen	
	vet's assistant [ˌvets‿ə'sɪstənt]	Tierarzthelfer/in	
	dentist's assistant [ˌdentɪsts‿ə'sɪstənt]	Zahnarzthelfer/in	
	logical ['lɒdʒɪkl]	logisch	a ~ person (ein logisch denkender Mensch) *French:* logique
	technology [tek'nɒlədʒi]	Technologie	! stress: **tech<u>no</u>logy** [tek'nɒlədʒi] *French:* la technologie
	builder ['bɪldə]	Bauarbeiter/in	
	technician [tek'nɪʃn]	Techniker/in	! stress: **tech<u>ni</u>cian** [tek'nɪʃn] *French:* le technicien, la technicienne
	punctual ['pʌŋktʃuəl]	pünktlich	You're late again. You must try to be more ~.
	bank clerk ['bæŋk klɑːk]	Bankangestellte(r)	
	nurse [nɜːs]	Krankenpfleger/in, -schwester	
p. 36/P 1	**indoors** [ˌɪn'dɔːz]	drinnen, im Haus; nach drinnen	The weather was awful so we stayed ~.
p. 36/P 2	**profile** ['prəʊfaɪl]	Profil, Beschreibung, Porträt	! stress and pronunciation: **<u>pro</u>file** ['prəʊfaɪl]
p. 37/P 4	**application** [ˌæplɪ'keɪʃn]	Bewerbung	a letter of ~ (ein Bewerbungsschreiben)
	form [fɔːm]	Formular	
p. 37/P 5	**to date**	bis heute	We need ten people to help with the party, but ~ ~ only six have volunteered.

PART B Applying for a job

p. 38	**CV** [siː 'viː] **(curriculum vitae** [kəˌrɪkjələm 'viːtaɪ]**)**	Lebenslauf	
	birth [bɜːθ]	Geburt	Write down your address, date of ~ (Geburtsdatum) and place of ~ (Geburtsort).
	sex [seks]	Geschlecht	
	nationality [ˌnæʃə'næləti]	Nationalität, Staatsangehörigkeit	My husband and I are different **nationalities**. He's French, I'm Canadian. *French:* la nationalité
	postcode ['pəʊstkəʊd]	Postleitzahl	
	primary school ['praɪməri]	Grundschule	*French:* l'école primaire *(f)*
	secondary school ['sekəndri]	weiterführende Schule	*French:* l'école secondaire *(f)*

first aid [ˌfɜːst‿ˈeɪd]	Erste Hilfe	
certificate [səˈtɪfɪkət]	Bescheinigung, Zertifikat	Do you get a ~ at the end of the course? *French:* le certificat
driving licence [ˈdraɪvɪŋ laɪsns]	Führerschein	
work experience *(no pl)* [ˈwɜːk‿ɪkˌspɪəriəns]	Praktikum; Arbeits-, Praxis-erfahrung(en)	! English: I have done **work experience** in a bank. German: ... **ein Praktikum** in einer Bank ...
reference [ˈrefrəns]	Referenz, Empfehlung	I got a ~ when the work experience finished. ! stress: **reference** [ˈrefrəns]
advertisement [ədˈvɜːtɪsmənt] (*infml:* **ad** [æd], *BE auch:* **advert** [ˈædvɜːt])	Anzeige, Inserat; *(im Fernsehen)* Werbespot	You find job **~s** in newspapers or on the internet. Lots of people change channels during the **~s**.
(to) **advertise** [ˈædvətaɪz]	Werbung machen (für); inserieren	! English: (to) **advertise** clothes/cars/furniture German: **für** Kleidung/Autos/Möbel **werben**
advertiser [ˈædvətaɪzə]	Inserent/in; Werbekunde/-kundin	
(to) **enclose** sth. [ɪnˈkləʊz]	etwas *(einem Brief)* beilegen	I **enclose** my CV. *or* My CV **is enclosed**.
(to) **be happy to do** sth. *(fml)*	gern bereit sein, etwas zu tun	We'll ~ ~ **to** help if you have any problems.
available [əˈveɪləbl]	verfügbar, erreichbar; vorrätig	Will you be ~ for an interview next week? Call me at the office. I'm usually ~ all morning. The guidebook to Paris isn't ~ at the moment.
(at) any time	jederzeit	I like online shopping: you can buy things ~ ~ ~.
formal [ˈfɔːml]	formell, förmlich	! stress: **formal** [ˈfɔːml] *French:* formel, le
informal [ɪnˈfɔːml]	informell; umgangssprachlich	**formal ◄► informal** *French:* informel, le
style [staɪl]	Stil	*French:* le style
Dear Sir/Madam [sɜː], [ˈmædəm]	Sehr geehrte Damen und Herren *(Briefbeginn)*	

Formal letters

Wenn der Name des Empfängers/der Empfängerin **unbekannt** ist:

Dear Sir/Madam	Sehr geehrte Damen und Herren,
...	...
...	...
Yours faithfully[1]	Mit freundlichen Grüßen
(+ your name)	(+ dein Name)

[1] [ˈfeɪθfəli]

Wenn der Name des Empfängers/der Empfängerin **bekannt** ist:

Dear Mrs Jones	Sehr geehrte Frau Jones,
...	...
...	...
Yours sincerely[2]	Mit freundlichen Grüßen
(+ your name)	(+ dein Name)

[2] [sɪnˈsɪəli]

p.39/P1 **similar (to** sb./sth.**)** [ˈsɪmɪlə]	(jm./etwas) ähnlich	Your flat is ~ **to** ours. It's almost the same size. *French:* similaire (à)
nature [ˈneɪtʃə]	Natur	! no article: I love **nature**. (Ich liebe **die** Natur.) stress: **nature** [ˈneɪtʃə] *French:* la nature
manager [ˈmænɪdʒə]	Geschäftsführer/in, Leiter/in	
technical [ˈteknɪkl]	technisch	
tractor [ˈtræktə]	Traktor	a **tractor**

	engineering [ˌendʒɪ'nɪərɪŋ]	Maschinenbau; Ingenieurswesen	
p.39/P 2	**level** ['levl]	(Lern-)Stand, Niveau, Grad	
	use [ju:s]	Gebrauch, Benutzung, Verwendung	The ~ of first names is more usual in England than in Germany. ! verb: (to) **use** [ju:z] – noun: **use** [ju:s]

PART C The Business: A reality TV show

p.40	**(job) interview**	Vorstellungsgespräch	
	candidate ['kændɪdət]	Kandidat/in, Bewerber/in	! stress: **candidate** ['kændɪdət] *French:* le candidat, la candidate
	(to) **impress** [ɪm'pres]	beeindrucken	*French:* impressionner
	(to) **dress** [dres]	sich kleiden	Emily has very nice clothes and always **~es** well. ! **„sich anziehen"** im Sinne von „sich ankleiden, Kleidung anziehen" = (to) **get dressed**: After I got up, I **got dressed** and went to school.
	suitable ['su:təbl]	geeignet, passend	Jeans aren't ~ clothes for a job interview. Dress **suitably** when you go for a job interview.
	strength [streŋθ]	Stärke, Kraft	adjective: **strong** – noun: **strength**
	weakness ['wi:knəs]	Schwäche, Schwachpunkt	adjective: **weak** – noun: **weakness**
	assessment [ə'sesmənt]	Einschätzung, Beurteilung	
	(to) **assess** [ə'ses]	einschätzen, beurteilen	Interviewers try to ~ a candidate's qualities.
	sheet [ʃi:t]	Blatt, Bogen *(Papier)*	
	look [lʊk]	(Gesichts-)Ausdruck	I knew something was wrong when I saw the ~ on her face.
	cheeky ['tʃi:ki]	frech, dreist	
p.42/P 3	**command** [kə'mɑ:nd]	Befehl, Aufforderung	To copy text use the ~ 'Strg C'.
	request [rɪ'kwest]	Bitte	Charities get a lot of **~s** for help every year.
p.43/P 5	**travel agent** ['trævl‿eɪdʒənt]	Reisebürokaufmann/-kauffrau	We went to a **travel agent's** to ask about holidays in Spain. (= ins **Reisebüro**)

PART D How to be a teenage millionaire

p.44	(to) **vote** [vəʊt]	zur Wahl gehen, wählen	At 17, he's old enough to drive, but too young to ~. *French:* voter
	design [dɪ'zaɪn]	Muster, Entwurf; Design, Gestaltung	This website has free **~s** for dresses and skirts. After school he wants to study ~ at art college.
	layout ['leɪaʊt]	Layout, Anordnung, Aufbau	
	(to) **borrow** sth. ['bɒrəʊ]	etwas (aus)leihen, sich etwas borgen	
	(to) **lend** sb. sth. [lend], **lent, lent** [lent]	jm. etwas leihen, etwas an jn. verleihen	

(to) lend – (to) borrow

You **lend** (= **give**) something to someone. You **borrow** (= **take**) something from someone.

within [wɪ'ðɪn]	innerhalb (von)	We were asked to finish our project ~ four weeks, but I didn't need so much time.
I **used to** be excited ... ['ju:st tə]	Früher war ich (immer) aufgeregt ...	! pronunciation: I **use** ... („benutzen") [ju:z] I **used to** ... [ju:st tə]

... used to be/do ...

Mit **used to ...** kannst du ausdrücken, dass etwas früher der Fall war, aber heute nicht mehr:

I **used to do** a lot of sport, but I haven't got the time now. — Ich habe früher (immer) viel Sport getrieben, ...
Dad **used to smoke**, but he gave up when I was born. — Dad hat (früher) geraucht, ...
We **used to live** in London, but now we live in Berlin. — Früher haben wir in London gewohnt, ...

! Frage und Verneinung mit **did** bzw. **didn't**:

Did you **use to cry** a lot when you were little? — Hast du viel geweint, als du klein warst?
He's changed a lot. He **didn't use to be** so shy. — ... Er war früher nicht so schüchtern.

(to) **receive** [rɪ'si:v]	erhalten, empfangen	a more formal word for '(to) get', '(to) be given' *French:* recevoir
cheque (for) [tʃek]	Scheck (über)	Ashley's mum was surprised when they received a ~ **for** $ 2,700. *French:* le chèque
p.45 **confident** ['kɒnfɪdənt]	zuversichtlich	The team had trained hard, so the coach was ~ that they would win. ! **confident** = **1.** selbstbewusst; **2.** zuversichtlich
(to) **trust** [trʌst]	trauen, vertrauen	He isn't very honest, you know. You can't really ~ him.
(to) **react (to)** [ri'ækt]	reagieren (auf)	How did your parents ~ **to** your plans?
shocked [ʃɒkt]	schockiert	We were ~ when we heard that he had died.
for a while [waɪl]	für eine Weile, eine Zeit lang	I haven't seen you **for a ~**. Where've you been?
set of rules [set]	Reihe von Regeln, Regelwerk	
set [set]	Reihe, Set, Satz	
ambitious [æm'bɪʃəs]	ehrgeizig	*French:* ambitieux, ambitieuse
(to) **be determined** [dɪ'tɜ:mɪnd]	(fest) entschlossen sein	Dad has given up cigarettes and **is ~** never to smoke again. *French:* déterminé, e
stressful ['stresfl]	anstrengend, stressig	

	(to) **graduate** ['grædʒueɪt] *(AE)*	den Schulabschluss machen *(an einer amerik. Highschool)*	
	definite ['defɪnət]	fest, bestimmt; endgültig, eindeutig	Have you got any ~ plans for the future? I need a ~ answer by tomorrow. *French:* définitif, définitive
p.46	**popular (with)** ['pɒpjələ]	beliebt (bei)	Chat rooms are very ~ **with** young people. ! stress: **popular** ['pɒpjələ]
	relationship [rɪ'leɪʃnʃɪp]	Beziehung	
	greedy ['gri:di]	gierig, habgierig	A ~ person is someone who wants more food or money than they really need.
	(to) **sum** sth. **up** **(-mm-)** [ˌsʌm‿'ʌp]	etwas zusammenfassen	At the end of her speech, she **~med up** her main ideas.

Unit 3: Teen world

p.48	**worldwide** [ˌwɜ:ld'waɪd]	weltweit; auf der ganzen Welt	Arsenal London has millions of supporters ~.
	lifestyle ['laɪfstaɪl]	Lebensstil	
	especially [ɪ'speʃəli]	besonders, vor allem	I love chocolate, ~ chocolate from Belgium or Switzerland.
	(to) **make friends (with** sb.**)**	Freunde finden; sich anfreunden (mit jm.)	The youth club is a great place to **make** new ~. At college I **made ~ with** a student from China.
	(to) **fancy** sb. ['fænsi] *(infml)*	auf jn. stehen	If I ~ a girl, I just ask her out on a date.
	(to) go **up to** sb./sth.	auf jn./etwas zugehen	 The artist went **up to** the piano.
p.49	**chore** [tʃɔ:]	(Haus-)Arbeit; *(lästige)* Pflicht	One ~ I really hate is washing the dishes.
	physics ['fɪzɪks]	Physik	! stress: **physics** ['fɪzɪks]
	chemistry ['kemɪstri]	Chemie	! stress: **chemistry** ['kemɪstri] *French:* la chimie
	candle ['kændl]	Kerze	 a **candle**

PART A Mobile

p.50	**secretly** ['si:krətli]	heimlich	• *(adv)* She **secretly** put some salt into his tea. • *(adj)* We had a **secret** meeting. (geheim) • *(n)* I can't tell you. It's a **secret**. (Geheimnis) *French:* secrètement
	funeral ['fju:nərəl]	Trauerfeier, Beerdigung	
	unwanted [ˌʌn'wɒntɪd]	unerwünscht, ungewollt	(to) feel **unwanted** an **unwanted** child (ein ungewolltes Kind)
	(to) **go by**	vergehen, vorübergehen *(Zeit)*	She said she'd be back in a minute, but a whole hour **went ~** before she came.
p.51/P 1	**outline** ['aʊtlaɪn]	Gliederung	

	(to) **introduce** sth. [ˌɪntrəˈdjuːs]	etwas einführen *(Thema, Mode, Methode)*	**!** (to) **introduce** sb. = jn. vorstellen (to) **introduce** sth. = etwas *(neu)* einführen *French:* introduire
	however [haʊˈevə]	jedoch, allerdings	The summer is usually very hot here. **However**, this year it has been quite cool.
	(to) **rate** [reɪt]	bewerten	He isn't a very nice person, but I ~ him highly as a footballer.
p.52/P 2	**false** [fɔːls]	falsch, unecht	Paris is the capital of France – true or ~?
p.52/P 3	(to) **save** [seɪv]	(ab)speichern *(Daten, Telefonnummern)*	
	Anyway, ... [ˈeniweɪ]	Aber egal, ... / Wie dem auch sei, ...	Sorry, I don't agree. **Anyway**, let's talk about something else. ...
p.53/P 4	**exchange rate** [ɪksˈtʃeɪndʒ reɪt]	Wechselkurs	What's the ~ ~? – 1.14 to the pound, I think.
	cash [kæʃ]	Bargeld	**!** (to) **pay cash** = bar bezahlen
	credit card [ˈkredɪt kɑːd]	Kreditkarte	(to) **pay by credit card** = mit Kreditkarte bezahlen **!** stress: **<u>cre</u>dit card** [ˈkredɪt kɑːd]
	receipt [rɪˈsiːt]	Quittung	
	(to) **order** [ˈɔːdə]	bestellen	
	note [nəʊt]	(Geld-)Schein, Banknote	My sister found a 10-euro ~ this morning.

PART B ASBO boy

p.54	**social** [ˈsəʊʃl]	sozial, Sozial-, gesellschaftlich	**!** stress: **<u>so</u>cial** [ˈsəʊʃl] *French:* social,e
	behaviour [bɪˈheɪvjə]	Verhalten, Benehmen	He used to make trouble in class but his ~ is better now.
	(to) **behave** [bɪˈheɪv]	sich verhalten, sich benehmen	He **~d** as if he hadn't seen me. **Behave** yourself, or you can go to your room.
	order [ˈɔːdə]	Befehl, Anweisung, Anordnung	The soldiers waited until they got the ~ to move. *French:* l'ordre *(m)*
	(to) **ban** **(-nn-)** [bæn]	sperren; ein (Aufenthalts-)Verbot erteilen	Sports stadiums should ~ people who use racist language. Radio stations have **~ned** the song because of its lyrics.
	punishment [ˈpʌnɪʃmənt]	Bestrafung, Strafe	Feeling sick was a kind of ~ for eating too much.
	(to) **punish** [ˈpʌnɪʃ]	bestrafen	When you did something wrong as a child, how were you **~ed**? *French:* punir

(to) **train as ...** [treɪn]	eine Ausbildung machen zu ...	She has **~ed as** a hairdresser and is looking for a job now.
(to) **straighten** sth. **up** [ˌstreɪtn‿'ʌp]	etwas aufräumen, etwas in Ordnung bringen	We'll have to **~ up** the house before the guests arrive. Give up smoking and drinking and try to **~ up** your life.
particular [pə'tɪkjələ]	bestimmte(r, s)	I'm looking for a pair of jeans, please. Size 30. – Any ~ colour, sir? *French:* particulier, -ière
prison ['prɪzn]	Gefängnis	**!** No article: (to) **be in prison** (im Gefängnis sein) (to) **go to prison** (ins Gefängnis kommen) *French:* la prison
graffiti [grə'fi:ti]	Graffiti	**Graffiti** was sprayed all over the wall. **!** *not:* **Graffiti** ~~were~~ sprayed ...
under age [ˌʌndər‿'eɪdʒ]	minderjährig	

a piece of **graffiti**

(to) **vandalize** ['vændəlaɪz]	mutwillig beschädigen, mutwillig zerstören	Cars and shop windows in the city centre have been **~d** again.
vandalism ['vændəlɪzəm]	Vandalismus, Zerstörungswut	**!** stress: **<u>van</u>dalism** ['vændəlɪzəm] *French:* le vandalisme
p.55 (to) **cause** [kɔ:z]	verursachen	Drinking too much alcohol **~s** headaches.
instead of *(prep)* [ɪn'sted‿əv]	statt, anstatt, anstelle von	This week's disco is on Friday **~ of** Saturday.
instead *(adv)* [ɪn'sted]	stattdessen, dafür	I don't like coffee. I'll have tea ~.
(to) **commit** a crime **(-tt-)** [kə'mɪt]	ein Verbrechen / eine Straftat verüben, begehen	*French:* commettre un crime
boot camp ['bu:t kæmp]	Erziehungslager *(für junge Straftäter/innen)*	
boot [bu:t]	Stiefel	a pair of **boots**
eagle ['i:gl]	Adler	
military ['mɪlətri]	militärisch, Militär-	**military**-style fashion (Mode im Militärstil) **!** stress: **<u>mil</u>itary** ['mɪlətri] *French:* militaire

instructor [ɪn'strʌktə]	Ausbilder/in	*French:* l'instructeur *(m)*, l'instructrice *(f)*
discipline ['dɪsəplɪn]	Disziplin	**!** spelling and stress: **<u>dis</u>cipline** ['dɪsəplɪn] *French:* la discipline
(to) **do well**	erfolgreich sein, gut abschneiden	Aidan **did** very ~ in last week's test. (to) **do well** ◄► (to) **do badly**
p.56/P1 (to) **express** [ɪk'spres]	ausdrücken, äußern	You'll all have a chance to ~ your opinion in a few moments. *French:* exprimer
clarification [ˌklærəfɪ'keɪʃn]	Klarstellung, Klärung	

p.57/P 2	(to) **worry** sb. ['wʌri]	jn. beunruhigen, jm. Sorgen machen	! • Something **is worrying** you. What is it? (= Etwas beunruhigt dich/macht dir Sorgen.) • You**'re worrying** about something. What is it? (= Du machst dir Sorgen wegen etwas.)
p.57/P 3	**youth** [juːθ], *pl* **youths** [juːðz]	Jugendliche(r)	Two policemen went up to the gang of **~s** in the park. Three **~s** were badly hurt in a road accident.
	(to) **do** sth. **about** sth.	etwas unternehmen gegen etwas	What can we **do ~** vandalism in the city centre? The TV isn't working. We'll have to **do** something **~** it.

Zusammengesetzte Adjektive: hard-working, warm-hearted, …

hard-working	a hard-working shop assistant	fleißig, hart arbeitend
good-looking	good-looking sportsmen and sportswomen	gut aussehend
never-ending	a never-ending story; a never-ending concert tour	endlos, unendlich
English-speaking	English-speaking countries; English-speaking tourists	englischsprachig; Englisch sprechend
oil-producing	oil-producing states	ölproduzierend
warm-hearted	warm-hearted grandparents	warmherzig
well-behaved	well-behaved children; a well-behaved dog	artig, gut erzogen
well-paid	well-paid jobs; a well-paid engineer	gut bezahlt
home-made	a home-made cake; home-made marmalade	hausgemacht, selbstgemacht

PART C Get involved

p.58	**spring** [sprɪŋ]	Quelle	a **spring** in the mountains
	along with sb./sth.	(zusammen) mit jm./etwas	We walked onto the ferry **~ with** hundreds of other travellers.
	trash [træʃ] *(AE)*	Abfall, Müll	
	such (a) [sʌtʃ]	so (ein/e), solch (ein/e); solche	The gold medal is a huge success for **~ a** young swimmer.

German 'so'

- ***so* + adjective**:

Helen is **so nice/beautiful**.	... **so** nett/schön
The book was **so good/interesting** that I read it twice.	... **so** gut/interessant

- ***such a*** (+ adjective) **+ noun**:

Helen is **such a** nice **person**.	... **so** ein netter Mensch
It was **such a** good **book** that I read it twice.	... **so** ein gutes Buch

It's **a shame**. [ʃeɪm]	Es ist ein Jammer/eine Schande.	**It's a ~** you can't come to our party.

a **turtle**

turtle ['tɜːtl]	Wasserschildkröte	
need [niːd]	Not; Notwendigkeit	We're trying to raise money for people in **~**. There's no **~** to shout. I can hear you perfectly.

	(to) **donate** [dəʊ'neɪt]	spenden, schenken	
	the **Bible** ['baɪbl]	die Bibel	
	coin [kɔɪn]	Münze	
	bill [bɪl] *(AE)*	(Geld-)Schein, Banknote	 some **coins** and **notes** *(BE)*/**bills** *(AE)*
	altogether [ˌɔːltə'geðə]	insgesamt, alles in allem	£ 3.75 for the postcards and £ 5.50 for the stamps. That's £ 9.25 ~.
	canned [kænd]	Dosen-; ... in Dosen	You can keep ~ food for a very long time.
	can [kæn]	Dose, Büchse	 a **can** of tomatoes  two **cans** of cola
	(to) **store** [stɔː]	(ein)lagern, aufbewahren	The bottle should be **~d** in a cool and dark place.
	overnight [ˌəʊvə'naɪt]	über Nacht	It was too late to go home, so we stayed ~.
p. 59	**community service** [kə'mjuːnəti ˌsɜːvɪs]	gemeinnützige Arbeit	
	service ['sɜːvɪs]	Dienst(leistung), Service	He was given a medal for ~ to his country. The ~ in that shop is a bit slow. *French:* le service
	minimum ['mɪnɪməm]	Minimum	a ~ of ten hours = at least ten hours *French:* le minimum
	(to) **encourage** [ɪn'kʌrɪdʒ]	*(jn.)* ermutigen, ermuntern; *(etwas)* fördern	My parents **~d** me to apply for the job. We'd like to ~ interest in local history. *French:* encourager
	opportunity [ˌɒpə'tjuːnəti]	Gelegenheit, Möglichkeit	! Verwende **opportunity** oder **chance** für „Möglichkeit" im Sinne von „Gelegenheit, Chance" (nicht *possibility*): a good **opportunity/chance** to speak English (eine gute Möglichkeit, Englisch zu sprechen) *French:* l'opportunité *(f)*
p. 60/P 1	**independence** [ˌɪndɪ'pendəns]	Unabhängigkeit	Australia got its ~ from Britain in 1901. *French:* l'indépendance *(f)*
	(to) **celebrate** ['selɪbreɪt]	feiern	They **~d** their grandma's 75th birthday in an expensive restaurant. *French:* célébrer
p. 61/P 4	**valuables** *(pl)* ['væljuəblz]	Wertgegenstände, Wertsachen	adjective: **valuable** – noun: **valuables** *(pl)*

PART D The caller

p. 64	(to) **create** [kri'eɪt]	schaffen, erschaffen	(to) make, (to) produce, (to) design, (to) invent *French:* créer
	suspense [sə'spens]	Spannung	There was so much ~ in the book that I couldn't put it down. *French:* le suspense

Unit 4: Big City Life

p.74	**polluted** [pə'lu:tɪd]	verseucht, verunreinigt	a **polluted** river *French:* pollué,e
	shiny ['ʃaɪni]	glänzend	**shiny** hair; **shiny** skyscrapers
p.75	**crowded** ['kraʊdɪd]	überfüllt, voll(gestopft)	London is always ~ with tourists.

PART A Mumbai

p.76	**lover** ['lʌvə]	Geliebte(r)	two **lovers**
	recently ['ri:sntli]	neulich, vor kurzem; in letzter Zeit	I met my old English teacher in London ~. I haven't done much sport ~.

	passenger ['pæsɪndʒə]	Passagier/in	
	carriage ['kærɪdʒ]	Eisenbahnwagen, Waggon	
	(to) **hold on (to** sth.**)** [həʊld], **held, held** [held]	sich festhalten (an etwas)	The **passengers hold on to** the top of the doors. *French:* le passager, la passagère
	(to) **reach out (for** sth.**)** [ri:tʃ]	die Hand/Hände ausstrecken (nach etwas); greifen (nach etwas)	I **~ed out** and touched his arm. He **~ed (out) for** my hand and held it tightly.
	space [speɪs]	Platz, Raum	There's not enough ~ in the living room for a second sofa. *French:* l'espace *(m)*
	wet [wet]	nass, feucht	
	dry [draɪ]	trocken	**dry ◄► wet**
	Hindu ['hɪndu:]	Hindu	
	Muslim ['mʊzlɪm]	Muslim/Muslima, Muslimin	
	Christian ['krɪstʃən]	Christ/in	
p.77	**power** ['paʊə]	Macht; Stärke	A new government came to ~ after the election. Electric cars don't have the ~ to drive very fast.
	financial [faɪ'nænʃl]	finanziell, Finanz-	**!** stress: **fi<u>nan</u>cial** [faɪ'nænʃl] *French:* financier, -ière
	Indian ['ɪndiən]	Inder/in; indisch	
	air conditioning *(no pl)* ['eəkənˌdɪʃnɪŋ]	Klimatisierung, Klimaanlage	**!** Does your new car have **air-conditioning**? (*not:* ... ~~an~~ air-conditioning)
p.78	**typical (of)** ['tɪpɪkl]	typisch (für)	**!** Alan arrived ten minutes late. – That's ~ **of** him. (*not:* ... typical ~~for~~ him) *French:* typique
	legend ['ledʒənd]	Legende, Sage	**!** stress: **<u>le</u>gend** ['ledʒənd] *French:* la légende
	colourful ['kʌləfl]	farbenfroh, farbenprächtig, farbig	

	costume ['kɒstjuːm]	(Bühnen-)Kostüm	❗ German „(Damen-)Kostüm“ = English **suit** stress: **costume** ['kɒstjuːm]
	whose [huːz]	deren, dessen *(Relativpronomen)*	What's the name of the boy ~ father comes from India?
	passion ['pæʃn]	Leidenschaft	❗ stress: **passion** ['pæʃn] *French:* la passion
	screen [skriːn]	Leinwand; Bildschirm	
	taboo [tə'buː]	tabu; Tabu	*French:* tabou,e; le tabou
p.79/P 1	**commuter** [kə'mjuːtə]	Pendler/in	
	motorway ['məʊtəweɪ] *(BE)*	Autobahn	
	suburb ['sʌbɜːb]	Vorort	
	fashionable ['fæʃnəbl]	modisch, schick	a **fashionable** restaurant, dress, area, idea, style
	stressed [strest]	gestresst	Drivers often feel ~ in traffic jams.
	stress [stres]	Stress	❗ **stress** = **1.** Stress; **2.** Betonung

PART B Johannesburg

p.80	**neighbourhood** ['neɪbəhʊd]	Viertel, Gegend; Nachbarschaft	
	baggy ['bægi]	weit (geschnitten) *(Hose)*	a **baggy** pair of jeans
	political [pə'lɪtɪkl]	politisch	
	cell [sel]	Zelle	
	slang [slæŋ]	Slang, Jargon	Using ~ can be a way of showing that you belong to a particular group.
	label ['leɪbl]	Marke, Label; Etikett	With these sweatshirts you're just paying for the ~. You could get cheaper ones. The instructions on the ~ will tell you how to wash your jacket.
	couple ['kʌpl]	Paar, Pärchen	❗ a **married couple** (ein Ehepaar) a **couple of kids** (ein paar/einige Jugendliche) *French:* le couple
	colour-blind ['kʌləblaɪnd]	farbenblind	❗ pronunciation: **blind** [blaɪnd]
	cultural ['kʌltʃərəl]	kulturell	❗ stress: **cultural** ['kʌltʃərəl] *French:* culturel,le
p.81	**racial** ['reɪʃl]	Rassen-, rassisch	It's important to protest against ~ discrimination. *French:* racial,e
	economic [ˌiːkə'nɒmɪk, ˌekə'nɒmɪk]	Wirtschafts-, wirtschaftliche(r, s)	Can the government solve our ~ problems? *French:* économique

rate [reɪt]	Rate, Quote	
official [ə'fɪʃl]	offiziell, amtlich, Amts-	Canada has two ~ languages: French and English. **!** stress: **official** [ə'fɪʃl] *French:* officiel, le
novel ['nɒvl]	Roman	
surrounded by [sə'raʊndɪd]	umgeben von; umstellt von	The garden was ~ **by** a tall wall. The terrorists were ~ **by** soldiers.
p.82 **peace** [pi:s]	Friede(n)	**peace** ◄► **war** *French:* la paix
embarrassed [ɪm'bærəst]	verlegen; peinlich berührt	I felt so ~ when I gave the wrong answer. *French:* embarrassé,e
This is where ...	Hier ...	**This is** ~ my dad went to school.
(to) **shoot** [ʃu:t], **shot, shot** [ʃɒt]	(er)schießen	She **shot** the thief in the leg. Do you know who **shot** Martin Luther King?
uprising ['ʌpraɪzɪŋ]	Aufstand	
cardboard ['kɑ:dbɔ:d]	Pappe	
metal ['metl]	Metall	**!** stress: **metal** ['metl] *French:* le métal
(to) **remind** sb. **(of/about** sth.**)** [rɪ'maɪnd]	jn. (an etwas) erinnern	Grandma always says that I ~ her **of** her brother. I'll ~ him **about** the meeting, or he'll forget.

(to) remind – (to) remember

- (to) **remind sb.** *(jemanden an etwas erinnern)*
  I mustn't forget to phone Grandpa. Please **remind** me. — ... Bitte **erinnere** mich daran.
- (to) **remember sth./sb.** *(sich an etwas/an jemanden erinnern)*
  I can still **remember** my first day at school. — Ich kann mich noch immer an meinen ersten Schultag **erinnern**.

the inside	das Innere, die Innenseite	**the inside** ◄► **the outside**
silent ['saɪlənt]	still, lautlos; schweigend	without a sound, quiet The whole room was ~. No one said a word. *French:* silencieux, se
(to) **hang** [hæŋ], **hung, hung** [hʌŋ]	hängen; *(etwas)* aufhängen	A photo of Big Ben **hung** on the wall. You can ~ your jacket over that chair.
(to) **wish** [wɪʃ]	wünschen	We all want to ~ you a very happy birthday.

Ich wünschte ... – I wish ...

I **wish** I **had** a brother or a sister. — Ich **wünschte**, ich **hätte** einen Bruder oder eine Schwester.

I **wish** I **could** fly. — Ich **wünschte**, ich **könnte** fliegen.

I **wish** I **knew** his phone number. — Ich **wünschte**, ich **wüsste** seine Telefonnummer.

Sätze mit ***I wish I had/could/knew/...*** drücken aus, dass etwas nicht so ist, wie ich es gern hätte.

(to) **stand** [stænd], **stood, stood** [stʊd]	aushalten, ertragen	Dan can't ~ the heat in Greece in the summer. I can't ~ waiting in queues. What I think of Pete? I can't ~ him! (... Ich kann ihn nicht ausstehen.)
somehow ['sʌmhaʊ]	irgendwie	The police locked the man into a cell, but ~ he was able to escape.

p.83/P 1	(to) **remember** sb./sth.	*einer Person/Sache* gedenken	The whole village came together to ~ the victims of the fire.

'I would have taken the bus' – *would* + *have* + past participle

p.84/P 4

A visit to the zoo **would have been** nice, but I didn't have the time.	Ein Besuch im Zoo **wäre** schön **gewesen** ...
Without your help, I **wouldn't have passed** the exam.	... **hätte** ich die Prüfung **nicht bestanden**.
He **would have gone** to the cinema, but his girlfriend didn't want to.	Er **wäre** ins Kino **gegangen**, ...

Mit ***I would have*** + **past participle** kannst du sagen, was <u>du</u> (anstelle von jemand anderem) in einer bestimmten Situation getan hättest:

In a situation like that, I **would have taken** the bus.	... **hätte** ich den Bus **genommen**.
I **wouldn't have waited** for Laura. I **would have left** without her.	Ich **hätte nicht** auf Laura **gewartet**. Ich **wäre** ohne sie **gegangen**.

p.85/P 5	**enquiry** [ɪn'kwaɪəri]	Anfrage, Erkundigung	Send us your ~ by e-mail, or phone 690809.
	(to) **enquire (about)** [ɪn'kwaɪə]	sich erkundigen (nach); anfragen (wegen)	You can phone this number to ~ about departure times.
	(to) **rent** [rent]	mieten, pachten	We don't own the flat, we just ~ it.
	subject line ['sʌbdʒɪkt laɪn]	Betreffzeile	

PART C Berlin

p.86	(to) **connect (to/with)** [kə'nekt]	verbinden (mit)	This hallway **~s** the kitchen **with** the dining room.
	gate [geɪt]	Tor; Pforte	
	guidebook ['gaɪdbʊk]	Reiseführer *(Buch)*	
	democratic [ˌdemə'krætɪk]	demokratisch	*French:* démocratique
	republic [rɪ'pʌblɪk]	Republik	! stress: **re<u>pub</u>lic** [rɪ'pʌblɪk] *French:* la république
	checkpoint ['tʃekpɔɪnt]	Kontrollpunkt; Grenzübergang	
	crossing ['krɒsɪŋ]	(Grenz-)Übergang; (Fußgänger-)Überweg	
	sector ['sektə]	Sektor, Bereich	You have to pay for your education if you go to a school in the private ~.
p.87	**reunification** [ˌriːˌjuːnɪfɪ'keɪʃn]	Wiedervereinigung	
	(to) **reunify** [ˌriː'juːnɪfaɪ]	wiedervereinigen	After Germany was **reunified**, the German parliament decided to move from Bonn to Berlin.
	(to) **prefer** sth. **(to** sth. else) **(-rr-)** [prɪ'fɜː]	etwas lieber tun/haben (als etwas anderes); etwas (etwas anderem) vorziehen	Which do you like better, tea or coffee? – I ~ tea. Linda **~s** tea **to** coffee. I don't get up early on Sundays. I ~ to stay in bed till 11.
	architect ['ɑːkɪtekt]	Architekt/in	! stress: **<u>ar</u>chitect** ['ɑːkɪtekt] *French:* l'architecte *(m, f)*
p.88	(to) **prevent** sth. [prɪ'vent]	etwas verhindern	Driving carefully is the best way to ~ road accidents.

	(to) **attract** [ə'trækt]	anziehen, anlocken	verb: (to) **attract** – noun: **attraction**
	institution [ˌɪnstɪ'tjuːʃn]	Institution, Einrichtung	! stress: **insti<u>tu</u>tion** [ˌɪnstɪ'tjuːʃn] *French:* l'institution *(f)*
	tourism ['tʊərɪzəm]	Tourismus	! stress: **<u>tou</u>rism** ['tʊərɪzəm] *French:* le tourisme
	(overhead) transparency [ˌəʊvəhed træns'pærənsi]	Folie *(für Overheadprojektoren)*	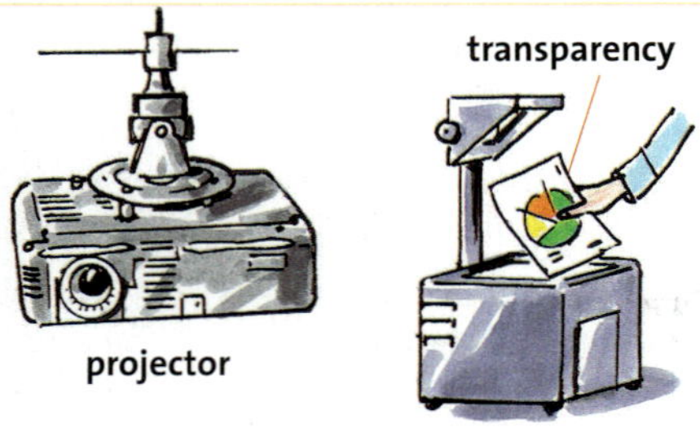
	talk [tɔːk]	Vortrag, Rede	
	(to) **give a talk (on** sth.**)**	einen Vortrag/eine Rede halten (über etwas)	
	projector [prə'dʒektə]	Projektor, Beamer	! Ein „Beamer" ist im Englischen ein **projector**. *French:* le projecteur
	visual ['vɪʒuəl]	visuell; optisch	! stress: **<u>vi</u>sual** ['vɪʒuəl] *French:* visuel, le
	material [mə'tɪəriəl]	Material	! stress: **ma<u>te</u>rial** [mə'tɪəriəl] *French:* le matériel
p. 89/P 2	**receptionist** [rɪ'sepʃənɪst]	Rezeptionist/in; Empfangsdame	*French:* le/la réceptionniste
	(to) **check in** [ˌtʃek‿'ɪn]	einchecken *(Hotel, Flughafen)*	(to) **check in** ◄► (to) **check out** (auschecken)
	(to) **include** [ɪn'kluːd]	(mit) einschließen, enthalten	Does the trip ~ a tour of London? An evening meal is **~d** in the price. *French:* inclure
	reservation [ˌrezə'veɪʃn]	Reservierung	When you make a ~ at a restaurant or hotel, you ~ a table or a room.
	(to) **book** [bʊk]	buchen, reservieren	
	dormitory ['dɔːmətri]	Schlafsaal	*French:* le dortoir
p. 89/P 3	(to) **rebuild** [ˌriː'bɪld], **rebuilt, rebuilt** [ˌriː'bɪlt]	wiederaufbauen	How long did it take to ~ the city after the earthquake?
p. 90/P 4	(to) **comment (on** sth.**)** ['kɒment]	sich (zu etwas) äußern; einen Kommentar abgeben (zu etwas)	A lot of people have **~ed on** the president's new hair style. 
	(to) **draw** sb.'s **attention to** sth. [ə'tenʃn], **drew, drawn**	jn. auf etwas aufmerksam machen; jemandes Aufmerksamkeit auf etwas lenken	I'm writing to you to **~ your ~ to** the number of accidents in Cork Street.
	Feel free to ask questions.	*etwa:* Ihr könnt jetzt gern Fragen stellen.	Please **feel ~** to phone us with any questions you might have.
	slide [slaɪd]	Dia; Folie *(in Präsentationsprogrammen)*	

Das **Dictionary** (S. 177–212) enthält den Wortschatz der Bände 1 bis 5 von *English G 21*.
Wenn du wissen möchtest, was ein Wort bedeutet, wie man es ausspricht oder wie es genau geschrieben wird, kannst du hier nachschlagen.

Im **Dictionary** werden folgende **Abkürzungen und Symbole** verwendet:

jm. = jemandem · sb. = somebody · *pl* = *plural* · *AE* = *American English*
jn. = jemanden · sth. = something · *no pl* = *no plural* · *infml* = *informal*

° Mit diesem Kringel sind Wörter markiert, die nicht zum Lernwortschatz gehören.
▸ Der Pfeil verweist auf Kästchen im **Vocabulary** (S. 156–176), in denen du weitere Informationen zu diesem Wort findest.

Die **Fundstellenangaben** zeigen, wo ein Wort zum ersten Mal vorkommt.
Die Ziffern in Klammern bezeichnen Seitenzahlen:

I = Band 1 • II = Band 2 • III = Band 3 • IV = Band 4 • V = Band 5
V 1 (8) = Band 5, Unit 1, Seite 8
V 1 (8/157) = Band 5, Unit 1, Seite 157 (im Vocabulary, zu Seite 8)

Tipps zur Arbeit mit einem Wörterbuch findest du im Skills File auf Seite 123.

A

a [ə]
1. ein, eine I
2. once/twice a week einmal/zweimal pro Woche III
a bit ein bisschen, etwas II • **a few** ein paar, einige II • **a little** ein bisschen, ein wenig IV • **a lot (of)** eine Menge, viel, viele II
He likes her a lot. Er mag sie sehr. I

able ['eɪbl]: **be able to do sth.** etwas tun können; fähig sein / in der Lage sein, etwas zu tun III

Aboriginal [ˌæbə'rɪdʒənl] Aborigine- *(die Ureinwohner/innen Australiens betreffend)* V 1 (8/157)

Aborigine [ˌæbə'rɪdʒəni] *Ureinwohner/in Australiens* V 1 (8)

about [ə'baʊt]
1. über I
2. ungefähr II
ask about sth. nach etwas fragen I • **be about to do sth.** im Begriff sein, etwas zu tun; kurz davor sein, etwas zu tun V 1 (6) • **do sth. about sth.** etwas unternehmen (gegen etwas) V 3 (57) • **This is about Mr Green.** Es geht um Mr Green. I • **How about ...?** Wie wär's mit ...? III • **What about ...?** **1.** Was ist mit ...? / Und ...? I; **2.** Wie wär's mit ...? I • **What are you talking about?** Wovon redest du? I • **°What are the pages about?** Wovon handeln die Seiten?
What was the best thing about ...? Was war das Beste an ...? II • **°Say what you like about ...** Sag, was du an ... magst

above [ə'bʌv]
1. oben III
2. über, oberhalb (von) III

abroad [ə'brɔːd] im Ausland II
go abroad ins Ausland gehen/fahren II

°academy [ə'kædəmi] Akademie

accent ['æksənt] Akzent II

°accessories *(pl)* [ək'sesəriz] Accessoires *(Modeartikel wie Schmuck, Gürtel usw.)*

accident ['æksɪdənt] Unfall II

ache [eɪk] wehtun IV

acid ['æsɪd] Säure IV

across [ə'krɒs]
1. (quer) über III
2. hinüber, herüber III

act [ækt]
1. handeln, sich verhalten IV
2. aufführen, spielen I
°Act out ... Spiele/Spielt ... vor.

active ['æktɪv] aktiv, tätig IV

activity [æk'tɪvəti] Aktivität, Tätigkeit I

actor ['æktə] Schauspieler/in II

actually ['æktʃuəli]
1. eigentlich; in Wirklichkeit III
2. nebenbei bemerkt; übrigens IV

ad [æd], *BE auch:* **advert** ['ædvɜːt] *(kurz für:* **advertisement***)* Anzeige, Inserat; *(im Fernsehen)* Werbespot V 2 (38)

°adapt [ə'dæpt] adaptieren, anpassen; bearbeiten

°adapted [ə'dæptɪd] adaptiert; bearbeitet

add (to) [æd] hinzufügen, ergänzen, addieren (zu) I • **°add up** addieren, zusammenzählen

address [ə'dres] Adresse V 1 (19)

adjective ['ædʒɪktɪv] Adjektiv I

admission [əd'mɪʃn] Eintritt, Eintrittspreis IV

adult ['ædʌlt] Erwachsene(r) III

advantage (over) [əd'vɑːntɪdʒ] Vorteil (gegenüber) IV

adventure [əd'ventʃə] Abenteuer IV

adverb ['ædvɜːb] Adverb I

advertise ['ædvətaɪz] Werbung machen (für); inserieren V 2 (38/164)

advertisement [əd'vɜːtɪsmənt] *(infml:* **ad** [æd], *BE auch:* **advert** ['ædvɜːt]*)* Anzeige, Inserat; *(im Fernsehen)* Werbespot V 2 (38)

advertiser ['ædvətaɪzə] Inserent/in; Werbekunde/-kundin V 2 (38/164)

advice *(no pl)* [əd'vaɪs] Rat, Ratschlag, Ratschläge V 2 (33/162)
take someone's advice auf jemandes Rat hören V 2 (33/162)

advise sb. [əd'vaɪz] jn. beraten V 2 (33) • **advise sb. to do sth.** jm. raten, etwas zu tun V 2 (33/162)

adviser [əd'vaɪzə] Berater/in V 2 (33)

afraid [ə'freɪd]
1. be afraid (of) Angst haben (vor) I
2. I'm afraid leider II

African-American [ˌæfrɪkən‿ə'merɪkən] afro-amerikanisch IV

°Afrikaans [ˌæfrɪ'kɑːns] Afrikaans *(eine der elf Amtssprachen Süd-*

afrikas, aus dem Niederländischen entstanden)
after ['ɑːftə] nach *(zeitlich)* I
after that danach I
after ['ɑːftə] nachdem II
afternoon [ˌɑːftə'nuːn] Nachmittag I • **in the afternoon** nachmittags, am Nachmittag I • **on Friday afternoon** freitagnachmittags, am Freitagnachmittag I
again [ə'gen] wieder; noch einmal I
once again noch einmal III
against [ə'genst] gegen I
age [eɪdʒ] Alter III • **for ages** ewig, eine Ewigkeit IV • **kids my age** Kinder/Jugendliche in meinem Alter V 1 (6) • **under age** minderjährig V 3 (54)
ago [ə'gəʊ]**: a minute ago** vor einer Minute I
agree (on) [ə'griː] sich einigen (auf) I • **agree with sb./sth.** jm./etwas zustimmen; mit jm./etwas übereinstimmen II
air [eə] Luft III
air conditioning *(no pl)* ['eə kənˌdɪʃnɪŋ] Klimatisierung, Klimaanlage V 4 (77)
airport ['eəpɔːt] Flughafen III
album ['ælbəm] Album III
alcohol ['ælkəhɒl] Alkohol V 1 (6)
alive [ə'laɪv] am Leben, lebendig IV
all [ɔːl] alle; alles I • **2 all** 2 beide (2:2 unentschieden) III • **all around the castle** ganz um die Burg herum II • **all day** den ganzen Tag (lang) I • **all over the world** auf der ganzen Welt III
all right [ɔːl 'raɪt] gut, in Ordnung II • **it's all right with her** es ist ihr recht; sie ist einverstanden V 4 (82)
all the time die ganze Zeit I • **all we have to do now ...** alles, was wir jetzt (noch) tun müssen, ... II
from all around Wales aus ganz Wales II • **from all over England/the UK** aus ganz England/aus dem gesamten Vereinigten Königreich III • **This is all wrong.** Das ist ganz falsch. I
all-day ticket [ˌɔːl deɪ 'tɪkɪt] Tagesfahrkarte III
allowed [ə'laʊd]**: be allowed** erlaubt sein IV • **be allowed to do sth.** etwas tun dürfen III
almost ['ɔːlməʊst] fast, beinahe II
alone [ə'ləʊn] allein I • **leave sb. alone** jn. in Ruhe lassen IV
along [ə'lɒŋ]**: along the road** entlang der Straße / die Straße entlang II • **along with sb./sth.** (zusammen) mit jm./etwas V 3 (58)
alphabet ['ælfəbet] Alphabet I
°**alphabetical** [ˌælfə'betɪkl] alphabetisch
already [ɔːl'redi] schon, bereits II
also ['ɔːlsəʊ] auch II
although [ɔːl'ðəʊ] obwohl III
altogether [ˌɔːltə'geðə] insgesamt, alles in allem V 3 (58)
always ['ɔːlweɪz] immer I
am [ˌeɪ_'em]**: 7 am** 7 Uhr morgens/vormittags I
amazing [ə'meɪzɪŋ] erstaunlich, unglaublich II
ambitious [æm'bɪʃəs] ehrgeizig V 2 (45)
ambulance ['æmbjələns] Krankenwagen III
American football [əˌmerɪkən 'fʊtbɔːl] Football I
amnesty ['æmnəsti] Amnestie, Begnadigung IV
an [ən] ein, eine I *siehe* **a**
analysis [ə'næləsɪs], *pl* **analyses** [ə'næləsiːz] Analyse, Auswertung IV
ancestor ['ænsestə] Vorfahre/Vorfahrin V 1 (16)
anchor ['æŋkə] Anker IV
anchorman/anchorwoman ['æŋkəmæn, 'æŋkəwʊmən] *(AE auch kurz:* **anchor)** Moderator/in *(von Nachrichtensendungen)* IV
and [ənd, ænd] und I • **and so on (etc.** [et'setərə]**)** und so weiter (usw.) IV
angel ['eɪndʒl] Engel II
angry (about sth./with sb.) ['æŋgri] wütend, böse (über etwas/auf jn.) II
animal ['ænɪml] Tier II
anniversary [ˌænɪ'vɜːsəri] Jahrestag IV • **anniversary of sb.'s death** js. Todestag IV
announce [ə'naʊns] ankündigen, bekanntgeben III
announcement [ə'naʊnsmənt] Durchsage, Ansage; Ankündigung, Bekanntgabe III
anorak ['ænəræk] Anorak, Windjacke III
another [ə'nʌðə] ein(e) andere(r, s); noch ein(e) I • **another 45p** weitere 45 Pence, noch 45 Pence II
one another einander, sich (gegenseitig) III
answer ['ɑːnsə] antworten; beantworten I
answer (to) ['ɑːnsə] Antwort (auf) I
anti- ['ænti] anti- V 3 (54)
any ['eni] jede(r, s) beliebige; irgendein(e) IV • **any ...?** (irgend) welche ...? I • **(at) any time** jederzeit V 2 (38) • **not (...) any** kein, keine I • **not (...) any more** nicht mehr II
anybody ['enibɒdi] (irgend)jemand II; jede(r) IV • **not (...) anybody** niemand II
anyone ['eniwʌn] IV *siehe* **anybody**
anything ['eniθɪŋ] (irgend)etwas II; alles IV • **not (...) anything** nichts II
anyway ['eniweɪ]
1. sowieso I
2. trotzdem II
3. Anyway, ... Aber egal, ... / Wie dem auch sei, ... V 3 (52)
anywhere ['eniweə] irgendwo(hin) II • **not (...) anywhere** nirgendwo(hin) II
apart [ə'pɑːt] auseinander, getrennt IV
°**apartheid** [ə'pɑːthaɪt, ə'pɑːtheɪt] Apartheid *(Rassentrennung in Südafrika, bis 1994)*
apartment [ə'pɑːtmənt] *(AE)* Wohnung IV
apologize (to sb. for sth.) [ə'pɒlədʒaɪz] sich (bei jm. für etwas) entschuldigen V 1 (17)
appear [ə'pɪə] erscheinen, auftauchen III
appetite ['æpɪtaɪt] Appetit III
apple ['æpl] Apfel I
application [ˌæplɪ'keɪʃn] Bewerbung V 2 (37) • **letter of application** Bewerbungsschreiben V 2 (37/163)
apply (for sth.) [ə'plaɪ] sich bewerben (um/für etwas); etwas beantragen IV
appointment [ə'pɔɪntmənt] Termin, Verabredung I
appreciate [ə'priːʃieɪt] schätzen, zu schätzen wissen IV
apprentice [ə'prentɪs] Auszubildende(r), Lehrling V 2 (32/161)
apprenticeship [ə'prentɪʃɪp] Lehre, Ausbildung V 2 (32)
April ['eɪprəl] April I
architect ['ɑːkɪtekt] Architekt/in V 4 (87)
archive ['ɑːkaɪv] Archiv IV
are [ɑː] bist; sind; seid I • **How are you?** Wie geht es dir/Ihnen/euch? II • **The pencils are 35p.** Die Bleistifte kosten 35 Pence. I • **You're joking, aren't you?** Du machst Witze, nicht wahr? / Das ist nicht dein Ernst, oder? II
area ['eəriə]
1. Bereich; Gebiet, Gegend III
2. Fläche V 1 (8)

argue ['ɑːgjuː]
1. sich streiten, sich zanken I
°**2.** argumentieren
argument ['ɑːgjumənt]
1. Argument, Begründung III
2. Streit III
arm [ɑːm] Arm I
armchair ['ɑːmtʃeə] Sessel I
around [ə'raʊnd] in ... umher, durch; um ... (herum) III • **all around the castle** ganz um die Burg herum II **around six** um sechs Uhr herum, gegen sechs III • **around the lake** um den See (herum) III • **around the town** in der Stadt umher, durch die Stadt III • **from all around Wales** aus ganz Wales II **look around** sich umsehen III **walk/run/jump around** herumgehen/-rennen/-springen, umhergehen/-rennen/-springen III
arrival (arr) [ə'raɪvl] Ankunft III
arrive [ə'raɪv] ankommen, eintreffen II
art [ɑːt] Kunst I
article ['ɑːtɪkl] (Zeitungs-)Artikel I
artificial [ˌɑːtɪ'fɪʃl] künstlich, Kunst- III
artist ['ɑːtɪst] Künstler/in III
artistic [ɑː'tɪstɪk] künstlerisch V 2 (33)
as *(conj)* [əz, æz] als, während II **as you can see** wie du sehen kannst II • **as if** als ob IV • **as long as** solange, sofern IV • **as soon as** sobald, sowie II
as *(prep)* [əz, æz] als II • **as a child** als Kind II
as ... as [əz, æz] so ... wie II • **as big/exciting as** so groß/aufregend wie II • **just as ... as** genauso ... wie V 1 (16)
°**ASBO** ['æzbəʊ] **(anti-social behaviour order)** einstweilige Verfügung wegen antisozialen Verhaltens
ask [ɑːsk] fragen I • **ask about sth.** nach etwas fragen I • **ask questions** Fragen stellen I • **ask sb. for sth.** jn. um etwas bitten II **ask sb. to do sth.** jn. darum bitten, etwas zu tun V 2 (34) • **ask sb. the way** jn. nach dem Weg fragen II
asleep [ə'sliːp]**: be asleep** schlafen I
Assembly [ə'sembli] Versammlung *(morgendliche Schulversammlung, oft mit Andacht)* III
assess [ə'ses] einschätzen, beurteilen V 2 (40/165)
assessment [ə'sesmənt] Einschätzung, Beurteilung V 2 (40)
assistant [ə'sɪstənt] Assistent/in V 2 (40)
°**association** [əˌsəʊsi'eɪʃn] Verband, Vereinigung
at [ət, æt]**: at 7 Hamilton Street** in der Hamiltonstraße 7 I • **at 8.45** um 8.45 I • **at 16** mit 16, im Alter von 16 Jahren II • **at any time** jederzeit V 2 (38) • **at break** in der Pause *(zwischen Schulstunden)* II **at first** zuerst, am Anfang IV • **at home** daheim, zu Hause I • **at last** endlich, schließlich I • **at least** zumindest, wenigstens I **at night** nachts, in der Nacht I **at school** in der Schule I • **at someone's place** bei jemandem zu Hause V 1 (6) • **at that table** an dem Tisch (dort) / an den Tisch (dort) I • **at the back (of the room)** hinten, im hinteren Teil (des Zimmers) II • **at the bottom (of)** unten, am unteren Ende (von) II **at the chemist's/hairdresser's** beim Apotheker/Friseur III • **at the end (of)** am Ende (von) I • **at the moment** im Moment, gerade II • **at the Shaws' house** im Haus der Shaws / bei den Shaws zu Hause I • **at the station** am Bahnhof I • **at the top (of)** oben, am oberen Ende, an der Spitze (von) I • **at the weekend** am Wochenende I • **at work** bei der Arbeit / am Arbeitsplatz I
ate [et, eɪt] *siehe* **eat**
athletics [æθ'letɪks] Leichtathletik III
Atlantic: the Atlantic (Ocean) [ətˌlæntɪk_'əʊʃn] der Atlantische Ozean, der Atlantik IV
atmosphere ['ætməsfɪə] Atmosphäre III
attach (to) [ə'tætʃ] anhängen, anheften (an) *(an Brief, Mail)* V 1 (12)
attack [ə'tæk] angreifen III
attack [ə'tæk] Angriff III
attention [ə'tenʃn] Aufmerksamkeit V 4 (90/176) • **draw sb.'s attention to sth.** jn. auf etwas aufmerksam machen; jemandes Aufmerksamkeit auf etwas lenken V 4 (90)
attitude (to, towards) ['ætɪtjuːd] Haltung (gegenüber), Einstellung (zu) IV
attract [ə'trækt] anziehen, anlocken V 4 (88)
attraction [ə'trækʃn] Attraktion, Anziehungspunkt II
audience ['ɔːdiəns] Publikum; Zuschauer/innen, Zuhörer/innen II
August ['ɔːgəst] August I
aunt [ɑːnt] Tante I • **auntie** ['ɑːnti] Tante II
Aussie ['ɒzi] *(infml)* Australier/in; australisch V 1 (13)
auto ['ɔːtəʊ] *(AE)* Auto, PKW IV
°**auto-rickshaw** ['ɔːtəʊˌrɪkʃɔː] Autorikscha *(motorisiertes, dreirädriges Fahrzeug zur preiswerten Personenbeförderung)*
autumn ['ɔːtəm] Herbst I
available [ə'veɪləbl] verfügbar, erreichbar; vorrätig V 2 (38)
avenue ['ævənjuː] Allee IV
average ['ævərɪdʒ] Durchschnitt; durchschnittlich IV
away [ə'weɪ] weg, fort I
awesome ['ɔːsəm] *(AE, infml)* klasse, großartig IV
awful ['ɔːfl] furchtbar, schrecklich II

B

baby ['beɪbi] Baby I • **have a baby** ein Baby/Kind bekommen II
back [bæk]
1. Rücken; Rückseite V 1 (11)
2. at the back (of) hinten, im hinteren Teil (von) II
back (to) [bæk] zurück (nach) I
back door [ˌbæk 'dɔː] Hintertür II
background ['bækgraʊnd] Hintergrund II • **background file** *etwa:* Hintergrundinformation(en) II
°**back inside cover** [ˌbæk_ˌɪnsaɪd 'kʌvə] hintere Umschlaginnenseite
bacon ['beɪkən] Schinkenspeck III
bad [bæd] schlecht, schlimm I **be bad at sth.** schlecht in etwas sein; etwas schlecht können III **bad timing** schlechtes Timing III
badly ['bædli]**: do badly** schlecht abschneiden *(in Prüfung)* V 3 (55/169)
badminton ['bædmɪntən] Badminton, Federball I • **badminton racket** ['rækɪt] Badmintonschläger III
bag [bæg] Tasche, Beutel, Tüte I
bagel ['beɪgl] Bagel *(ringförmiges Brötchen)* IV
baggy ['bægi] weit (geschnitten) *(Hose)* V 4 (80)
bagpipes *(pl)* ['bægpaɪps] Dudelsack III
ball [bɔːl]
1. Ball I
2. Ball *(Tanzveranstaltung)* IV
ballet ['bæleɪ] Ballett V 1 (11)
ban (-nn-) [bæn] sperren; ein (Aufenthalts-)Verbot erteilen

V 3 (54) • **ban sb. from sth.** jn. von etwas ausschließen IV
banana [bəˈnɑːnə] Banane I
band [bænd] Band, (Musik-)Gruppe I
bank [bæŋk] Bank, Sparkasse I
bank clerk [ˈbæŋk klɑːk] Bankangestellte(r) V 2 (35)
bank robber [ˈbæŋk ˌrɒbə] Bankräuber/in I
bar [bɑː] Bar II
barbecue [ˈbɑːbɪkjuː] Grillfest, Grillparty V 1 (6)
bar chart [ˈbɑː tʃɑːt] Balkendiagramm V 1 (10)
°**barman**, *pl* **barmen** [ˈbɑːmən] Barkeeper
baseball [ˈbeɪsbɔːl] Baseball I
baseball cap [ˈbeɪsbɔːl kæp] Baseballmütze II
basic [ˈbeɪsɪk] grundlegend; Grund-, Haupt- V 1 (19)
basket [ˈbɑːskɪt] Korb I • **a basket of apples** ein Korb Äpfel I
basketball [ˈbɑːskɪtbɔːl] Basketball I
bat [bæt]: **table tennis bat** Tischtennisschläger III
bath [bɑːθ] Bad, Badewanne II
have a bath baden, ein Bad nehmen II
bathroom [ˈbɑːθruːm] Badezimmer I
bay [beɪ] Bucht III
be [biː], **was/were, been** sein I
be a farmer, a teacher, ... Bauer, Lehrer/in, ... werden IV
beach [biːtʃ] Strand II • **on the beach** am Strand II
bean [biːn] Bohne IV
bear [beə] Bär II
beard [bɪəd] Bart II
beat [biːt], **beat, beaten** schlagen; besiegen III
beaten [ˈbiːtn] *siehe* **beat**
beautiful [ˈbjuːtɪfl] schön I
beauty [ˈbjuːti] Schönheit III
became [bɪˈkeɪm] *siehe* **become**
because [bɪˈkɒz] weil I
► S.157 because – because of
because of [bɪˈkɒz_əv] wegen V 1 (9)
► S.157 because – because of
become [bɪˈkʌm], **became, become** werden II
bed [bed] Bett I • **Bed and Breakfast (B&B)** [ˌbed_ən ˈbrekfəst] Frühstückspension I • **go to bed** ins Bett gehen I
bedroom [ˈbedruːm] Schlafzimmer I
bedspread [ˈbedspred] Tagesdecke III
beef [biːf] Rindfleisch III
been [biːn] *siehe* **be**
before [bɪˈfɔː] vor *(zeitlich)* I
before [bɪˈfɔː] bevor II
before [bɪˈfɔː] (vorher) schon mal II
the night/week/... before in der Nacht/Woche/... zuvor III
began [bɪˈgæn] *siehe* **begin**
begin (-nn-) [bɪˈgɪn], **began, begun** beginnen, anfangen (mit) III
beginning [bɪˈgɪnɪŋ] Beginn, Anfang; Einleitung II
begun [bɪˈgʌn] *siehe* **begin**
behave [bɪˈheɪv] sich verhalten, sich benehmen V 3 (54/168) • **Behave yourself.** Benimm dich (anständig)! V 3 (54/168)
behaviour [bɪˈheɪvjə] Verhalten, Benehmen V 3 (54)
behind [bɪˈhaɪnd] hinter II • **stay behind** zurückbleiben, daheimbleiben IV
belief [bɪˈliːf] Glaube, Überzeugung V 1 (16)
believable [bɪˈliːvəbl] glaubhaft IV
believe (in) [bɪˈliːv] glauben (an) IV
bell [bel] Klingel, Glocke I
belong (to) [bɪˈlɒŋ] gehören (zu) II
below [bɪˈləʊ]
1. unten III
2. unter, unterhalb (von) III
bench [bentʃ] (Sitz-)Bank IV
besides [bɪˈsaɪdz] außerdem IV
best [best] am besten II • **the best ...** der/die/das beste ...; die besten I • **like sth. best** etwas am liebsten mögen III • **What was the best thing about ...?** Was war das Beste an ...? II • **Best wishes** *etwa:* Alles Gute / Mit besten Grüßen *(als Briefschluss)* IV
bet (-tt-) [bet], **bet, bet** wetten IV
You bet! *(infml)* Aber klar! / Und ob! IV
better [ˈbetə] besser I • **like sth. better** etwas lieber mögen II
between [bɪˈtwiːn] zwischen II
Bible [ˈbaɪbl]: **the Bible** die Bibel V 3 (58)
big [bɪg] groß I
big wheel [ˌbɪg ˈwiːl] Riesenrad III
bike [baɪk] Fahrrad I • **ride a bike** Rad fahren I
bilingual [ˌbaɪˈlɪŋgwəl] zweisprachig IV
bill [bɪl] *(AE)* (Geld-)Schein, Banknote V 3 (58)
bin [bɪn] Mülltonne II
biography [baɪˈɒgrəfi] Biografie III
biology [baɪˈɒlədʒi] Biologie I
bird [bɜːd] Vogel I
birth [bɜːθ] Geburt V 2 (38) • **date of birth** Geburtsdatum V 2 (38)
place of birth Geburtsort V 2 (38/163)
birthday [ˈbɜːθdeɪ] Geburtstag I
for his birthday zu seinem Geburtstag III • **Happy birthday.** Herzlichen Glückwunsch zum Geburtstag. I • **My birthday is in May.** Ich habe im Mai Geburtstag. I • **My birthday is on 13th June.** Ich habe am 13. Juni Geburtstag. I
When's your birthday? Wann hast du Geburtstag? I
biscuit [ˈbɪskɪt] Keks, Plätzchen I
bit [bɪt]: **a bit** ein bisschen, etwas II
black [blæk] schwarz I
black bear [ˈblæk beə] Schwarzbär III
blame sb. (for) [bleɪm] jn. die Schuld geben (an); jn. Vorwürfe machen (wegen) III
blanket [ˈblæŋkɪt] Decke *(zum Zudecken)* III
bleep [bliːp] piepsen II
bleep [bliːp] Piepton II
blew [bluː] *siehe* **blow**
blind [blaɪnd] blind V 4 (80)
block [blɒk] (Häuser-, Wohn-)Block IV
block [blɒk] blockieren, (ver)sperren IV
blog [blɒg] *digitales Tagebuch* IV
blond *(bei Frauen oft:* **blonde***)* [blɒnd] blond, hell IV; V 1 (17/160)
blood [blʌd] Blut III
bloody [ˈblʌdi] blutig V 4 (89)
blouse [blaʊz] Bluse II
blow [bləʊ], **blew, blown** wehen, blasen III
blown [bləʊn] *siehe* **blow**
blue [bluː] blau I
board [bɔːd]
1. (Wand-)Tafel I • **on the board** an der/die Tafel I
2. **on board** an Bord V 4 (76)
boat [bəʊt] Boot, Schiff I
body [ˈbɒdi] Körper I
bodyguard [ˈbɒdigɑːd] Leibwächter/in, Leibwache IV
°**Boer** [bɔː] Bure/Burin *(Südafrikaner/in niederländischer Herkunft)*
bold print [ˌbəʊld ˈprɪnt] Fettdruck III
book [bʊk] Buch I
book [bʊk] buchen, reservieren V 4 (89)
booklet [ˈbʊklət] Broschüre II
bookshelf [ˈbʊkʃelf], *pl* **bookshelves** [ˈ-ʃelvz] Bücherregal V 3 (62)
boot [buːt] Stiefel I; V 3 (55)

boot camp ['bu:t kæmp] Erziehungslager *(für junge Straftäter/-täterinnen)* V 3 (55)
border ['bɔ:də] Grenze IV
bored [bɔ:d]: **be/feel bored** gelangweilt sein, sich langweilen IV
get bored sich langweilen IV
boring ['bɔ:rɪŋ] langweilig I
born [bɔ:n]: **be born** geboren sein/werden II
borough ['bʌrə, *AE:* 'bɜ:rəʊ] (Stadt-)Bezirk IV
borrow sth. ['bɒrəʊ] etwas (aus)leihen, sich etwas borgen V 2 (44)
► S.166 (to) lend – (to) borrow
boss [bɒs] Chef/in, Boss III
both [bəʊθ] beide I
bottle ['bɒtl] Flasche I • **a bottle of milk** eine Flasche Milch I
bottom ['bɒtəm] unteres Ende II
at the bottom (of) unten, am unteren Ende (von) II
bought [bɔ:t] *siehe* **buy**
boulevard ['bu:ləvɑ:d] Boulevard IV
bowl [bəʊl] Schüssel I • **a bowl of cornflakes** eine Schale Cornflakes I
box [bɒks] Kasten, Kästchen, Kiste I
boy [bɔɪ] Junge I
boyfriend ['bɔɪfrend] (fester) Freund IV
°**bracket** ['brækɪt] Klammer *(in Texten)*
brainstorm ['breɪnstɔ:m] brainstormen *(so viele Ideen wie möglich sammeln)* III
brave [breɪv] mutig IV
bread *(no pl)* [bred] Brot I
break [breɪk] Pause I • **at break** in der Pause *(zwischen Schulstunden)* II • **take a break** eine Pause machen IV
break [breɪk], **broke, broken** (zer-)brechen; kaputt gehen IV
breakable ['breɪkəbl] zerbrechlich IV
breakfast ['brekfəst] Frühstück I
have breakfast frühstücken I
bridge [brɪdʒ] Brücke I
bridle path ['braɪdl pɑ:θ] Reitweg III
bright [braɪt] hell, leuchtend II
bring [brɪŋ], **brought, brought** (mit-, her)bringen I
British ['brɪtɪʃ] britisch; Brite, Britin II
°**brochure** ['brəʊʃə] Prospekt, Broschüre
broke [brəʊk] *siehe* **break**
broken ['brəʊkən] gebrochen; zerbrochen, kaputt II *siehe* **break**

brother ['brʌðə] Bruder I
brought [brɔ:t] *siehe* **bring**
brown [braʊn] braun I
budgie ['bʌdʒi] Wellensittich I
build [bɪld], **built, built** bauen II
builder ['bɪldə] Bauarbeiter/in V 2 (35)
building ['bɪldɪŋ] Gebäude II
built [bɪlt] *siehe* **build**
bulletin board ['bʊlətɪn bɔ:d] *(AE)* Anschlagtafel, „schwarzes Brett" IV
bully ['bʊli] einschüchtern, tyrannisieren II
bully ['bʊli] (Schul-)Tyrann III
bunk (bed) [bʌŋk] Etagenbett, Koje II
burn [bɜ:n] brennen; verbrennen IV
burn sth. down etwas niederbrennen IV
bus [bʌs] Bus I
bush [bʊʃ] Busch, Strauch V 1 (6)
the bush der Busch *(unkultiviertes, „wildes" Land in Australien, Afrika)* V 1 (6)
business ['bɪznəs] Unternehmen; Geschäft(e) IV • **do business with** Handel treiben mit; Geschäfte machen mit V 1 (8) • **Mind your own business.** Das geht dich nichts an! / Kümmere dich um deine eigenen Angelegenheiten! II
start a business ein Unternehmen gründen V 2 (44)
businesswoman/-man ['bɪznəswʊmən, -mæn] Geschäftsfrau/Geschäftsmann IV
bus pass ['bʌs pɑ:s] Monatskarte *(für den Bus)* III
bus stop ['bʌs stɒp] Bushaltestelle III
busy ['bɪzi] belebt, verkehrsreich; hektisch III; beschäftigt IV
but [bət, bʌt] aber I
butter ['bʌtə] Butter IV
button ['bʌtn] Knopf III
buy [baɪ], **bought, bought** kaufen I
°**buzz** [bʌz] *hier:* den Summer/die Glocke betätigen
by [baɪ]
1. von I
2. an; (nahe) bei II
by car/bike/... mit dem Auto/Rad/... II • **by ten o'clock** bis (spätestens) zehn Uhr III • **by two degrees / ten per cent** um zwei Grad / zehn Prozent V 1 (9)
by the way [ˌbaɪ ðə 'weɪ] übrigens; nebenbei (bemerkt) III
go by vergehen, vorübergehen *(Zeit)* V 3 (50)
Bye. [baɪ] Tschüs! I

C

cab [kæb] Taxi IV
cabin ['kæbɪn] Hütte III
cable ['keɪbl] Kabel *(auch kurz für* Kabelfernsehen) IV
café ['kæfeɪ] *(kleines)* Restaurant, Imbissstube, Café I
cage [keɪdʒ] Käfig I
cake [keɪk] Kuchen, Torte I
calendar ['kælɪndə] Kalender I
call [kɔ:l] rufen; anrufen; nennen I
call sb. names jn. mit Schimpfwörtern hänseln, jm. Schimpfwörter nachrufen III
call [kɔ:l] Anruf, Telefongespräch I
make a call ein Telefongespräch führen II
called [kɔ:ld]: **be called** heißen, genannt werden III
calm [kɑ:m] ruhig, still V 2 (33)
calm down [ˌkɑ:m 'daʊn] sich beruhigen II
calorie ['kæləri] Kalorie IV
came [keɪm] *siehe* **come**
camel ['kæml] Kamel II
camera ['kæmərə] Kamera, Fotoapparat I
camp [kæmp] Camp, (Ferien-)Lager IV
camp [kæmp] zelten III
camping gear ['kæmpɪŋ gɪə] Campingausrüstung, Campingsachen IV
can [kən, kæn]
1. können I
2. dürfen I
Can I help you? Kann ich Ihnen helfen? / Was kann ich für Sie tun? *(im Geschäft)* I
can [kæn] Dose, Büchse V 3 (58/171)
canal [kə'næl] Kanal III
cancer ['kænsə] Krebs *(Krankheit)* V 1 (9)
candidate ['kændɪdət] Kandidat/in, Bewerber/in V 2 (40)
candle ['kændl] Kerze V 3 (49)
canned [kænd] Dosen-; ... in Dosen V 3 (58)
canoe [kə'nu:] paddeln, Kanu fahren III
canoe [kə'nu:] Kanu, Paddelboot III
canyon ['kænjən] Cañon IV
cap [kæp] Mütze, Kappe II
capital ['kæpɪtl] Hauptstadt III
capital letter [ˌkæpɪtl 'letə] Großbuchstabe III
captain ['kæptɪn] Kapitän/in V 1 (8)
caption ['kæpʃn] Bildunterschrift III
car [kɑ:] Auto I • **car park** Parkplatz III

caravan ['kærəvæn] Wohnwagen II
card [kɑːd] (Spiel-, Post-)Karte I
cardboard ['kɑːdbɔːd] Pappe V 4 (82)
care about sth. [keə] etwas wichtig nehmen IV • **I don't care.** Es/Das ist mir egal. IV • **I didn't care.** Es war mir egal. IV
career [kə'rɪə] Karriere III
careful ['keəfl]
1. vorsichtig II
2. sorgfältig II
caretaker ['keəteɪkə] Hausmeister/Hausmeisterin II
car park ['kɑː pɑːk] Parkplatz III
carriage ['kærɪdʒ] Eisenbahnwagen, Waggon V 4 (76)
carrot ['kærət] Möhre, Karotte I
carry ['kæri] tragen V 1 (6)
cartoon [kɑː'tuːn] Cartoon (Zeichentrickfilm; Bilderwitz) II
case [keɪs] Fall II
cash [kæʃ] Bargeld V 3 (53) • **pay cash** bar bezahlen V 3 (53/168)
castle ['kɑːsl] Burg, Schloss II
cat [kæt] Katze I
catch [kætʃ]**, caught, caught** fangen; erwischen II
cathedral [kə'θiːdrəl] Kathedrale, Dom III
caught [kɔːt] *siehe* **catch**
cause [kɔːz] verursachen V 3 (55)
°**cave** [keɪv] Höhle
CD [ˌsiː'diː] CD I • **CD player** CD-Spieler I
ceilidh ['keɪli] *Musik- und Tanzveranstaltung, vor allem in Schottland und Irland* III
celebrate ['selɪbreɪt] feiern V 3 (60)
cell [sel] Zelle V 4 (80)
cellphone ['selfəʊn] *(AE)* Handy, Mobiltelefon III
Celsius (C) ['selsiəs] Celsius III
cent (c) [sent] Cent I
centimetre (cm) ['sentɪmiːtə] Zentimeter III
central ['sentrəl] Zentral-, Mittel- III
centre ['sentə] Zentrum, Mitte I
century ['sentʃəri] Jahrhundert II
certificate [sə'tɪfɪkət] Bescheinigung, Zertifikat V 2 (38)
°**chain** [tʃeɪn] Kette
chair [tʃeə] Stuhl I
champion ['tʃæmpiən] Meister/in, Champion I
championship ['tʃæmpiənʃɪp] Meisterschaft III
chance [tʃɑːns] Chance, Möglichkeit, Aussicht II
change [tʃeɪndʒ]
1. (sich) ändern; (sich) verändern IV
2. wechseln IV
3. umsteigen III
4. sich umziehen IV
change channels umschalten *(Fernsehen)* IV
change [tʃeɪndʒ]
1. (Ver-)Änderung; Wechsel IV
2. Wechselgeld I; Kleingeld IV
channel ['tʃænl] Kanal, Sender II
character ['kærəktə]
1. Charakter, Persönlichkeit IV
2. Person, Figur *(in Roman, Film)* IV
charity ['tʃærəti] Wohlfahrtsorganisation II
chart [tʃɑːt] Tabelle, Diagramm, Schaubild V 1 (10)
°**charts** *(pl)* [tʃɑːts] Hitliste, Charts
chat (-tt-) [tʃæt] chatten, plaudern II
chat [tʃæt] Chat, Unterhaltung II
chat room ['tʃæt ruːm] Chatroom III
cheap [tʃiːp] billig, preiswert II
check [tʃek] (über)prüfen, kontrollieren I
check in [ˌtʃek‿'ɪn] einchecken *(Hotel, Flughafen)* V 4 (89)
check out [ˌtʃek‿'aʊt] auschecken *(aus Hotel)* V 4 (89)
checkpoint ['tʃekpɔɪnt] Kontrollpunkt I; Grenzübergang V 4 (86)
cheek [tʃiːk] Wange IV
cheeky ['tʃiːki] frech, dreist V 2 (40)
cheer [tʃɪə] jubeln, Beifall klatschen II
cheerleader ['tʃɪəliːdə] Cheerleader *(Stimmungsanheizer/in bei Sportereignissen)* IV
cheese [tʃiːz] Käse I
chef [ʃef] Koch, Köchin *(Berufsbezeichnung)* V 2 (32)
chemist ['kemɪst] Drogerie, Apotheke II • **at the chemist's** beim Apotheker III
chemistry ['kemɪstri] Chemie V 3 (49)
cheque (for) [tʃek] Scheck (über) V 2 (44)
chicken ['tʃɪkɪn] Huhn; (Brat-)Hähnchen I
child [tʃaɪld]**,** ***pl*** **children** ['tʃɪldrən] Kind I
childcare ['tʃaɪldkeə] Kinderbetreuung V 2 (33)
childcare assistant ['tʃaɪldkeər‿əˌsɪstənt] Kinderpfleger/in; Erzieher/in V 2 (33)
childproof ['tʃaɪldpruːf] kindersicher *(Flasche, Verschluss)* V 1 (17/161)
chips *(pl)* [tʃɪps]
1. *(BE)* Pommes frites I
2. *(AE)* (Kartoffel-)Chips IV
chocolate ['tʃɒklət] Schokolade I
°**choice** [tʃɔɪs] (Aus-)Wahl, Entscheidung
choir ['kwaɪə] Chor I
choose [tʃuːz]**, chose, chosen** (sich) aussuchen, (aus)wählen I
chore [tʃɔː] (Haus-)Arbeit; *(lästige)* Pflicht V 3 (49)
chorus ['kɔːrəs] Refrain III
chose [tʃəʊz] *siehe* **choose**
chosen ['tʃəʊzn] *siehe* **choose**
Christian ['krɪstʃən] Christ/in V 4 (76)
church [tʃɜːtʃ] Kirche I
cigarette [ˌsɪgə'ret] Zigarette IV
cinema ['sɪnəmə] Kino II • **go to the cinema** ins Kino gehen II
circle ['sɜːkl] Kreis IV
circus ['sɜːkəs]
1. Zirkus III
2. (runder) Platz *(in der Stadt)* III
city ['sɪti] Stadt, Großstadt I
city centre [ˌsɪti 'sentə] Stadtzentrum, Innenstadt I
civil ['sɪvl]**: civil rights** *(pl)* Bürgerrechte IV • **civil war** Bürgerkrieg IV
°**claim an island (for sb.)** [kleɪm] eine Insel in Besitz nehmen (für jn.)
clap (-pp-) [klæp] (Beifall) klatschen IV
clarification [ˌklærəfɪ'keɪʃn] Klarstellung, Klärung V 3 (56)
class [klɑːs]
1. (Schul-)Klasse I
2. Unterricht; Kurs IV
class teacher Klassenlehrer/in I
classical ['klæsɪkl] klassisch III
classmate ['klɑːsmeɪt] Klassenkamerad/in, Mitschüler/in I
classroom ['klɑːsruːm] Klassenzimmer I
°**clause** [klɔːz] (Teil-, Glied-)Satz
clean [kliːn] sauber II
clean [kliːn] sauber machen, putzen I • **I clean my teeth.** Ich putze mir die Zähne. I
cleaner ['kliːnə] Putzfrau, -mann II
°**clean-up** ['kliːn‿ʌp] Säuberung
clear [klɪə] klar, deutlich I
clever ['klevə] klug, schlau I
cleverness ['klevənəs] Klugheit, Schlauheit IV
click on sth. [klɪk] etwas anklicken II
°**climax** ['klaɪmæks] Höhepunkt
climb [klaɪm] klettern; hinaufklettern (auf) I • **Climb a tree.** Klettere auf einen Baum. I
clinic ['klɪnɪk] Klinik II
clock [klɒk] (Wand-, Stand-, Turm-)Uhr I
clone [kləʊn] Klon III
close [kləʊs]
1. eng V 1 (8)

2. close (to) nahe (bei, an) III
That was close. Das war knapp. II
close [kləʊz] schließen, zumachen I
closed [kləʊzd] geschlossen II
°**closely** ['kləʊsli]: **Look closely at ...** Sieh dir ... genau an.
°**closing phrase** ['kləʊzɪŋ freɪz] Schlusswort(e) *(am Briefende)*
clothes *(pl)* [kləʊðz, kləʊz] Kleider, Kleidung(sstücke) II
cloud [klaʊd] Wolke II
cloudless ['klaʊdləs] wolkenlos IV
cloudy ['klaʊdi] bewölkt II
club [klʌb] Klub; Verein I
coach [kəʊtʃ] Trainer/in III
coast [kəʊst] Küste III
coffee ['kɒfi] Kaffee IV • **coffee to go** Kaffee zum Mitnehmen IV
coin [kɔɪn] Münze V 3 (58)
cola ['kəʊlə] Cola I
cold [kəʊld] kalt I • **be cold** frieren I
cold [kəʊld]
1. Kälte IV
2. Erkältung II
have a cold erkältet sein, eine Erkältung haben II
°**collage** ['kɒlɑːʒ] Collage
collapse [kə'læps] zusammenbrechen; einstürzen IV
collect [kə'lekt] sammeln I
collection [kə'lekʃn] Sammlung IV
collector [kə'lektə] Sammler/in II
college ['kɒlɪdʒ] Hochschule, Fachhochschule IV
collocation [ˌkɒlə'keɪʃn] Kollokation *(Wörter, die oft zusammen vorkommen)* IV
colony ['kɒləni] Kolonie V 1 (8)
colour ['kʌlə] Farbe I • **What colour is ...?** Welche Farbe hat ...? I
colour ['kʌlə] kolorieren, färben; bunt an-, ausmalen III
colour-blind ['kʌləblaɪnd] farbenblind V 4 (80)
colourful ['kʌləfl] farbenfroh, farbenprächtig, farbig V 4 (78)
column ['kɒləm] Säule III
°**combine** [kəm'baɪn] kombinieren, verbinden
come [kʌm], **came, come** kommen I • °**come down** fallen *(Mauer; Preise)* • **come home** nach Hause kommen I • **come in** hereinkommen I • **Come on. 1.** Na los, komm. II; **2.** Ach komm! / Na hör mal! II • **come out** rauskommen; veröffentlicht werden *(Film, DVD)* IV
comedian [kə'miːdiən] Komiker/in IV
comedy ['kɒmədi] Komödie; Comedy IV
comfortable ['kʌmftəbl] bequem IV • **Make yourself comfortable.** Machen Sie es sich bequem. / Mach es dir bequem. IV
comic ['kɒmɪk] Comic-Heft I
command [kə'mɑːnd] Befehl, Aufforderung V 2 (42)
comment ['kɒment] Kommentar, Bemerkung IV
comment (on sth.) ['kɒment] sich (zu etwas) äußern; einen Kommentar abgeben (zu etwas) V 4 (90)
commit a crime (-tt-) [kə'mɪt] ein Verbrechen / eine Straftat verüben, begehen V 3 (55)
common ['kɒmən] weit verbreitet, häufig V 1 (6)
Commonwealth ['kɒmənwelθ]: **the Commonwealth** *Gemeinschaft der Länder des ehemaligen Britischen Weltreichs* III
community [kə'mjuːnəti]: **community centre** Gemeinschaftszentrum, Gemeindezentrum III • **community hall** Gemeinschaftshalle, -saal, Gemeindehalle, -saal III • **community service** gemeinnützige Arbeit V 3 (59)
commuter [kə'mjuːtə] Pendler/in V 4 (79)
company ['kʌmpəni] Firma, Gesellschaft III
compare [kəm'peə] vergleichen IV
°**compared to** [kəm'peəd] verglichen mit
comparison [kəm'pærɪsn] Steigerung; Vergleich II • °**make comparisons** Vergleiche anstellen, vergleichen
compete [kəm'piːt] konkurrieren, mithalten IV
competition [ˌkɒmpə'tɪʃn] Wettbewerb, Wettkampf IV
°**complete** [kəm'pliːt] vollständig, komplett
°**complete** [kəm'pliːt] vervollständigen, ergänzen
°**compromise** ['kɒmprəmaɪz] Kompromiss
computer [kəm'pjuːtə] Computer I
°**computer geek** [giːk] *(bes. AE, infml)* Computerfreak
concert ['kɒnsət] Konzert III
conclusion [kən'kluːʒn] Schluss(folgerung) IV • **draw conclusions** Schlüsse ziehen, schlussfolgern IV
confident ['kɒnfɪdənt]
1. selbstbewusst, (selbst)sicher V 2 (35)
2. zuversichtlich V 2 (45)
°**confused** [kən'fjuːzd] verwirrt
connect (to/with) [kə'nekt] verbinden (mit) V 4 (86)
contact sb. ['kɒntækt] sich mit jm. in Verbindung setzen; mit jm. Kontakt aufnehmen III
contact ['kɒntækt] Kontakt V 2 (38)
contacts *(pl) Liste von Bekannten/ Kontakten (im Handy, im Mailprogramm)* V 3 (52)
contain [kən'teɪn] enthalten IV
content ['kɒntent] Gehalt, Inhalt IV
contestant [kən'testənt] Kandidat/ Kandidatin *(in Fernsehshow)*, (Wettkampf-)Teilnehmer/in IV
context ['kɒntekst] Kontext, Zusammenhang IV
continent ['kɒntɪnənt] Kontinent, Erdteil V 1 (8)
continue [kən'tɪnjuː] fortsetzen; weitermachen (mit) V 1 (14)
conversation [ˌkɒnvə'seɪʃn] Gespräch, Unterhaltung V 1 (14)
convict ['kɒnvɪkt] Sträfling, Strafgefangene(r) V 1 (8)
cook [kʊk] kochen, zubereiten II
cook [kʊk] Koch/Köchin III
cooker ['kʊkə] Herd I
cookie ['kʊki] *(AE)* Keks IV
cool [kuːl]
1. kühl II
2. cool I
copy ['kɒpi] kopieren II
copy ['kɒpi]
1. Kopie II
2. Exemplar III
°**coral** ['kɒrəl] Koralle
corner ['kɔːnə] Ecke I • **on the corner of Sand Street and London Road** Sand Street, Ecke London Road II
cornflakes ['kɔːnfleɪks] Cornflakes I
correct [kə'rekt] berichtigen, korrigieren II • °**correcting circle** *etwa:* Korrekturkreis
correct [kə'rekt] korrekt, richtig III
°**correction** [kə'rekʃn] Korrektur, Berichtigung
cost [kɒst], **cost, cost** kosten IV
costume ['kɒstjuːm] (Bühnen-)Kostüm V 4 (78)
cotton ['kɒtn] Baumwolle IV
could [kəd, kʊd]: **he could ...**
1. er konnte ... II
2. er könnte ... III
count [kaʊnt] zählen II
counter ['kaʊntə]
1. Spielstein II
2. Theke, Ladentisch IV
country ['kʌntri] Land *(auch als Gegensatz zur Stadt)* II • **in the country** auf dem Land II

couple ['kʌpl] Paar, Pärchen V 4 (80)
a couple of ein paar, einige V 4 (80/173) • **married couple** Ehepaar V 4 (80/173)
course [kɔːs] Kurs, Lehrgang III
course: of course [əv 'kɔːs] natürlich, selbstverständlich I
court [kɔːt]
1. Platz, Court *(für Squash, Badminton)* III
2. Gericht(shof) IV
cousin ['kʌzn] Cousin, Cousine I
cover ['kʌvə]
1. (CD-)Hülle I
°2. **inside cover** Umschlaginnenseite
cow [kaʊ] Kuh II
crash sth. [kræʃ] einen Unfall mit etwas haben IV
crazy ['kreɪzi] verrückt III
cream [kriːm] Sahne; Creme IV
cream cheese [ˌkriːm 'tʃiːz] Frischkäse IV
create [kri'eɪt] schaffen, erschaffen V 3 (64)
credit card ['kredɪt kɑːd] Kreditkarte V 3 (53) • **pay by credit card** mit Kreditkarte bezahlen V 3 (53/168)
cricket ['krɪkɪt] Kricket *(Schlagballspiel)* V 1 (13)
crime [kraɪm] Kriminalität; Verbrechen IV
crime series ['kraɪm ˌsɪəriːz] Krimiserie IV
crisps *(pl)* [krɪsps] Kartoffelchips I
crocodile ['krɒkədaɪl] Krokodil II
cross [krɒs] überqueren; (sich) kreuzen II
°**cross** [krɒs] Kreuz, Kreuzchen
crossing ['krɒsɪŋ] (Grenz-)Übergang; (Fußgänger-)Überweg V 4 (86)
crowd [kraʊd] (Menschen-)Menge IV
crowded ['kraʊdɪd] überfüllt, voll(gestopft) V 4 (75) • °**crowded together** zusammengedrängt
cruel [kruːəl] grausam IV
crush [krʌʃ]: **have a crush on sb.** in jn. verknallt sein III
cry [kraɪ]
1. weinen IV
2. schreien, rufen IV
cry out aufschreien IV
°**crystal clear** [ˌkrɪstl 'klɪə] kristallklar
cultural ['kʌltʃərəl] kulturell V 4 (80)
culture ['kʌltʃə] Kultur IV
cup [kʌp]
1. Tasse III
2. Pokal III
a cup of tea eine Tasse Tee III
cupboard ['kʌbəd] (Küchen-)Schrank I
curriculum vitae [kəˌrɪkjələm 'viːtaɪ] **(CV)** Lebenslauf V 2 (38)
curtain ['kɜːtn] Vorhang III
customer ['kʌstəmə] Kunde, Kundin II
customer adviser [əd'vaɪzə] Kundenbetreuer/in, -berater/in V 2 (33)
cut (-tt-) [kʌt], **cut, cut** schneiden III • **cut sth. off** etwas abschneiden, abtrennen III • **cut the grass** Rasen mähen IV
CV [siː 'viː] **(curriculum vitae** [kəˌrɪkjələm 'viːtaɪ]**)** Lebenslauf V 2 (38)
cycle ['saɪkl] (mit dem) Rad fahren II • **cycle path** Radweg II

D

dad [dæd] Papa, Vati; Vater I
daily ['deɪli] täglich, Tages- IV
dance [dɑːns] tanzen I
dance [dɑːns] Tanz I
dance floor ['dɑːns flɔː] Tanzfläche, Tanzboden IV
dancer ['dɑːnsə] Tänzer/in II
dancing ['dɑːnsɪŋ] Tanzen I
dancing lessons Tanzstunden, Tanzunterricht I
danger ['deɪndʒə] Gefahr I
dangerous ['deɪndʒərəs] gefährlich II
dark [dɑːk]
1. dunkel I
2. dunkelhaarig V 1 (17/160)
date [deɪt]
1. Datum I
2. Date, Verabredung III
date of birth Geburtsdatum V 2 (38) • **to date** bis heute V 2 (37)
date sb. [deɪt] mit jm. (aus)gehen; sich (regelmäßig) mit jm. treffen III
daughter ['dɔːtə] Tochter I
day [deɪ] Tag I • °**a day out** ein Tagesausflug • **one day** eines Tages I • **days of the week** Wochentage I • **the day she was stolen** der Tag, an dem sie gestohlen wurde V 1 (17) • **that day** an jenem Tag III
dead [ded] tot I
deal [diːl]: **It's a deal!** Abgemacht! III • **make a deal** ein Abkommen / eine Abmachung treffen III
°**deal drugs** [diːl], **dealt, dealt** mit Drogen handeln
°**dealt** [delt] *siehe* **deal**
dear [dɪə] Schatz, Liebling I • **Oh dear!** Oje! II
dear [dɪə]: **Dear Jay ...** Lieber Jay, ... I • **Dear Sir/Madam** Sehr geehrte Damen und Herren *(Briefbeginn)* V 2 (38)
► S.164 Formal letters
death [deθ] Tod IV
debate [dɪ'beɪt] debattieren IV
debate [dɪ'beɪt] Debatte IV
December [dɪ'sembə] Dezember I
decide (on) [dɪ'saɪd] beschließen; sich entscheiden (für) III
decision [dɪ'sɪʒn] Entscheidung V 2 (33) • **make a decision** eine Entscheidung fällen V 2 (33/161)
deer, *pl* **deer** [dɪə] Reh, Hirsch II
definite ['defɪnət] fest, bestimmt; endgültig, eindeutig V 2 (45)
°**definition** [ˌdefɪ'nɪʃn] Definition
degree [dɪ'griː] Grad II
deli ['deli] Deli *(Lebensmittelgeschäft mit Fastfoodrestaurant)* IV
delicious [dɪ'lɪʃəs] köstlich, lecker II
democratic [ˌdemə'krætɪk] demokratisch V 4 (86)
dentist ['dentɪst] Zahnarzt, -ärztin IV
dentist's assistant [ˌdentɪsts‿ə'sɪstənt] Zahnarzthelfer/in V 2 (35)
department store [dɪ'pɑːtmənt stɔː] Kaufhaus II
departure (dep) [dɪ'pɑːtʃə] Abfahrt, Abflug; Abreise III
depressed [dɪ'prest] deprimiert, niedergeschlagen IV
depressing [dɪ'presɪŋ] trostlos, deprimierend IV
describe sth. (to sb.) [dɪ'skraɪb] (jm.) etwas beschreiben II
description [dɪ'skrɪpʃn] Beschreibung II
desert ['dezət] Wüste V 1 (9)
design [dɪ'zaɪn] entwerfen, gestalten II
design [dɪ'zaɪn] Muster, Entwurf; Design, Gestaltung V 2 (44)
designer [dɪ'zaɪnə] Designer/in V 4 (80)
desk [desk] Schreibtisch I
detail ['diːteɪl] Detail, Einzelheit III
detective [dɪ'tektɪv] Detektiv/in I
determined [dɪ'tɜːmɪnd]: **be determined** (fest) entschlossen sein V 2 (45)
°**diagram** ['daɪəgræm] Diagramm, Schaubild
dialogue ['daɪəlɒg] Dialog IV
diary ['daɪəri] Tagebuch; Terminkalender I • °**keep a diary** ein Tagebuch führen
dice, *pl* **dice** [daɪs] Würfel II

°**dictate** [dɪk'teɪt] diktieren
dictionary ['dɪkʃənri] Wörterbuch, *(alphabetisches)* Wörterverzeichnis I
did [dɪd] *siehe* **do** • **Did you know ...?** Wusstest du ...? I • **we didn't go** ['dɪdnt] wir gingen nicht / wir sind nicht gegangen I
°**didgeridoo** [ˌdɪdʒəri'du:] Didgeridoo
die (of) *(-ing form:* **dying***)* [daɪ] sterben (an) II
difference ['dɪfrəns] Unterschied III
different (from) ['dɪfrənt] verschieden, unterschiedlich; anders (als) I
difficult ['dɪfɪkəlt] schwierig, schwer I
dining room ['daɪnɪŋ ru:m] Esszimmer I
dinner ['dɪnə] Abendessen, Abendbrot I • **have dinner** Abendbrot essen I
dinosaur ['daɪnəsɔ:] Dinosaurier III
direct [də'rekt, daɪ'rekt]**: direct question** direkte Frage II • **direct speech** direkte Rede, wörtliche Rede IV
directions *(pl)* [də'rekʃnz] Wegbeschreibung(en) II
dirt [dɜ:t] Schmutz, Dreck V 1 (12)
dirt bike ['dɜ:t baɪk] Geländemotorrad V 1 (12)
dirty ['dɜ:ti] schmutzig II
disabled [dɪs'eɪbld] (körper)behindert III
disadvantage [ˌdɪsəd'vɑ:ntɪdʒ] Nachteil IV
disagree (with) [ˌdɪsə'gri:] nicht übereinstimmen (mit); anderer Meinung sein (als) III
disappear [ˌdɪsə'pɪə] verschwinden II
discipline ['dɪsəplɪn] Disziplin V 3 (55)
disc jockey (DJ) ['dɪsk dʒɒki, 'di: dʒeɪ] Diskjockey III
disco ['dɪskəʊ] Disko I
discover [dɪ'skʌvə] entdecken; herausfinden II
discriminate against sb. [dɪ'skrɪmɪneɪt] jn. diskriminieren, jn. benachteiligen IV
discrimination (against) [dɪˌskrɪmɪ'neɪʃn] Diskriminierung (von), Benachteiligung (von) IV
°**discuss** [dɪ'skʌs] diskutieren, besprechen
discussion [dɪ'skʌʃn] Diskussion II
disease [dɪ'zi:z] Krankheit V 1 (8)
dish [dɪʃ] Gericht *(Speise)* III
dishes ['dɪʃɪz]**: wash the dishes** das Geschirr abwaschen V 1 (19)
dishwasher ['dɪʃwɒʃə] Geschirrspülmaschine I
display: be on display [dɪ'spleɪ] ausgestellt sein/werden IV
°**distance** ['dɪstəns] Entfernung
divide sth. (into) [dɪ'vaɪd] etwas (auf)teilen (in) V 1 (10)
divorced [dɪ'vɔ:st] geschieden I
get divorced sich scheiden lassen V 1 (11/158)
DJ ['di: dʒeɪ] Diskjockey III
DJ ['di: dʒeɪ] (Musik/CDs/Platten) auflegen *(in der Disko)* III
do [du:]**, did, done** tun, machen I
Do you like ...? Magst du ...? I
do sth. about sth. etwas unternehmen gegen etwas V 3 (57)
do an exam eine Prüfung ablegen IV • **do a gig** einen Auftritt haben, ein Konzert geben III • **do a good job** gute Arbeit leisten II • **do a project** ein Projekt machen, durchführen II • **do an exercise** eine Übung machen II • **do badly** schlecht abschneiden *(in Prüfung)* V 3 (55/169) • **do business with** Handel treiben mit; Geschäfte machen mit V 1 (8) • **do jobs** Arbeiten/Aufträge erledigen V 2 (34)
do research recherchieren IV • **do sport** Sport treiben I • **do well** erfolgreich sein, gut abschneiden V 3 (55) • **do work experience** ein Praktikum machen V 2 (38)
doable ['du:əbl] machbar IV
doctor ['dɒktə] Doktor; Arzt/Ärztin II • **to the doctor's** zum Arzt III
documentary [ˌdɒkju'mentri] Dokumentarfilm, -beitrag IV
°**dodge a call** [dɒdʒ] einen Anruf nicht annehmen
dog [dɒg] Hund I
dollar ($) ['dɒlə] Dollar IV
dolphin ['dɒlfɪn] Delfin V 1 (9)
°**domain** [də'meɪn] Domain, Domäne
donate [dəʊ'neɪt] spenden, schenken V 3 (58)
done [dʌn] *siehe* **do**
don't [dəʊnt]**: Don't listen to Dan.** Hör/Hört nicht auf Dan. I • **I don't like ...** Ich mag ... nicht. / Ich mag kein(e) ... I
door [dɔ:] Tür I
doorbell ['dɔ:bel] Türklingel I
dormitory ['dɔ:mətri] Schlafsaal V 4 (89)
dossier ['dɒsieɪ] Mappe, Dossier *(des Sprachenportfolios)* I
double ['dʌbl] zweimal, doppelt, Doppel- I • **double room** Doppelzimmer V 4 (89)
double-click ['dʌblklɪk] doppelklicken II
down [daʊn] hinunter, herunter, nach unten I • **down there** dort unten II • **fall down** hinfallen II
download [ˌdaʊn'ləʊd] runterladen, downloaden II
downloadable [ˌdaʊn'ləʊdəbl] herunterladbar IV
downstairs [ˌdaʊn'steəz] unten; nach unten I
downtown [ˌdaʊn'taʊn] *(AE)* (im/in das) Stadtzentrum IV • **the downtown bus** *(AE)* der Bus in Richtung Stadtzentrum IV
°**Down Under** [ˌdaʊn‿'ʌndə] *umgangssprachliche Bezeichnung für Australien*
°**dragon boat** ['drægən bəʊt] Drachenboot
drama ['drɑ:mə]
1. Schauspiel, darstellende Kunst I
2. Fernsehspiel; Drama IV
drank [dræŋk] *siehe* **drink**
draw [drɔ:] Unentschieden III
draw [drɔ:]**, drew, drawn**
1. zeichnen III
2. draw conclusions Schlüsse ziehen, schlussfolgern IV • **draw sb.'s attention to sth.** jn. auf etwas aufmerksam machen; jemandes Aufmerksamkeit auf etwas lenken V 4 (90)
drawing ['drɔ:ɪŋ] Zeichnung III
drawn [drɔ:n] *siehe* **draw**
°**dreadful** ['dredfl] schrecklich, fürchterlich
dream [dri:m] Traum I
dream (of, about) [dri:m] träumen (von) III • **dream on** weiterträumen III
dreamer ['dri:mə] Träumer/in V 2 (34)
dress [dres] Kleid I
dress [dres] sich kleiden V 2 (40)
dressed [drest]**: get dressed** sich anziehen I
drew [dru:] *siehe* **draw**
°**drill instructor** ['drɪl‿ɪnˌstrʌktə] Ausbilder/in *(beim Militär)*
drink [drɪŋk] Getränk I
drink [drɪŋk]**, drank, drunk** trinken I
drinkable ['drɪŋkəbl] trinkbar, genießbar IV
drive [draɪv]**, drove, driven** *(ein Auto / mit dem Auto)* fahren II
drive [draɪv] (Auto-)Fahrt III
driven ['drɪvn] *siehe* **drive**
driver ['draɪvə] Fahrer/in II
driving licence ['draɪvɪŋ laɪsns] Führerschein V 2 (38)

drop (-pp-) [drɒp]
1. fallen lassen I
2. fallen I
drop sb. off jn. absetzen *(aussteigen lassen)* IV
drove [drəʊv] *siehe* **drive**
drug [drʌg] Droge, Rauschgift; Medikament IV
drum [drʌm] Trommel III • **play the drums** Schlagzeug spielen III
drunk [drʌŋk] betrunken IV *siehe* **drink**
dry [draɪ] trocken V 4 (76/172)
during *(prep)* ['djʊərɪŋ] während IV
dustbin ['dʌstbɪn] Mülltonne II
dusty ['dʌsti] staubig IV
DVD [ˌdiː viː' diː] DVD I
DVD recorder DVD-Rekorder IV

E

each [iːtʃ] jeder, jede, jedes (einzelne) I • **each other** einander, sich (gegenseitig) III
eagle ['iːgl] Adler V 3 (55)
ear [ɪə] Ohr I
earache ['ɪəreɪk] Ohrenschmerzen II
early ['ɜːli] früh I
earn [ɜːn] verdienen *(Geld, Respekt usw.)* V 1 (19)
earring ['ɪərɪŋ] Ohrring I
earth [ɜːθ] Erde III • **on earth** auf der Erde III
earthquake ['ɜːθkweɪk] Erdbeben III
east [iːst] Osten; nach Osten; östlich III
eastbound ['iːstbaʊnd] Richtung Osten III
easy ['iːzi] leicht, einfach I
easy-going [ˌiːzi'gəʊɪŋ] gelassen, locker III
eat [iːt]**, ate, eaten** essen I
eaten ['iːtn] *siehe* **eat**
economic [ˌiːkə'nɒmɪk, ˌekə'nɒmɪk] Wirtschafts-, wirtschaftliche(r, s) V 4 (81)
editor ['edɪtə] Redakteur/in III
education [ˌedʒu'keɪʃn] (Schul-)Bildung, Ausbildung; Erziehung IV
e-friend ['iːfrend] Brieffreund/in *(im Internet)* I
e.g. [ˌiː'dʒiː] *(from Latin:* **exempli gratia***)* z.B. (zum Beispiel) V 1 (10)
egg [eg] Ei III
°**either ... or ...** ['aɪðə ... ɔː, 'iːðə ... ɔː] entweder ... oder
elect sb. sth. [ɪ'lekt] jn. zu etwas wählen IV
election [ɪ'lekʃn] Wahl *(von Kandidaten bei einer Abstimmung)* IV
electric [ɪ'lektrɪk] elektrisch, Elektro- III
electricity [ɪˌlek'trɪsəti] Strom, Elektrizität III
electronic [ɪˌlek'trɒnɪk] elektronisch III
elementary school [ˌelɪ'mentri skuːl] *(USA)* Grundschule *(für 6- bis 11-Jährige)* IV
elephant ['elɪfənt] Elefant I
elevator ['elɪveɪtə] *(AE)* Fahrstuhl, Aufzug II
else [els]**: anybody else** (sonst) noch jemand / irgendjemand anderes IV • **anything else** (sonst) noch etwas / irgendetwas anderes IV • **somebody else** (noch) jemand anderes IV • **somewhere else** woanders(hin); sonst irgendwo(hin) IV • **what else?** was (sonst) noch? IV • **What else do you know?** Was weißt du sonst noch? II • **who else?** wer/wen/wem (sonst) noch? IV
e-mail, email ['iːmeɪl] E-Mail I
e-mail, email ['iːmeɪl] mailen V 2 (39)
embarrassed [ɪm'bærəst] verlegen; peinlich berührt V 4 (82)
°**embrace** [ɪm'breɪs] Umarmung
empty ['empti] leer I
emu ['iːmjuː] Emu V 1 (9)
enclose sth. [ɪn'kləʊz] etwas *(einem Brief)* beilegen V 2 (38)
encourage [ɪn'kʌrɪdʒ] *(jn.)* ermutigen, ermuntern; *(etwas)* fördern V 3 (59)
°**encyclopedia** [ɪnˌsaɪklə'piːdiə] Enzyklopädie, Lexikon
end [end] Ende, Schluss I • **at the end (of)** am Ende (von) I • **in the end** schließlich, zum Schluss III
end [end] enden; beenden III
ending ['endɪŋ]
1. Ende, (Ab-)Schluss *(einer Geschichte, eines Films usw.)* III
2. Endung IV
endless ['endləs] endlos IV
enemy ['enəmi] Feind/in II
energetic [ˌenə'dʒetɪk] dynamisch, tatkräftig, energisch V 2 (35)
energy ['enədʒi] Energie; Kraft II
engine ['endʒɪn] Motor IV
engineer [ˌendʒɪ'nɪə] Ingenieur/in II
engineering [ˌendʒɪ'nɪərɪŋ] Maschinenbau; Ingenieurswesen V 2 (39)
English ['ɪŋglɪʃ] Englisch; englisch I
English-speaking ['ɪŋglɪʃ ˌspiːkɪŋ] englischsprachig; Englisch sprechend V 3 (57/170)
enjoy [ɪn'dʒɔɪ] genießen II
enough [ɪ'nʌf] genug I
enquire (about) [ɪn'kwaɪə] sich erkundigen (nach); anfragen (wegen) V 4 (85)
enquiry [ɪn'kwaɪəri] Anfrage, Erkundigung V 4 (85)
enter ['entə]
1. betreten; eintreten (in) III
2. enter sth. etwas eingeben, eintragen II
enter a country in ein Land einreisen IV
entry ['entri] Eintrag, Eintragung *(in Wörterbuch/Tagebuch)* III
°**epic** ['epɪk] Epos; *hier etwa:* Monumentalfilm
episode ['epɪsəʊd] Folge, Episode *(einer Fernsehserie)* IV
equipment [ɪ'kwɪpmənt] Ausrüstung III
eraser [ɪ'reɪzə, *AE:* ɪ'reɪsər] *(AE)* Radiergummi IV
escape (from sb./sth.) [ɪ'skeɪp] fliehen (vor jm./aus etwas); entkommen III
especially [ɪ'speʃəli] besonders, vor allem V 3 (48)
essay (about, on) ['eseɪ] Aufsatz (über) I
etc. (et cetera) [et'setərə] usw. (und so weiter) IV
ethnic ['eθnɪk] ethnisch IV
°**eucalyptus** [ˌjuːkə'lɪptəs] Eukalyptus
euro (€) ['jʊərəʊ] Euro I
even ['iːvn] sogar II • **even if** selbst wenn; obwohl IV • **not even** (noch) nicht einmal III
evening ['iːvnɪŋ] Abend I • **in the evening** abends, am Abend I • **on Friday evening** freitagabends, am Freitagabend I
event [ɪ'vent] Ereignis; Veranstaltung IV
ever? ['evə] je? / jemals? / schon mal? II
every ['evri] jeder, jede, jedes I
everybody ['evribɒdi] jeder, alle II
everyday *(adj)* ['evrideɪ] Alltags-; alltägliche(r, s) III
everyone ['evriwʌn] IV *siehe* **everybody**
everything ['evriθɪŋ] alles I
everywhere ['evriweə] überall I
exact [ɪg'zækt] exakt, genau IV
exactly [ɪg'zæktli] genau III
exam [ɪg'zæm] Prüfung, Examen IV • **fail an exam** eine Prüfung nicht bestehen; durchfallen IV • **take/do an exam** eine Prüfung ablegen IV

example [ɪɡ'zɑːmpl] Beispiel I
for example zum Beispiel I
excellent ['eksələnt] ausgezeichnet, hervorragend IV
except [ɪk'sept] außer IV
°**exchange** [ɪks'tʃeɪndʒ] austauschen
exchange [ɪks'tʃeɪndʒ] (Schüler-) Austausch III
exchange rate [ɪks'tʃeɪndʒ reɪt] Wechselkurs V 3 (53)
exchange student [ɪks'tʃeɪndʒ ˌstjuːdənt] Austauschschüler/in III
excited [ɪk'saɪtɪd] aufgeregt, begeistert III
exciting [ɪk'saɪtɪŋ] aufregend, spannend II
Excuse me, ... [ɪk'skjuːz miː] Entschuldigung, ... / Entschuldigen Sie, ... I
exercise ['eksəsaɪz]
1. Übung, Aufgabe I
2. *(no pl)* (körperliche) Bewegung, Training IV
exercise book ['eksəsaɪz bʊk] Schulheft, Übungsheft I
expect [ɪk'spekt] erwarten III
expensive [ɪk'spensɪv] teuer I
experience [ɪk'spɪəriəns] erleben, erfahren IV
experience [ɪk'spɪəriəns] Erlebnis, Erfahrung IV
explain sth. to sb. [ɪk'spleɪn] jm. etwas erklären, erläutern II
explanation [ˌeksplə'neɪʃn] Erklärung II
explore [ɪk'splɔː] erkunden, erforschen I
explorer [ɪk'splɔːrə] Entdecker/in, Forscher/in II
explosion [ɪk'spləʊʒn] Explosion IV
express [ɪk'spres] ausdrücken, äußern V 3 (56)
extra ['ekstrə] zusätzlich I
extracurricular activities *(kurz:* **extracurriculars***)* [ˌekstrəkə'rɪkjələz] *schulische Angebote außerhalb des regulären Unterrichts, oft als Arbeitsgemeinschaften* IV
eye [aɪ] Auge I
°**e-zine** ['iːziːn] elektronisches Magazin, elektronische Zeitschrift

F

face [feɪs] Gesicht I
fact [fækt] Tatsache, Fakt III
factory ['fæktri] Fabrik II
fail an exam [feɪl] eine Prüfung nicht bestehen; durchfallen IV
failure *(n)* ['feɪljə] ungenügend *(USA, Schulnote)* IV
fair [feə]
1. fair, gerecht II
2. hell *(Haut; Haare)* V 1 (17)
faithfully ['feɪθfəli]**: Yours faithfully** Mit freundlichen Grüßen *(Briefschluss bei namentlich unbekanntem Empfänger)* V 2 (38)
► S.164 Formal letters
fall [fɔːl]**, fell, fallen** fallen, stürzen; hinfallen II • **fall down** hinfallen II • **fall in love (with sb.)** sich verlieben (in jn.) IV • **fall off** herunterfallen (von) II
fallen ['fɔːlən] *siehe* **fall**
false [fɔːls] falsch, unecht V 3 (52)
family ['fæməli] Familie I • **family tree** (Familien-)Stammbaum I
famous (for) ['feɪməs] berühmt (für, wegen) II
fan [fæn] Fan I
fancy sb. ['fænsi] *(infml)* auf jn. stehen V 3 (48)
fantastic [fæn'tæstɪk] fantastisch, toll I
far [fɑː] weit (entfernt) I • **so far** bis jetzt, bis hierher I
farm [fɑːm] Bauernhof, Farm II
farmer ['fɑːmə] Bauer/Bäuerin, Landwirt/in; (Fisch-)Züchter/in III
fashion ['fæʃn] Mode II
fashionable ['fæʃnəbl] modisch, schick V 4 (79)
fast [fɑːst] schnell II • **fast food** Fastfood III
fat [fæt] dick IV
father ['fɑːðə] Vater I
fault [fɔːlt]**: It's not my fault.** Es/Das ist nicht meine Schuld. IV
favourite ['feɪvərɪt] Favorit/in; Liebling III; Lieblings- I
February ['februəri] Februar I
fed [fed] *siehe* **feed** • **be fed up (with sth.)** [ˌfed‿'ʌp] die Nase voll haben (von etwas) II
feed [fiːd]**, fed, fed** füttern I
feel [fiːl]**, felt, felt** fühlen; sich fühlen; sich anfühlen II • **Feel free to ask questions.** *etwa:* Ihr könnt jetzt gern Fragen stellen. V 4 (90)
How do they feel about ...? Was halten sie von ...? III • **I feel sick.** Mir ist schlecht. IV
feeling ['fiːlɪŋ] Gefühl III
feet [fiːt] *pl von „foot"*
fell [fel] *siehe* **fall**
felt [felt] *siehe* **feel**
felt tip ['felt tɪp] Filzstift I
fence [fens] Zaun IV
ferry ['feri] Fähre III
festival ['festɪvl] Fest, Festival III
few: a few [ə 'fjuː] ein paar, einige II
fiddle ['fɪdl] *(infml)* Fiedel, Geige III
play the fiddle Geige spielen III
field [fiːld] Feld, Acker, Weide II; Sportplatz, Spielfeld III • **in the field** auf dem Feld II
FIFA World Cup [ˌfiːfə wɜːld 'kʌp] FIFA-Fußball-WM V 4 (81)
fight (for) [faɪt]**, fought, fought** kämpfen (für, um) III • **fight sth.** etwas bekämpfen III
fight [faɪt] Kampf; Schlägerei IV
figure ['fɪɡə] Zahl, Ziffer V 1 (8)
°**file** [faɪl] (Akten-)Ordner, Hefter
file [faɪl]**: background file** *etwa:* Hintergrundinformation(en) II
grammar file *Grammatikanhang* I
skills file *Anhang mit Lern- und Arbeitstechniken* I • **sound file** Tondatei, Soundfile III
fill [fɪl] füllen, ausfüllen V 1 (6)
fill in **1.** ausfüllen *(Formular)* V 2 (37); °**2.** einsetzen
film [fɪlm] filmen III
film [fɪlm] Film I
film star ['fɪlm stɑː] Filmstar I
final ['faɪnl] letzte(r, s); End- III
final score Endstand *(beim Sport)* III
final ['faɪnl] Finale, Endspiel III
finally ['faɪnəli] schließlich, endlich V 1 (17)
financial [faɪ'nænʃl] finanziell, Finanz- V 4 (77)
find [faɪnd]**, found, found** finden I
find out (about) herausfinden (über) I
fine [faɪn]
1. gut, schön; in Ordnung II
2. *(gesundheitlich)* gut II
I'm/He's fine. Es geht mir/ihm gut. II
finger ['fɪŋɡə] Finger I
finish ['fɪnɪʃ] beenden, zu Ende machen; enden I
fire ['faɪə] Feuer, Brand II
firefighter ['faɪəfaɪtə] Feuerwehrmann, -frau IV
fireman ['faɪəmən] Feuerwehrmann II
fireproof ['faɪəpruːf] feuerfest V 1 (17/161)
fire station ['faɪə steɪʃn] Feuerwache IV
firewoman ['faɪəˌwʊmən] Feuerwehrfrau II
fireworks *(pl)* ['faɪəwɜːks] Feuerwerk(skörper) II
first [fɜːst]
1. erste(r, s) I
2. zuerst, als Erstes I
at first zuerst, am Anfang IV
be first der/die Erste sein I

first aid [ˌfɜːst_ˈeɪd] Erste Hilfe V 2 (38)
first floor [ˌfɜːst flɔː] erster Stock *(BE)* / Erdgeschoss *(AE)* IV
fish, *pl* **fish** [fɪʃ] Fisch I
fish [fɪʃ] fischen, angeln III
fist [fɪst] Faust IV
fit (-tt-) [fɪt] passen I • **fit in** hineinpassen; sich einfügen, sich anpassen IV
fit [fɪt] fit III
fitness [ˈfɪtnəs] Fitness V 2 (33)
fitness instructor [ˈfɪtnəs_ɪnˌstrʌktə] Fitnesstrainer/in V 2 (33)
flash [flæʃ] Lichtblitz III
flat [flæt] Wohnung I
°**flat** [flæt] flach, eben
flavour [ˈfleɪvə] Geschmack, Geschmacksrichtung II
flew [fluː] *siehe* **fly**
flight [flaɪt] Flug II
floor [flɔː]
1. Fußboden I
2. Stock(werk) IV
first floor erster Stock *(BE)* / Erdgeschoss *(AE)* IV • **ground floor** *(BE)* Erdgeschoss IV • **on the second floor** im zweiten Stock *(BE)* / im ersten Stock *(AE)* IV
°**floppy hat** [ˌflɒpi ˈhæt] Schlapphut
flow chart [ˈfləʊ tʃɑːt] Flussdiagramm I
flower [ˈflaʊə] Blume; Blüte III
flown [fləʊn] *siehe* **fly**
flute [fluːt] Querflöte III
fly [flaɪ], **flew, flown** fliegen II
fog [fɒg] Nebel II
foggy [ˈfɒgi] neblig II
folk (music) [fəʊk] Folk *(englische, schottische, irische oder nordamerikanische Volksmusik des 20. Jahrhunderts)* III
follow [ˈfɒləʊ] folgen; verfolgen I
the following ... die folgenden ... II
food [fuːd]
1. Essen; Lebensmittel I
2. Futter I
foot [fʊt], *pl* **feet** [fiːt] Fuß I; Fuß *(Längenmaß; ca. 30 cm)* IV
on foot zu Fuß III
football [ˈfʊtbɔːl] Fußball I
football boots [ˈfʊtbɔːl buːts] Fußballschuhe, -stiefel I
football pitch [ˈfʊtbɔːl pɪtʃ] Fußballplatz, -feld II
football shirt [ˈfʊtbɔːl ʃɜːt] (Fußball-)Trikot III
for [fə, fɔː] für I • **for ages** ewig, eine Ewigkeit IV • **for a while** für eine Weile, eine Zeit lang V 2 (45)
for breakfast/lunch/dinner zum Frühstück/Mittagessen/Abendbrot I • **for example** zum Beispiel I
for his birthday zu seinem Geburtstag III • **for lots of reasons** aus vielen Gründen I • **for miles** meilenweit II • **for sale** *(auf Schild)* zu verkaufen IV • **for the first time** zum ersten Mal IV • **for 20 minutes** seit 20 Minuten; 20 Minuten lang IV • **just for fun** nur zum Spaß I • **What for?** Wofür? II • **What's for homework?** Was haben wir als Hausaufgabe auf? I
foreground [ˈfɔːgraʊnd] Vordergrund II
foreign [ˈfɒrən] ausländisch, fremd IV • **foreign language** Fremdsprache IV
forest [ˈfɒrɪst] Wald II
forever [fərˈevə] ewig, für immer IV
forgave [fəˈgeɪv] *siehe* **forgive**
forget (-tt-) [fəˈget], **forgot, forgotten** vergessen III
forgive [fəˈgɪv], **forgave, forgiven** vergeben, verzeihen IV
forgiven [fəˈgɪvn] *siehe* **forgive**
forgot [fəˈgɒt] *siehe* **forget**
forgotten [fəˈgɒtn] *siehe* **forget**
fork [fɔːk] Gabel III
form [fɔːm]
1. (Schul-)Klasse I
2. Form IV
3. Formular V 2 (37)
form teacher Klassenlehrer/in I
form [fɔːm] (sich) bilden, formen IV
formal [ˈfɔːml] formell, förmlich V 2 (38)
former [ˈfɔːmə] ehemalige(r, s), frühere(r, s) V 1 (8)
forum [ˈfɔːrəm] Forum V 2 (40)
forward [ˈfɔːwəd]: **look forward to sth.** sich auf etwas freuen IV
fought [fɔːt] *siehe* **fight**
found [faʊnd] gründen IV
found [faʊnd] *siehe* **find**
fox [fɒks] Fuchs II
free [friː]
1. frei I
2. kostenlos I
free time Freizeit, freie Zeit I
Feel free to ask questions. *etwa:* Ihr könnt jetzt gern Fragen stellen. V 4 (90)
freedom [ˈfriːdəm] Freiheit IV
French [frentʃ] Französisch I
French fries [ˌfrentʃ ˈfraɪz] *(AE)* Pommes frites IV
fresh [freʃ] frisch IV
Friday [ˈfraɪdeɪ, ˈfraɪdi] Freitag I
fridge [frɪdʒ] Kühlschrank I
friend [frend] Freund/in I • **make friends (with sb.)** Freunde finden; sich anfreunden (mit jm.) V 3 (48)
friendliness [ˈfrendlinəs] Freundlichkeit IV
friendly [ˈfrendli] freundlich II
°**friendship** [ˈfrendʃɪp] Freundschaft
frog [frɒg] Frosch II
from [frəm, frɒm]
1. aus I
2. von I
from all around Wales aus ganz Wales II • **from all over England/the UK** aus ganz England/aus dem gesamten Vereinigten Königreich III • **from Monday to Friday** von Montag bis Freitag III • **from my point of view** aus meiner Sicht; von meinem Standpunkt aus gesehen II • **I'm from ...** Ich komme aus .../bin aus ... I • **Where are you from?** Wo kommst du her? I
front [frʌnt]: **in front of** vor *(räumlich)* I • **to the front** nach vorn I
front door [ˌfrʌnt ˈdɔː] Wohnungstür, Haustür I
°**front inside cover** [ˌfrʌnt_ˌɪnsaɪd ˈkʌvə] vordere Umschlaginnenseite
fruit [fruːt] Obst, Früchte; Frucht I
fruit salad [ˈfruːt ˌsæləd] Obstsalat I
fruity [ˈfruːti] fruchtig V 4 (89)
full [fʊl] voll I
fun [fʌn] Spaß I • **have fun** Spaß haben, sich amüsieren I • **Have fun!** Viel Spaß! I • **just for fun** nur zum Spaß I • **Riding is fun.** Reiten macht Spaß. I
funeral [ˈfjuːnərəl] Trauerfeier, Beerdigung V 3 (50)
funny [ˈfʌni] witzig, komisch I
furniture *(no pl)* [ˈfɜːnɪtʃə] Möbel III
a piece of furniture ein Möbelstück III
future [ˈfjuːtʃə] Zukunft I

G

gallery [ˈgæləri] (Bilder-)Galerie V 1 (6)
game [geɪm] Spiel I • **a game of football** ein Fußballspiel II
gangster [ˈgæŋstə] Gangster/in V 4 (80)
°**gap** [gæp] Lücke
garage [ˈgærɑːʒ]
1. Garage II
2. Autowerkstatt *(oft mit Tankstelle)* V 2 (32)
garbage [ˈgɑːbɪdʒ] *(AE)* Müll, Abfall IV
garden [ˈgɑːdn] Garten I
gardener [ˈgɑːdnə] Gärtner/in IV

gas [gæs]
°**1.** Gas
2. *(AE)* Benzin IV
gasp [gɑːsp] nach Luft schnappen *(auch: vor Überraschung)* IV
gas station ['gæs steɪʃn] *(AE)* Tankstelle IV
gate [geɪt]
1. Tor; Pforte V 4 (86)
2. Flugsteig III
gave [geɪv] *siehe* **give**
°**GCSE (General Certificate of Secondary Education)** [səˈtɪfɪkət] *Schulabschlussprüfungen für 16-Jährige in England, Wales und Nordirland, vergleichbar der mittleren Reife oder der Fachoberschulreife*
gear *(no pl)* [gɪə]**: camping gear** Campingausrüstung, Campingsachen IV • **sports gear** Sportausrüstung, Sportsachen II
°**geek** [giːk]**: computer geek** *(bes. AE, infml)* Computerfreak
general ['dʒenrəl] allgemeine(r, s) III
generation [ˌdʒenəˈreɪʃn] Generation V 1 (17)
geography [dʒiˈɒgrəfi] Geografie, Erdkunde I
German ['dʒɜːmən] Deutsch; deutsch; Deutsche(r) I
Germany ['dʒɜːməni] Deutschland I
get (-tt-) [get]**, got, got**
1. bekommen, kriegen II
2. holen, besorgen II
3. gelangen, (hin)kommen I
4. get angry/hot/... wütend/heiß/... werden II
5. get off (the train/bus) (aus dem Zug/Bus) aussteigen I • **get on (the train/bus)** (in den Zug/Bus) einsteigen I
6. get up aufstehen I
I didn't get that. *(infml)* Das habe ich nicht mitbekommen. / Ich habe das nicht verstanden. V 1 (14) • **get bored** sich langweilen IV • **get divorced** sich scheiden lassen V 1 (11/158) • **get dressed** sich anziehen I • **get in trouble** in Schwierigkeiten geraten V 3 (56) • **get involved (in)** sich engagieren (für, bei); sich beteiligen (an) IV • **get married (to sb.)** (jn.) heiraten V 1 (11) • **get ready (for)** sich fertig machen (für), sich vorbereiten (auf) I • **get rid of sb./sth.** jn./etwas loswerden IV • **get sth. off the ground** etwas auf den Weg bringen; etwas auf die Beine stellen III • **get things ready** Dinge fertig machen, vorbereiten I • **get tired of sth.** einer Sache überdrüssig werden, die Lust an etwas verlieren IV • **get to know sb.** jn. kennenlernen IV
getting by in English [ˌgetɪŋ ˈbaɪ] *etwa:* auf Englisch zurechtkommen I
gig [gɪg] *(infml)* Gig, Auftritt III
do a gig einen Auftritt haben, ein Konzert geben III
giraffe [dʒəˈrɑːf] Giraffe II
girl [gɜːl] Mädchen I
girlfriend ['gɜːlfrend] (feste) Freundin IV
give [gɪv]**, gave, given** geben I
give a talk (on sth.) einen Vortrag/eine Rede halten (über etwas) V 4 (88) • **give up** aufgeben IV
given ['gɪvn] *siehe* **give**
°**glad** [glæd] froh
glass [glɑːs] Glas I • **a glass of water** ein Glas Wasser I
glasses *(pl)* ['glɑːsɪz] (eine) Brille I
°**glitter** ['glɪtə] Glitter; Glitzerkram
glue [gluː] (auf-, ein)kleben II
glue [gluː] Klebstoff I
glue stick ['gluː stɪk] Klebestift I
go [gəʊ]**, went, gone** gehen I; fahren II • **coffee to go** Kaffee zum Mitnehmen IV • **go abroad** ins Ausland gehen/fahren II • **go by** vergehen, vorübergehen *(Zeit)* V 3 (50) • **go by car/train/bike/...** mit dem Auto/Zug/Rad/... fahren II • °**go crazy** durchdrehen, verrückt werden • **go for a walk** spazieren gehen, einen Spaziergang machen II • **go home** nach Hause gehen I • **go on 1.** weitermachen I; weiterreden III; **2.** angehen *(Licht)* III • **go on a trip** einen Ausflug machen II • **go on holiday** in Urlaub fahren II • **go out** weg-, raus-, ausgehen I • **go to bed** ins Bett gehen I • **go to the cinema** ins Kino gehen II • **go together** zusammenpassen IV
go up to sb./sth. auf jn./etwas zugehen V 3 (48) • **go well!** gut (ver-) laufen, gutgehen III • **go with** gehören zu, passen zu III • **go wrong** schiefgehen III • **Let's go.** Auf geht's! I • **There you go!** *(infml) etwa:* So, das hätten wir. IV
goal [gəʊl] Tor *(im Sport)* III
goalkeeper ['gəʊlkiːpə] Torwart, Torfrau III
God [gɒd] Gott IV
gold [gəʊld] Gold III
golden ['gəʊldən] golden IV
golf [gɒlf] Golf III
gone [gɒn] *siehe* **go**
°**gonna** ['gɒnə, gənə]**: it's gonna happen** *(infml) = it's going to happen*
good [gʊd]
1. gut I
2. brav II
be good at sth. gut in etwas sein; etwas gut können III • **Good afternoon.** Guten Tag. *(nachmittags)* I • **Good luck (with ...)!** Viel Glück (bei/mit ...)! I • **Good morning.** Guten Morgen. I
Goodbye. [ˌgʊdˈbaɪ] Auf Wiedersehen. I • **say goodbye** sich verabschieden I
good-looking [ˌgʊdˈlʊkɪŋ] gut aussehend V 3 (57/170)
got [gɒt] *siehe* **get**
got [gɒt]**: I've got ...** Ich habe ... I
I haven't got a chair. Ich habe keinen Stuhl. I
government ['gʌvənmənt] Regierung (*als Schulfach etwa:* Staatskunde) IV
governor ['gʌvənə] Gouverneur/in IV
grab (-bb-) [græb] schnappen, packen III
grade [greɪd]
1. (Schul-)Note, Zensur IV
2. *(AE)* Jahrgangsstufe, Klasse IV
graduate ['grædʒueɪt] *(AE)* den Schulabschluss machen *(an einer amerik. Highschool)* V 2 (45)
graffiti [grəˈfiːti] Graffiti V 3 (54)
grain [greɪn] Korn IV
grammar ['græmə] Grammatik I
grammar file *Grammatikanhang* I
grand [grænd] eindrucksvoll, beeindruckend IV
grandchild ['græntʃaɪld]**,** *pl* **grandchildren** ['-tʃɪldrən] Enkel/in I
granddaughter ['grændɔːtə] Enkelin II
grandfather ['grænfɑːðə] Großvater I
grandma ['grænmɑː] Oma I
grandmother ['grænmʌðə] Großmutter I
grandpa ['grænpɑː] Opa I
grandparents ['grænpeərənts] Großeltern I
grandson ['grænsʌn] Enkel II
granny ['græni] Oma II
grape [greɪp] Weintraube IV
°**graph** [grɑːf] Graph, Kurve, Schaubild
grass [grɑːs] Rasen IV
great [greɪt] großartig, toll I
great-grandfather [ˌgreɪt ˈgrænfɑːðə] Urgroßvater III
great-grandmother [ˌgreɪt ˈgrænmʌðə] Urgroßmutter III

greedy ['gri:di] gierig, habgierig V 2 (46)
green [gri:n] grün I
°**greeting** ['gri:tɪŋ] Gruß, Begrüßung
grew [gru:] *siehe* **grow**
grey [greɪ] grau II
ground [graʊnd] (Erd-)Boden III
get sth. off the ground etwas auf den Weg bringen; etwas auf die Beine stellen III
ground floor [ˌgraʊnd 'flɔ:] *(BE)* Erdgeschoss IV
ground zero [ˌgraʊnd 'zɪərəʊ] Bodennullpunkt *(Bezeichnung für das zerstörte World Trade Center in New York; ursprünglich: Explosionsstelle einer Bombe oder Rakete über dem Boden)* IV
group [gru:p] Gruppe I • **group word** Oberbegriff II
grow [grəʊ], **grew, grown**
1. wachsen II
2. *(Getreide usw.)* anbauen, anpflanzen II
grow up erwachsen werden; aufwachsen III
grown [grəʊn] *siehe* **grow**
grumble ['grʌmbl] murren, nörgeln I
guess [ges] raten, erraten, schätzen II • **Guess what!** Stell dir vor! II
°**guess** [ges] Vermutung, Schätzung
guest [gest] Gast I
guide [gaɪd] (Fremden-)Führer/in, Reiseleiter/in IV
guidebook ['gaɪdbʊk] Reiseführer *(Buch)* V 4 (86)
guilty ['gɪlti] schuldbewusst; schuldig IV
guinea pig ['gɪni pɪg] Meerschweinchen I
guitar [gɪ'tɑ:] Gitarre I • **play the guitar** Gitarre spielen I
gun [gʌn] (Schuss-)Waffe II
guy [gaɪ] *(infml)* Typ, Kerl IV • **guys** *(pl) (AE, infml)* Leute III
gym [dʒɪm] Sporthalle, Turnhalle IV

H

had [hæd] *siehe* **have**
hair *(no pl)* [heə] Haar, Haare I
hairdresser ['heədresə] Friseur/in III
at the hairdresser's beim Friseur III
hairy ['heəri] haarig, behaart V 4 (89)
half [hɑ:f], *pl* **halves** [hɑ:vz]
1. Hälfte III
2. Halbzeit III
the first half die erste Halbzeit III
half [hɑ:f]: **half an hour** eine halbe Stunde III • **half past 11** halb zwölf (11.30 / 23.30) I • **three and a half days/weeks** dreieinhalb Tage/Wochen IV
half-pipe ['hɑ:fpaɪp] Halfpipe *(halbierte Röhre für Inlineskater)* III
half-time [ˌhɑ:f 'taɪm] Halbzeit(pause) III
hall [hɔ:l]
1. Flur, Diele I
2. Halle, Saal III
study hall *Zeit zum selbstständigen Lernen in der Schule* IV
hallway ['hɔ:lweɪ] *(AE)* Korridor, Gang IV
halves [hɑ:vz] *pl von „half"*
hamburger ['hæmbɜ:gə] Hamburger I
hamster ['hæmstə] Hamster I
hand [hænd] Hand I
hang [hæŋ], **hung, hung** hängen; *(etwas)* aufhängen V 4 (82) • **hang out** *(infml)* rumhängen, abhängen III • °**hang sth. up** etwas aufhängen
happen (to) ['hæpən] geschehen, passieren (mit) I
happiness ['hæpinəs] Glück IV
happy ['hæpi] glücklich, froh I
Happy birthday. Herzlichen Glückwunsch zum Geburtstag. I
happy ending Happyend II • **be happy to do sth.** *(fml)* gern bereit sein, etwas zu tun V 2 (38)
harbour ['hɑ:bə] Hafen II
hard [hɑ:d]
1. hart; schwer, schwierig II
2. *(adv)* heftig, kräftig IV
work hard hart arbeiten II
hard-working [ˌhɑ:d 'wɜ:kɪŋ] fleißig, tüchtig, hart arbeitend V 2 (33); V 3 (57/170)
harvest ['hɑ:vɪst] Ernte IV
hat [hæt] Hut II
hate [heɪt] hassen, gar nicht mögen I
have [həv, hæv], **had, had** haben, besitzen II • **have a baby** ein Baby/Kind bekommen II • **have a bath** baden, ein Bad nehmen II
have a cold erkältet sein, eine Erkältung haben II • **have a crush on sb.** in jn. verknallt sein III
Have a good time! Viel Spaß! / Viel Vergnügen! III • **have a party** eine Party feiern/veranstalten II
have a sauna in die Sauna gehen II • **have a shower** (sich) duschen I • **have a sore throat** Halsschmerzen haben II • **have a temperature** Fieber haben II • **have breakfast** frühstücken I • **have dinner** Abendbrot essen I • **have ... for breakfast** ... zum Frühstück essen/trinken I • **have fun** Spaß haben, sich amüsieren I • **Have fun!** Viel Spaß! I • **have to do** tun müssen I
have got: I've got ... [aɪv 'gɒt] Ich habe ... I • **I haven't got a chair.** ['hævnt gɒt] Ich habe keinen Stuhl. I
he [hi:] er I
head [hed] Kopf I • °**head of state** Staatsoberhaupt • °**running head** Leitwort *(am Kopf einer Wörterbuchseite)*
headache ['hedeɪk] Kopfschmerzen II
°**head boy** [ˌhed 'bɔɪ] Schulsprecher
heading ['hedɪŋ] Überschrift IV
headless ['hedləs] kopflos IV
headline ['hedlaɪn] Schlagzeile IV
headphones *(pl)* ['hedfəʊnz] Kopfhörer III
head teacher [ˌhed 'ti:tʃə] Schulleiter/in III
health [helθ] Gesundheit; Gesundheitslehre IV
healthy ['helθi] gesund II
hear [hɪə], **heard, heard** hören I
heard [hɜ:d] *siehe* **hear**
heart [hɑ:t] Herz II
°**heat** [hi:t] Hitze
heaven ['hevn] Himmel *(im religiösen Sinn)* IV
hedgehog ['hedʒhɒg] Igel II
held [held] *siehe* **hold**
helicopter ['helɪkɒptə] Hubschrauber, Helikopter II
Hello. [hə'ləʊ] Hallo. / Guten Tag. I
helmet ['helmɪt] Helm III
help [help] helfen I • **Can I help you?** Kann ich Ihnen helfen? / Was kann ich für Sie tun? *(im Geschäft)* I
help [help] Hilfe I
helpful ['helpfl] hilfreich, nützlich IV; hilfsbereit V 2 (35)
helpless ['helpləs] hilflos IV
her [hə, hɜ:]
1. ihr, ihre I
2. sie; ihr I
here [hɪə]
1. hier I
2. hierher I
Here you are. Bitte sehr. / Hier bitte. I
hero ['hɪərəʊ], *pl* **heroes** ['hɪərəʊz] Held, Heldin II
hers [hɜ:z] ihrer, ihre, ihrs II
herself [hə'self, hɜ:'self] sich (selbst) III

Hi! [haɪ] Hallo! I • **Say hi to Dilip for me.** Grüß Dilip von mir. I
hid [hɪd] *siehe* **hide**
hidden ['hɪdn] *siehe* **hide**
hide [haɪd], **hid, hidden** sich verstecken; *(etwas)* verstecken I
high [haɪ] hoch III
high school ['haɪ sku:l] *(USA) Schule für 14- bis 18-Jährige* IV
highlight ['haɪlaɪt] Höhepunkt V 4 (90)
°**highlighted** ['haɪlaɪtɪd] hervorgehoben, markiert *(mit Textmarker)*
highway ['haɪweɪ] *(USA)* Fernstraße *(oft mit vier oder mehr Spuren)* IV
hijacker ['haɪdʒækə] (Flugzeug-)Entführer/in IV
hike [haɪk] wandern IV
hike [haɪk] Wanderung, Marsch IV
hill [hɪl] Hügel II
hilly ['hɪli] hügelig III
him [hɪm] ihn; ihm I
himself [hɪm'self] sich (selbst) III
Hindu ['hɪndu:] Hindu V 4 (76)
°**hinterland** ['hɪntəlænd] Hinterland
hip hop ['hɪp hɒp] Hiphop III
hippo ['hɪpəʊ] Flusspferd II
his [hɪz]
1. sein, seine I
2. seiner, seine, seins II
Hispanic *(n; adj)* [hɪ'spænɪk] *US-amerikanischer Ausdruck für Menschen mit Wurzeln in spanischsprachigen Ländern, besonders in Mittelamerika* IV
history ['hɪstri] Geschichte I
hit (-tt-) [hɪt], **hit, hit** schlagen I
hit the windscreen gegen/auf die Windschutzscheibe schlagen/prallen III
hit [hɪt] Hit III
hobby ['hɒbi] Hobby I
hockey ['hɒki] Hockey I
hockey pitch ['hɒki pɪtʃ] Hockeyplatz, Hockeyfeld II
hockey shoes ['hɒki ʃu:z] Hockeyschuhe I
hold [həʊld], **held, held** halten II
hold on (to sth.) sich festhalten (an etwas) V 4 (76) • °**hold sth. up** etwas hochhalten
hole [həʊl] Loch I
holiday ['hɒlədeɪ]
1. Feiertag IV
2. holiday(s) Ferien I
be on holiday in Urlaub sein; Ferien haben/machen II • **go on holiday** in Urlaub fahren II
home [həʊm] Heim, Zuhause I
at home daheim, zu Hause I
come home nach Hause kommen I • **get home** nach Hause kommen I • **go home** nach Hause gehen I
homeless ['həʊmləs] obdachlos IV
home-made [ˌhəʊm'meɪd] hausgemacht, selbstgemacht V 3 (57/170)
hometown ['həʊmtaʊn] Heimatstadt IV
homework *(no pl)* ['həʊmwɜ:k] Hausaufgabe(n) I • **do homework** die Hausaufgabe(n) machen I
What's for homework? Was haben wir als Hausaufgabe auf? I
honest ['ɒnɪst] ehrlich V 1 (12) • **I honestly think ...** Ich glaube, ehrlich gesagt, dass ... V 1 (12)
Hooray! [hu'reɪ] Hurra! II
hope [həʊp] hoffen II
hope [həʊp] Hoffnung III
hopeless ['həʊpləs] hoffnungslos, verzweifelt IV
horrible ['hɒrəbl] scheußlich, grauenhaft II
horse [hɔ:s] Pferd I
hospital ['hɒspɪtl] Krankenhaus II
host [həʊst] *(Radio-, Fernseh-)* Moderator/in IV
hostel ['hɒstl] Herberge, Wohnheim III
hostess ['həʊstəs] Gastgeberin *(in USA auch: Frau, die im Restaurant die Gäste empfängt und an ihren Platz führt)* IV
hot [hɒt] heiß I • **hot-water bottle** Wärmflasche II
hotel [həʊ'tel] Hotel II
hotline ['hɒtlaɪn] Hotline II
hour ['aʊə] Stunde II • **a 14-hour flight** ein 14-stündiger Flug, ein 14-Stunden-Flug III • **a 24-hour supermarket** ein Supermarkt, der 24 Stunden geöffnet ist III • **half an hour** eine halbe Stunde III
opening hours *(pl)* Öffnungszeiten IV • **work long hours** lange arbeiten V 2 (33)
house [haʊs] Haus I • **at the Shaws' house** im Haus der Shaws/bei den Shaws zu Hause I
how [haʊ] wie I • **How about ...?** Wie wär's mit ...? III • **How am I doing?** Wie komme ich voran? *(Wie sind meine Fortschritte?)* III
How are you? Wie geht es dir/Ihnen/euch? II • **How do you feel about ...?** Was hältst du von ...? III
How do you know ...? Woher weißt/kennst du ...? I • **How long ...?** Seit wann ...? / Wie lange ...? IV • **how many?** wie viele? I
how much? wie viel? I • **How much is ...?** Was kostet ...? / Wie viel kostet ...? I • **how to do sth.** wie man etwas tut / tun kann / tun soll IV
however [haʊ'evə] jedoch, allerdings V 3 (51)
°**HTML (Hypertext Markup Language)** ['haɪpətekst] Hypertext-Auszeichnungssprache *(Formatierungssprache zur Erstellung von Hypertextseiten im WWW)*
huge [hju:dʒ] riesig, sehr groß III
human ['hju:mən] Menschen-, menschlich IV
hundred ['hʌndrəd] hundert I
hung [hʌŋ] *siehe* **hang**
hungry ['hʌŋgri] hungrig I • **be hungry** Hunger haben, hungrig sein I
hunt [hʌnt] jagen III
hunt [hʌnt] Jagd III
hunter ['hʌntə] Jäger/in III
hurry ['hʌri] eilen; sich beeilen II
hurry up sich beeilen I
hurry ['hʌri]: **be in a hurry** in Eile sein, es eilig haben I
hurt [hɜ:t], **hurt, hurt** wehtun; verletzen I
hurt [hɜ:t] verletzt II
husband ['hʌzbənd] Ehemann II
hutch [hʌtʃ] (Kaninchen-)Stall I

I

I [aɪ] ich I • **I'm** [aɪm] ich bin I
I'm from ... Ich komme aus ... / Ich bin aus ... I • **I'm ... years old.** Ich bin ... Jahre alt. I • **I'm sorry.** Entschuldigung. / Tut mir leid. I
ice [aɪs] Eis II
ice cream [ˌaɪs 'kri:m] (Speise-)Eis I
ice hockey ['aɪs hɒki] Eishockey III
ice rink ['aɪs rɪŋk] Schlittschuhbahn II
icy ['aɪsi] eisig; vereist V 4 (89)
idea [aɪ'dɪə] Idee, Einfall I
ideal [aɪ'di:əl] Ideal, Idealvorstellung V 1 (17)
if [ɪf]
1. falls, wenn II
2. ob II
as if als ob IV • **even if** selbst wenn; obwohl IV
ill [ɪl] krank II
illegal [ɪ'li:gl] illegal, ungesetzlich IV
illness ['ɪlnəs] Krankheit IV
°**imaginary** [ɪ'mædʒɪnəri] imaginär *(nur in der Vorstellung vorhanden)*
°**imaginary journey** Fantasiereise
imagination [ɪˌmædʒɪ'neɪʃn] Fantasie, Vorstellung(skraft) IV

imagine sth. [ɪ'mædʒɪn] sich etwas vorstellen III
immediately [ɪ'mi:diətli] sofort IV
immigrant ['ɪmɪgrənt] Einwanderer/Einwanderin IV
important [ɪm'pɔ:tnt] wichtig II
important to sb. wichtig für jn. III
impossible [ɪm'pɒsəbl] unmöglich II
impress [ɪm'pres] beeindrucken V 2 (40)
impressed [ɪm'prest] beeindruckt IV
°**impression** [ɪm'preʃn] Eindruck
impressive [ɪm'presɪv] beeindruckend V 4 (89)
°**improve** [ɪm'pru:v] verbessern
in [ɪn] in I • **in 1948** im Jahr 1948 II • **in ... Street** in der ...straße I **in English** auf Englisch I • **in front of** vor *(räumlich)* I • **in here** hier drinnen I • **in my opinion** meiner Meinung nach IV • **in my/your view** meiner/deiner Ansicht nach III • **in other places** an anderen Orten, anderswo III • °**in the 1970s** in den 70er-Jahren *(des 20. Jahrhunderts)* • **in the afternoon** nachmittags, am Nachmittag I • **in the country** auf dem Land II • **in the end** schließlich, zum Schluss III • **in the evening** abends, am Abend I • **in the field** auf dem Feld II • **in the morning** am Morgen, morgens I • **in the photo** auf dem Foto I • **in the picture** auf dem Bild I • **in the sky** am Himmel II • **in there** dort drinnen I • **in the world** auf der Welt V 4 (77) • **in time** rechtzeitig II
°**inch** [ɪntʃ] Zoll, Inch *(= 2,54 cm)*
include [ɪn'klu:d] (mit) einschließen, enthalten V 4 (89)
°**incorrect** [,ɪnkə'rekt] falsch
independence [,ɪndɪ'pendəns] Unabhängigkeit V 3 (60)
independent [,ɪndɪ'pendənt] unabhängig V 1 (8)
Indian ['ɪndiən]
1. Indianer/in; indianisch IV
2. Inder/in; indisch V 4 (77)
indirect question [,ɪndərekt 'kwestʃən] indirekte Frage II
indoors [,ɪn'dɔ:z]
1. drinnen, im Haus V 2 (36)
2. nach drinnen V 2 (36)
industrial [ɪn'dʌstriəl] industriell, Industrie- IV
industry ['ɪndəstri] Industrie IV
infinitive [ɪn'fɪnətɪv] Infinitiv *(Grundform des Verbs)* I
informal [ɪn'fɔ:ml] informell; umgangssprachlich V 2 (38/164)
information (about/on) *(no pl)* [,ɪnfə'meɪʃn] Information(en) (über) I
insect ['ɪnsekt] Insekt IV
inside [,ɪn'saɪd]
1. innen (drin), drinnen I
2. nach drinnen II
3. inside the car ins Auto (hinein), ins Innere des Autos II
inside [,ɪn'saɪd]**: the inside** das Innere, die Innenseite V 4 (82)
°**inside cover** [,ɪnsaɪd 'kʌvə] Umschlaginnenseite
install [ɪn'stɔ:l] installieren, einrichten II
installation [,ɪnstə'leɪʃn] Installation, Einrichtung II
instant messages *(pl)* [,ɪnstənt 'mesɪdʒɪz] *Nachrichten, die man im Internet austauscht (in Echtzeit)* III
instead *(adv)* [ɪn'sted] stattdessen, dafür V 3 (55/169)
instead of *(prep)* [ɪn'sted_əv] statt, anstatt, anstelle von V 3 (55)
institution [,ɪnstɪ'tju:ʃn] Institution, Einrichtung V 4 (88)
instructions *(pl)* [ɪn'strʌkʃnz] (Gebrauchs-)Anweisung(en), Anleitung(en) II
instructor [ɪn'strʌktə] Ausbilder/in V 3 (55)
instrument ['ɪnstrəmənt] Instrument II
interactive [,ɪntər'æktɪv] interaktiv IV
interest (in) ['ɪntrəst] Interesse (an) IV
°**interest sb.** ['ɪntrəst] jn. interessieren
interested ['ɪntrəstɪd]**: be interested (in)** interessiert sein (an), sich interessieren (für) III
interesting ['ɪntrəstɪŋ] interessant I
international [,ɪntə'næʃnəl] international III
internet ['ɪntənet] Internet I
interrupt [,ɪntə'rʌpt] unterbrechen IV
interview ['ɪntəvju:] interviewen, befragen II
interview ['ɪntəvju:] Interview II **(job) interview** Vorstellungsgespräch V 2 (40)
into ['ɪntə, 'ɪntʊ] in ... (hinein) I **run into sth./sb.** gegen etwas fahren / jn. anfahren IV
intolerant [ɪn'tɒlərənt] intolerant III
introduce sb. to sb. [,ɪntrə'dju:s] jn. jm. vorstellen; jn. mit jm. bekanntmachen V 1 (14) • **introduce sth.** etwas einführen *(Thema, Mode, Methode)* V 3 (51)
► S.159 Introducing people
introduction [,ɪntrə'dʌkʃn] Einführung, Einleitung III
invitation (to) [,ɪnvɪ'teɪʃn] Einladung (zu) I
invite (to) [ɪn'vaɪt] einladen (zu) I
involved [ɪn'vɒlvd]**: get involved (in)** sich engagieren (für, bei); sich beteiligen (an) IV
irregular [ɪ'regjələ] unregelmäßig I
is [ɪz] ist I
island ['aɪlənd] Insel II
it [ɪt] er/sie/es I • **It's £1.** Er/Sie/Es kostet 1 Pfund. I • **It says here: ...** Hier steht: ... / Es heißt hier: ... II
IT [,aɪ 'ti:]**, information technology** [tek'nɒlədʒi] IT, Informationstechnologie II
°**italics** [ɪ'tælɪks]**: in italics** kursiv; in Kursivschrift
its [ɪts] sein/seine; ihr/ihre I
itself [ɪt'self] sich (selbst) III

J

jacket ['dʒækɪt] Jacke, Jackett II
jail [dʒeɪl] Gefängnis IV
January ['dʒænjuəri] Januar I
jazz [dʒæz] Jazz I
jealous (of) ['dʒeləs] neidisch (auf); eifersüchtig (auf) III
jeans *(pl)* [dʒi:nz] Jeans I
jewellery *(no pl)* ['dʒu:əlri] Schmuck II
Jewish ['dʒu:ɪʃ] jüdisch IV
job [dʒɒb] Aufgabe, Job I • **do jobs** Arbeiten/Aufträge erledigen V 2 (34) • **job interview** Vorstellungsgespräch V 2 (40)
jobless ['dʒɒbləs] arbeitslos IV
join sb. [dʒɔɪn] sich jm. anschließen; bei jm. mitmachen II • °**join up (with)** sich zusammentun (mit)
joke [dʒəʊk] Witz I
joke [dʒəʊk] scherzen, Witze machen II
journalist ['dʒɜ:nəlɪst] Journalist/in IV
journey ['dʒɜ:ni] Reise, Fahrt II
judge (by) [dʒʌdʒ] beurteilen, einschätzen (nach) IV
judo ['dʒu:dəʊ] Judo I • **do judo** Judo machen I
jug [dʒʌg] Krug I • **a jug of milk** ein Krug Milch I
juice [dʒu:s] Saft I
juicy ['dʒu:si] saftig V 4 (89)
July [dʒu'laɪ] Juli I

°**jumble** [ˈdʒʌmbl] gebrauchte Sachen, Trödel
jumble sale [ˈdʒʌmbl seɪl] Wohltätigkeitsbasar I
jump [dʒʌmp] springen II
June [dʒuːn] Juni I
junior [ˈdʒuːniə] Junioren-, Jugend- I
just [dʒʌst]
1. (einfach) nur, bloß I
2. einfach III • **I just can't find them.** Ich kann sie einfach nicht finden. III
3. gerade (eben), soeben II • **just then** genau in dem Moment; gerade dann II
4. **just like you** genau wie du II
just as ... as genauso ... wie V 1 (16)

K

kangaroo [ˌkæŋɡəˈruː] Känguru II
keep [kiːp], **kept, kept** (be)halten; aufbewahren III • **keep in touch** in Verbindung bleiben, Kontakt halten III • **keep sth. warm/cool/open/...** etwas warm/kühl/offen/... halten II • °**keep a diary** ein Tagebuch führen
kept [kept] *siehe* **keep**
ketchup [ˈketʃəp] Ketschup V 3 (58)
key [kiː] Schlüssel I • **key word** Stichwort, Schlüsselwort I
keyboard [ˈkiːbɔːd] Keyboard *(elektronisches Tasteninstrument)* III
key card [ˈkiː kɑːd] Schlüsselkarte V 4 (89)
kick [kɪk] treten IV
kid [kɪd] Kind, Jugendliche(r) I
kill [kɪl] töten I
kilogram (kg) [ˈkɪləɡræm], **kilo** [ˈkiːləʊ] Kilogramm, Kilo III
a 90-kilogram bear ein 90 Kilogramm schwerer Bär III
kilometre (km) [ˈkɪləmiːtə] Kilometer III • **a ten-kilometre walk** eine Zehn-Kilometer-Wanderung III
kind (of) [kaɪnd] Art III • **What kind of car ...?** Was für ein Auto ...? III
kind of scary [kaɪnd] *(infml)* irgendwie unheimlich III
kindergarten [ˈkɪndəɡɑːtn] Kindergarten; *(USA)* Vorschule *(für 5- bis 6-Jährige)* IV
king [kɪŋ] König I
kiss [kɪs] küssen IV
kiss [kɪs] Kuss IV
kitchen [ˈkɪtʃən] Küche I
kite [kaɪt] Drachen I
knee [niː] Knie I
knew [njuː] *siehe* **know**
knife [naɪf], *pl* **knives** [naɪvz] Messer III
knock (on) [nɒk] (an)klopfen (an) I
know [nəʊ], **knew, known**
1. wissen I
2. kennen I
know about sth. von etwas wissen; über etwas Bescheid wissen II
get to know sb. jn. kennenlernen IV • **How do you know ...?** Woher weißt du ...? / Woher kennst du ...? I • **I don't know.** Ich weiß es nicht. I • **..., you know.** ..., wissen Sie. / ..., weißt du. I • **You know what, Sophie?** Weißt du was, Sophie? I
known [nəʊn] bekannt IV
siehe **know**
koala [kəʊˈɑːlə] Koala V 1 (6)
kph (kilometres per hour) [ˌkeɪ piː ˈeɪtʃ] km/h (Stundenkilometer, Kilometer pro Stunde) III

L

label [ˈleɪbl] Marke, Label; Etikett V 4 (80)
°**label** [ˈleɪbl] beschriften, etikettieren
°**ladder** [ˈlædə] *(die)* Leiter
laid [leɪd] *siehe* **lay**
lake [leɪk] (Binnen-)See II
lamb [læm] Lamm III
lamp [læmp] Lampe I
land [lænd] Land, Grund und Boden II • **on land** auf dem Land III
land [lænd] landen II
°**landscape** [ˈlændskeɪp] Landschaft
lane [leɪn] Gasse, Weg III
language [ˈlæŋɡwɪdʒ] Sprache I
laptop [ˈlæptɒp] Laptop V 1 (12)
large [lɑːdʒ] groß II
lasagne [ləˈzænjə] Lasagne I
last [lɑːst] letzte(r, s) I • **the last day** der letzte Tag I • **last name** Nachname V 2 (38) • **at last** endlich, schließlich I
last (for) [lɑːst] dauern IV
late [leɪt] spät; zu spät I • **be late** zu spät sein/kommen I • **Sorry, I'm late.** Entschuldigung, dass ich zu spät bin/komme. I
later [ˈleɪtə] später I
latest [ˈleɪtɪst] neueste(r, s) III
°**latrine** [ləˈtriːn] Latrine
laugh [lɑːf] lachen I • **laugh at sb.** jn. auslachen, über jn. lachen III
laugh out loud laut lachen II
laughable [ˈlɑːfəbl] lächerlich, lachhaft IV
laughter [ˈlɑːftə] Gelächter II
law [lɔː] Gesetz IV
lay the table [leɪ], **laid, laid** den Tisch decken I
layout [ˈleɪaʊt] Layout, Anordnung, Aufbau V 2 (44)
leader [ˈliːdə] (An-)Führer/in, Leiter/in III
leaf [liːf], *pl* **leaves** [liːvz] Blatt *(an Pflanzen)* V 1 (11)
lean [liːn] sich beugen, sich lehnen IV • **lean over** sich herüberbeugen, -lehnen IV
learn [lɜːn] lernen I • **learn sth. about sth.** etwas über etwas erfahren, etwas über etwas herausfinden II
least [liːst] am wenigsten III • **at least** zumindest, wenigstens I
leather [ˈleðə] Leder III
leave [liːv], **left, left**
1. (weg)gehen; abfahren II
2. verlassen II
3. zurücklassen II
leave school von der Schule abgehen V 2 (39) • **leave sb. alone** jn. in Ruhe lassen IV • **leave sth. out** etwas weglassen/auslassen IV
leaves [liːvz] *pl von „leaf"*
left [left] *siehe* **leave**
left [left] linke(r, s) II • **look left** nach links schauen II • **on the left** links, auf der linken Seite I • **turn left** (nach) links abbiegen II
leg [leɡ] Bein I
legal [ˈliːɡl] legal IV
legend [ˈledʒənd] Legende, Sage V 4 (78)
leisure centre [ˈleʒə sentə] Freizeitzentrum, -park II
lemonade [ˌleməˈneɪd] Limonade I
lend sb. sth. [lend], **lent, lent** jm. etwas leihen, etwas an jn. verleihen V 2 (44/165)
► S.166 (to) lend – (to) borrow
lent [lent] *siehe* **lend**
leotard [ˈliːətɑːd] Gymnastikanzug; Turnanzug III
less [les] weniger IV
lesson [ˈlesn] (Unterrichts-)Stunde I • **lessons** *(pl)* [ˈlesnz] Unterricht I
let (-tt-) [let], **let, let** lassen II
Let's ... Lass uns ... / Lasst uns ... I
Let's go. Auf geht's! I • **Let's look at the list.** Sehen wir uns die Liste an. / Lasst uns die Liste ansehen. I
let sb. do sth. jm. erlauben, etwas zu tun; zulassen, dass jd. etwas tut III
letter [ˈletə]
1. Buchstabe I

2. letter (to) Brief (an) II • **letter of application** Bewerbungsschreiben V 2 (37/163)
lettuce ['letɪs] (Kopf-)Salat II
level ['levl] (Lern-)Stand, Niveau, Grad V 2 (39) • °**UV level** Grad der UV-Strahlenbelastung
library ['laɪbrəri] Bibliothek, Bücherei I
license plate ['laɪsns pleɪt] *(AE)* Nummernschild IV
life [laɪf], *pl* **lives** [laɪvz] Leben I
lifesaver ['laɪfseɪvə] Rettungsschwimmer/in V 3 (48)
lifestyle ['laɪfstaɪl] Lebensstil V 3 (48)
lifetime ['laɪftaɪm] Leben, Lebensdauer V 4 (76)
lift [lɪft] Fahrstuhl, Aufzug II
light [laɪt] Licht III
light [laɪt], **lit, lit** anzünden IV
like [laɪk] wie I • **just like you** genau wie du II • **What was the weather like?** Wie war das Wetter? II • **like that / like this** so IV
like [laɪk] mögen, gernhaben I
like sth. better etwas lieber mögen II • **like sth. best** etwas am liebsten mögen III • **I like swimming/dancing/...** Ich schwimme/tanze/... gern. I • **I'd like ... (= I would like ...)** Ich hätte gern ... / Ich möchte gern ... I • **I'd like to go (= I would like to go)** Ich würde gern gehen / Ich möchte gehen I
I wouldn't like to go Ich würde nicht gern gehen / Ich möchte nicht gehen I • **Would you like ...?** Möchtest du ...? / Möchten Sie ...? I
°**Say what you like about ...** Sag, was du an ... magst
likeable ['laɪkəbl] sympathisch, liebenswert IV
line [laɪn]
1. Zeile II
2. (U-Bahn-)Linie III
3. Leitung *(Telefon)* IV
4. *(AE)* Schlange, Reihe *(wartender Menschen)* IV
link [lɪŋk] verbinden, verknüpfen I
link [lɪŋk] Verbindung, Verknüpfung III
linking word ['lɪŋkɪŋ wɜːd] Bindewort II
lion ['laɪən] Löwe II
list [lɪst] Liste I
list [lɪst] auflisten, aufzählen II
listen (to) ['lɪsn] zuhören; sich *etwas* anhören I • **listen for sth.** auf etwas horchen, achten III
listener ['lɪsnə] Zuhörer/in II
lit [lɪt] *siehe* **light**

little ['lɪtl]
1. klein I
2. wenig IV
live [lɪv] leben, wohnen I
live music ['laɪv ˌmjuːzɪk] Livemusik II
lives [laɪvz] *pl von „life"*
living room ['lɪvɪŋ ruːm] Wohnzimmer I
lobby ['lɒbi] Eingangshalle IV
local ['ləʊkl] Lokal-, örtlich; am/vom Ort IV
location [ləʊ'keɪʃn] (Einsatz-)Ort, Platz III
lock [lɒk] Schleuse III
lock up [ˌlɒk‿'ʌp] abschließen II
lodge [lɒdʒ] Landhaus IV
logical ['lɒdʒɪkl] logisch V 2 (35)
logo ['ləʊgəʊ], *pl* **logos** Logo, Markenzeichen III
lonely ['ləʊnli] einsam III
long [lɒŋ] lang I • **a long time** lange III • **as long as** *(conj)* solange, sofern IV • **How long ...?** Seit wann ...? / Wie lange ...? IV
work long hours lange arbeiten V 2 (33)
look [lʊk]
1. schauen, gucken I
2. look different/great/old anders/toll/alt aussehen I
look after sth./sb. auf etwas/jn. aufpassen; sich um etwas/jn. kümmern II • **look around** sich umsehen III • **look at** ansehen, anschauen I • **look for** suchen II
look forward to sth. sich auf etwas freuen IV • **look left/right** nach links/rechts schauen II
look round sich umsehen I • **look sth. up** etwas nachschlagen III
look up (from) hochsehen, aufschauen (von) II
look [lʊk]
1. (Gesichts-)Ausdruck V 2 (40)
2. Blick V 4 (90)
take a look (at) einen Blick werfen (auf) V 4 (90)
lose [luːz], **lost, lost** verlieren II
lost [lɒst] *siehe* **lose**
lot [lɒt]: **a lot (of)** eine Menge, viel, viele II • **Thanks a lot!** Vielen Dank! I • **He likes her a lot.** Er mag sie sehr. I • **lots more** viel mehr I • **lots of ...** eine Menge ..., viele ..., viel ... I
°**lottery** ['lɒtəri] Lotterie
loud [laʊd] laut I
love [lʌv] lieben, sehr mögen II
I'd love to ... Ich würde liebend gern ... V 1 (12)

love [lʌv]
1. Liebe II
2. Liebes, Liebling III
fall in love (with sb.) sich verlieben (in jn.) IV • **Love ...** Liebe Grüße, ... *(Briefschluss)* I
lover ['lʌvə] Geliebte(r) V 4 (76)
luck [lʌk]: **Good luck (with ...)!** Viel Glück (bei/mit ...)! I
luckily ['lʌkɪli] zum Glück, glücklicherweise II
lucky ['lʌki]: **be lucky (with)** Glück haben (mit) II
lunch [lʌntʃ] Mittagessen I
lunch break Mittagspause I
lunchtime ['lʌntʃtaɪm] Mittagszeit IV
lyrics *(pl)* ['lɪrɪks] Liedtext(e), Songtext(e) III

M

machine [mə'ʃiːn] Maschine, Gerät III
mad [mæd] verrückt I • **be mad about sth.** verrückt nach/auf etwas sein III
Madam ['mædəm]: **Dear Sir/Madam** Sehr geehrte Damen und Herren *(Briefbeginn)* V 2 (38)
► S.164 Formal letters
made [meɪd] *siehe* **make**
magazine [ˌmægə'ziːn] Zeitschrift, Magazin I
magical ['mædʒɪkl] zauberhaft, wundervoll V 1 (6)
maid [meɪd] Hausangestellte, Zimmermädchen IV
mail [meɪl] schicken, senden *(per Post oder E-Mail)* I • **mail sb.** jn. anmailen II
mailbox ['meɪlbɒks] Mailbox V 3 (52)
main [meɪn] Haupt- III
majority [mə'dʒɒrəti] Mehrheit IV
make [meɪk], **made, made** machen; bauen I • **make a call** ein Telefongespräch führen II • **make a deal** ein Abkommen/eine Abmachung treffen III • **make a decision** eine Entscheidung fällen V 2 (33/161)
make a mess alles durcheinanderbringen, alles in Unordnung bringen I • **make a point** ein Argument vorbringen III • **make a speech** eine Rede halten IV
°**make comparisons** Vergleiche anstellen, vergleichen • **make friends (with sb.)** Freunde finden; sich anfreunden (mit jm.) V 3 (48)
make money Geld verdienen IV
°**make notes** (sich) Notizen ma-

chen • **make sb. do sth.** jn. dazu bringen, etwas zu tun V 2 (34)
make sure that ... sich vergewissern, dass ...; dafür sorgen, dass ... IV • **°make sth. up** sich etwas ausdenken • **°What makes a game a good game?** Was macht ein Spiel zu einem guten Spiel?
make-up ['meɪkʌp] Make-up II
make-up artist ['ɑ:tɪst] Maskenbildner/in V 2 (32)
mall [mɔ:l], **shopping mall** *(großes)* Einkaufszentrum III
man [mæn], *pl* **men** [men] Mann I
manager ['mænɪdʒə] Manager/in III; Geschäftsführer/in, Leiter/in V 2 (39)
°manatee [ˌmænə'ti:] Seekuh
many ['meni] viele I • **how many?** wie viele? I
°Maori ['maʊri] Maori; maorisch
map [mæp] Landkarte, Stadtplan II
marathon ['mærəθən] Marathon IV
march [mɑ:tʃ] Marsch, Demonstration IV
March [mɑ:tʃ] März I
mark [mɑ:k] (Schul-)Note, Zensur IV
mark sth. up [ˌmɑ:k_'ʌp] etwas markieren, kennzeichnen II
°marked [mɑ:kt] markiert
market ['mɑ:kɪt] Markt II
marmalade ['mɑ:məleɪd] (Orangen-)Marmelade I
married (to) ['mærɪd] verheiratet (mit) I • **get married (to sb.)** (jn.) heiraten V 1 (11) • **married couple** Ehepaar V 4 (80/173)
match [mætʃ] Spiel, Wettkampf I
°match [mætʃ]
1. passen zu
2. zuordnen
°Match the letters and numbers. Ordne die Buchstaben den Zahlen zu.
match day ['mætʃ deɪ] Spieltag V 2 (41)
mate [meɪt] *(infml)* Freund/in, Kumpel III
material [mə'tɪəriəl] Material V 4 (88)
math [mæθ] *(AE)* Mathematik IV
maths [mæθs] Mathematik I
matter ['mætə]: **What's the matter?** Was ist los? / Was ist denn? II
mattress ['mætrəs] Matratze V 1 (17)
may [meɪ] dürfen I
May [meɪ] Mai I
maybe ['meɪbi] vielleicht I
mayor [meə] Bürgermeister/in IV
me [mi:] mir; mich I • **Me too.** Ich auch. I • **more than me** mehr als ich II • **That's me.** Das bin ich. I
Why me? Warum ich? I
meal [mi:l] Mahlzeit, Essen III
set meal Menü III
mean [mi:n], **meant, meant**
1. bedeuten II
2. meinen *(sagen wollen)* II
What do you mean by ...? Was meinst du mit ...? IV
meaning ['mi:nɪŋ] Bedeutung III
meant [ment] *siehe* **mean**
meat [mi:t] Fleisch I
meaty ['mi:ti] fleischig; Fleisch-; mit viel Fleisch V 4 (89)
mechanic [mə'kænɪk] Mechaniker/ Mechanikerin V 2 (32)
medal ['medl] Medaille III
media *(pl)* ['mi:diə] Medien III
mediation [ˌmi:di'eɪʃn] Vermittlung, Sprachmittlung, Mediation II
medium ['mi:diəm] mittel(groß) II
meet [mi:t], **met, met**
1. treffen; kennenlernen I
2. sich treffen I
Nice to meet you. Nett, dich kennenzulernen. III
meeting ['mi:tɪŋ] Versammlung, Besprechung; Treffen, Begegnung IV
member (of) ['membə] Mitglied (in, von) IV
men [men] *pl von „man"*
menu ['menju:]
1. Speisekarte III
2. Menü *(Computer)* III
merry-go-round ['merigəʊraʊnd] Karussell IV
mess [mes]: **be a mess** sehr unordentlich sein; fürchterlich aussehen *(Zimmer)* II • **make a mess** alles durcheinanderbringen, alles in Unordnung bringen I
message ['mesɪdʒ] Nachricht III
met [met] *siehe* **meet**
metal ['metl] Metall V 4 (82)
°method ['meθəd] Methode, Art und Weise
metre ['mi:tə] Meter II
mice [maɪs] *pl von „mouse"*
microphone ['maɪkrəfəʊn] Mikrofon III
middle (of) ['mɪdl] Mitte I; Mittelteil II • **in the middle of nowhere** *(infml) etwa:* am Ende der Welt V 1 (12)
middle school ['mɪdl sku:l] *(USA) Schule für 11- bis 14-Jährige* IV
might [maɪt]: **you might need help** du könntest (vielleicht) Hilfe brauchen III
mild [maɪld] mild III
mile [maɪl] Meile *(= ca. 1,6 km)* II
for miles meilenweit II
military ['mɪlətri] militärisch, Militär- V 3 (55) • **military-style fashion** Mode im Militärstil V 3 (55/169)
milk [mɪlk] Milch I
million ['mɪljən] Million III
millionaire [ˌmɪljə'neə] Millionär/in IV
mime [maɪm] pantomimisch darstellen, vorspielen II
°mime [maɪm] Pantomime
mind [maɪnd]: **I don't mind helping/ working/...** Es macht mir nichts aus zu helfen / zu arbeiten / ... V 2 (34) • **Do you mind?** Stört es Sie? V 2 (34/162) • **if you don't mind** wenn Sie nichts dagegen haben V 2 (34/162) • **Mind your own business.** Das geht dich nichts an! / Kümmere dich um deine eigenen Angelegenheiten! II • **Never mind.** *etwa:* Nicht so wichtig. / Ist (doch) egal. / Das willst du gar nicht wissen. IV
► S.162 (to) mind
mind map ['maɪnd mæp] Mindmap („Gedankenkarte", „Wissensnetz") I
mine [maɪn] meiner, meine, meins II
mini- ['mɪni] Mini- II
minimum ['mɪnɪməm] Minimum V 3 (59)
minister ['mɪnɪstə] Pastor/in, Pfarrer/in IV
minority [maɪ'nɒrəti] Minderheit IV
mints *(pl)* [mɪnts] Pfefferminzbonbons I
minus ['maɪnəs] minus III
minute ['mɪnɪt] Minute I • **Wait a minute.** Warte mal! / Moment mal! II
mirror ['mɪrə] Spiegel II
miss [mɪs]
1. vermissen II
2. verpassen II
3. Miss a turn. Einmal aussetzen. II
Miss White [mɪs] Frau White *(unverheiratet)* I
missing ['mɪsɪŋ]: **be missing** fehlen II
mistake [mɪ'steɪk] Fehler I
mix [mɪks] mischen, mixen III
°mix up durcheinanderbringen
°be mixed up durcheinander/ in der falschen Reihenfolge sein
mix [mɪks] Mix, Mischung III
mixed-race gemischtrassische(r,s) V 1 (17)

mixture ['mɪkstʃə] Mischung III
mobile ['məʊbaɪl] mobil, beweglich V 3 (50)
°**mobile** ['məʊbaɪl] Mobile
mobile (phone) ['məʊbaɪl] Mobiltelefon, Handy I
model ['mɒdl] Modell*(-flugzeug, -schiff usw.)* I; (Foto-)Modell II
modelling ['mɒdəlɪŋ] Arbeit als (Foto-)Modell V 1 (18)
modern ['mɒdən] modern III
mole [məʊl] Maulwurf II
mom [mɒm, *AE:* mɑ:m] *(AE)* Mama, Mutti; Mutter III
moment ['məʊmənt] Moment, Augenblick II • **at the moment** im Moment, gerade II
Monday ['mʌndeɪ, 'mʌndi] Montag I • **Monday morning** Montagmorgen I
money ['mʌni] Geld I
monitor ['mɒnɪtə] Bildschirm, Monitor III
monkey ['mʌŋki] Affe II
monster ['mɒnstə] Monster, Ungeheuer III
month [mʌnθ] Monat I
monument ['mɒnjumənt] Denkmal, Monument IV
moon [mu:n] Mond II
moped ['məʊped] Moped V 2 (38)
more [mɔ:] mehr I • **lots more** viel mehr I • **more boring (than)** langweiliger (als) II • **more quickly (than)** schneller (als) II • **more than** mehr als II • **more than me** mehr als ich II • **no more music** keine Musik mehr I • **not (...) any more** nicht mehr II • **once more** noch einmal III • **one more** noch ein(e), ein(e) weitere(r, s) I
morning ['mɔ:nɪŋ] Morgen, Vormittag I • **in the morning** morgens, am Morgen I • **Monday morning** Montagmorgen I • **on Friday morning** freitagmorgens, am Freitagmorgen I
mosque [mɒsk] Moschee III
most [məʊst] (der/die/das) meiste ...; am meisten II • **most people** die meisten Leute I • **(the) most boring** der/die/das langweiligste ...; am langweiligsten II
mostly ['məʊstli] hauptsächlich, überwiegend V 2 (35)
motel [məʊ'tel] Motel IV
mother ['mʌðə] Mutter I
motorbike ['məʊtəbaɪk] Motorrad V 3 (54)
motorway ['məʊtəweɪ] Autobahn V 4 (79)
mountain ['maʊntən] Berg II
mouse [maʊs], *pl* **mice** [maɪs] Maus I
mouth [maʊθ] Mund I
move [mu:v]
1. bewegen; sich bewegen II
Move back one space. Geh ein Feld zurück. II • **Move on one space.** Geh ein Feld vor. II
2. transportieren; verrücken *(Möbel)* V 3 (61)
3. move (to) umziehen (nach, in) II
move in einziehen II • **move out** ausziehen II
movement ['mu:vmənt] Bewegung II
movie ['mu:vi] Film III
MP3 player [ˌempi:'θri: ˌpleɪə] MP3-Spieler I
Mr ... ['mɪstə] Herr ... I
Mrs ... ['mɪsɪz] Frau ... I
Ms ... [mɪz, məz] Frau ... II
much [mʌtʃ] viel I • **how much?** wie viel? I • **How much is/are ...?** Was kostet/kosten ...? / Wie viel kostet/kosten ...? I • **like/love sth. very much** etwas sehr mögen/ sehr lieben II
muesli ['mju:zli] Müsli IV
mule [mju:l] Maultier IV
multi- ['mʌlti] viel-, mehr-; multi-, Multi- IV • **multi-coloured** vielfarbig, mehrfarbig IV • **multicultural** multikulturell V 4 (80)
multi-millionaire Multimillionär/in IV
multiple choice [ˌmʌltɪpl 'tʃɔɪs] Multiple-Choice II
mum [mʌm] Mama, Mutti; Mutter I
murder ['mɜ:də] Mord III
murder ['mɜ:də] (er)morden III
murderer ['mɜ:dərə] Mörder/in III
museum [mju'zi:əm] Museum I
mushroom ['mʌʃrʊm, -ru:m] Pilz III
music ['mju:zɪk] Musik I
musical ['mju:zɪkl] Musical I
musical instrument [ˌmju:zɪkl‿'ɪnstrəmənt] Musikinstrument III
musician [mju:'zɪʃn] Musiker/in III
Muslim ['mʊzlɪm] Muslim/Muslima, Muslimin V 4 (76)
must [mʌst] müssen I
must *(n)* [mʌst] Muss IV
mustn't do ['mʌsnt] nicht tun dürfen II
my [maɪ] mein/e I • **My name is ...** Ich heiße ... / Mein Name ist ... I
It's my turn. Ich bin dran / an der Reihe. I
myself [maɪ'self] mir/mich (selbst) III
mystery ['mɪstri] Rätsel, Geheimnis II

N

name [neɪm] Name I • **call sb. names** jn. mit Schimpfwörtern hänseln, jm. Schimpfwörter nachrufen III • **My name is ...** Ich heiße ... / Mein Name ist ... I
What's your name? Wie heißt du? I
name [neɪm] nennen; benennen II
nanny ['næni] Kindermädchen IV
nation ['neɪʃn] Nation IV
national ['næʃnəl] national, National- III • **National Park** Nationalpark IV
nationality [ˌnæʃə'næləti] Nationalität, Staatsangehörigkeit V 2 (38)
Native American [ˌneɪtɪv‿ə'merɪkən] amerikanische(r) Ureinwohner/in, Indianer/in IV
natural ['nætʃrəl] Natur-, natürlich IV • **natural history** Naturkunde III; Naturgeschichte IV
nature ['neɪtʃə] Natur V 2 (39)
near [nɪə] in der Nähe von, nahe (bei) I
nearly ['nɪəli] fast, beinahe V 1 (10)
neat [ni:t] gepflegt II; ordentlich V 2 (37) • **neat and tidy** schön ordentlich II
necessary ['nesəsəri] nötig, notwendig IV
need [ni:d] Not; Notwendigkeit V 3 (58)
need [ni:d] brauchen, benötigen I
need to do sth. etwas tun müssen; etwas zu tun brauchen V 1 (16)
► S.160 'need' als Hilfsverb / als Vollverb
needn't do ['ni:dnt] nicht tun müssen, nicht zu tun brauchen II
► S.160 'need' als Hilfsverb / als Vollverb
neighbour ['neɪbə] Nachbar/in I
neighbourhood ['neɪbəhʊd] Viertel, Gegend; Nachbarschaft V 4 (80)
nephew ['nefju:, 'nevju:] Neffe IV
nervous ['nɜ:vəs] nervös, aufgeregt I
network ['netwɜ:k] *(Radio-, Fernseh-)*Sendernetz IV; (Wörter-)Netz I
never ['nevə] nie, niemals I
Never mind. *etwa:* Nicht so wichtig. / Ist (doch) egal. / Das willst du gar nicht wissen. IV
never-ending [ˌnevər‿'endɪŋ] endlos, unendlich V 3 (57/170)
new [nju:] neu I
news *(no pl)* [nju:z] Nachrichten II
newspaper ['nju:speɪpə] Zeitung I
next [nekst]**: be next** der/die Nächste sein I • **the next morning/day** am nächsten Morgen/Tag

I • **the next photo** das nächste Foto I • **What have we got next?** Was haben wir als Nächstes? I
next to [nekst] neben I
nice [naɪs] schön, nett I • **Nice to meet you.** Nett, dich kennenzulernen. III
niece [niːs] Nichte IV
night [naɪt] Nacht, später Abend I • **at night** nachts, in der Nacht I • **on Friday night** freitagnachts, Freitagnacht I
nil [nɪl] null III
no [nəʊ] nein I
no [nəʊ] kein, keine I • **no more music** keine Musik mehr I • **no one** niemand IV • **No way!** Auf keinen Fall! / Kommt nicht in Frage! II
nobody ['nəʊbədi] niemand II
nod (-dd-) [nɒd] nicken (mit) II
noise [nɔɪz] Geräusch; Lärm I
noisy ['nɔɪzi] laut, lärmend II
non-violent [ˌnɒn'vaɪələnt] gewaltlos, gewaltfrei IV
°**noon** [nuːn] Mittag, zwölf Uhr mittags
normal ['nɔːml] normal V 2 (34)
north [nɔːθ] Norden; nach Norden; nördlich III
northbound ['nɔːθbaʊnd] Richtung Norden III
north-east [ˌnɔːθ'iːst] Nordosten; nach Nordosten; nordöstlich III
°**northern** ['nɔːðən] Nord-, nördlich
north-west [ˌnɔːθ'west] Nordwesten; nach Nordwesten; nordwestlich III
nose [nəʊz] Nase I
not [nɒt] nicht I • **not (...) any** kein, keine I • **not (...) any more** nicht mehr II • **not (...) anybody** niemand II • **not (...) anything** nichts II • **not (...) anywhere** nirgendwo(hin) II • **not even** (noch) nicht einmal III • **not ... till / not ... until** erst (um); nicht vor III **not (...) yet** noch nicht II
note [nəʊt]
1. Mitteilung, Notiz I
2. (Geld-)Schein, Banknote V 3 (53)
°**make notes** sich Notizen machen
take notes sich Notizen machen I
nothing ['nʌθɪŋ] nichts II
notice ['nəʊtɪs] Mitteilung, Aushang V 1 (19)
notice board ['nəʊtɪs bɔːd] Anschlagtafel, „schwarzes Brett" IV
novel ['nɒvl] Roman V 4 (81)
November [nəʊ'vembə] November I
now [naʊ] nun, jetzt I
nowhere ['nəʊweə] nirgendwo(hin) V 1 (12) • **in the middle of nowhere** *(infml) etwa:* am Ende der Welt V 1 (12)
number ['nʌmbə] Zahl, Ziffer, Nummer I
°**numbered** ['nʌmbəd] nummeriert
number plate ['nʌmbə pleɪt] Nummernschild IV
nun [nʌn] Nonne V 1 (17)
nurse [nɜːs] Krankenpfleger/in, Krankenschwester V 2 (35)
nut [nʌt] Nuss III

O

o [əʊ] null I
ocean ['əʊʃn] Ozean IV
o'clock [ə'klɒk]**: eleven o'clock** elf Uhr I
October [ɒk'təʊbə] Oktober I
°**odd** [ɒd]**: What word is the odd one out?** Welches Wort passt nicht dazu? / Welches Wort gehört nicht dazu?
of [əv, ɒv] von I • **of the summer holidays** der Sommerferien I
of course [əv 'kɔːs] natürlich, selbstverständlich I
off [ɒf]**: cut sth. off** etwas abschneiden, abtrennen III • **drop sb. off** jn. absetzen *(aussteigen lassen)* IV **fall off** herunterfallen (von) II **get off (the train/bus)** (aus dem Zug/Bus) aussteigen I • **get sth. off the ground** etwas auf den Weg bringen; etwas auf die Beine stellen III • **take off** *(infml)* sich davonmachen, sich aus dem Staub machen IV • **take sth. off** etwas ausziehen *(Kleidung)* II; etwas absetzen *(Hut, Helm)* III • **take 10c off** 10 Cent abziehen I • **tear sth. off** etwas abreißen IV • **turn sth. off** etwas ausschalten II
offer ['ɒfə] anbieten IV
office ['ɒfɪs] Büro III
official [ə'fɪʃl] offiziell, amtlich, Amts- V 4 (81)
often ['ɒfn] oft, häufig I
Oh dear! [əʊ 'dɪə] Oje! II
Oh well ... [əʊ 'wel] Na ja ... / Na gut ... I
°**OHP** [ˌəʊ‿eɪtʃ 'piː] *(kurz für:* **overhead projector** [ˌəʊvəhed prə'dʒektə]*)* Overheadprojektor
oil [ɔɪl] Öl III
oil-producing ['ɔɪl prəˌdjuːsɪŋ] ölproduzierend V 3 (57/170)
OK [əʊ'keɪ] okay, gut, in Ordnung I
old [əʊld] alt I • **How old are you?** Wie alt bist du? I • **I'm ... years old.** Ich bin ... Jahre alt. I • **thirteen-year-old** Dreizehnjährige(r) III
old-fashioned [ˌəʊld'fæʃnd] altmodisch III
Olympic Games [əˌlɪmpɪk 'geɪmz] Olympische Spiele IV
on [ɒn]
1. auf I
2. weiter III
3. an, eingeschaltet *(Radio, Licht usw.)* II
and so on *(short:* **etc.** [et'setərə]*)* und so weiter (usw.) IV • **be on** gezeigt werden, laufen *(im Fernsehen)* IV • **be on holiday** in Urlaub sein; Ferien haben/machen II • **go on** angehen *(Licht)* III • **go on holiday** in Urlaub fahren II • **on 13th June** am 13. Juni I • **on earth** auf der Erde III • **on foot** zu Fuß III • **on Friday** am Freitag I • **on Friday afternoon** freitagnachmittags, am Freitagnachmittag I **on Friday evening** freitagabends, am Freitagabend I • **on Friday morning** freitagmorgens, am Freitagmorgen I • **on Friday night** freitagnachts, Freitagnacht I • **on my/our/... own** allein, selbstständig *(ohne Hilfe)* IV • **on the beach** am Strand II • **on the board** an die Tafel I • **on the corner of Sand Street and London Road** Sand Street, Ecke London Road II • **on the left** links, auf der linken Seite I • **on the phone** am Telefon I **on the plane** im Flugzeug II • **on the radio** im Radio I • **on the right** rechts, auf der rechten Seite I • **on the second floor** im zweiten Stock *(BE)* / im ersten Stock *(AE)* IV **on the train** im Zug I • **on TV** im Fernsehen I • **straight on** geradeaus weiter II • **What page are we on?** Auf welcher Seite sind wir? I
once [wʌns]
1. einst, früher einmal III
2. einmal III
once more / once again noch einmal III
one [wʌn] eins, ein, eine I • **a new one** ein neuer / eine neue / ein neues II • **my old ones** meine alten II • **no one** niemand IV **one another** einander, sich (gegenseitig) III • **one day** eines Tages I • **one more** noch ein/e, ein/e weitere(r, s) I
onion ['ʌnjən] Zwiebel III

online [ˌɒn'laɪn] online, Online- III
only ['əʊnli]
1. nur, bloß I; erst III
2. **the only guest** der einzige Gast I
onto ['ɒntə, 'ɒntʊ] auf (... hinauf) III
open ['əʊpən]
1. öffnen, aufmachen I
2. sich öffnen I
open ['əʊpən] offen, geöffnet II
open-air im Freien; Freilicht- III
open-top bus oben offener (Doppeldecker-)Bus III
opening hours *(pl)* ['əʊpənɪŋ‿ˌaʊəz] Öffnungszeiten IV
°**opening sentence** [ˌəʊpənɪŋ 'sentəns] Einleitungssatz
opera ['ɒprə] Oper III
operation (on) [ˌɒpə'reɪʃn] Operation (an) III
opinion (of) [ə'pɪnjən] Meinung (von, zu) IV • **in my opinion** meiner Meinung nach IV
opportunity [ˌɒpə'tju:nəti] Gelegenheit, Möglichkeit V 3 (59)
opposite ['ɒpəzɪt] gegenüber (von) II
opposite ['ɒpəzɪt] Gegenteil I
opposite ['ɒpəzɪt] gegenteilige(r, s), entgegengesetzte(r, s) V 3 (51)
or [ɔ:] oder I • °**either ... or ...** ['aɪðə ... ɔ:, 'i:ðə ... ɔ:] entweder ... oder
orange ['ɒrɪndʒ] orange(farben) I
orange ['ɒrɪndʒ] Orange, Apfelsine I
orange juice ['ɒrɪndʒ dʒu:s] Orangensaft I
order ['ɔ:də]
1. Reihenfolge III
2. Befehl, Anweisung, Anordnung V 3 (54)
°**word order** Wortstellung
order ['ɔ:də] bestellen V 3 (53)
organ ['ɔ:gən] Orgel II
organize ['ɔ:gənaɪz] organisieren V 2 (33)
organized ['ɔ:gənaɪzd] (gut) organisiert V 2 (33)
original *(n; adj)* [ə'rɪdʒənl] Original; Original- IV
orphan ['ɔ:fn] Waise, Waisenkind V 1 (17)
other ['ʌðə] andere(r, s) I • **the others** die anderen I • **the other way round** anders herum II
Ouch! [aʊtʃ] Autsch! I
our ['aʊə] unser, unsere I
ours ['aʊəz] unserer, unsere, unseres II
ourselves [aʊə'selvz] uns (selbst) III
out [aʊt] heraus, hinaus; draußen II
be out weg sein, nicht da sein I
out of ... aus ... (heraus/hinaus) I
°**a day out** ein Tagesausflug
°**two out of three** zwei von drei
outback ['aʊtbæk]: **the outback** *(Australien)* das Hinterland V 1 (6)
outdoor ['aʊtdɔ:] im Freien, Außen- III
outdoors [ˌaʊt'dɔ:z] draußen, im Freien; nach draußen V 1 (9)
outfit ['aʊtfɪt] Outfit *(Kleidung; Ausrüstung)* II
°**outhouse** ['aʊthaʊs] Nebengebäude; Außentoilette
outline ['aʊtlaɪn] Gliederung V 3 (51)
outside [ˌaʊt'saɪd]
1. draußen I
2. nach draußen II
3. **outside his room** vor seinem Zimmer; außerhalb seines Zimmers I
outside [ˌaʊt'saɪd]: **the outside** das Äußere, die Außenseite V 4 (82/174)
over ['əʊvə]
1. über, oberhalb von I
2. über, mehr als II
3. **be over** vorbei/zu Ende sein I
all over the world auf der ganzen Welt III • **from all over England/the UK** aus ganz England/aus dem gesamten Vereinigten Königreich III • **over there** da drüben, dort drüben I • **over to ...** hinüber zu/nach ... II
overhead transparency [ˌəʊvəhed træns'pærənsi] Folie *(für Overheadprojektoren)* V 4 (88)
overnight [ˌəʊvə'naɪt] über Nacht V 3 (58)
own [əʊn]: **on my/our/... own** allein, selbstständig *(ohne Hilfe)* IV • **our own pool** unser eigenes Schwimmbad II • °**a statement of your own** eine eigene Aussage
owner ['əʊnə] Besitzer/in V 1 (19)
ozone layer ['əʊzəʊn leɪə] Ozonschicht V 1 (9)

P

Pacific: the Pacific (Ocean) [pəˌsɪfɪk‿'əʊʃn] der Pazifische Ozean, der Pazifik IV
°**Pacific Islander** [pəˌsɪfɪk‿'aɪləndə] Pazifikinsulaner/in
pack [pæk] packen, einpacken II
packet ['pækɪt] Päckchen, Packung, Schachtel I • **a packet of mints** ein Päckchen/eine Packung Pfefferminzbonbons I
paddle ['pædl] paddeln III
paddle ['pædl] Paddel III
pads *(pl)* [pædz] *(Knie- usw.)* Schützer *(für Inlineskater)*; Schulterpolster *(beim American Football)* III
page [peɪdʒ] (Buch-, Heft-)Seite I
What page are we on? Auf welcher Seite sind wir? I
paid [peɪd] *siehe* **pay**
pain [peɪn] Schmerz(en) IV
painful ['peɪnfl] schmerzhaft; schmerzlich V 4 (89)
paint [peɪnt] malen, anmalen I
painter ['peɪntə] Maler/in II
painting ['peɪntɪŋ] Gemälde IV
pair [peə]: **a pair (of)** ein Paar II
palace ['pæləs] Palast, Schloss III
panic ['pænɪk]: **Don't panic.** Keine Panik. / Bleib ruhig. IV
pants *(pl)* [pænts] *(AE)* Hose IV
paper ['peɪpə]
1. Papier I
2. Zeitung II
paragraph ['pærəgrɑ:f] Absatz *(in einem Text)* II
Paralympics *(pl)* [ˌpærə'lɪmpɪks] *olympischer Wettkampf für Behindertensportler/innen* III
paramedic [ˌpærə'medɪk] Sanitäter/in II
paraphrase ['pærəfreɪz] umschreiben, anders ausdrücken III
parcel ['pɑ:sl] Paket I
parents ['peərənts] Eltern I
park [pɑ:k] Park I
parking ['pɑ:kɪŋ] (das) Parken IV
park ranger ['reɪndʒə] *Ranger sind eine Art Aufseher/in in Nationalparks, die auch Führungen machen und als Wald- und Wildhüter/innen arbeiten* IV
parliament ['pɑ:ləmənt] Parlament III
parrot ['pærət] Papagei I
part [pɑ:t] Teil I • **take part (in)** teilnehmen (an) IV
particular [pə'tɪkjələ] bestimmte(r, s) V 3 (54)
partner ['pɑ:tnə] Partner/in I
party ['pɑ:ti] Party I • **have a party** eine Party feiern/veranstalten II
party ['pɑ:ti] (Partys) feiern IV
pass [pɑ:s]
1. (herüber)reichen, weitergeben I
pass round herumgeben I
°**pass sth. on** etwas weitergeben
2. **pass an exam** eine Prüfung bestehen IV
passenger ['pæsɪndʒə] Passagier/in V 4 (76)

passion ['pæʃn] Leidenschaft V 4 (78)
past [pɑːst] Vergangenheit II
past [pɑːst] vorbei (an), vorüber (an) II • **half past 11** halb zwölf (11.30 / 23.30) I • **quarter past 11** Viertel nach 11 (11.15 / 23.15) I
pasta *(no pl)* ['pæstə] Nudeln, Teigwaren IV
path [pɑːθ] Pfad, Weg II • **bridle path** ['braɪdl pɑːθ] Reitweg III
patrol [pə'trəʊl] Streife, Patrouille IV
pavement ['peɪvmənt] Gehweg, Bürgersteig IV
pay [peɪ] Bezahlung, Lohn V 1 (19)
pay (for sth.) [peɪ], **paid, paid** etwas bezahlen II • **pay by credit card** mit Kreditkarte bezahlen V 3 (53/168) **pay cash** bar bezahlen V 3 (53/168)
PE [,piː‿'iː], **Physical Education** [,fɪzɪkəl‿edʒu'keɪʃn] Sportunterricht, Turnen I
pea [piː] Erbse III
peace [piːs] Friede(n) V 4 (82)
pen [pen] Kugelschreiber, Füller I
pence (p) *(pl)* [pens] Pence *(pl von „penny")* I
pencil ['pensl] Bleistift I
pencil case ['pensl keɪs] Federmäppchen I
pencil sharpener ['pensl ʃɑːpnə] Bleistiftanspitzer I
penny ['peni] *kleinste britische Münze* I
people ['piːpl] Menschen, Leute I
pepper ['pepə] Pfeffer III
per [pɜː, pə] pro III
per cent (%) [pə'sent] Prozent III
percentage [pə'sentɪdʒ] Prozentsatz, prozentualer Anteil V 1 (10)
perfect ['pɜːfɪkt] perfekt, ideal, vollkommen IV
period ['pɪəriəd]
1. (Unterrichts-/Schul-)Stunde IV
°**2. period of time** Zeitspanne, Zeitraum
person ['pɜːsn] Person II
personal ['pɜːsənl] persönliche(r, s) III
personality [,pɜːsə'næləti] Persönlichkeit V 2 (34)
pet [pet] Haustier I
petrol ['petrəl] Benzin IV
petrol station ['petrəl steɪʃn] Tankstelle IV
pet shop ['pet ʃɒp] Tierhandlung I
phone [fəʊn] Telefon I • **on the phone** am Telefon I • **phone call** Anruf, Telefongespräch I • **phone number** Telefonnummer I
phone [fəʊn] anrufen II
photo ['fəʊtəʊ] Foto I • **in the photo** auf dem Foto I • **take photos** Fotos machen, fotografieren I
°**photocopy** ['fəʊtəʊkɒpi] Fotokopie
photographer [fə'tɒgrəfə] Fotograf/in II
phrase [freɪz] Ausdruck, (Rede-) Wendung I
physics ['fɪzɪks] Physik V 3 (49)
piano [pi'ænəʊ] Klavier, Piano I **play the piano** Klavier spielen I
pick [pɪk]: **pick fruit/flowers** Obst/ Blumen pflücken IV • **pick sb. up** jn. abholen III • **pick sth. up** etwas hochheben, aufheben II
picnic ['pɪknɪk] Picknick II
picture ['pɪktʃə] Bild I • **in the picture** auf dem Bild I
picture sth. ['pɪktʃə] sich etwas (bildlich) vorstellen IV
pie [paɪ] Obstkuchen; Pastete II
pie chart ['paɪ tʃɑːt] Tortendiagramm V 1 (10)
piece [piːs]: **a piece of** ein Stück I **a piece of paper** ein Stück Papier I
pig [pɪg] Schwein III
pink [pɪŋk] pink(farben), rosa I
pipe [paɪp] Pfeife III
pirate ['paɪrət] Pirat, Piratin I
pitch [pɪtʃ]: **football/hockey pitch** Fußball-/Hockeyplatz, -feld II
pizza ['piːtsə] Pizza I
place [pleɪs] Ort, Platz I • **at someone's place** bei jemandem zu Hause V 1 (6) • **in other places** an anderen Orten, anderswo III **place of birth** Geburtsort V 2 (38/163) • **take place** stattfinden IV
°**placemat** ['pleɪsmæt] Set, Platzdeckchen
plan [plæn] Plan I
plan (-nn-) [plæn] planen II
plane [pleɪn] Flugzeug II • **on the plane** im Flugzeug II
planet ['plænɪt] Planet II
plant [plɑːnt] Pflanze IV
plant [plɑːnt] pflanzen, einpflanzen IV
plantation [plɑːn'teɪʃn] Plantage IV
plastic ['plæstɪk] Plastik, Kunststoff V 3 (58)
plate [pleɪt] Teller I • **a plate of chips** ein Teller Pommes frites I **license plate** *(AE)* Nummernschild IV • **number plate** Nummernschild IV
platform ['plætfɔːm] Bahnsteig, Gleis III
play [pleɪ] spielen I • **play a trick on sb.** jm. einen Streich spielen II **play the drums** Schlagzeug spielen III • **play the fiddle** Geige spielen III • **play the guitar** Gitarre spielen I • **play the piano** Klavier spielen I
play [pleɪ] Theaterstück I
player ['pleɪə] Spieler/in I
playlist ['pleɪlɪst] Titelliste *(von zu spielenden Songs)* III
please [pliːz] bitte *(in Fragen und Aufforderungen)* I
plot [plɒt] Handlung *(eines Romans, Films)* IV
plug [plʌg] Stecker III
plus [plʌs] plus III
pm [,piː‿'em]: **7 pm** 7 Uhr abends/ 19 Uhr I
pocket ['pɒkɪt] Tasche *(an Kleidungsstück)* II
pocket money ['pɒkɪt ,mʌni] Taschengeld II
poem ['pəʊɪm] Gedicht I
point [pɔɪnt] Punkt II • **make a point** ein Argument vorbringen III °**point in time** Zeitpunkt • **point of view** Standpunkt II • **from my point of view** aus meiner Sicht; von meinem Standpunkt aus gesehen II • **10.4 (ten point four)** 10,4 (zehn Komma vier) III
point (at/to sth.) [pɔɪnt] zeigen, deuten (auf etwas) II
police *(pl)* [pə'liːs] Polizei I
policeman, policewoman [pə'liːsmən, pə'liːswʊmən] Polizist, Polizistin II
police officer [pə'liːs‿,ɒfɪsə] Polizist/ Polizistin V 2 (32)
police station [pə'liːs steɪʃn] Polizeiwache, Polizeirevier II
polite [pə'laɪt] höflich IV
political [pə'lɪtɪkl] politisch V 4 (80)
polluted [pə'luːtɪd] verseucht, verunreinigt V 4 (74)
poltergeist ['pəʊltəgaɪst] Poltergeist I
ponytail ['pəʊniteɪl] Pferdeschwanz *(Frisur)* III
poor [pɔː, pʊə] arm I • **poor Sophie** (die) arme Sophie I
pop (music) [pɒp] Pop(musik) III
popcorn ['pɒpkɔːn] Popcorn II
popular (with) ['pɒpjələ] beliebt (bei) V 2 (46)
population [,pɒpju'leɪʃn] Bevölkerung, Einwohner(zahl) III
pork [pɔːk] Schweinefleisch III
°**possession** [pə'zeʃn] Besitz
possibility [,pɒsə'bɪləti] Möglichkeit IV
possible ['pɒsəbl] möglich II

post [pəʊst] Post *(Briefe, Päckchen, ...)* III
post [pəʊst] posten *(ins Netz stellen)* V 1 (6)
postcard ['pəʊstkɑ:d] Postkarte II
postcode ['pəʊstkəʊd] Postleitzahl V 2 (38)
poster ['pəʊstə] Poster I
post office ['pəʊst‿ɒfɪs] Postamt II
potato [pə'teɪtəʊ], *pl* **potatoes** Kartoffel I
potato chips [pə'teɪtəʊ tʃɪps] *(AE)* Kartoffelchips IV
°**pouch** [paʊtʃ] Beutel
poultry ['pəʊltri] Geflügel IV
pound (£) [paʊnd] Pfund *(britische Währung)* I
power ['paʊə] Macht; Stärke V 4 (77)
practice ['præktɪs] *hier:* Übungsteil I
practice ['præktɪs] *(AE)* üben; trainieren IV
practise ['præktɪs]
1. üben; trainieren I
°**2.** ausüben *(Religion)*
prefer sth. (to sth. else) (-rr-) [prɪ'fɜ:] etwas lieber tun/haben (als etwas anderes); etwas (etwas anderem) vorziehen V 4 (87)
prejudice (against) ['predʒudɪs] Voreingenommenheit (gegen), Vorurteil (gegenüber) IV
prejudiced ['predʒədɪst]: **be prejudiced (against)** voreingenommen sein (gegen), Vorurteile haben (gegenüber) IV
prepare [prɪ'peə] vorbereiten; sich vorbereiten II • **prepare for** sich vorbereiten auf II
present ['preznt]
1. Gegenwart I
2. Geschenk I
present sth. (to sb.) [prɪ'zent] (jm.) etwas präsentieren, vorstellen I
presentation [ˌprezn'teɪʃn] Präsentation, Vorstellung I
presenter [prɪ'zentə] Moderator/in II
president ['prezɪdənt] Präsident/in IV
press sth. [pres] etwas drücken; auf etwas drücken IV
pretty ['prɪti] hübsch I
pretty cool/good/... ['prɪti] ziemlich cool/gut/... II
prevent sth. [prɪ'vent] etwas verhindern V 4 (88)
price [praɪs] (Kauf-)Preis I
primary school ['praɪməri sku:l] Grundschule V 2 (38)
prime time ['praɪm taɪm] Hauptsendezeit IV

print [prɪnt] drucken, abdrucken V 1 (9) • **print sth. out** etwas ausdrucken II
print: bold print [ˌbəʊld 'prɪnt] Fettdruck III
printer ['prɪntə] Drucker V 2 (34)
prison ['prɪzn] Gefängnis V 3 (54)
go to prison ins Gefängnis kommen V 3 (54/169)
private ['praɪvət] privat IV
private detective [ˌpraɪvət dɪ'tektɪv] Privatdetektiv/in V 2 (35)
prize [praɪz] Preis, Gewinn I
probably ['prɒbəbli] wahrscheinlich II
problem ['prɒbləm] Problem II
process ['prəʊses] Prozess, Verfahren IV
produce [prə'dju:s] produzieren, herstellen III
product ['prɒdʌkt] Produkt, Erzeugnis IV
production [prə'dʌkʃn] Produktion, Herstellung IV
profile ['prəʊfaɪl] Profil, Beschreibung, Porträt V 2 (36)
program ['prəʊgræm] *(AE)* Programm V 3 (58)
programme ['prəʊgræm] Programm I
project (about, on) ['prɒdʒekt] Projekt (über, zu) I
projector [prə'dʒektə] Projektor, Beamer V 4 (88)
promise ['prɒmɪs] versprechen II
°**pronounce** [prə'naʊns] aussprechen
pronunciation [prəˌnʌnsi'eɪʃn] Aussprache I
proof *(no pl)* [pru:f] Beweis(e) II
protect sb. (from) [prə'tekt] jn. (be)schützen (vor) III
protest ['prəʊtest] Protest IV
protest [prə'test] protestieren IV
protester [prə'testə] Demonstrant/-in, Protestierer/in V 4 (83)
proud (of sb./sth.) [praʊd] stolz (auf jn./etwas) II
province ['prɒvɪns] Provinz III
°**Prussia** ['prʌʃə] Preußen
PS [ˌpi:‿'es] **(postscript** ['pəʊstskrɪpt]**)** PS *(Nachschrift unter Briefen)* III
pub [pʌb] Kneipe, Lokal II
public ['pʌblɪk] öffentliche(r, s) III
public transport *(no pl)* öffentliche Verkehrsmittel, öffentlicher Personennahverkehr III
publish ['pʌblɪʃ] veröffentlichen III
pull [pʊl] ziehen I
pullover ['pʊləʊvə] Pullover II
punctual ['pʌŋktʃuəl] pünktlich V 2 (35)

punish ['pʌnɪʃ] bestrafen V 3 (54/160)
punishment ['pʌnɪʃmənt] Bestrafung, Strafe V 3 (54)
punk (rock) [pʌŋk] Punk(rock) III
purple ['pɜ:pl] violett; lila I
purse [pɜ:s] Geldbörse II
push [pʊʃ] drücken, schieben, stoßen I
put (-tt-) [pʊt], **put, put** legen, stellen, *(etwas wohin)* tun I • **put sth. down** etwas hinlegen IV • **put sth. on** etwas anziehen *(Kleidung)* II; etwas aufsetzen *(Hut, Helm)* III
put out a fire ein Feuer löschen IV
°**Put up your hand.** Heb deine Hand. / Hebt eure Hand.
puzzle ['pʌzl] Rätsel IV
puzzled ['pʌzld] verwirrt II
pyjamas *(pl)* [pə'dʒɑ:məz] Schlafanzug II
pyramid ['pɪrəmɪd] Pyramide IV

Q

qualification [ˌkwɒlɪfɪ'keɪʃn] Abschluss, Qualifikation V 2 (32)
quality ['kwɒləti] Qualität IV
quarter ['kwɔ:tə]: **quarter past 11** Viertel nach 11 (11.15 / 23.15) I
quarter to 12 Viertel vor 12 (11.45 / 23.45) I
queen [kwi:n] Königin III
question ['kwestʃn] Frage I • **ask questions** Fragen stellen
°**questionnaire** [ˌkwestʃə'neə] Fragebogen
°**question word** ['kwestʃn wɜ:d] Fragewort
queue [kju:] Schlange, Reihe *(wartender Menschen)* IV
quick [kwɪk] schnell I
quiet ['kwaɪət] leise, still, ruhig I
°**quit** [kwɪt], **quit, quit** verlassen
quite quickly/well/... [kwaɪt] ziemlich schnell/gut/... II
quiz [kwɪz], *pl* **quizzes** ['kwɪzɪz] Quiz, Ratespiel I
°**quotation marks** [kwəʊ'teɪʃn mɑ:ks] Anführungszeichen, -striche

R

rabbit ['ræbɪt] Kaninchen I
rabbit-proof ['ræbɪt pru:f] kaninchen-sicher, kaninchen-fest V 1 (17)
race [reɪs] Rasse V 1 (17/160)
racial ['reɪʃl] Rassen-, rassisch V 4 (81)
°**racing** ['reɪsɪŋ] Rennsport, Rennen

racing car ['reɪsɪŋ kɑː] Rennwagen V 2 (35)
racist ['reɪsɪst] rassistisch; Rassist/Rassistin V 1 (17)
racket ['rækɪt]: **badminton racket** Badmintonschläger III
radio ['reɪdiəʊ] Radio I • **on the radio** im Radio I
raft [rɑːft] Schlauchboot *(wildwassertauglich)* IV
railway ['reɪlweɪ] Eisenbahn II
rain [reɪn] Regen II
rain [reɪn] regnen II
°**rainfall** ['reɪnfɔːl] Niederschlag(s-menge)
rainforest ['reɪnfɒrɪst] Regenwald V 1 (9)
rainproof ['reɪnpruːf] regendicht, wasserdicht V 1 (17/161)
rainy ['reɪni] regnerisch II
raise money (for) [reɪz] Geld sammeln (für) IV
ran [ræn] *siehe* **run**
rang [ræŋ] *siehe* **ring**
ranger ['reɪndʒə]: **(park) ranger** *Ranger sind eine Art Aufseher/in in Nationalparks, die auch Führungen machen und als Wald- und Wildhüter/innen arbeiten* IV
rap [ræp] Rap *(rhythmischer Sprechgesang)* I
rap (-pp-) [ræp] rappen III
rapids *(pl)* ['ræpɪdz] Stromschnellen III
rapper ['ræpə] Rapper/in III
rate [reɪt] bewerten V 3 (51)
rate [reɪt] Rate, Quote V 4 (81) • **exchange rate** Wechselkurs V 3 (53)
ray [reɪ] Strahl V 1 (9) • **ultraviolet rays** ultraviolette Strahlen V 1 (9)
RE [ˌɑːr_'iː], **Religious Education** [rɪˌlɪdʒəs_edʒu'keɪʃn] Religion, Religionsunterricht I
Re: ... [riː] Betreff: ... IV
reach [riːtʃ] erreichen IV • **reach for sth.** nach etwas greifen V 4 (76)
reach out (for sth.) die Hand/Hände ausstrecken (nach etwas); greifen (nach etwas) V 4 (76)
react (to) [ri'ækt] reagieren (auf) V 2 (45)
read [riːd], **read, read** lesen I
read on weiterlesen III • °**read out** vorlesen • °**Read out loud.** Lies laut vor. • °**Read the poem to a partner.** Lies das Gedicht einem Partner/einer Partnerin vor.
read [red] *siehe* **read**
reader ['riːdə] Leser/in II
ready ['redi] bereit, fertig I • **get ready (for)** sich fertig machen (für), sich vorbereiten (auf) I • **get things ready** Dinge fertig machen, vorbereiten I
real [rɪəl] echt, wirklich I • **real late** *(AE, infml)* wirklich spät, richtig spät III
realistic [ˌriːə'lɪstɪk] realistisch, wirklichkeitsnah III
reality [ri'æləti] Realität, Wirklichkeit IV
really ['rɪəli] wirklich I
reason ['riːzn] Grund, Begründung I • **for lots of reasons** aus vielen Gründen I
rebuild [ˌriː'bɪld], **rebuilt, rebuilt** wiederaufbauen V 4 (89)
rebuilt [ˌriː'bɪlt] *siehe* **rebuild**
receipt [rɪ'siːt] Quittung V 3 (53)
receive [rɪ'siːv] erhalten, empfangen V 2 (44)
recently ['riːsntli] neulich, vor kurzem; in letzter Zeit V 4 (76)
receptionist [rɪ'sepʃənɪst] Rezeptionist/in; Empfangsdame V 4 (89)
record ['rekɔːd] Schallplatte III
record [rɪ'kɔːd] *(Musik)* aufnehmen, aufzeichnen III
recorded message [rɪˌkɔːdɪd 'mesɪdʒ] (automatische) Telefonansage IV
recorder [rɪ'kɔːdə] Blockflöte III
recording [rɪ'kɔːdɪŋ] Aufnahme, Aufzeichnung III
recycled [ˌriː'saɪkld] wiederverwertet, wiederverwendet, recycelt II
recycling [ˌriː'saɪklɪŋ] Wiederverwertung, Recycling II
red [red] rot I
reef [riːf] Riff V 1 (9)
refer to (-rr-) [rɪ'fɜː] sich beziehen auf III
reference ['refrəns] Referenz, Empfehlung V 2 (38)
reflex ['riːfleks] Reflex IV
reggae ['regeɪ] Reggae III
rehearsal [rɪ'hɜːsl] Probe *(am Theater)* I
rehearse [rɪ'hɜːs] proben *(am Theater)* I
relations *(pl)* [rɪ'leɪʃnz] Beziehungen IV
relationship [rɪ'leɪʃnʃɪp] Beziehung V 2 (46)
relax [rɪ'læks] (sich) entspannen, sich ausruhen II
relaxed [rɪ'lækst] locker, entspannt III
release [rɪ'liːs] herausbringen, auf den Markt bringen *(CD, Film usw.)* III
reliable [rɪ'laɪəbl] zuverlässig, verlässlich V 2 (34)
remember sth. [rɪ'membə]
1. sich an etwas erinnern I
2. sich etwas merken I
3. remember sb./sth. *einer Person/Sache* gedenken V 4 (83)
°**Remember ...** Denk dran, ...
► S.174 (to) remind – (to) remember
remind sb. (of/about sth.) [rɪ'maɪnd] jn. (an etwas) erinnern V 4 (82)
► S.174 (to) remind – (to) remember
rent [rent] mieten, pachten V 4 (85)
repair [rɪ'peə] reparieren V 2 (33)
repeat sth. [rɪ'piːt] etwas wiederholen V 1 (14)
repeat [rɪ'piːt] Wiederholung *(einer Fernsehsendung)* IV
report (on) [rɪ'pɔːt] Bericht, Reportage (über) I
report (to sb.) [rɪ'pɔːt] (jm.) berichten II
reporter [rɪ'pɔːtə] Reporter/in IV
represent [ˌreprɪ'zent] repräsentieren, vertreten III
republic [rɪ'pʌblɪk] Republik V 4 (86)
request [rɪ'kwest] Bitte V 2 (42)
rerun ['riːrʌn] *(AE)* Wiederholung *(einer Fernsehsendung)* IV
research *(no pl)* [rɪ'sɜːtʃ, 'riːsɜːtʃ] Recherche; Nachforschung(en) IV
do research recherchieren IV
reservation [ˌrezə'veɪʃn] Reservierung V 4 (89)
respect [rɪ'spekt] achten, respektieren V 1 (16)
rest [rest] Rest II
restaurant ['restrɒnt] Restaurant II
result [rɪ'zʌlt] Ergebnis, Resultat I
°**retell** [ˌriː'tel], **retold, retold** nacherzählen
°**retold** [ˌriː'təʊld] *siehe* **retell**
return [rɪ'tɜːn] zurückkehren IV
return ticket [rɪ'tɜːn ˌtɪkɪt] Rückfahrkarte II
reunification [ˌriːˌjuːnɪfɪ'keɪʃn] Wiedervereinigung V 4 (87)
reunify [ˌriː'juːnɪfaɪ] wiedervereinigen V 4 (87/175)
revise [rɪ'vaɪz]
1. überarbeiten III
2. wiederholen III
revision [rɪ'vɪʒn] Wiederholung *(des Lernstoffs)* I
°**rewrite** [ˌriː'raɪt], **rewrote, rewritten** umschreiben, neu schreiben
°**rewritten** [ˌriː'rɪtn] *siehe* **rewrite**
°**rewrote** [ˌriː'rəʊt] *siehe* **rewrite**
rhino ['raɪnəʊ] Nashorn II
rice [raɪs] Reis IV
rich [rɪtʃ] reich II
rid [rɪd]: **get rid of sb./sth.** jn./etwas loswerden IV
ridden ['rɪdn] *siehe* **ride**
riddle ['rɪdl] Rätsel III

ride [raɪd], **rode, ridden** reiten I
go riding ['raɪdɪŋ] reiten gehen I
ride a bike Rad fahren I
ride [raɪd] Ritt V 4 (79) • **(bike) ride** (Rad-)Fahrt, (Rad-)Tour II • **take a ride** eine Fahrt machen III
rider ['raɪdə] Reiter/in IV
riding boots *(pl)* ['raɪdɪŋ bu:ts] Reitstiefel III
riding hat ['raɪdɪŋ hæt] Reitkappe, Reiterhelm III
right [raɪt] Recht IV
right [raɪt] richtig I • **all right** [ɔ:l 'raɪt] gut, in Ordnung II • **it's all right with her** es ist ihr recht; sie ist einverstanden V 4 (82) • **be right** Recht haben I • **That's right.** Das ist richtig. / Das stimmt. I • **You need a school bag, right?** Du brauchst eine Schultasche, stimmt's? / nicht wahr? I
right [raɪt] rechte(r, s) II • **look right** nach rechts schauen II • **on the right** rechts, auf der rechten Seite I • **turn right** (nach) rechts abbiegen II
right [raɪt]: **right after lunch** direkt/gleich nach dem Mittagessen I
right now jetzt sofort; jetzt gerade I • **right behind you** direkt/genau hinter dir II
rim [rɪm] Rand, Kante IV
ring [rɪŋ] Ring II
ring [rɪŋ], **rang, rung** klingeln, läuten II
ringtone ['rɪŋtəʊn] Klingelton III
rise [raɪz], **rose, risen** (auf)steigen IV
risen ['rɪzn] *siehe* **rise**
river ['rɪvə] Fluss II
road [rəʊd] Straße I • **Park Road** [,pɑ:k 'rəʊd] Parkstraße I
rock [rɒk] Fels, Felsen III
rock (music) [rɒk] Rock(musik) III
rode [rəʊd] *siehe* **ride**
role [rəʊl] Rolle III
°**role model** ['rəʊl mɒdl] Vorbild
role play ['rəʊl pleɪ] Rollenspiel II
roll [rəʊl] Brötchen I
Roman ['rəʊmən] römisch; Römer, Römerin II
°**romance** [rəʊ'mæns] Romanze
room [ru:m, rʊm] Raum, Zimmer I
rose [rəʊz] *siehe* **rise**
round [raʊnd] rund II
round [raʊnd] um ... (herum); in ... umher II • **the other way round** anders herum II
route [ru:t] Strecke, Route IV
royal ['rɔɪəl] königlich III
rubber ['rʌbə] Radiergummi I
rubbish ['rʌbɪʃ] (Haus-)Müll, Abfall II
rucksack ['rʌksæk] Rucksack III
rude [ru:d] unhöflich, unverschämt II
rugby ['rʌgbi] Rugby V 3 (48)
rule [ru:l] Regel, Vorschrift III
ruler ['ru:lə] Lineal I
run [rʌn] (Wett-)Lauf II
run (-nn-) [rʌn], **ran, run**
1. laufen, rennen I
2. verlaufen *(Straße; Grenze)* IV
3. run sth. etwas leiten *(Hotel, Firma usw.)* V 1 (17)
run into sth./sb. gegen etwas fahren / jn. anfahren IV
rung [rʌŋ] *siehe* **ring**
runner ['rʌnə] Läufer/in II
°**running head** [,rʌnɪŋ 'hed] Leitwort *(am Kopf einer Wörterbuchseite)*
running shoes ['rʌnɪŋ ʃu:z] Laufschuhe III
running track ['rʌnɪŋ træk] Laufbahn *(Sport)* III
rush hour ['rʌʃ‿aʊə] Hauptverkehrszeit III

S

sad [sæd] traurig II
saddle ['sædl] Sattel III
sadness ['sædnəs] Traurigkeit IV
safe (from) [seɪf] sicher, in Sicherheit (vor) II
safe [seɪf] Safe V 3 (62)
safety ['seɪfti] Sicherheit IV
said [sed] *siehe* **say**
sail [seɪl] segeln II
salad ['sæləd] Salat *(als Gericht oder Beilage)* I
sale [seɪl] Verkauf; Schlussverkauf IV • **for sale** *(auf Schild)* zu verkaufen IV
salmon ['sæmən], *pl* **salmon** Lachs III
salt [sɔ:lt] Salz III
same [seɪm]: **the same ...** der-/die-/dasselbe ...; dieselben ... I • **be the same** gleich sein I • **look the same** gleich aussehen I
sandal ['sændl] Sandale II
sandwich ['sænwɪtʃ, 'sænwɪdʒ] Sandwich, *(zusammengeklapptes)* belegtes Brot I
sang [sæŋ] *siehe* **sing**
sat [sæt] *siehe* **sit**
Saturday ['sætədeɪ, 'sætədi] Samstag, Sonnabend I
sauna ['sɔ:nə] Sauna II • **have a sauna** in die Sauna gehen II
sausage ['sɒsɪdʒ] (Brat-, Bock-) Würstchen, Wurst I
save [seɪv]
1. retten II
2. sparen II
3. (ab)speichern *(Daten, Telefonnummern)* V 3 (52)
saw [sɔ:] *siehe* **see**
saxophone ['sæksəfəʊn] Saxophon III
say [seɪ], **said, said** sagen I • **It says here: ...** Hier steht: ... / Es heißt hier: ... II • **say goodbye** sich verabschieden I • **Say hi to your parents for me.** Grüß deine Eltern von mir. I • **say sorry** sich entschuldigen II
°**scale** [skeɪl] Maßstab
scan (-nn-) [skæn]
°**1.** (ein)scannen
2. scan a text einen Text schnell nach bestimmten Wörtern/Informationen absuchen II
scared [skeəd] verängstigt II • **be scared (of)** Angst haben (vor) I
scary ['skeəri] unheimlich; gruselig I
scene [si:n] Szene I
scenery ['si:nəri] *(schöne)* Landschaft IV
schedule [*AE:* 'skedʒu:l, *BE:* 'ʃedju:l] *(AE)*
1. Stundenplan IV
2. Fahrplan IV
school [sku:l] Schule I • **at school** in der Schule I
school bag ['sku:l bæg] Schultasche I
school subject ['sʌbdʒɪkt] Schulfach I
science ['saɪəns] Naturwissenschaft I
score [skɔ:] Spielstand; Punktestand III • **final score** Endstand *(beim Sport)* III • **What's the score?** Wie steht es? *(beim Sport)* III
score (a goal) [skɔ:] ein Tor schießen, einen Treffer erzielen III
scrapbook ['skræpbʊk] Sammelalbum IV
scream [skri:m] schreien, kreischen IV
screen [skri:n] Leinwand; Bildschirm V 4 (78)
°**screw up** [,skru:‿'ʌp] *(infml)* Mist bauen; alles vermasseln
sea [si:] Meer, *(die)* See I
search (for) [sɜ:tʃ] suchen (nach) II
search engine ['sɜ:tʃ‿endʒɪn] Suchmaschine IV

sea snake ['si: sneɪk] Seeschlange V 1 (9)
second ['sekənd] zweite(r, s) I
second-hand [ˌsekənd 'hænd] gebraucht; aus zweiter Hand III
secondary school ['sekəndri sku:l] weiterführende Schule V 2 (38)
secret ['si:krət] Geheimnis V 3 (50/167)
secret ['si:krət] geheim V 3 (50/167)
secretly ['si:krətli] heimlich V 3 (50)
section ['sekʃn] Abschnitt, Teil, (Themen-)Bereich III
sector ['sektə] Sektor, Bereich V 4 (86)
security [sɪ'kjʊərəti] Sicherheit(svorkehrungen) IV
see [si:], **saw, seen**
1. sehen I
2. see sb. jn. besuchen, jn. aufsuchen II
See? Siehst du? I • **See you.** Tschüs. / Bis bald. I • **Wait and see!** Wart's ab! III
seem (to be/to do) [si:m] (zu sein/zu tun) scheinen IV
seen [si:n] *siehe* **see**
see-through ['si:θru:] durchsichtig IV
segregate ['segrɪgeɪt] trennen *(nach Rasse, Religion, Geschlecht)* IV
segregation [ˌsegrɪ'geɪʃn] (Rassen-)Trennung IV
sell [sel], **sold, sold** verkaufen I
be sold out ausverkauft sein, vergriffen sein III
semester [sɪ'mestə] Semester *(Schulhalbjahr in den USA)* IV
semi-final [ˌsemi'faɪnl] Halbfinale III
send [send], **sent, sent** senden, schicken II
sent [sent] *siehe* **send**
sentence ['sentəns] Satz I
separate ['seprət] getrennt, separat IV
September [sep'tembə] September I
series, *pl* **series** ['sɪəri:z] (Sende-)Reihe, Serie II
serious ['sɪəriəs] ernst, ernsthaft IV
Seriously? Im Ernst? IV
servant ['sɜ:vənt] Diener/in, Bedienstete(r) IV
serve [sɜ:v] bedienen *(Kunden)* V 2 (33)
service ['sɜ:vɪs] Dienst(leistung), Service V 3 (59)
set [set] Reihe, Set, Satz V 2 (45)
set of rules Reihe von Regeln, Regelwerk V 2 (45)
set a trap (for sb.) (-tt-) [set], **set, set** (jm.) eine Falle stellen II
set meal [ˌset 'mi:l] Menü III
settle ['setl] sich niederlassen, siedeln; besiedeln V 1 (16) • **settle down** sich eingewöhnen III
°**several** ['sevrəl] einige; mehrere
sew (on) [səʊ], **sewed, sewn** (an)nähen IV
sewn [səʊn] *siehe* **sew**
sex [seks] Geschlecht V 2 (38)
°**shack** [ʃæk] Baracke, Hütte
shadow ['ʃædəʊ] Schatten III
shake [ʃeɪk], **shook, shaken** schütteln; zittern IV
shaken ['ʃeɪkən] *siehe* **shake**
shame [ʃeɪm]: **It's a shame.** Es ist ein Jammer/eine Schande. V 3 (58)
share sth. (with) [ʃeə] sich etwas teilen (mit) I
she [ʃi:] sie I
sheep, *pl* **sheep** [ʃi:p] Schaf II
sheep station Schaffarm *(in Australien)* V 1 (12)
sheet [ʃi:t] Blatt, Bogen *(Papier)* V 2 (40)
shelf [ʃelf], *pl* **shelves** [ʃelvz] Regal(brett) I
shift [ʃɪft] Schicht *(bei der Arbeit)* IV • **on his shift** in seiner Schicht IV
shine [ʃaɪn], **shone, shone** scheinen *(Sonne)* II
shiny ['ʃaɪni] glänzend V 4 (74)
ship [ʃɪp] Schiff I
shirt [ʃɜ:t] Hemd I
shiver ['ʃɪvə] zittern II
shock [ʃɒk] Schock, Schreck V 1 (6)
shocked [ʃɒkt] schockiert V 2 (45)
shocking ['ʃɒkɪŋ] schockierend, erschreckend, schrecklich V 3 (55)
shoe [ʃu:] Schuh I
shone [ʃɒn] *siehe* **shine**
shook [ʃʊk] *siehe* **shake**
shoot [ʃu:t], **shot, shot** (er)schießen V 4 (82)
shop [ʃɒp] Laden, Geschäft I
shop (-pp-) [ʃɒp] einkaufen (gehen) I • **shop for sth.** etwas einkaufen V 3 (48)
shop assistant ['ʃɒp‿əˌsɪstənt] Verkäufer/in I
shopping ['ʃɒpɪŋ] (das) Einkaufen I
go shopping einkaufen gehen I
shopping list ['ʃɒpɪŋ lɪst] Einkaufsliste I
shopping mall ['ʃɒpɪŋ mɔ:l] *(großes)* Einkaufszentrum III
shop window [ˌʃɒp 'wɪndəʊ] Schaufenster II
short [ʃɔ:t] kurz I; klein *(Person)* IV
shorts *(pl)* [ʃɔ:ts] Shorts, kurze Hose I
shot [ʃɒt] *siehe* **shoot**
shot [ʃɒt]
1. Schuss III
°**2.** Szene *(beim Filmen)*
winning shot Siegtreffer, Siegesschuss III
should [ʃəd, ʃʊd]: **we should ...** wir sollten ... IV
shoulder ['ʃəʊldə] Schulter I
shout [ʃaʊt] schreien, rufen I
shout at sb. jn. anschreien I
show [ʃəʊ] Show, Vorstellung I
show [ʃəʊ], **showed, shown** zeigen I
shower ['ʃaʊə] Dusche I • **have a shower** (sich) duschen I
shown [ʃəʊn] *siehe* **show**
shut up [ˌʃʌt‿'ʌp], **shut, shut** den Mund halten II
shy [ʃaɪ] schüchtern, scheu II
sick [sɪk]: **I feel sick.** Mir ist schlecht. IV
side [saɪd] Seite II
sidewalk ['saɪdwɔ:k] *(AE)* Gehweg, Bürgersteig IV
sights *(pl)* [saɪts] Sehenswürdigkeiten III
sign [saɪn] Schild; Zeichen III
silence ['saɪləns] Stille; Schweigen III
silent ['saɪlənt] still, lautlos; schweigend V 4 (82) • **silent letter** „stummer" Buchstabe *(nicht gesprochener Buchstabe)* II
silly ['sɪli] albern, dumm III
similar (to sb./sth.) ['sɪmɪlə] (jm./etwas) ähnlich V 2 (39)
simple ['sɪmpl] simpel, einfach V 2 (44)
since [sɪns]
1. da (ja), weil IV
2. since April 4th seit dem 4. April IV • **since then** seitdem IV
sincerely [sɪn'sɪəli]: **Yours sincerely** Mit freundlichen Grüßen *(Briefschluss bei namentlich bekanntem Empfänger)* V 2 (38)
► S.164 Formal letters
sing [sɪŋ], **sang, sung** singen I
singer ['sɪŋə] Sänger/in II
single ['sɪŋgl] ledig, alleinstehend I
single ['sɪŋgl] Single III
single (ticket) ['sɪŋgl] einfache Fahrkarte *(nur Hinfahrt)* III
single room Einzelzimmer V 4 (89)
sink [sɪŋk] Spüle, Spülbecken I
sir [sɜ:] Sir *(höfliche Anrede für einen Unbekannten (z.B. einen Kunden) oder einen Vorgesetzten* IV
Dear Sir/Madam Sehr geehrte Damen und Herren *(Briefbeginn)* V 2 (38)
► S.164 Formal letters

sister ['sɪstə] Schwester I
sister city ['sɪstə sɪti] *(AE)* Partnerstadt IV
sit (-tt-) [sɪt]**, sat, sat** sitzen; sich setzen I • **sit down** sich hinsetzen II • **Sit with me.** Setz dich zu mir. / Setzt euch zu mir. I
°**situation** [ˌsɪtʃu'eɪʃn] Situation
size [saɪz] Größe I
skate [skeɪt] Inliner/Skateboard fahren I; Schlittschuh laufen, eislaufen II
skateboard ['skeɪtbɔːd] Skateboard I
skates *(pl)* [skeɪts] Inliner I
sketch [sketʃ] Sketch I
ski [skiː] Ski III
ski [skiː] Ski laufen/fahren III
skill [skɪl] Fähigkeit, Fertigkeit V 2 (33)
skills file ['skɪlz faɪl] *Anhang mit Lern- und Arbeitstechniken* I
skim a text (-mm-) [skɪm] einen Text überfliegen *(um den Inhalt grob zu erfassen)* III
skin [skɪn] Haut IV
skirt [skɜːt] Rock II
ski slope ['skiː sləʊp] Skipiste III
sky [skaɪ] Himmel II • **in the sky** am Himmel II
skydiving ['skaɪdaɪvɪŋ] Fallschirmspringen V 1 (13)
skyscraper ['skaɪskreɪpə] Wolkenkratzer IV
slang [slæŋ] Slang, Jargon V 4 (80)
slave [sleɪv] Sklave, Sklavin II
sledge [sledʒ] Schlitten III
sleep [sliːp] Schlaf III
sleep [sliːp]**, slept, slept** schlafen I
sleeping bag ['sliːpɪŋ bæg] Schlafsack V 1 (6)
sleepless ['sliːpləs] schlaflos IV
sleepover ['sliːpəʊvə] Schlafparty III
slept [slept] *siehe* **sleep**
slice [slaɪs] Scheibe; (Kuchen-)Stück V 1 (10)
slide [slaɪd] Dia; Folie *(in Präsentationsprogrammen)* V 4 (90)
°**Slip! Slop! Slap!** [slɪp, slɒp, slæp] *kurz für:* Schlüpf in ein Hemd! Trag Sonnenschutz auf! Setz einen Hut auf! *(als Schutzmaßnahmen gegen UV-Strahlung)*
slogan ['sləʊgən] Slogan, Parole V 4 (80)
slow [sləʊ] langsam II
slum [slʌm] Slum, Elendsviertel V 4 (74)
small [smɔːl] klein II
smart [smɑːt] clever, schlau IV
smell [smel] riechen II
smell [smel] Geruch II
smile [smaɪl] lächeln I • **smile at sb.** jn. anlächeln II
smile [smaɪl] Lächeln II
smoke [sməʊk] rauchen II
smoke [sməʊk] Rauch II
snack [snæk] Snack, Imbiss II
snake [sneɪk] Schlange I
°**snorkel** *(BE:* **-ll-***)* ['snɔːkl] schnorcheln
snow [snəʊ] Schnee II
snowball ['snəʊbɔːl] Schneeball IV
snowshoe ['snəʊʃuː] Schneeschuh III
snowshoeing ['snəʊʃuːɪŋ] Schneeschuhwandern III
so [səʊ]
1. also; deshalb, daher I • **So?** Und? / Na und? II
2. so sweet so süß I • **so far** bis jetzt, bis hierher I
3. so that sodass, damit III
4. I think so. Ich glaube (ja). I
I don't think so. Das finde/glaube ich nicht. I • **Do you really think so?** Meinst du wirklich? / Glaubst du das wirklich? II
► S.170 German 'so'
soap [səʊp]
1. Seife I
2. *(infml)* Seifenoper IV
soap opera ['səʊp‿ɒprə] *(infml auch:* **soap***)* Seifenoper IV
soccer ['sɒkə] Fußball IV
social ['səʊʃl] sozial, Sozial-, gesellschaftlich V 3 (54)
social worker ['səʊʃl ˌwɜːkə] Sozialarbeiter/in V 3 (57)
sock [sɒk] Socke, Strumpf I
soda ['səʊdə] *(AE)* Limonade IV
sofa ['səʊfə] Sofa I
soft [sɒft] weich IV • **soft drink** alkoholfreies Getränk IV
software ['sɒftweə] Software II
sold [səʊld] *siehe* **sell** • **be sold out** ausverkauft sein, vergriffen sein III
soldier ['səʊldʒə] Soldat/in IV
solve [sɒlv] lösen; aufklären V 2 (34)
some [səm, sʌm] einige, ein paar I
some cheese/juice/money etwas Käse/Saft/Geld I
somebody ['sʌmbədi] jemand I
Find/Ask somebody who ... Finde/Frage jemanden, der ... II
somehow ['sʌmhaʊ] irgendwie V 4 (82)
someone ['sʌmwʌn] IV *siehe* **somebody**
something ['sʌmθɪŋ] etwas I
something to eat etwas zu essen I
sometimes ['sʌmtaɪmz] manchmal I
somewhere ['sʌmweə] irgendwo(hin) II
son [sʌn] Sohn I
song [sɒŋ] Lied, Song I
soon [suːn] bald I • **as soon as** sobald, sowie II
sooner ['suːnə] eher, früher V 1 (18)
sore [sɔː]**: be sore** wund sein, wehtun II • **have a sore throat** Halsschmerzen haben II
sorry ['sɒri]**: (I'm) sorry.** Entschuldigung. / Tut mir leid. I • **Sorry, I'm late.** Entschuldigung, dass ich zu spät bin/komme. I • **Sorry?** Wie bitte? I • **say sorry** sich entschuldigen II
°**SOS** [ˌes‿əʊ‿'es] SOS(-Ruf) *(Notsignal)*
sound [saʊnd] klingen, sich *(gut usw.)* anhören I
sound [saʊnd] Laut; Klang I
sound file ['saʊnd faɪl] Tondatei, Soundfile III
soup [suːp] Suppe II
source [sɔːs] *(Informations-, Text-)* Quelle IV
south [saʊθ] Süden; nach Süden; südlich III
southbound ['saʊθbaʊnd] Richtung Süden III
south-east [ˌsaʊθ'iːst] Südosten; nach Südosten; südöstlich III
south-west [ˌsaʊθ'west] Südwesten; nach Südwesten; südwestlich III
°**souvenir** [ˌsuːvə'nɪə] Andenken, Souvenir
space [speɪs]
1. Platz, Raum V 4 (76)
°**2.** Weltraum
Move back one space. Geh ein Feld zurück. II • **Move on one space.** Geh ein Feld vor. II
spaghetti [spə'geti] Spaghetti II
spat [spæt] *siehe* **spit**
speak (to) [spiːk]**, spoke, spoken** sprechen (mit), reden (mit) II
special ['speʃl] besondere(r, s) III
What's special about ...? Was ist das Besondere an ...? III
specific [spə'sɪfɪk] bestimmte(r, s), spezifische(r, s) IV
°**speculate (about)** ['spekjuleɪt] Vermutungen anstellen (über), spekulieren (über)
speech [spiːtʃ] Rede IV • **make a speech** eine Rede halten IV
°**speech bubble** ['spiːtʃ bʌbl] Sprechblase
spell [spel] buchstabieren I

spelling ['spelɪŋ] (Recht-)Schreibung, Schreibweise III
spend [spend], **spent, spent: spend money (on)** Geld ausgeben (für) II • **spend time (on)** Zeit verbringen (mit) II
spent [spent] *siehe* **spend**
spicy ['spaɪsi] würzig, scharf gewürzt III
spit (at sb.) (-tt-) [spɪt], **spat, spat** (jn. an)spucken IV
splash [splæʃ] spritzen IV
spoke [spəʊk] *siehe* **speak**
spoken ['spəʊkən] *siehe* **speak**
spoon [spu:n] Löffel III
sport [spɔ:t] Sport; Sportart I **do sport** Sport treiben I
sports gear *(no pl)* ['spɔ:ts gɪə] Sportausrüstung, Sportsachen II
sports hall ['spɔ:ts hɔ:l] Sporthalle III
sportsman, -woman ['spɔ:tsmən, -ˌwʊmən] Sportler/in IV
sporty ['spɔ:ti] sportlich V 2 (33)
spot (-tt-) [spɒt] entdecken III
spray [spreɪ] sprühen; besprühen IV
spring [sprɪŋ]
1. Frühling I
2. Quelle V 3 (58)
spy [spaɪ] Spion/in I
square [skweə] Platz *(in der Stadt)* II
square km (sq km) [skweə] Quadratkilometer III
°**squatter** ['skwɒtə] Hausbesetzer/in; Landbesetzer/in
squeeze [skwi:z] drücken; (aus-)pressen III
squirrel ['skwɪrəl] Eichhörnchen II
stadium ['steɪdiəm] Stadion III
stage [steɪdʒ] Bühne I
stairs *(pl)* [steəz] Treppe; Treppenstufen I
stamp [stæmp] Briefmarke I
stand [stænd], **stood, stood**
1. stehen; sich (hin)stellen II
stand up aufstehen II
2. aushalten, ertragen V 4 (82)
I can't stand him. Ich kann ihn nicht ausstehen. V 4 (82/174)
star [stɑ:]
1. Stern II
2. (Film-, Pop-)Star I
start [stɑ:t] starten, anfangen, beginnen (mit) I • **start a business** ein Unternehmen gründen V 2 (44)
start [stɑ:t] Start, Anfang, Beginn II
state [steɪt] Staat III
statement ['steɪtmənt] Aussage, Feststellung III

station ['steɪʃn]
1. Bahnhof I • **at the station** am Bahnhof I
2. **(radio/pop) station** (Radio-/Pop-)Sender III • **fire station** Feuerwache IV • **gas station** *(AE)* Tankstelle IV • **petrol station** Tankstelle IV • **sheep station** Schaffarm *(in Australien)* V 1 (12)
statue ['stætʃu:] Statue II
stay [steɪ] bleiben; wohnen, übernachten II • **stay behind** zurückbleiben, daheimbleiben IV • **stay out** draußen bleiben, wegbleiben III
stay [steɪ] Aufenthalt V 4 (89)
steak [steɪk] Steak III
steal [sti:l], **stole, stolen** stehlen II
steel [sti:l] Stahl III
steel drum [ˌsti:l 'drʌm] Steeldrum III
step [step]
1. Stufe IV
2. Schritt I
stew [stju:] Eintopf(gericht) III
stick out of sth. [stɪk], **stuck, stuck** aus etwas herausragen, herausstehen III
still [stɪl]
1. (immer) noch I
2. trotzdem, dennoch V 1 (12)
stole [stəʊl] *siehe* **steal**
stolen ['stəʊlən] gestohlen V 1 (17) *siehe* **steal**
stomach ['stʌmək] Magen II
stomach ache ['stʌmək_eɪk] Magenschmerzen, Bauchweh II
stone [stəʊn] Stein II
stood [stʊd] *siehe* **stand**
stop (-pp-) [stɒp]
1. aufhören I
2. anhalten I
Stop that! Hör auf damit! / Lass das! I
store [stɔ:] (ein)lagern, aufbewahren V 3 (58)
store [stɔ:]: **department store** Kaufhaus II
storm [stɔ:m] Sturm; Gewitter II
stormy ['stɔ:mi] stürmisch II
story ['stɔ:ri] Geschichte, Erzählung I
straight [streɪt]
°1. gerade, aufrecht
2. **straight on** geradeaus weiter II
straight towards sb. direkt auf jn. zu IV
straighten sth. up [ˌstreɪtn_'ʌp] etwas aufräumen, etwas in Ordnung bringen V 3 (54)
strange [streɪndʒ] seltsam, sonderbar; fremd III

strawberry ['strɔ:bəri] Erdbeere II
street [stri:t] Straße I • **at 7 Hamilton Street** in der Hamiltonstraße 7 I
strength [streŋθ] Stärke, Kraft V 2 (40)
stress [stres]
1. Stress V 4 (79/173)
2. Betonung III
stressed [strest]
1. gestresst V 4 (79)
°2. betont
stressful ['stresfl] anstrengend, stressig V 2 (45)
strict [strɪkt] streng III
strike [straɪk] Streik III • **be on strike** streiken, sich im Streik befinden III • **go on strike** streiken, in den Streik treten III
strong [strɒŋ] stark II
structure ['strʌktʃə] Struktur; Gliederung III
structure ['strʌktʃə] strukturieren, aufbauen II
stuck [stʌk] *siehe* **stick**
student ['stju:dənt] Schüler/in; Student/in I
studio ['stju:diəʊ] Studio I
study ['stʌdi] studieren; sorgfältig durchlesen; lernen IV
study hall ['stʌdi hɔ:l] *Zeit zum selbstständigen Lernen in der Schule* IV
study skills *(pl)* ['stʌdi skɪlz] Lern- und Arbeitstechniken I
stuff [stʌf] Zeug, Kram II
stupid ['stju:pɪd] blöd, dumm III
style [staɪl] Stil V 2 (38) • **military-style fashion** Mode im Militärstil V 3 (55/169)
subject ['sʌbdʒɪkt] Schulfach I
subject line ['sʌbdʒɪkt laɪn] Betreffzeile V 4 (85)
suburb ['sʌbɜ:b] Vorort V 4 (79)
subway ['sʌbweɪ]: **the subway** *(AE)* die U-Bahn II
succeed (in sth.) [sək'si:d] Erfolg haben, erfolgreich sein (mit etwas, bei etwas) IV
success [sək'ses] Erfolg III
successful [sək'sesfl] erfolgreich III
such (a) [sʌtʃ] so (ein/e), solch (ein/e); solche V 3 (58)
► S.170 German 'so'
suddenly ['sʌdnli] plötzlich, auf einmal I
sugar ['ʃʊgə] Zucker II
suggest sth. (to sb.) [sə'dʒest] (jm.) etwas vorschlagen IV
suggestion [sə'dʒestʃən] Vorschlag IV

suit [su:t] Anzug; (Damen-)Kostüm IV
suitable ['su:təbl] geeignet, passend V 2 (40)
suitcase ['su:tkeɪs] Koffer II
sum sth. up (-mm-) [ˌsʌm_'ʌp] etwas zusammenfassen V 2 (46)
°**summarize** ['sʌməraɪz] zusammenfassen
summary ['sʌməri] Zusammenfassung IV
summer ['sʌmə] Sommer I
sun [sʌn] Sonne II
Sunday ['sʌndeɪ, 'sʌndi] Sonntag I
sung [sʌŋ] *siehe* **sing**
sunglasses *(pl)* ['sʌŋglɑ:sɪz] (eine) Sonnenbrille I
sunny ['sʌni] sonnig II
sunscreen ['sʌnskri:n] Sonnenschutzmittel V 1 (9)
supermarket ['su:pəmɑ:kɪt] Supermarkt II
supper ['sʌpə] Abendessen IV
support [sə'pɔ:t] unterstützen IV
support a team eine Mannschaft unterstützen; Fan einer Mannschaft sein III
supporter [sə'pɔ:tə] Anhänger/in, Fan III
suppose [sə'pəʊz] annehmen, vermuten II
sure [ʃʊə, ʃɔ:] sicher I • **make sure that ...** sich vergewissern, dass ...; dafür sorgen, dass ... IV
surf [sɜ:f] surfen IV • **surf the internet** im Internet surfen II
surfboard ['sɜ:fbɔ:d] Surfbrett II
surfer ['sɜ:fə] Surfer/in IV
surfing ['sɜ:fɪŋ]: **go surfing** wellenreiten gehen, surfen gehen II
surprise [sə'praɪz] Überraschung II
surprise sb. [sə'praɪz] jn. überraschen III
surprised (at sth.) [sə'praɪzd] überrascht (über etwas) III
surprising [sə'praɪzɪŋ] überraschend, erstaunlich III
surrounded by [sə'raʊndɪd] umgeben von; umstellt von V 4 (81)
survey (on) ['sɜ:veɪ] Umfrage, Untersuchung (über) II
survival [sə'vaɪvl] Überleben II
survive [sə'vaɪv] überleben II
suspense [sə'spens] Spannung V 3 (64)
swam [swæm] *siehe* **swim**
swap sth. (for sth.) (-pp-) [swɒp] etwas (ein)tauschen (für etwas/gegen etwas) IV
sweat [swet] schwitzen IV
sweat [swet] Schweiß IV
sweatshirt ['swetʃɜ:t] Sweatshirt I
sweet [swi:t] süß I
sweetheart ['swi:thɑ:t] Liebling, Schatz II
sweets *(pl)* [swi:ts] Süßigkeiten I
swim (-mm-) [swɪm], **swam, swum** schwimmen I • **go swimming** schwimmen gehen I
swimmer ['swɪmə] Schwimmer/in II
swimming pool ['swɪmɪŋ pu:l] Schwimmbad, Schwimmbecken I
swimming trunks *(pl)* ['swɪmɪŋ trʌŋks] Badehose III
swimsuit ['swɪmsu:t] Badeanzug III
swum [swʌm] *siehe* **swim**
syllable ['sɪləbl] Silbe I
°**symbol** ['sɪmbl] Symbol
synagogue ['sɪnəgɒg] Synagoge III
synonym ['sɪnənɪm] Synonym *(Wort mit gleicher oder sehr ähnlicher Bedeutung)* IV
system ['sɪstəm] System IV

T

table ['teɪbl] Tisch I
table tennis ['teɪbl tenɪs] Tischtennis I • **table tennis bat** Tischtennisschläger III
taboo [tə'bu:] tabu; Tabu V 4 (78)
take [teɪk], **took, taken**
1. nehmen I
2. (weg-, hin)bringen I
3. dauern, *(Zeit)* brauchen III
I can take it. Ich halt's aus. / Ich kann's aushalten. IV • **I'll take it from here.** *etwa:* Ich übernehme das jetzt. / Ich komme jetzt allein klar. IV • **take a break** eine Pause machen IV • **take an exam** eine Prüfung ablegen IV • **take a look (at)** einen Blick werfen (auf) V 4 (90) • **take a ride** eine Fahrt machen III • **take notes** sich Notizen machen I • **take off** *(infml)* sich davonmachen, sich aus dem Staub machen IV • **take someone's advice** auf jemandes Rat hören V 2 (33/162) • **take sth. off** etwas ausziehen *(Kleidung)* II; etwas absetzen *(Hut, Helm)* III
take 10c off 10 Cent abziehen I
take sth. out etwas herausnehmen I • **take sth. over** etwas übernehmen; etwas in seine Gewalt bringen IV • **take part (in)** teilnehmen (an) IV • **take photos** Fotos machen, fotografieren I
take place stattfinden IV • °**Take turns.** Wechselt euch ab.
taken ['teɪkən] *siehe* **take**
talent ['tælənt] Talent, Begabung III
talk [tɔ:k]
1. Gespräch IV
2. Vortrag, Rede V 4 (88)
give a talk (on sth.) einen Vortrag/eine Rede halten (über etwas) V 4 (88)
talk (to sb. about sth.) [tɔ:k] (mit jm. über etwas) reden, sich (mit jm. über etwas) unterhalten I
tall [tɔ:l] hoch *(Bäume, Türme usw.)*; groß *(Person)* IV
tank [tæŋk] Tank III
taught [tɔ:t] *siehe* **teach**
taxi ['tæksi] Taxi III
tea [ti:] Tee *(auch: leichte Nachmittags- oder Abendmahlzeit)* I
tea bag ['ti: bæg] Teebeutel IV
teach [ti:tʃ], **taught, taught** unterrichten, lehren I
teacher ['ti:tʃə] Lehrer/in I
team [ti:m] Team, Mannschaft I
tear [tɪə] Träne IV
tear sth. off [teə], **tore, torn** etwas abreißen IV
teaspoon ['ti:spu:n] Teelöffel III
°**techie** ['teki] *(infml)* Technikfreak
technical ['teknɪkl] technisch V 2 (39)
technician [tek'nɪʃn] Techniker/in V 2 (35)
technology [tek'nɒlədʒi] Technologie V 2 (35)
teddy bear ['tedi beə] Teddybär III
teen [ti:n] Teenager-, Jugend- III
teenager ['ti:neɪdʒə] Teenager, Jugendliche(r) II
teeth [ti:θ] *pl von „tooth"*
telephone ['telɪfəʊn] Telefon I
telephone number Telefonnummer I
television (TV) ['telɪvɪʒn] Fernsehen I
tell (about) [tel], **told, told** erzählen (von), berichten (über) I • **Tell me your names.** Sagt mir eure Namen. I • **tell sb. the way** jm. den Weg beschreiben II • **tell sb. to do sth.** jn. auffordern, etwas zu tun; jm. sagen, dass er/sie etwas tun soll II
temperature ['temprətʃə] Temperatur II • **have a temperature** Fieber haben II
tennis ['tenɪs] Tennis I
tense [tens] (grammatische) Zeit, Tempus III
tent [tent] Zelt IV
term [tɜ:m] Trimester II
terrible ['terəbl] schrecklich, furchtbar I

terrified ['terɪfaɪd]: **be terrified (of)** schreckliche Angst haben (vor) IV
°**territory** ['terətri] Revier, Gebiet, Territorium
terrorist ['terərɪst] Terrorist/in IV
terrorist ['terərɪst] terroristisch, Terror- IV
test [test] Klassenarbeit, Test, Prüfung II
°**test** [test] prüfen, testen
text [tekst] Text I
text message ['tekst ˌmesɪdʒ] SMS III
text sb. [tekst] jm. eine SMS schicken III
than [ðæn, ðən] als II • **more than** mehr als II • **more than me** mehr als ich II
Thank you. ['θæŋk juː] Danke (schön). I • **Thanks.** [θæŋks] Danke. I • **Thanks a lot!** Vielen Dank! I • **Thanks very much!** Danke sehr! / Vielen Dank! II
that [ðət, ðæt]
1. das (dort) I
2. jene(r, s) I
that day an jenem Tag III • **That's me.** Das bin ich. I • **That's right.** Das ist richtig. / Das stimmt. I
That's up to you. Das liegt bei dir./ Das kannst/musst du (selbst) entscheiden. III • **that's why** deshalb, darum I • **That way ...** So .../ Auf diese Weise ... III
that [ðət, ðæt] der, die, das; die *(Relativpronomen)* III
that [ðət, ðæt] dass I • **so that** sodass, damit III
that far/good/bad/... [ðæt] so weit/ gut/schlecht/... III
the [ðə, ði] der, die, das; die I
theatre ['θɪətə] Theater II
their [ðeə] ihr, ihre *(Plural)* I
theirs [ðeəz] ihrer, ihre, ihrs *(Plural)* II
them [ðəm, ðem] sie; ihnen I
theme park ['θiːm pɑːk] Themenpark *(Freizeitpark mit Attraktionen zu einem bestimmten Thema)* IV
themselves [ðəm'selvz] sich (selbst) III
then [ðen] dann, danach I • **since then** seitdem IV
there [ðeə]
1. da, dort I
2. dahin, dorthin I
down there dort unten II • **in there** dort drinnen I • **over there** da drüben, dort drüben I • **there are** es sind (vorhanden); es gibt I
there's es ist (vorhanden); es gibt I • **there isn't a ...** es ist kein/e ...; es gibt kein/e ... I • **There you go!** *(infml) etwa:* So, das hätten wir. IV
up there dort oben III
thermometer [θə'mɒmɪtə] Thermometer II
these [ðiːz] diese, die (hier) I
they [ðeɪ] sie *(Plural)* I
thief [θiːf], *pl* **thieves** [θiːvz] Dieb/in II
thing [θɪŋ] Ding, Sache I • **What was the best thing about ...?** Was war das Beste an ...? II
think [θɪŋk], **thought, thought** glauben, meinen, denken I • **I think so.** Ich glaube (ja). I • **I don't think so.** Das finde/glaube ich nicht. I • **think about** 1. nachdenken über II; 2. denken über, halten von II • **think of** 1. denken über, halten von II; 2. denken an; sich ausdenken II
third [θɜːd] dritte(r, s) I
thirsty ['θɜːsti] durstig I • **be thirsty** Durst haben, durstig sein I
this [ðɪs]
1. dies (hier) I
2. diese(r, s) I
like this so IV • **This is Isabel.** Hier spricht Isabel. / Hier ist Isabel. *(am Telefon)* II • **This is where ...** Hier ... V 4 (82) • **this morning/ afternoon/evening** heute Morgen/Nachmittag/Abend I • **this way** 1. hier entlang, in diese Richtung II; 2. so; auf diese Weise III
those [ðəʊz] die (da), jene (dort) I
though [ðəʊ] obwohl V 1 (12)
thought [θɔːt] *siehe* **think**
thought [θɔːt] Gedanke IV
thousand ['θaʊznd] tausend I
threw [θruː] *siehe* **throw**
throat [θrəʊt] Hals, Kehle II • **have a sore throat** Halsschmerzen haben II
through [θruː] durch II
throw [θrəʊ], **threw, thrown** werfen I • **throw up** sich übergeben IV
thrown [θrəʊn] *siehe* **throw**
Thursday ['θɜːzdeɪ, 'θɜːzdi] Donnerstag I
°**tick** [tɪk] Häkchen
ticket ['tɪkɪt]
1. Eintrittskarte I
2. Fahrkarte II
all-day ticket Tagesfahrkarte III
return ticket Rückfahrkarte II
single ticket einfache Fahrkarte *(nur Hinfahrt)* III
ticket agent ['tɪkɪt‿eɪdʒənt] *Angestellte(r) in Kartenvorverkaufsstelle* IV
ticket machine ['tɪkɪt məˌʃiːn] Fahrkartenautomat III
ticket office ['tɪkɪt‿ɒfɪs] Kasse *(für den Verkauf von Eintrittskarten)*; Fahrkartenschalter IV
tide [taɪd] Gezeiten, Ebbe und Flut II • **the tide is in** es ist Flut II
the tide is out es ist Ebbe II
tidy ['taɪdi] aufräumen I
tidy ['taɪdi] ordentlich, aufgeräumt II
tie *(-ing form:* **tying***)* [taɪ] binden IV
tie [taɪ] Krawatte, Schlips IV
tiger ['taɪgə] Tiger II
tight [taɪt] fest IV
tights *(pl)* [taɪts] Strumpfhose III
till [tɪl] bis *(zeitlich)* I • **not ... till** erst (um); nicht vor III
time [taɪm]
1. Zeit; Uhrzeit I • **What's the time?** Wie spät ist es? I • **a long time** lange III • **in time** rechtzeitig II • **time of day** Tageszeit V 1 (9)
2. **time(s)** Mal(e); -mal II • **for the first time** zum ersten Mal IV
timeline ['taɪmlaɪn] Zeitstrahl III
timetable ['taɪmteɪbl]
1. Stundenplan I
2. Fahrplan III
timing ['taɪmɪŋ]: **bad timing** schlechtes Timing III
tip [tɪp]
1. Spitze IV
2. Tipp III
tired ['taɪəd] müde I • **be tired of sth.** genug von etwas haben, etwas satt haben IV • **get tired of sth.** einer Sache überdrüssig werden, die Lust an etwas verlieren IV
title ['taɪtl] Titel, Überschrift I
to [tə, tu]
1. zu, nach I • **an e-mail to** eine E-Mail an I • **to Jenny's** zu Jenny I • **to the doctor's** zum Arzt III
to the front nach vorn I • **I've never been to Bath.** Ich bin noch nie in Bath gewesen. II • **write to** schreiben an I
2. **quarter to 12** Viertel vor 12 (11.45 / 23.45) I • **from Monday to Friday** von Montag bis Freitag III
to date bis heute V 2 (37) • **to this day** bis heute, bis zum heutigen Tag V 1 (16)
3. **something to eat** etwas zu essen I • **try to do** versuchen, zu tun I • **we know what to do** wir wissen, was wir tun müssen; wir wissen, was zu tun ist III
4. um zu I

toast [təʊst] Toast(brot) I
tobacco [tə'bækəʊ] Tabak II
today [tə'deɪ] heute I; heutzutage V 2 (33)
toe [təʊ] Zeh I
together [tə'geðə] zusammen I
go together zusammenpassen IV
toilet ['tɔɪlət] Toilette I
told [təʊld] *siehe* **tell**
tolerant ['tɒlərənt] tolerant III
tomato [tə'mɑːtəʊ], *pl* **tomatoes** Tomate II
tomorrow [tə'mɒrəʊ] morgen I
tomorrow's weather das Wetter von morgen II
°**tongue-twister** ['tʌŋtwɪstə] Zungenbrecher
tonight [tə'naɪt] heute Nacht, heute Abend I • **tonight's programme** das Programm von heute Abend; das heutige Abendprogramm II
too [tuː]**: from Bristol too** auch aus Bristol I • **Me too.** Ich auch. I
too much/big/... [tuː] zu viel/groß/... I
took [tʊk] *siehe* **take**
tool [tuːl] Werkzeug IV
tooth [tuːθ], *pl* **teeth** [tiːθ] Zahn I
toothache ['tuːθeɪk] Zahnschmerzen II
toothless ['tuːθləs] zahnlos IV
top [tɒp]
1. Spitze, oberes Ende I • **at the top (of)** oben, am oberen Ende, an der Spitze (von) I
2. Top, Oberteil I
topic ['tɒpɪk] Thema, Themenbereich I • **topic sentence** *Satz, der in das Thema eines Absatzes einführt* II
tore [tɔː] *siehe* **tear**
torn [tɔːn] *siehe* **tear**
tornado [tɔː'neɪdəʊ] Tornado, Wirbelsturm II
tortoise ['tɔːtəs] Schildkröte I
touch [tʌtʃ] berühren, anfassen II
touch [tʌtʃ]**: keep in touch** in Verbindung bleiben, Kontakt halten III
tour [tʊə] Tour, Rundgang I • **tour of the house** Rundgang durch das Haus I
tourism ['tʊərɪzəm] Tourismus V 4 (88)
tourist ['tʊərɪst] Tourist/in II
tourist information Fremdenverkehrsamt II
towards sb./sth. [tə'wɔːdz] auf jn./etwas zu II • °**feel ... towards sb.** sich ... fühlen gegenüber jm.
towel ['taʊəl] Handtuch IV
tower ['taʊə] Turm I
town [taʊn] Stadt I
°**township** ['taʊnʃɪp] *Bezeichnung für die während der Apartheid in Südafrika eingerichteten Wohngegenden für die nicht weiße Bevölkerung*
track [træk]
1. Stück, Titel, Track *(auf einer CD)* III
2. running track Laufbahn *(Sport)* III
tractor ['træktə] Traktor V 2 (39)
tradition [trə'dɪʃn] Tradition IV
traditional [trə'dɪʃənl] traditionell III
traffic ['træfɪk] Verkehr II
traffic jam ['træfɪk dʒæm] (Verkehrs-)Stau IV
trail [treɪl]
1. (Lehr-)Pfad IV
°**2.** Route, Weg
train [treɪn] Zug I • **on the train** im Zug I
train [treɪn] trainieren III • **train as ...** eine Ausbildung machen zu ... V 3 (54)
trainers *(pl)* ['treɪnəz] Turnschuhe II
training ['treɪnɪŋ] *(berufliche)* Ausbildung V 2 (32)
training session ['treɪnɪŋ ˌseʃn] Trainingsstunde, -einheit III
train times *(pl)* ['treɪn taɪmz] (Zug-)Abfahrtszeiten IV
tram [træm] Straßenbahn III
translate [træns'leɪt] übersetzen III
translation [træns'leɪʃn] Übersetzung III
transparency [træns'pærənsi] Folie *(für Overheadprojektoren)* V 4 (88)
transport *(no pl)* ['trænspɔːt] Verkehrsmittel III • **public transport** *(no pl)* öffentliche Verkehrsmittel, öffentlicher Personennahverkehr III
trap [træp] Falle II
trash [træʃ] *(AE)* Abfall, Müll V 3 (58)
travel (*BE:* **-ll-**) ['trævl] reisen II
travel agent ['trævl‿eɪdʒənt] Reisebürokaufmann/-kauffrau V 2 (43) • **travel agent's** Reisebüro V 2 (43)
Travelcard ['trævlkɑːd] Tagesfahrkarte *(der Londoner Verkehrsbetriebe)* III
tree [triː] Baum I
trendy ['trendi] modisch, schick III
trick [trɪk]
1. (Zauber-)Kunststück, Trick I • **do tricks** (Zauber-)Kunststücke machen I
2. Streich II • **play a trick on sb.** jm. einen Streich spielen II
trick sb. [trɪk] jn. reinlegen V 1 (17)
trick sb. into doing sth. jn. mit einer List / einem Trick dazu bringen, etwas zu tun V 1 (17)
tricky ['trɪki] verzwickt, heikel V 1 (15)
trip [trɪp] Reise; Ausflug I • **go on a trip** einen Ausflug machen II
trombone [trɒm'bəʊn] Posaune III
trouble ['trʌbl] Schwierigkeiten, Ärger II • **be in trouble** in Schwierigkeiten sein; Ärger kriegen II
get in trouble in Schwierigkeiten geraten V 3 (56)
trousers *(pl)* ['traʊzəz] Hose II
truck [trʌk] Last(kraft)wagen, LKW V 1 (17)
true [truː] wahr II
trumpet ['trʌmpɪt] Trompete III
trust [trʌst] trauen, vertrauen V 2 (45)
try [traɪ]
1. versuchen I
2. probieren, kosten I
try and do sth. / try to do sth. versuchen, etwas zu tun I • **try on** anprobieren *(Kleidung)* I
T-shirt ['tiːʃɜːt] T-Shirt I
tube [tjuːb]**: the Tube** *(no pl)* die Londoner U-Bahn III
Tuesday ['tjuːzdeɪ, 'tjuːzdi] Dienstag I
tune [tjuːn] Melodie III
tunnel ['tʌnl] Tunnel II
turkey ['tɜːki] Truthahn, Pute/Puter III
turn [tɜːn]
1. sich umdrehen II • **turn left/right** (nach) links/rechts abbiegen II • **turn to sb.** sich jm. zuwenden; sich an jn. wenden II
2. turn sth. on etwas einschalten I
turn sth. off etwas ausschalten II
turn sth. up/down etwas lauter/leiser stellen III
turn [tɜːn]**: (It's) my turn.** Ich bin dran / an der Reihe. I • **Miss a turn.** Einmal aussetzen. II • °**Take turns.** Wechselt euch ab. • **Whose turn is it?** Wer ist dran / an der Reihe? II
turtle ['tɜːtl] Wasserschildkröte V 3 (58)
TV [tiː'viː] Fernsehen I • **on TV** im Fernsehen I • **watch TV** fernsehen I
TV listings *(pl)* ['lɪstɪŋz] das Fernsehprogramm IV
twice [twaɪs] zweimal III
twin [twɪn]**: twin brother** Zwillingsbruder I • **twins** *(pl)* Zwillinge I

twin towers Zwillingstürme IV
twin town Partnerstadt I
type [taɪp] *(infml)* Typ III
typical (of) ['tɪpɪkl] typisch (für) V 4 (78)

U

ultraviolet (UV) [ˌʌltrə'vaɪələt] ultraviolett V 1 (9) • **ultraviolet rays** ultraviolette Strahlen V 1 (9)
unbelievable [ˌʌnbɪ'liːvəbl] unglaublich IV
uncle ['ʌŋkl] Onkel I
unconscious [ʌn'kɒnʃəs] bewusstlos II
uncool [ˌʌn'kuːl] *(infml)* uncool III
under ['ʌndə] unter I • **under age** minderjährig V 3 (54)
underground ['ʌndəgraʊnd]**: the underground** die U-Bahn II
°**underline** [ˌʌndə'laɪn] unterstreichen
°**underlined** [ˌʌndə'laɪnd] unterstrichen
understand [ˌʌndə'stænd]**, understood, understood** verstehen, begreifen I
understandable [ˌʌndə'stændəbl] verständlich IV
understood [ˌʌndə'stʊd] *siehe* **understand**
unfair [ˌʌn'feə] unfair, ungerecht III
unforgettable [ˌʌnfə'getəbl] unvergesslich V 4 (89)
unforgiveable [ˌʌnfə'gɪvəbl] unverzeihlich V 4 (89)
unfriendly [ʌn'frendli] unfreundlich III
unhappy [ʌn'hæpi] unglücklich III
unhealthy [ʌn'helθi] ungesund III
uniform ['juːnɪfɔːm] Uniform I
unit ['juːnɪt] Kapitel, Lektion I
unite [ju'naɪt] vereinen, vereinigen, verbinden V 1 (16)
united [ju'naɪtɪd]**: the United Kingdom (UK)** [juˌnaɪtɪd 'kɪŋdəm] das Vereinigte Königreich *(Großbritannien und Nordirland)* III • **the United States (US)** [juˌnaɪtɪd 'steɪts] die Vereinigten Staaten (von Amerika) III
university [ˌjuːnɪ'vɜːsəti] Universität IV
unsafe [ʌn'seɪf] nicht sicher, gefährlich III
untidy [ʌn'taɪdi] unordentlich III
until [ən'tɪl] bis III • **not … until** erst (um); nicht vor III
unwanted [ˌʌn'wɒntɪd] unerwünscht, ungewollt V 3 (50)
up [ʌp] hinauf, herauf, nach oben I
up (the hill) (den Hügel) hinauf II
up there dort oben III • **go up to sb./sth.** auf jn./etwas zugehen V 3 (48) • **That's up to you.** Das liegt bei dir. / Das kannst/musst du (selbst) entscheiden. III
°**update** [ˌʌp'deɪt] aktualisieren, auf den neuesten Stand bringen
uprising ['ʌpraɪzɪŋ] Aufstand V 4 (82)
upset (about) [ˌʌp'set] aufgebracht, gekränkt, mitgenommen (wegen) III
upset sb. (-tt-) [ʌp'set]**, upset, upset** jn. ärgern, kränken, aus der Fassung bringen III
upstairs [ˌʌp'steəz] oben; nach oben I
us [əs, ʌs] uns I
use [juːz] benutzen, verwenden I
use [juːs] Gebrauch, Benutzung, Verwendung V 2 (39)
°**used** [juːzd] gebraucht
used to ['juːst tə]**: I used to be excited …** Früher war ich (immer) aufgeregt … V 2 (44)
► S.166 … used to be/do
useful ['juːsfl] nützlich III
useless ['juːsləs] nutzlos, unbrauchbar V 4 (89)
usually ['juːʒuəli] meistens, gewöhnlich, normalerweise I

V

vacation [və'keɪʃn, *AE:* veɪ'keɪʃn] *(AE)* Urlaub, Ferien III
valley ['væli] Tal II • **valley floor** Talboden II
valuable ['væljuəbl] wertvoll; nützlich IV
valuables *(pl)* ['væljuəblz] Wertgegenstände, Wertsachen V 3 (61)
vandalism ['vændəlɪzəm] Vandalismus, Zerstörungswut V 3 (54/169)
vandalize ['vændəlaɪz] mutwillig beschädigen, mutwillig zerstören V 3 (54)
vegetable ['vedʒtəbl] *(ein)* Gemüse III • **vegetable oil** Pflanzenöl IV
vegetarian [ˌvedʒə'teəriən] vegetarisch; Vegetarier/in IV
very ['veri] sehr I • **like/love sth. very much** etwas sehr mögen/sehr lieben II • **Thanks very much!** Danke sehr! / Vielen Dank! II
vet [vet] Tierarzt/-ärztin V 2 (35)
vet's assistant [ˌvets‿ə'sɪstənt] Tierarzthelfer/in V 2 (35)
victim ['vɪktɪm] Opfer III
video ['vɪdiəʊ] Video III
view [vjuː] Aussicht, Blick II • **in my/your view** meiner/deiner Ansicht nach III • **point of view** Standpunkt II • **from my point of view** aus meiner Sicht; von meinem Standpunkt aus gesehen II
°**view** [vjuː] betrachten; *(im Fernsehen/Kino)* anschauen
viewer ['vjuːə] Zuschauer/in IV
village ['vɪlɪdʒ] Dorf I
violence ['vaɪələns] Gewalt, Gewalttätigkeit IV
violent ['vaɪələnt] gewalttätig; gewaltsam IV
virus ['vaɪrəs] Virus I
visibility [ˌvɪzə'bɪləti] Sicht(weite) IV
visit ['vɪzɪt] besuchen, aufsuchen II
visit ['vɪzɪt] Besuch II
visitor ['vɪzɪtə] Besucher/in, Gast I
visual ['vɪʒuəl] visuell; optisch V 4 (88)
vocabulary [və'kæbjələri] Vokabelverzeichnis, Wörterverzeichnis I
voice [vɔɪs] Stimme I
volleyball ['vɒlibɔːl] Volleyball I
volunteer [ˌvɒlən'tɪə] Freiwillige(r) IV
volunteer [ˌvɒlən'tɪə] sich freiwillig melden, sich bereit erklären IV
volunteer with ehrenamtliche Arbeit leisten für/bei V 3 (54)
vote [vəʊt] zur Wahl gehen, wählen V 2 (44) • **vote for sb.** für jn. stimmen IV
vowel sound ['vaʊəl saʊnd] Vokallaut II

W

wait (for) [weɪt] warten (auf) I
I can't wait to see … ich kann es kaum erwarten, … zu sehen I
Wait a minute. Warte mal! / Moment mal! II • **Wait and see!** Wart's ab! III
waiter ['weɪtə] Kellner II
waiting room ['weɪtɪŋ ruːm] Wartezimmer IV
waitress ['weɪtrəs] Kellnerin II
wake [weɪk]**, woke, woken:**
1. wake sb. (up) jn. (auf)wecken III
2. wake up aufwachen III
walk [wɔːk] (zu Fuß) gehen I
walk on weitergehen III
walk [wɔːk] Spaziergang II • **go for a walk** spazieren gehen, einen Spaziergang machen II
wall [wɔːl] Wand; Mauer II

walrus ['wɔ:lrəs] Walross III
want [wɒnt] (haben) wollen I
want to do tun wollen I • **want sb. to do sth.** wollen, dass jd. etwas tut IV
war [wɔ:] Krieg IV
wardrobe ['wɔ:drəʊb] Kleiderschrank I
warm [wɔ:m] warm II
warm-hearted [,wɔ:m'hɑ:tɪd] warmherzig V 3 (57/170)
warn sb. (about sth.) [wɔ:n] jn. (vor etwas) warnen III
was [wəz, wɒz]: **I/he/she/it was** *siehe* **be**
wash [wɒʃ] waschen I; (auf-) wischen *(Fußboden)* II • **I wash my face.** Ich wasche mir das Gesicht. • **wash the dishes** das Geschirr abwaschen V 1 (19)
waste (on) [weɪst] verschwenden, vergeuden (für) III
watch [wɒtʃ] beobachten, sich *etwas* ansehen; zusehen I
°**watch for sth.** auf etwas achten, nach etwas Ausschau halten
watch TV fernsehen I
watch [wɒtʃ] Armbanduhr I
water ['wɔ:tə] Wasser I
waterproof ['wɔ:təpru:f] wasserdicht, wasserfest V 1 (17/161)
wave [weɪv] winken II
wave [weɪv] Welle V 1 (6)
way [weɪ]
1. Weg II • **ask sb. the way** jn. nach dem Weg fragen II • **on the way (to)** auf dem Weg (zu/nach) II • **tell sb. the way** jm. den Weg beschreiben II
2. Richtung II • **the other way round** anders herum II • **the wrong way** in die falsche Richtung II • **this way** hier entlang, in diese Richtung II • **which way?** in welche Richtung? / wohin? II
3. Art und Weise III • **that way/ this way** so; auf diese Weise III
the way you ... so wie du ..., auf dieselbe Weise wie du ... IV
4. **by the way** übrigens; nebenbei (bemerkt) III • **No way!** Auf keinen Fall! / Kommt nicht in Frage! II
we [wi:] wir I
weak [wi:k] schwach II
weakness ['wi:knəs] Schwäche, Schwachpunkt V 2 (40)
wear [weə], **wore, worn** tragen, anhaben *(Kleidung)* I
weather ['weðə] Wetter II
weatherproof ['weðəpru:f] wetterfest V 1 (17/161)
webcam ['webkæm] Webcam, Internetkamera II
website ['websaɪt] Website II
Wednesday ['wenzdeɪ, 'wenzdi] Mittwoch I
week [wi:k] Woche I • **days of the week** Wochentage I • **a two-week holiday** ein zweiwöchiger Urlaub III
weekend [,wi:k'end] Wochenende I
at the weekend am Wochenende I
welcome ['welkəm]
1. **Welcome (to Bristol).** Willkommen (in Bristol). I
2. **You're welcome.** Gern geschehen. / Nichts zu danken. I
welcome sb. (to) ['welkəm] jn. begrüßen, willkommen heißen (in) I
They welcome you to ... Sie heißen dich in ... willkommen I
well [wel]
1. gut II • **do well** erfolgreich sein, gut abschneiden V 3 (55) • **go well** gut (ver)laufen, gutgehen III
You did well. Das hast du gut gemacht. II • **Oh well ...** Na ja ... / Na gut ... I • **Well, ...** Nun, ... / Also, ... I
2. *(gesundheitlich)* gut; gesund, wohlauf II
well-behaved [,welbɪ'heɪvd] artig, gut erzogen V 3 (57/170)
well-paid [,wel'peɪd] gut bezahlt V 3 (57/170)
Welsh [welʃ] walisisch; Walisisch II
went [went] *siehe* **go**
were [wə, wɜ:]: **we/you/they were** *siehe* **be**
west [west] Westen; nach Westen; westlich III
westbound ['westbaʊnd] Richtung Westen III
western ['westən] westlich, West- III
wet [wet] nass, feucht V 4 (76)
wetsuit ['wetsu:t] Surfanzug, Taucheranzug V 1 (15)
whale [weɪl] Wal(fisch) V 1 (9)
what [wɒt]
1. was I
2. welche(r, s) I
we know what to do wir wissen, was wir tun müssen; wir wissen, was zu tun ist III • **What about ...?** 1. Was ist mit ...? / Und ...? I; 2. Wie wär's mit ...? I • **What an interesting life!** Was für ein interessantes Leben! III • °**What are the pages about?** Wovon handeln die Seiten? • **What are you talking about?** Wovon redest du? I • **What colour is ...?** Welche Farbe hat ...? I • **What else do you know ...?** Was weißt du sonst noch ...? II • **What for?** Wofür? II
What have we got next? Was haben wir als Nächstes? I • **What kind of car ...?** Was für ein Auto ...? III • **What page are we on?** Auf welcher Seite sind wir? I • **What's for homework?** Was haben wir als Hausaufgabe auf? I • **What's for lunch?** Was gibt es zum Mittagessen? III • **What's the matter?** Was ist los? / Was ist denn? II
What's the time? Wie spät ist es? I • **What's wrong with you?** Was fehlt dir? II • **What's your name?** Wie heißt du? I • **What was the weather like?** Wie war das Wetter? II
whatever [wɒt'evə] was (auch) immer IV
wheel [wi:l] Rad III • **big wheel** Riesenrad III
wheelchair ['wi:ltʃeə] Rollstuhl I
when [wen] wann I • **When's your birthday?** Wann hast du Geburtstag? I
when [wen]
1. wenn I
2. als I
whenever [wen'evə] wann (auch) immer IV
where [weə]
1. wo I
2. wohin I
This is where ... Hier ... V 4 (82)
Where are you from? Wo kommst du her? I
wherever [weər'evə] wo(hin) (auch) immer IV
which [wɪtʃ] welche(r, s) I • **Which picture ...?** Welches Bild ...? I
which way? in welche Richtung? / wohin? II
which [wɪtʃ] der, die, das; die *(Relativpronomen)* III
while *(conj)* [waɪl] während III
while [waɪl] Weile V 2 (45) • **for a while** für eine Weile, eine Zeit lang V 2 (45)
whisky ['wɪski] Whisky II
whisper ['wɪspə] flüstern I
whistle ['wɪsl] pfeifen II
whistle ['wɪsl] (Triller-)Pfeife; Pfiff III
white [waɪt] weiß I
who [hu:]
1. wer I
2. wen / wem II
who [hu:] der, die, das; die *(Relativpronomen)* III

whoever [huː'evə] wer (auch) immer; wen/wem (auch) immer IV
whole [həʊl] ganze(r, s), gesamte(r, s) III
whole-grain ['həʊlgreɪn] Vollkorn- IV
whose [huːz] deren, dessen *(Relativpronomen)* V 4 (78)
whose? [huːz] wessen? II
Whose are these? Wem gehören diese? II • **Whose turn is it?** Wer ist dran? / Wer ist an der Reihe? II
why [waɪ] warum I • **Why me?** Warum ich? I • **that's why** deshalb, darum I
°**wide** [waɪd] breit
wife [waɪf], *pl* **wives** [waɪvz] Ehefrau II
wild [waɪld] wild II
will [wɪl]: **you'll be cold (= you will be cold)** du wirst / ihr werdet frieren II
win (-nn-) [wɪn], **won, won** gewinnen I
win [wɪn] Sieg III
wind [wɪnd] Wind I
window ['wɪndəʊ] Fenster I
windproof ['wɪndpruːf] winddicht V 1 (17/161)
windscreen ['wɪndskriːn] Windschutzscheibe III
windy ['wɪndi] windig I
wine [waɪn] Wein IV
wing [wɪŋ] Flügel IV
winner ['wɪnə] Gewinner/in, Sieger/in II
winning shot [ˌwɪnɪŋ 'ʃɒt] Siegtreffer, Siegesschuss III
winter ['wɪntə] Winter I
wish [wɪʃ] wünschen V 4 (82)
► S.174 Ich wünschte ... – I wish ...
wish [wɪʃ]: **Best wishes** *etwa:* Alles Gute / Mit besten Grüßen *(als Briefschluss)* IV
with [wɪð]
1. mit I
2. bei I
be with sb. mit jm. zusammen sein IV • **go with** gehören zu, passen zu III • **Sit with me.** Setz dich zu mir. / Setzt euch zu mir. I
within [wɪ'ðɪn] innerhalb (von) V 2 (44)
without [wɪ'ðaʊt] ohne I
wives [waɪvz] *pl von „wife"* II
woke [wəʊk] *siehe* **wake**
woken ['wəʊkən] *siehe* **wake**
wolf [wʊlf], *pl* **wolves** [wʊlvz] Wolf II
woman ['wʊmən], *pl* **women** ['wɪmɪn] Frau I
won [wʌn] *siehe* **win**
wonder ['wʌndə] sich fragen, gern wissen wollen II
°**wonderful** ['wʌndəfl] wunderbar
won't [wəʊnt]: **you won't be cold (= you will not be cold)** du wirst nicht frieren / ihr werdet nicht frieren II
wood [wʊd] Holz II
woodpecker ['wʊdpekə] Specht II
woods *(pl)* [wʊdz] Wald, Wälder II
word [wɜːd] Wort I • **word building** Wortbildung II • **word field** Wortfeld III • °**word order** Wortstellung
wore [wɔː] *siehe* **wear**
work [wɜːk]
1. arbeiten I
2. funktionieren III
work hard hart arbeiten II • **work long hours** lange arbeiten V 2 (33)
work on sth. an etwas arbeiten I
work out gut ausgehen IV
work sth. out etwas herausarbeiten, herausfinden IV
work [wɜːk] Arbeit I • **at work** bei der Arbeit / am Arbeitsplatz I
worker ['wɜːkə] Arbeiter/in II
work experience *(no pl)* ['wɜːk‿ɪkˌspɪəriəns] Praktikum; Arbeits-, Praxiserfahrung(en) V 2 (38) • **do work experience** ein Praktikum machen V 2 (38)
worksheet ['wɜːkʃiːt] Arbeitsblatt I
workshop ['wɜːkʃɒp] Workshop, Werkstatt III
world [wɜːld] Welt I • **all over the world** auf der ganzen Welt III
in the world auf der Welt V 4 (77)
world war [ˌwɜːld 'wɔː] Weltkrieg V 1 (8)
worldwide [ˌwɜːld'waɪd] weltweit; auf der ganzen Welt V 3 (48)
worn [wɔːn] *siehe* **wear**
worried ['wʌrid]: **be worried (about)** beunruhigt sein, besorgt sein (wegen/um) IV
worry ['wʌri] Sorge, Kummer II
worry (about) ['wʌri] sich Sorgen machen (wegen, um) I • **Don't worry.** Mach dir keine Sorgen. I
worry sb. jn. beunruhigen, jm. Sorgen machen V 3 (57)
worse [wɜːs] schlechter, schlimmer II
worst [wɜːst]: **(the) worst** am schlechtesten, schlimmsten; der/die/das schlechteste, schlimmste II
would [wəd, wʊd]: **you would ...** du würdest ... III • **I'd like ... (= I would like ...)** Ich hätte gern ... / Ich möchte gern ... I • **Would you like ...?** Möchtest du ...? / Möchten Sie ...? I • **I'd like to go (= I would like to go)** ich würde gern gehen / ich möchte gehen I • **I wouldn't like to go** ich würde nicht gern gehen / ich möchte nicht gehen I
I'd love to ... (= I would love to ...) Ich würde liebend gern ... V 1 (12)
write [raɪt], **wrote, written** schreiben I • **write down** aufschreiben I • °**write sth. out** etwas ausschreiben • **write to** schreiben an I • °**write sth. up** etwas (schriftlich) ausarbeiten
writer ['raɪtə] Schreiber/in; Schriftsteller/in II
written ['rɪtn] *siehe* **write**
wrong [rɒŋ] falsch, verkehrt I
be wrong 1. falsch sein I; **2.** sich irren, Unrecht haben II • **go wrong** schiefgehen III • **the wrong way** in die falsche Richtung II • **What's wrong with you?** Was fehlt dir? II
wrote [rəʊt] *siehe* **write**

Y

yard [jɑːd] Hof II • **in the yard** auf dem Hof II
yawn [jɔːn] gähnen II
year [jɪə]
1. Jahr I
2. Jahrgangsstufe I
thirteen-year-old Dreizehnjährige(r) III
yellow ['jeləʊ] gelb I
yes [jes] ja I
yesterday ['jestədeɪ, 'jestədi] gestern I • **yesterday morning/afternoon/evening** gestern Morgen/Nachmittag/Abend I • **yesterday's homework** die Hausaufgaben von gestern II
yet [jet]: **not (...) yet** noch nicht II
yet? schon? II
°**YMCA** [ˌwaɪ‿em siː‿'eɪ] **(Young Men's Christian Association)** *dem CVJM (Christlicher Verein Junger Menschen) vergleichbare Organisation*
yoga ['jəʊgə] Yoga I
you [juː]
1. du; Sie I
2. man III
3. ihr I • **you two** ihr zwei I
4. dir; dich; euch I
You bet! *(infml)* Aber klar! / Und ob! IV • **There you go!** *(infml)* *etwa:* So, das hätten wir. IV

young [jʌŋ] jung I
your [jɔː]
1. dein/e I
2. Ihr I
3. euer/eure I
yours [jɔːz]
1. deiner, deine, deins II
2. Ihrer, Ihre, Ihrs II
3. eurer, eure, eures II
Yours faithfully Mit freundlichen Grüßen *(Briefschluss bei namentlich unbekanntem Empfänger)* V 2 (38) • **Yours sincerely** Mit freundlichen Grüßen *(Briefschluss bei namentlich bekanntem Empfänger)* V 2 (38)
► S.164 Formal letters
yourself [jə'self, jɔː'self] dir/dich (selbst) III • **about yourself** über dich selbst III
yourselves [jə'selvz, jɔː'selvz] euch (selbst) III
youth [juːθ]
1. Jugend III
2. *(pl* **youths** [juːðz]*)* Jugendliche(r) V 3 (57)

Z

zebra ['zebrə] Zebra II
zero ['zɪərəʊ] null I
zone [zəʊn] Zone, Bereich III
zoo [zuː] Zoo IV

Infinitive	Simple past form	Past participle	
(to) **be**	**was/were**	**been**	sein
(to) **beat**	**beat**	**beaten**	schlagen; besiegen
(to) **become**	**became**	**become**	werden
(to) **begin**	**began**	**begun**	beginnen, anfangen (mit)
(to) **bet**	**bet**	**bet**	wetten
(to) **blow**	**blew**	**blown**	wehen, blasen
(to) **break** [eɪ]	**broke**	**broken**	(zer)brechen; kaputt gehen
(to) **bring**	**brought**	**brought**	(mit-, her)bringen
(to) **build**	**built**	**built**	bauen
(to) **buy**	**bought**	**bought**	kaufen
(to) **catch**	**caught**	**caught**	fangen; erwischen
(to) **choose** [uː]	**chose** [əʊ]	**chosen** [əʊ]	(aus)wählen; (sich) aussuchen
(to) **come**	**came**	**come**	kommen
(to) **cost**	**cost**	**cost**	kosten
(to) **cut**	**cut**	**cut**	schneiden
(to) **do**	**did**	**done** [ʌ]	tun, machen
(to) **draw**	**drew**	**drawn**	zeichnen; ziehen
(to) **drink**	**drank**	**drunk**	trinken
(to) **drive** [aɪ]	**drove**	**driven** [ɪ]	*(ein Auto)* fahren
(to) **eat**	**ate** [et, eɪt]	**eaten**	essen
(to) **fall**	**fell**	**fallen**	(hin)fallen, stürzen
(to) **feed**	**fed**	**fed**	füttern
(to) **feel**	**felt**	**felt**	(sich) fühlen; sich anfühlen
(to) **fight**	**fought**	**fought**	kämpfen
(to) **find**	**found**	**found**	finden
(to) **fly**	**flew**	**flown**	fliegen
(to) **forget**	**forgot**	**forgotten**	vergessen
(to) **forgive**	**forgave**	**forgiven**	vergeben, verzeihen
(to) **get**	**got**	**got**	bekommen; holen; werden; (hin)kommen
(to) **give**	**gave**	**given**	geben
(to) **go**	**went**	**gone** [ɒ]	gehen, fahren
(to) **grow**	**grew**	**grown**	wachsen; anbauen, anpflanzen
(to) **hang**	**hung**	**hung**	hängen; *(etwas)* aufhängen
(to) **have (have got)**	**had**	**had**	haben, besitzen
(to) **hear** [ɪə]	**heard** [ɜː]	**heard** [ɜː]	hören
(to) **hide** [aɪ]	**hid** [ɪ]	**hidden** [ɪ]	(sich) verstecken
(to) **hit**	**hit**	**hit**	schlagen
(to) **hold**	**held**	**held**	halten
(to) **hurt**	**hurt**	**hurt**	wehtun; verletzen
(to) **keep**	**kept**	**kept**	(be)halten
(to) **know** [nəʊ]	**knew** [njuː]	**known** [nəʊn]	wissen; kennen
(to) **lay** the table	**laid**	**laid**	den Tisch decken
(to) **leave**	**left**	**left**	(weg)gehen; abfahren; verlassen; zurücklassen
(to) **lend**	**lent**	**lent**	(ver)leihen

Infinitive	Simple past form	Past participle	
(to) **let**	**let**	**let**	lassen
(to) **light**	**lit**	**lit**	anzünden
(to) **lose** [uː]	**lost** [ɒ]	**lost** [ɒ]	verlieren
(to) **make**	**made**	**made**	machen; bauen; bilden
(to) **mean** [iː]	**meant** [e]	**meant** [e]	bedeuten; meinen
(to) **meet**	**met**	**met**	(sich) treffen
(to) **pay**	**paid**	**paid**	bezahlen
(to) **put**	**put**	**put**	legen, stellen, *(wohin)* tun
(to) **read** [iː]	**read** [e]	**read** [e]	lesen
(to) **ride** [aɪ]	**rode**	**ridden** [ɪ]	reiten; *(Rad)* fahren
(to) **ring**	**rang**	**rung**	klingeln, läuten
(to) **rise** [aɪ]	**rose**	**risen** [ɪ]	(auf)steigen
(to) **run**	**ran**	**run**	rennen, laufen; verlaufen *(Straße, Grenze)*; leiten *(Hotel, Firma)*
(to) **say** [eɪ]	**said** [e]	**said** [e]	sagen
(to) **see**	**saw**	**seen**	sehen; besuchen, aufsuchen
(to) **sell**	**sold**	**sold**	verkaufen
(to) **send**	**sent**	**sent**	schicken, senden
(to) **set** a trap	**set**	**set**	eine Falle stellen
(to) **sew** [əʊ]	**sewed**	**sewn**	nähen
(to) **shake**	**shook**	**shaken**	schütteln; zittern
(to) **shine**	**shone** [ɒ]	**shone** [ɒ]	scheinen *(Sonne)*
(to) **shoot**	**shot**	**shot**	(er)schießen
(to) **show**	**showed**	**shown**	zeigen
(to) **shut up**	**shut**	**shut**	den Mund halten
(to) **sing**	**sang**	**sung**	singen
(to) **sit**	**sat**	**sat**	sitzen; sich setzen
(to) **sleep**	**slept**	**slept**	schlafen
(to) **speak**	**spoke**	**spoken**	sprechen
(to) **spend**	**spent**	**spent**	*(Zeit)* verbringen; *(Geld)* ausgeben
(to) **spit**	**spat**	**spat**	spucken
(to) **stand**	**stood**	**stood**	stehen; sich (hin)stellen
(to) **steal**	**stole**	**stolen**	stehlen
(to) **stick**	**stuck**	**stuck**	herausragen, herausstehen
(to) **swim**	**swam**	**swum**	schwimmen
(to) **take**	**took**	**taken**	nehmen; (weg-, hin)bringen; dauern, *(Zeit)* brauchen
(to) **teach**	**taught**	**taught**	unterrichten, lehren
(to) **tear off** [eə]	**tore**	**torn**	abreißen
(to) **tell**	**told**	**told**	erzählen, berichten
(to) **think**	**thought**	**thought**	denken, glauben, meinen
(to) **throw**	**threw**	**thrown**	werfen
(to) **understand**	**understood**	**understood**	verstehen
(to) **upset**	**upset**	**upset**	ärgern, kränken, aus der Fassung bringen
(to) **wake** up	**woke**	**woken**	aufwachen; wecken
(to) **wear** [eə]	**wore** [ɔː]	**worn** [ɔː]	tragen *(Kleidung)*
(to) **win**	**won** [ʌ]	**won** [ʌ]	gewinnen
(to) **write**	**wrote**	**written**	schreiben

First names
(Vornamen)

Abby ['æbi]
Adam ['ædəm]
Aggie ['ægi]
Akeem [ɑ:'ki:m, ɒ'ki:m]
Alex ['ælɪks]
Alfie ['ælfi]
Alice ['ælɪs]
Amy ['eɪmi]
Andrew ['ændru:]
Anna ['ænə]
Ashley ['æʃli]
Beyoncé [bi'jɒnseɪ]
Binita [bə'ni:tə, bɪ'ni:tə]
Brad [bræd]
Brian ['braɪən]
Carla ['kɑ:lə]
Carolyn ['kærəlɪn]
Cath [kæθ]
Chia-Wen [ˌtʃiə 'wen]
Chloe ['kləʊi]
Colm [kɒlm, 'kɒləm]
Craig [kreɪg]
Dave [deɪv]
David ['deɪvɪd]
Desmond ['dezmənd]
Elin ['elɪn]
Ethan ['i:θən]
Ewan ['ju:ən]
Framji ['fræmdʒɪ]
Frank [fræŋk]
George [dʒɔ:dʒ]
Gino ['dʒi:nəʊ]
Grace [greɪs]
Hannah ['hænə]
Jacob ['dʒeɪkəb]
Jade [dʒeɪd]
Jake [dʒeɪk]
James [dʒeɪmz]
Jamie ['dʒeɪmi]
Jane [dʒeɪn]
Jay [dʒeɪ]
Jeannie ['dʒi:ni]
Jemma ['dʒemə]
Jennifer ['dʒenɪfə]
Jeremy ['dʒerəmi]
Jess [dʒes]
Joseph ['dʒəʊzɪf, 'dʒəʊsef]
Judith ['dʒu:dɪθ]
Katherine ['kæθrɪn]
Katy ['keɪti]
Keith [ki:θ]
Kirsty ['kɜ:sti]
Lara ['lɑ:rə]
Laura ['lɔ:rə]
Lea ['liə]
Leena ['leənə]
Letitia [lə'tɪʃə]
Lina ['li:nə]
Louise [lu'i:z]
Lucy ['lu:si]
Luke [lu:k]
Madonna [mə'dɒnə]
Mahatma [mə'hɑ:tmə]
Mani ['mæni]
Margaret ['mɑ:grət]
Maria [mə'ri:ə]
Mary ['meəri]
Nate [neɪt]
Nelson ['nelsən]
Nicole [nɪ'kɒl, nɪ'kəʊl]
Nina ['ni:nə]
Norman ['nɔ:mən]
Nova ['nəʊvə]
Paul [pɔ:l]
Pedro ['pedrəʊ, 'peɪdrəʊ]
Reece [ri:s]
Rita ['ri:tə]
Rochelle, Roche [rə'ʃel], [rɒʃ]
Rubin ['ru:bɪn]
Ryan ['raɪən]
Samantha [sə'mænθə]
Sandra ['sændrə]
Shane [ʃeɪn]
Sheila [ʃi:lə]
Shireen [ʃə'ri:n]
Simon ['saɪmən]
Sinita [sɪ'ni:tə]
Steve [sti:v]
Suketu [sʊ'keɪtu]
Tom [tɒm]
Tyler ['taɪlə]
Tyson ['taɪsn]
Uma ['u:mə]
Victor ['vɪktə]
Woody ['wʊdi]
Zach [zæk]
Zita ['zi:tə]

Family names
(Familiennamen)

Allen ['ælən]
Armstrong ['ɑ:mstrɒŋ]
Beckham ['bekəm]
Bond [bɒnd]
Carter ['kɑ:tə]
Collins ['kɒlɪnz]
Coman ['kəʊmən]
Cruise [kru:z]
Denham ['denəm]
Ejogo [ɪ'dʒəʊgəʊ]
Ford [fɔ:d]
Foster ['fɒstə]
Gandhi ['gændi]
Gubbins ['gʌbɪnz]
Harris ['hærɪs]
Hunter ['hʌntə]
Kidman ['kɪdmən]
Lin [lɪn]
Lucas ['lu:kəs]
Mackintosh ['mækɪntɒʃ]
Mandela [mæn'delə]
McQueen [mə'kwi:n]
Mehta ['metə]
Murray ['mʌri]
Nobel [nəʊ'bel]
Otambo [əʊ'tæmbəʊ]
Parton ['pɑ:tn]
Peris ['perɪs]
Preston ['prestən]
Qualls [kwɒlz, kwɔ:lz]
Ravenhill ['reɪvnhɪl]
Robinson ['rɒbɪnsən]
Saunders ['sɔ:ndəz]
Smith [smɪθ]
Tay [teɪ]
Tilling ['tɪlɪŋ]
Tutu ['tu:tu:]
Urban ['ɜ:bən]
Wallace ['wɒlɪs]
Williams ['wɪljəmz]
Wilson ['wɪlsn]
Yates [jeɪts]

Place names
(Ortsnamen)

Auckland ['ɔ:klənd]
Ayers Rock [ˌeəz 'rɒk]
Bangkok [ˌbæŋ'kɒk]
Berlin [bɜ:'lɪn]
Bombay [ˌbɒm'beɪ]
Brisbane ['brɪzbən]
Broome [bru:m]
Cairns [keənz]
California [ˌkælə'fɔ:niə]
Cambridge ['keɪmbrɪdʒ]
Canberra ['kænbərə]
Ceduna [sə'du:nə]
The **Chauncy School** ['tʃɔ:nsi sku:l]
Checkpoint Charlie [ˌtʃekpɔɪnt 'tʃɑ:li]
Cologne [kə'ləʊn]
Colorado [ˌkɒlə'rɑ:dəʊ]
Coral Sea [ˌkɒrəl 'si:]
Daintree ['deɪntri:]
Darlington ['dɑ:lɪŋtən]
Darwin ['dɑ:wɪn]
Derby ['dɑ:bi]
Detroit [di'trɔɪt]
El Paso [el 'pæsəʊ]
Eno ['i:nəʊ]
Eugene [ju:'dʒi:n]
Florida ['flɒrɪdə]
Forster ['fɔ:stə]
Fountain Valley [ˌfaʊntɪn 'væli]
Georgia ['dʒɔ:dʒə]
Gibson Desert [ˌgɪbsn 'dezət]
Gordon Street ['gɔ:dn ˌstri:t]
Great Australian Bight [ˌgreɪt‿ɒˌstreɪliən 'baɪt]
Great Barrier Reef [ˌgreɪt 'bæriə ri:f]
Gulf of Carpentaria [ˌgʌlf‿əv kɑ:pən'teəriə]
Harston ['hɑ:stən]
Hawaii [hə'waɪi]
Hertford ['hɑ:tfəd]
Hertfordshire ['hɑ:tfədʃə]
Hickory ['hɪkəri]
Hollywood ['hɒliwʊd]
Hong Kong [ˌhɒŋ 'kɒŋ]
Humber Road [ˌhʌmbə 'rəʊd]
Ife ['i:feɪ]
Johannesburg, Joburg, Jozi [dʒəʊ'hænɪsbɜ:g], ['dʒəʊbɜ:g], ['dʒəʊzi]
Kimberley Plateau [ˌkɪmbəli 'plætəʊ]
Knysna ['naɪznə]
Kuala Pilah [ˌkwɑ:lə 'pi:lə]
Lawn Hill Road [ˌlɔ:n hɪl 'rəʊd]
Lincoln Park [ˌlɪŋkən ˌpɑ:k]
Little Hadham [ˌlɪtl 'hædəm]
Meadows Home Farm [ˌmedəʊz ˌhəʊm 'fɑ:m]
Melbourne ['melbən]
Melville ['melvɪl]
Mumbai [ˌmʊm'baɪ]
New Delhi [ˌnju: 'deli]
New Mexico [ˌnju: 'meksɪkəʊ]
New South Wales [ˌnju: saʊθ 'weɪlz]
New York [ˌnju: 'jɔ:k]
Northern Territory [ˌnɔ:ðən 'terətri]
Oakwood Close [ˌəʊkwʊd 'kləʊs]
Oldham School ['əʊldəm sku:l]
Oregon ['ɒrɪgən]
Perth [pɜ:θ]
Port Jackson [ˌpɔ:t 'dʒæksən]
Pretoria [pri'tɔ:riə]
Prussia ['prʌʃə]
Queensland ['kwi:nzlænd]
Rockhampton [rɒk'hæmptən]
Rosebank ['rəʊzbæŋk]
Sanjay Gandhi Nagar [ˌsændʒeɪ ˌgændi næ'gɑ:]
Soweto [sə'wetəʊ]
Swindon ['swɪndən]
Sydney ['sɪdni]
Tara Downs Homestead [ˌtɑ:rə ˌdaʊnz 'həʊmsted]
Tasmania [tæz'meɪniə]
Timor Sea [ˌti:mɔ: 'si:]
Townsville ['taʊnzvɪl]
Tweed Heads [ˌtwi:d 'hedz]
Uluru [ˌu:lə'ru:, 'u:ləru:]
Uluru-Kata Tjuta [ˌu:ləru: ˌkætə 'tju:tə]
Victoria [vɪk'tɔ:riə]
Ware [weə]
Weeki Wachee Springs [ˌwi:ki ˌwɑ:tʃi 'sprɪŋz]
Wiltshire ['wɪltʃə]
Worita [wə'ri:tə]
Yarra ['jærə]

Other names
(Andere Namen)

Bollywood ['bɒlɪwʊd]
Herts Gazette [ˌhɑ:ts gə'zet]
IMAX ['aɪmæks]
Rusty ['rʌsti]
Toadzilla [təʊd'zɪlə]
UNICEF ['ju:nisef]

Country/Continent	Adjective	Person	People
Africa ['æfrɪkə] *Afrika*	African ['æfrɪkən]	an African	the Africans
America [ə'merɪkə] *Amerika*	American [ə'merɪkən]	an American	the Americans
Asia ['eɪʃə, 'eɪʒə] *Asien*	Asian ['eɪʃn, 'eɪʒn]	an Asian	the Asians
Australia [ɒ'streɪliə] *Australien*	Australian [ɒ'streɪliən]	an Australian	the Australians
Austria ['ɒstriə] *Österreich*	Austrian ['ɒstriən]	an Austrian	the Austrians
Belgium ['beldʒəm] *Belgien*	Belgian ['beldʒən]	a Belgian	the Belgians
Canada ['kænədə] *Kanada*	Canadian [kə'neɪdiən]	a Canadian	the Canadians
China ['tʃaɪnə] *China*	Chinese [ˌtʃaɪ'ni:z]	a Chinese	the Chinese
Croatia [krəʊ'eɪʃə] *Kroatien*	Croatian [krəʊ'eɪʃn]	a Croatian	the Croatians
the Czech Republic [ˌtʃek rɪ'pʌblɪk] *Tschechien, die Tschechische Republik*	Czech [tʃek]	a Czech	the Czechs
Denmark ['denmɑ:k] *Dänemark*	Danish ['deɪnɪʃ]	a Dane [deɪn]	the Danes
England ['ɪŋglənd] *England*	English ['ɪŋglɪʃ]	an Englishman/-woman	the English
Europe ['jʊərəp] *Europa*	European [ˌjʊərə'pi:ən]	a European	the Europeans
Finland ['fɪnlənd] *Finnland*	Finnish ['fɪnɪʃ]	a Finn [fɪn]	the Finns
France [frɑ:ns] *Frankreich*	French [frentʃ]	a Frenchman/-woman	the French
Georgia ['dʒɔ:dʒə] *Georgien*	Georgian ['dʒɔ:dʒən]	a Georgian	the Georgians
Germany ['dʒɜ:məni] *Deutschland*	German ['dʒɜ:mən]	a German	the Germans
(Great) Britain ['brɪtn] *Großbritannien*	British ['brɪtɪʃ]	a Briton ['brɪtn]	the British
Greece [gri:s] *Griechenland*	Greek [gri:k]	a Greek	the Greeks
Holland ['hɒlənd] *Holland, die Niederlande*	Dutch [dʌtʃ]	a Dutchman/-woman	the Dutch
Hungary ['hʌŋgəri] *Ungarn*	Hungarian [hʌŋ'geəriən]	a Hungarian	the Hungarians
India ['ɪndiə] *Indien*	Indian ['ɪndiən]	an Indian	the Indians
Ireland ['aɪələnd] *Irland*	Irish ['aɪrɪʃ]	an Irishman/-woman	the Irish
Italy ['ɪtəli] *Italien*	Italian [ɪ'tæliən]	an Italian	the Italians
Japan [dʒə'pæn] *Japan*	Japanese [ˌdʒæpə'ni:z]	a Japanese	the Japanese
Malaysia [mə'leɪʒə, mə'leɪziə] *Malaysia*	Malaysian [mə'leɪʒn, mə'leɪziən]	a Malaysian	the Malaysians
the Netherlands ['neðələndz] *die Niederlande, Holland*	Dutch [dʌtʃ]	a Dutchman/-woman	the Dutch
New Zealand [ˌnju: 'zi:lənd] *Neuseeland*	New Zealand [ˌnju: 'zi:lənd]	a New Zealander	the New Zealanders
Nigeria [naɪ'dʒɪəriə] *Nigeria*	Nigerian [naɪ'dʒɪəriən]	a Nigerian	the Nigerians
Norway ['nɔ:weɪ] *Norwegen*	Norwegian [nɔ:'wi:dʒən]	a Norwegian	the Norwegians
Pakistan [ˌpækɪ'stæn, ˌpɑ:kɪ'stɑ:n] *Pakistan*	Pakistani [ˌpækɪ'stæni, ˌpɑ:kɪ'stɑ:ni]	a Pakistani	the Pakistanis
the Philippines ['fɪlɪpi:nz] *die Philippinen*	Philippine ['fɪlɪpi:n]	a Filipino [ˌfɪlɪ'pi:nəʊ]/ Filipina [ˌfɪlɪ'pi:nə]	the Filipinos/ Filipinas
Poland ['pəʊlənd] *Polen*	Polish ['pəʊlɪʃ]	a Pole [pəʊl]	the Poles
Portugal ['pɔ:tʃʊgl] *Portugal*	Portuguese [ˌpɔ:tʃu'gi:z]	a Portuguese	the Portuguese
Russia ['rʌʃə] *Russland*	Russian ['rʌʃn]	a Russian	the Russians
Scotland ['skɒtlənd] *Schottland*	Scottish ['skɒtɪʃ]	a Scotsman/-woman, a Scot [skɒt]	the Scots, the Scottish
Slovakia [sləʊ'vɑ:kiə, sləʊ'vækiə] *die Slowakei*	Slovak ['sləʊvæk]	a Slovak	the Slovaks
Slovenia [sləʊ'vi:niə] *Slowenien*	Slovenian [sləʊ'vi:niən], Slovene ['sləʊvi:n]	a Slovene, a Slovenian	the Slovenes, the Slovenians
Spain [speɪn] *Spanien*	Spanish ['spænɪʃ]	a Spaniard ['spænɪəd]	the Spaniards
Sweden ['swi:dn] *Schweden*	Swedish ['swi:dɪʃ]	a Swede [swi:d]	the Swedes
Switzerland ['swɪtsələnd] *die Schweiz*	Swiss [swɪs]	a Swiss	the Swiss
Turkey ['tɜ:ki] *die Türkei*	Turkish ['tɜ:kɪʃ]	a Turk [tɜ:k]	the Turks
the United Kingdom (the UK) [juˌnaɪtɪd 'kɪŋdəm, ju:'keɪ] *das Vereinigte Königreich (Großbritannien und Nordirland)*	British ['brɪtɪʃ]	a Briton ['brɪtn]	the British
the United States of America (the USA) [juˌnaɪtɪd ˌsteɪts‿əv‿ə'merɪkə, ˌju:‿es‿'eɪ] *die Vereinigten Staaten von Amerika*	American [ə'merɪkən]	an American	the Americans
Wales [weɪlz] *Wales*	Welsh [welʃ]	a Welshman/-woman	the Welsh

Key to 'How am I doing?'

Unit 1 ► p. 25

1 Brisbane, Canberra, Melbourne, Sydney, Perth
3 of these, 1 point each
2 emu, kangaroo, koala, wombat, crocodile, ... 3 of these, 1 point each
3 wear a hat, use sunscreen, wear a shirt, wear sunglasses
2 of these, 1 point each
4 surfing, Aussie rules football, cricket, tennis, swimming, rugby
3 of these, 1 point each
5 C autumn 1 point
6 B outback 1 point
7 D the Whites. 1 point
8 B were taken away by Whites. 1 point
9 a) Kim said (that) she would/she'd have a great time Down Under. 1 point
b) Jess said (that) she just loved kangaroos. 1 point
c) Tom said that Frank had visited Sydney in 2009. 1 point
d) Lara said that they/we could go again next year / the following year. 1 point
10 A was once 1 point
11 D done by many people. 1 point
12 C have to do it. 1 point
13 B attach 1 point
14 The chart below is a pie chart. It shows the percentage of Australia's population that lives in big cities, near big cities and far from the cities. More than two thirds of Australians live in the cities, about 30% live more or less near the cities, and only 2.3% far from the cities.
1 point for each answer

Getting ready for a test 1 ► pp. 26–31

1 LISTENING Travelling to Australia ► p. 28
1 B Gate 17
2 C chicken with a salad or pasta
3 A just over there
4 B $ 52.50
5 C 07:00–10:30

2 LISTENING Shark attack ► p. 29
a) 1 C New South Wales
2 A surfing
3 D leg
4 B 5 seconds
5 C Jon swam back to the beach
6 C scariest
b) 1 ... they tied a rope round his leg ...
2 ... but he didn't lose his leg / survived / is alive.
3 ... attack / kill people.
4 ... in Australia every day than from shark attacks in ten years
5 ... always swim in groups, so your friends can help you. And never swim in the early morning or in the evening ...

3 LISTENING Young Australians and the internet ► p. 30
1 False
2 True
3 False
4 True
5 True
6 True

4 WRITING An online magazine for young Europeans ► p. 30
(Individuelle Lösungen)

Key to 'How am I doing?'

Unit 2 ▸ p. 47

1 sporty 1 point
2 popular 1 point
3 reliable 1 point
4 cheeky 1 point
5 ambitious 1 point
6 punctual 1 point
7 calm, organized
2 points if both answers are correct
8 punctual, reliable
2 points if both answers are correct
9 ambitious, confident
2 points if both answers are correct
10 a) ... to come next week. 1 point
b) ... not to worry if next week wasn't possible. 3 points
c) ... if she could come in two weeks 2 points
d) ... if she needed directions for getting there 2 points
11 nurse 1 point
12 mechanic 1 point
13 travel agent 1 point
14 childcare assistant 1 point
15 customer adviser 1 point
16 fitness instructor 1 point
17 vet's assistant 1 point
18 Personal statement, Education, Qualifications, (Other) skills, Work experience, Hobbies and interests, References
1 point each for any of these headings
19 B you don't know 1 point
20 A at the beginning of the letter. 1 point
21 B long verb forms. 1 point
22 A usually a good idea. 1 point
23 A your CV. 1 point
24 B Yours sincerely ... 1 point

Key to 'How am I doing?'

Unit 3 ▸ p. 65

1 C anti-social behaviour 1 point
2 A the courts 1 point
3 C want to help others. 1 point
4 C note 1 point
5 B contacts 1 point
6 a) store
b) donate
c) order
d) receive
1 point each
7 a) move
b) commit
c) train
d) get
1 point each
8 a) oil-producing
b) well-behaved
c) home-made
1 point each
9 a) instead of
b) by
c) up to
d) along with
1 point each
10 c) 2 points
11 a) was taken
b) cannot be printed
c) will be taken
d) must be punished
2 points
12 arguments 2 points
13 a) In my opinion ... / I think ... / I feel ...
b) I agree (with you). / That's a good point. / You're right.
c) I don't think you can say ... / I see what you mean but ... / No, that's not right. / Sorry, I don't agree with you.
d) Could you say that again? / Sorry, but I don't understand what you mean.
1 point for each phrase

Getting ready for a test 2 ▸ pp. 66–73

1 READING Choosing a book ▸ p. 68
Student A – Book 7
Student B – Book 5
Student C – Book 3
Student D – Book 1
Student E – Book 4

2 MEDIATION A note to your friend ▸ p. 69
(Individuelle Lösungen)

3 READING Dev Patel ▸ pp. 70–71
a) 1 C the young English actor Dev Patel
2 D he looked a bit like a 'slumdog'.
3 B becomes a millionaire.
4 C had only played a small role in a TV series
5 A has Indian parents but grew up in England
6 B acting
7 D He replied to a newspaper advertisement.
b) 1 ... looked more like a 'slumdog'.
2 ... his daughter.
3 ... he didn't think he'd/he would get the part.
4 ... he grew up five years in five months.
5 ... they are happy.

4 SPEAKING Talking about a picture ▸ p. 72
(Individuelle Lösungen)

5 SPEAKING Hobbies and interests ▸ p. 72
(Individuelle Lösungen)

Key to 'How am I doing?'

Unit 4 ▸ *p. 91*

1 B British 1 point
2 A gun fights 1 point
3 C is South Africa's main business centre. 1 point
4 C eleven 1 point
5 World War II 1 point
6 Reunification. 1 point
7 A If you had done all the homework, you would have done better in the test. 1 point
8 C we would have won the match. 1 point
9 a) fashionable
b) recently
c) suburb
d) enquire
1 point each
10 a) comment on
b) live in
c) prefer small towns to
d) typical of
1 point each
11 a) peace
b) wet
c) inside
d) check out
1 point each
12 a) cultural
b) racial
c) official
1 point each
13 A the second paragraph. 1 point

Was DU im Klassenzimmer sagen kannst / What YOU can say in the classroom

Du brauchst Hilfe	You need help
Tut mir leid, ich habe das nicht verstanden.	**Sorry, I don't understand.**
Können Sie/Kannst du das bitte noch einmal sagen?	**Can you say that again, please?**
Können Sie/Kannst du bitte lauter sprechen.	**Can you speak louder, please?**
Kann ich eine Frage stellen?	**Can I ask a question, please?**
Können Sie/Kannst du mir bitte helfen?	**Can you help me, please?**
Was bedeutet ...?	**What does ... mean?**
Ist ... das richtige Wort für ... ?	**Is ... the right word for ...?**
Ich habe ... – ist das auch richtig?	**I've got ... – is that right too?**
Können Sie ... bitte buchstabieren?	**Can you spell ..., please?**
Wie spricht man das erste Wort in Zeile 2 aus?	**How do you say the first word in line 2?**
Können Sie es bitte an die Tafel schreiben?	**Can you write that on the board, please?**
Können wir das bitte noch einmal hören?	**Can we listen to that again, please?**
Tut mir leid, ich finde es nicht. Auf welcher Seite sind wir?	**Sorry, I can't find it. What page are we on?**
Was haben wir (als Hausaufgabe) auf?	**What's for homework?**

Du hast ein Problem	You're in trouble
Entschuldigung, dass ich zu spät komme/meine Hausaufgaben nicht gemacht habe, Herr .../Frau ...	**Sorry, I'm late / I haven't done my homework, Mr/Mrs/Ms/Miss ...**
Tut mir leid, dass ich mein Schulheft vergessen habe.	**Sorry, I've forgotten my exercise book.**
Ich bin noch nicht fertig.	**I haven't finished yet.**
Entschuldigung, ich habe nicht zugehört/ das weiß ich nicht.	**Sorry, I wasn't listening / I don't know.**
Ich kann Nummer 3 nicht lösen.	**I can't do number 3.**

Über Texte reden	Talking about texts
Die Geschichte/Das Theaterstück/Das Gedicht/ Das Lied/Der Film handelt von ...	**The story/play/poem/ song/film is about ...**
Die Handlung spielt während/in ...	**The action takes place during/in ...**
In Zeile 15–20 steht, dass ...	**In lines 15–20 it says that ...**
Die Hauptfigur ist ...	**The main character is ...**
Der Mann/Die Frau/... scheint sehr einsam/zornig/ traurig/... zu sein.	**The man/woman/... seems to be very lonely/angry/ sad/...**
Die Beziehung zwischen ... und ... ist sonderbar/...	**The relationship between ... and ... is strange/...**
Es war lustig/unheimlich/langweilig/... als ...	**It was funny/scary/boring/... when ...**
Ich fand es gut/nicht gut als ...	**I liked it/didn't like it when ...**
Ich fand den Schluss überraschend/enttäuschend/ blöd/... , weil ...	**I found the ending surprising/disappointing/ stupid/... because ...**
Ich finde die Geschichte ist lustig/aufregend/...,weil ...	**I think the story is funny/exciting/... because ...**
Die Geschichte hat mich glücklich/wütend/... gemacht.	**The story made me (feel) happy/angry/...**

In einer Diskussion	In a discussion
Meiner Meinung nach ...	**In my opinion ...**
Ich will dir ein Beispiel geben: ...	**Let me give you an example: ...**
Erstens ... /Zweitens ... /Und schließlich ...	**First ... / Second ... / And finally ...**
Ich stimme (...) zu/nicht zu, weil ...	**I agree/disagree (with ...) because ...**
Ja, du hast Recht./Genau!	**Yes, you're right. / Exactly!**
Was Tim sagt, ist richtig/falsch.	**What Tim says is right/wrong.**
Du sagst ..., aber ...	**You say ..., but ...**
Was genau meinst du?	**What do you mean exactly?**
Du könntest Recht haben, aber ...	**You may be right, but ...**
Ich bin mir nicht sicher. Vielleicht ...	**I'm not so sure. Maybe/Perhaps ...**
Was meinst du (zu ...)?	**What do you think (about ...)?**

Bei der Partner- oder Gruppenarbeit	Working with a partner or in a group
Kann ich mit ... arbeiten?	**Can I work with ...?**
Was machen wir als Erstes?	**What are we going to do first?**
Lass/Lasst uns die Aufgabe noch einmal lesen.	**Let's read the task again.**
Wer ist dran? – Ich bin/Du bist dran, das zu schreiben/ die Fragen zu stellen.	**Whose turn is it? – It's my/your turn to write/ ask questions.**
Ich finde, wir sollten/könnten ...	**I think we should/could ...**
Hast du eine Idee/einen Vorschlag?	**Have you got any ideas?**
Mir gefällt deine Idee sehr gut. / Das klingt gut.	**I really like your idea. / That sounds good.**
Wo können wir etwas finden zu ...?	**Where can we find out about ...?**
Was hast du im Internet gefunden?	**What did you find on the internet?**
Was hältst du von meinem Text/Bild/...?	**What do you think of my text/picture/...?**
Ich verstehe nicht, was du meinst. / Ich bin mir da nicht sicher.	**I don't understand what you mean. / I'm not sure about that.**
Lass/Lasst uns ... auf unser Poster schreiben.	**Let's write ... on our poster.**
Lass/Lasst uns das Bild hier hinsetzen/-kleben.	**Let's put the picture here.**
Wie viel Zeit haben wir (noch)?	**How much (more) time do we have?**
Wir haben nur noch ... Minuten Zeit.	**We've only got ... minutes left.**
Lass/Lasst uns ... schnell machen und dann mit ... fortfahren.	**Let's do ... quickly and then go on to ...**
Vielleicht sollten wir ... weglassen/ etwas zu ... sagen.	**Maybe we should leave out ... / say something about ...**
Wir sind fast fertig.	**We've nearly finished.**

Bei einer Präsentation	Giving a talk / presentation
Das Thema meines Vortrags ist ...	**The topic of my talk/presentation is ...**
Ich werde meinen Vortrag in ... Teile gliedern.	**I'm going to divide my talk into ... parts.**
Erstens/Als nächstes/... würde ich gern ...	**First/Next/... I would like to ...**
Zum Schluss werde ich etwas über ... erzählen.	**Finally, I'll tell you something about ...**
Auf der ersten Folie links/rechts könnt ihr sehen ...	**On the first slide on the left/right you can see ...**
Zusammenfassend möchte ich sagen ...	**To sum up I'd like to say ...**
Gibt es/Habt ihr Fragen oder Kommentare dazu?	**Are there any questions or comments?**

What YOUR TEACHER says / Was DEIN/E LEHRER/IN sagt

What YOUR TEACHER says	Was DEIN/E LEHRER/IN sagt
Copy/Fill in the chart/form.	Kopiert/Füllt die Tabelle/das Formular aus.
Correct the mistakes.	Verbessert die Fehler.
Don't forget to check your spelling.	Vergesst nicht die Rechtschreibung zu überprüfen.
Be careful with the word order.	Achtet auf die Satzstellung.
Write it on the board, please.	Schreibe es bitte an die Tafel.
Compare your sentences/answers/... with your partner.	Vergleiche deine Sätze/Antworten/... mit deinem Partner/deiner Partnerin.
Discuss ... in your group.	Diskutiert ... in der Gruppe.
Practise/Act out the dialogues with a partner, please.	Bitte übe/spiele den Dialog mit deinem Partner/deiner Partnerin.
Walk around the class and ask other students.	Geht durch die Klasse und fragt andere Schüler/innen.
Take/Make notes.	Macht euch Notizen.
Imagine you are ...	Stellt euch vor, ihr seid ...
What do you think of ...?	Was haltet ihr von ...?
Have you got any other ideas?	Habt ihr andere/sonstige Ideen?
Give three reasons.	Nenne drei Gründe.
Have you finished?	Seid ihr/Bist du fertig?
Present your talk/poster/... to the class.	Präsentiere dein Referat/Poster/... vor der Klasse.
Do exercise 3 for homework, please.	Macht bitte Übung 3 als Hausaufgabe.

Illustrationen

Silke Bachmann, Hamburg (S. 14; 24; 108 unten; 109 oben); **Roland Beier**, Berlin (S. 9; 13 oben re.; 15; 53 unten; 60; 120-121; 122 oben-125; 127-176); **Carlos Borrell**, Berlin (vordere und hintere Umschlaginnenseite; S. 10; 11; 25; 77 li.; 81; S. 98/99 Hintergrund); **Dylan Gibson**, Pitlochry (S. 34 Bild 1, 3, 7; S. 97 4. v. unten; S. 105-107); **Christian Görke**, Berlin (S. 103; 108 oben; 126 oben); **Jeongsook Lee**, Köln (S. 122 unten); **Alfred Schüssler**, Frankfurt/Main (S. 102 Vignetten (M))

Bildquellen

A1PIX, Taufkirchen (Inhaltsverz. oben 2. v. li. (u. 32 Mitte re.): REO); **Alamy**, Abingdon (Inhaltsverz. unten theme park (M) (u. 32 oben li.): Teddy, girl (M): Images-USA; S. 12 2. v. unten (u.121): photocay; S. 13 Mitte li.: Buzz Pictures; S. 16 unten li.: PCL; S. 17 unten: Photos 12; S. 30 unten re.: Brownstock Inc. (RF); S. 33 Mitte: Brownstock Inc. (RF); S. 36 oben: Picture Partners, Bild 3: Image Source White; S. 41 Mitte re. (M) (u. 94 u. 96): artpartner-images. com; S. 49 Mitte re.: Bloom Works Inc. (RF), unten: Steve Skjold; S. 53 re.: Digital Vision (RF); S. 54: Janine Wiedel Photolibrary; S. 58 oben tin (M): FB-StockPhoto; S. 59 oben kids (M): Steve Skjold (RF), unten li.: Jim West, unten Mitte: Bubbles Photolibrary, unten re.: PhotoAlto (RF); S. 72 unten: Digital Vision (RF); S. 78 unten li.: Dinodia Images (RF); S. 80 unten: Greatstock Photographic Library (RF); S. 85 unten: Images of Africa Photobank; S. 100 Bild 3: David Page; S. 101 oben: Alex Maddox); **Argus**, Hamburg (S. 69: Peter Frischmuth); **Associated Press**, Frankfurt/Main (S. 76 unten: Gurinder Osan); **Richard Baxter Photography**, Sheffield (Inhaltsverz. oben re. (u. 75 oben re.)); **www.Berlin-Bilder.com** (S. 75 unten re.: Andreas Schwiede); **Chuck Braverman. Art and Design ©2004 New Video Group, Inc.** (S. 55; S. 56 oben re.: film stills taken from "High school boot camp"); **Caro Fotoagentur**, Berlin (S. 75 unten li.: Jürgen Blume); **cartoonStock**, Bath (S. 51 unten: Dave Carpenter; S. 52: Dave Parker; S. 97 3. v. unten (u. 109 unten): Kes); **Cinetext**, Frankfurt/Main (S. 77 re. Cinetext Bildarchiv; S. 78 Mitte oben u. unten: Cinetext Bildarchiv); **Corbis**, Düsseldorf (Inhaltsverz. girls (u. 50): Creasource; S. 6 Bild 1: Dennis Degnan; S. 7 Bild 2: Aurora Open/Lars Schneider (RF); S. 12 unten: Hannah Mason (RF); S. 42: Simon Jarratt (RF); S. 48 Mitte li.: Jack Hollingsworth (RF); S. 49 li.: James Marshall; S. 81 unten li.: Sygma/Yves Forestier); **Cornelsen Verlag**, Berlin (S. 40 oben: Michael Weihrauch); **Rob Cousins**, Bristol (S. 43); **Fotolia**, New York (S. 56 oben li. u. Mitte: Klaus-Peter Adler (RF)); **Fotosearch**, Waukesha (S. 97 4. v. oben (u. 104) (RF)); **Fountain Valley School of Colorado**, Colorado Springs (S. 59 oben website u. Logo (M)); **Getty Images**, München (Inhaltsverz. girl with laptop (u. 49 oben re.): Allan Shoemake (RF); S. 6/7 Hintergrund Uluru: Ted Mead; S. 7 Bild 3: Bec Parsons, Bild 6: Doug Armand; S. 9 unten li. (M): Jeff Hunter; S. 11 unten: Stephen Lovekin; S. 12 oben girl (M): Jack Hollingsworth (RF); S. 13 oben li.: Anthony Ong (RF), unten re.: Tony Lewis, unten li.: James Knowler; S. 19 oben: Matt Turner, unten; S. 22 oben: Ian Waldie; S. 29 li.: Annie Griffiths Belt; S. 33 unten: Andersen Ross; S. 36 Bild 1: Image Source (RF); S. 53 Mitte: Jason Dewey; S. 72 oben: Adrian Weinbrecht; S. 74 club: Per-Anders Pettersson; S. 76 oben: AFP; S. 78 oben Bachchan: AFP, Rampal: WireImage; S. 80 Mitte: Per-Anders Pettersson; S. 83 oben li. u. re.: Time Life Pictures, unten: AFP; S. 95 li.: Popperfoto, re.; S. 97 toad (u. 103 oben), 2. v. unten (u. 118 re.): AFP; S. 99 unten re.); **Bonnie Glänzer**, Berlin (S. 44 unten); **Guardian News & Media Ltd 2008** (S. 17 oben: Barbara McMahon); **The Hickory Daily Record**, Hickory (S. 58 unten website u. Logo, unten li.: Robert Reed); **David Hoffman Photo Library**, London (S. 32 unten li.); **iStockphoto**, Calgary (S. 6 li.: Renee Lee; S. 12 sheep: John Simmons; S. 20 re.: Timothy Ball; S. 26 unten li.: Gene Chutka, re.: Jeffrey Smith; S. 27 (u. 99 Mitte re.): susan flashman; S. 28 oben: Carlos Santa Maria, Mitte li.: Elnur Amikishiyev; S. 29 re.: Chuck Babbitt; S. 30 oben: Pali Rao, unten monitor (M): zak, question mark (M): Zeffss1; S. 34 Bild A: wrangle, Bild B: btrenkel; S. 40 unten: dawn liljenquist; S. 51 oben: Eduardo Jose Bernardino; S. 66 unten re.: Diane White Rosier; S. 67: Chris Schmidt; S. 68 li.: Søren Sielemann, 2. v. li.: Rich Legg, Mitte: Chris Schmidt, 2. v. re.: ronen, re.: Suzanne Tucker; S. 75 pink pattern (u. 77): Niels Laan; S. 84: Joselito Briones; S. 85 oben hiker (M): Christy Seely; S. 97 Beware (u. 101 Bild 5): James Bowyer; S. 100/101: Linda & Colin McKie; S. 100 Bild 2 u. 4: david franklin; S. 102 background (M): Paul Morton); **Lonely Planet Images**, London (S. 75 oben li.: Anders Blomqvist); **http://manateens.blogspot.com/** (S. 58 oben website, Hintergrund u. Logo (M): used with permission of Volunteer ManaTEE. Volunteer Services of Manatee County, Inc. (Stand 15.06.2009)); **Masterfile**, Düsseldorf (S. 32 Mitte li.: Ron Fehling); **mauritius images**, Mittenwald (S. 59 Mitte: Cultura Images Ltd. (RF)); **melalouise.net**, East St Kilda (S. 16 oben re.); **Okapia**, Frankfurt/Main: (S. 22 unten: Hans Reinhard; S. 79; S. 92: BIOS/ Klein & Hubert); **Photofusion Picture Library**, London (S. 33 oben: Melanie Friend); **Photolibrary**, London (S. 48 Mitte re.: Banana Stock; S. 53 li.: Banana Stock; S. 89: Britain on View; S. 98 oben re.: Jörg Reuther); **Picture-Alliance**, Frankfurt/Main (Inhaltsverz. unten (u. 74 oben): dpa - Report; S. 13 Mitte re.: dpa – Report; S. 34 Bild D: dpa – Report; S. 36 Bild 2: Okapia/Christine Steimer; S. 56 unten re.: Sander; S. 70: empics; S. 77 unten li.: dpa; S. 78 Khan: Photoshot, Rai: Jazz Archiv; S. 81 unten re.: Sven Simon; S. 99 oben re.: NHPA/ photoshot; S. 103 unten: NHPA/photoshot; S. 118 li.: Godong/Philippe Lissac); **The Picture Desk**, London (S. 71: Film 4/Celador Films/Pathe International/The Kobal Collection; S. 78 unten re.: Pathe Pictures LTC/The Kobal Collection); **Marion Schönenberger**, Berlin (S. 86-87 (Bild 10 (M))); **Jakob Schröck**, Berlin (S. 90); **Shooting Jozi, a project of Global Studio 2007 and the individuals who participated** (S. 74 township; S. 97 unten (u. S. 119 Bild A); S. 119); **Shutterstock**, New York (Inhaltsverz. oben li.: Tap10, Inhaltsverz. Mitte (u. 16 oben li.): Ronald Sumners; S. 7 Bild 4: markrhiggins, Bild 5: BlueSoul Photography; S. 8 oben re.: Dimitrios Kaisaris, Mitte li.: Jennifer King, Mitte re.: Andrei Marincas; S. 9 unten re.: Ian Scott (M); S. 11 oben: aliciahh; S. 12 oben trees (M): aliciahh; S. 16 unten re.: Kaspars Grinvalds; S. 20 li.: Ashley Whitworth; S. 21: aliciahh; S. 26 oben: Rob Wilson; S. 28 Mitte u. re.: Robyn Mackenzie, unten Mitte: Nayashkova Olga, unten li. u. re.: Joe Gough; S. 32 oben re.: sirtravelalot; S. 34 Bild C: Ilja Mašík; S. 41 oben: Yuri Arcurs, unten li.: fizkes; S. 48 oben re.: Alhovic, unten: Rannev; S. 61: Andresr; S. 66 oben li.: Robert Ranson, oben re.: Rick Becker-Leckrone, unten li.: Amy Myers; S. 74 Hintergrund (u. 81): Ferin; S. 75 green pattern (u. 88): claus+mutschler; S. 85 oben (M): André Klaassen; S. 97 oben (u. 99 Mitte li.): Patsy A. Jacks; S. 98 oben li.: tororo reaction, unten: alysta; S. 99 unten li.: hocus-focus; S. 128: Holger Mette); **ullstein bild**, Berlin (S. 75 Berlin emblem (u. 88): Probst; S. 87 Bild 10 Hintergrund (M): Xamax; S. 88 oben re.: C.T. Fotostudio); **vario-images**, Bonn (S. 58 oben snorkeling (M)); **Vector-Images**, Bradenton (S. 75 Mumbai emblem (u. 77); **Visum Foto**, Hamburg (S. 32 unten re.: Bernd Arnold); **Martynka Wawrzyniak**, New York (S. 44 oben; S. 45); **Courtesy YFM radio** (S. 80 oben)

Titelbild

Corbis, Düsseldorf (sign and bus (M): zefa/Theo Allofs); **Corel Library** (flag Hintergrund (M)); **Plainpicture**, Hamburg (jeans with map (M): Sina Preikschat)

Textquellen

S. 17 *Children were stolen for a racist ideal. Now a nation says sorry.* Adapted from "Snatched from home for a racist ideal. Now a nation says sorry" by Barbara McMahon, 11.2.2008. http://www.guardian.co.uk/world/2008/feb/11/australia. Copyright Guardian News & Media Ltd 2008; **S. 20 – 23** *In the outback.* Abridged and adapted from „Children of the Wind - A Prayer for Blue Delaney" by Kirsty Murray. Allen & Unwin, Crows Nest, Australia, 2005 (www.allenandunwin.com); **S. 54** *ASBO boy.* Abridged and adapted from „ASBO made me give up life as a yob". From http://www.mirror.co.uk/news/top-stories/2007/11/13/asbo-made-me-give-up-life-as-a-yob-115875-20099323/ by Jeremy Armstrong, 13.11.2007. Mirror Syndication International, London; **S. 58** *Springs Clean-up.* Text adapted from http://manateens.blogspot.com/ (Stand 15.06.2009) used with permission of Volunteer ManaTEE. Volunteer Services of Manatee County, Inc., Hickory Soup Kitchen. Adapted from "Students soup up kitchen" by Sarah Newell Williamson, 6.8.2008. http://www2.hickoryrecord.com/content/2008/aug/06/students-soup-kitchen/. Used with permission of The Hickory Daily Record, Hickory; **S. 59** *Community Service.* Adapted from http://www.fvs.edu/podium/default.aspx?t=39763. Used with permission of Fountain Valley School of Colorado, Colorado Springs; **S. 61** *Ein Beitrag für sich und die Gesellschaft.* Auszug aus der Informationsbroschüre "Für mich und für andere". http://www.bmfsfj.de/bmfsfj/generator/RedaktionBMFSFJ/Broschuerenstelle/Pdf-Anlagen/Fuer-mich-und-fuer-andere-FSJ-FOEJ GFD,property=pdf,bereich=bmfsfj,sprache=de,rwb=true.pdf. Herausgegeben vom Bundesministerium für Familie, Senioren, Frauen und Jugend. Berlin, 2008; **S. 62 – 64** *The caller.* Abridged and adapted. Reprinted by permission of Carus Publishing Company, from DARE TO BE SCARED: THIRTEEN STORIES TO CHILL AND THRILL by Daniel D. San Souci, text © 2003 by Robert D. San Souci; **S. 76** *A lover's embrace.* Abridged and adapted from "Mumbai" by Suketu Mehta. Copyright © 1997 by Suketu Mehta. Originally published by Granta Books. Reprinted by permission of William Morris Endeavor Entertainment, LLC on behalf of the Author; **S. 80** *The Y Generation.* Adapted from travel and leisure article from go2southafrica.com,
http://www.go2southafrica.com/About-South-Africa/About-South-Africa/Johannesburg-Travel-&-Leisure-Article/ (Stand 4.3.2009). Used with permission; **S. 81 – 82** *A tour of Soweto.* Abridged and adapted from "Many Stones" by Carolyn Coman. (Front Street, an imprint of Boyds Mills Press, 2000). Reprinted with the permission of Boyds Mills Press, Inc. Text copyright © by Carolyn Coman; **S. 108 – 110** *Bus attack Part 1, Bus attack Part 2.* Abridged and adapted from case study 4, taken from http://www.restorativejustice.org.uk/Media/pdf/Case%20Study%20-%20Bus%20Co.pdf (30.06.2009). Used by permission of Restorative Justice Consortium, London; **S. 111 – 117** *Famous.* Abridged and adapted from "TOTALLY OVER YOU" Copyright © Mark Ravenhill, 2003. All rights whatsoever in this play are strictly reserved and application for performance etc., must be made before rehearsal to Casarotto Ramsey & Associates Ltd., 7-12 Noel Street, London W1F 8GQ. No performance may be given unless a license has been obtained; **S. 118** *Mumbai slums.* Abridged and adapted from „Shadow Cities: A Billion Squatters, A New Urban World" by Robert Neuwirth. Routledge. New York, 2004. Reprinted by permission of Dunow, Carlson & Lerner Literary Agency. Copyright 2004, Robert Neuwirth. First appeared in "Shadow Cities"; **S. 123** Auszug aus „English G 2000 Wörterbuch - Das Wörterbuch zum Lehrwerk". Herausgegeben von der Langenscheidt-Redaktion Wörterbücher und der Cornelsen-Redaktion Englisch. © 2002 Cornelsen Verlag GmbH & Co. OHG, Berlin und Langenscheidt KG, Berlin und München

Liedquellen

S. 104 *Nine to five.* Text, OT: Parton, Dolly. © Velvet Apple Music. Neue Welt Musikverlag GmbH, Hamburg